T0380817

NGO STRATEGIES BY CHRISTIANS TO CHANGE THE WORLD

MAKING A DIFFERENCE ONE VILLAGE, ONE FAMILY, ONE PERSON AT A TIME

WARNER WOODWORTH, Ph.D.

WESTBOW
PRESS®
A DIVISION OF THOMAS NELSON
& ZONDERVAN

WestBow Press books may be ordered through booksellers or by contacting:

WestBow Press
A Division of Thomas Nelson & Zondervan
1663 Liberty Drive
Bloomington, IN 47403
www.westbowpress.com
844-714-3454

Scripture quotations taken from The Holy Bible, New International Version® NIV® Copyright © 1973 1978 1984 2011 by Biblica, Inc. TM. Used by permission. All rights reserved worldwide.

ISBN: 978-1-6642-9134-8 (sc)
ISBN: 978-1-6642-9133-1 (e)

Library of Congress Control Number: 2023902214

Print information available on the last page.

WestBow Press rev. date: 05/10/2023

PRAISE FOR THE AUTHOR

Robert A. Rees

Warner Woodworth is widely recognized for his pioneering work as a global social entrepreneur. He has trained and mentored several generations of social entrepreneurs while helping to organize more than four dozen NGOs that now operate in 62 countries and raise nearly $30 million annually in donations. Every serious Christian takes seriously Jesus's call to "feed my sheep" and to "love your neighbor as yourself," but in a real sense we all stand condemned before one of Jesus's last great parables, which is found in the 25th chapter of St. Matthew's gospel. There Jesus puts himself in the place of any whom we consider "the least," those that Mother Teresa calls "Jesus in disguise." Although in truth he is the greatest among us, Jesus puts himself in the place of the stranger, any we consider our enemy, the person least desiring of our love or nurture, and the most wicked person we know or can think of—and then He urges us to treat that person as if he or she were Jesus himself. For over half a century, Warner Woodworth's personal ministry has been to "the least" of our brothers and sisters throughout the world. His ministry is an invitation to all of us to take Jesus seriously.

PhD, former Professor of Religion, Graduate Theological Union, Berkeley; Poet; Author; Professor and Assistant Dean of Fine Arts, UCLA; Danforth Fellow; Claremont University Scholar; Fulbright Scholar in Lithuania; Founder of Liahona Foundation serving severely malnourished children globally

Monty Lynn

Are Christians making a difference in global development? Warner Woodworth responds with an emphatic "yes," and he offers evidence and innovative examples as support. He is a seasoned poverty alleviation activist. In *NGO Strategies by Christians to Change the World*, he shares his deep experience and introduces us to a diverse array of communities and faith-based organizations collaborating for the common good. His examples and insights are rare gifts, able to inspire and instruct current and future efforts in transformational development.

PhD, Professor of Management, Abilene Christian University endowed chair; author of Development in Mission; *two master's degrees from Cornell and the University of London*

Tim Stay

Father Greg Boyle, of Homeboys Industry, taught that the way to truly become a community before God is to go to those on the margins. As we go to the margins, we change and the margins are erased and we become one before God. All the great ones, such as Christ, Mohammed, Gandhi, Martin Luther King, Jr., and Mother Teresa, among others, have done this. Warner has spent his life serving those on the margins: the poor, the disadvantaged, the disempowered, the exploited, and the disenfranchised, working toward the day when "there need be no poor people among you" (Deuteronomy 15:4) and when we will be one before God. This powerful Christian book shares efforts around the world that are working toward erasing the margins so that we can find godly kinship with those "on the other side."
CEO, The Other Side Academy; former CEO of Unitus Global Microfinance Accelerator in 26 nations; Founder of several tech firms, and the new Other Side Village for the homeless

The Rev. Daniel Haas

Warner Woodworth continues to practice servant leadership locally and globally. As a Christian leader he understands profoundly why Jesus talks about money a great deal: True discipleship happens with your checkbook.
BCC, Pastor, Thomaskirche, Wuppertal, Germany; Studied at Hebrew University of Jerusalem; Chaplain at Episcopal Community Services; Former Pastor at St. John's United Church of Christ, Houston; Pastor at Community Congregational United Church of Christ; currently Lead Staff Chaplain in U.S. Army Reserve and also at Japanese Church of Christ

Tracy M. Maylett

One of my most treasured life experiences was sitting next to Warner Woodworth in a small room in Guatemala after two weeks of planting gardens, constructing ovens, building roads, and digging village wells. I labored there with a group of Warner's teary-eyed (and exhausted) volunteers from four universities. He lives Biblical values brilliantly, illustrating how social entrepreneurship and simple caring for our brothers and sisters blesses and improves the lives not only of those who receive, but of those who give.
E.D.; CEO of DecisionWise; university professor; social entrepreneur and board member of HELP International NGO; author of two best-selling books The Employee Experience *and* Engagement Magic: Five Keys for Engaging People, Leaders, and Organizations

Ronald Miller

Warner Woodworth has written extremely compelling cases that show how to succeed in accomplishing great good in difficult circumstances. Many wonder how they might contribute, what change they can accomplish, what good they can do. Woodworth not only gives insights into the success others have achieved across a wide swath of needs, along with specifics of their worthy causes, but gives a template for those who have the desire to make positive change in the world. Woodworth's book is a wonderful examination of how good can be accomplished in our troubled world. It is inspiring, yet as a guide it is indispensable.

Perdue PhD; Lifetime Academic Scholar at Oxford University's SAID Business School for Social Entrepreneurship; Professor of Statistics, Woodbury School of Business

The Rev. Canon Elizabeth Hunter

Dr. Woodworth's devout faith, belief in Christian principles, and experience with worldwide social enterprise organizations give him a unique perspective to highlight examples of successful programs, many of which he and his students have developed that continue to change the world. His life's work in social responsibility exemplifies the teaching from Micah 6:8: "He has shown you, O mortal, what is good. And what does the Lord require of you? To act justly and to love mercy and to walk humbly with your God." Dr. Woodworth's example of living his faith and his commitment to social enterprise have enlightened interfaith understanding and dialogue between diverse religious communities.

Board member of Coalition of Religious Communities (CORC); Retired Deacon at Cathedral Church of St. Mark; worked at Episcopal Diocese of Utah

Shon Hiatt

Dr. Warner Woodworth has devoted his life and career to addressing the challenges facing the poor and needy. In this latest book, he highlights numerous innovations that followers of Christ undertake while fulfilling the commandment to love God *and* their neighbor. These humanitarian initiatives not only provide individuals with education, health, and financial opportunities; they also change the destiny of generations.

PhD; Associate Professor of Business Administration, University of Southern California and USC Center for Sustainability Solutions; former Assistant Professor at Harvard Business School; Visiting Scholar at Lisbon Catholic School of Business and Economics; author of articles in the London School of Economics Review, *the* Academy of Management Journal, *and various Harvard Business cases*

Scott Leckman

Warner has done it again! If you want to make a difference in people's lives as an expression of your Christian values, then this book is for you. Warner provides you with examples and inspiration.

Stanford MD and general surgeon; Director at RESULTS Educational Fund in Washington, DC; informal Protestant leader; Grameen Bank NGO advisor; Rotary Foundation Chair at Rotary International

Geoff Davis

Professor Woodworth has been practicing what he preaches for decades and has inspired and mentored hundreds of people in his wake. This great book captures much of his thinking and much of what he has learned along the way, and does so in a way that is both enlightening and inspiring. The world would be a better place and we'd have Zion in our midst if we all applied these principles as diligently as Warner has.

CEO, Sorenson Impact Center, President of Unitus Global Accelerator, and Warner Woodworth mentee

Peter J. Sorenson

I have known Professor Warner Woodworth since fall 1976. For over 45 years, I have known him as a good and honest man who has devoted his life to serving others. He and I have been in the classroom together, consulting together, and more importantly—regarding this book—we have been "boots on the ground" doing humanitarian work in the developing world. What he shares with you in this book is *real*. He shows that it is possible to have values and live by them and also to be of service to others in ways that will change both their lives and your own life. We went to Thailand in 2005 after the destructive Asian tsunami, helping the people with years of rebuilding—rebuilding not just homes, but also lives. And dignity, self-sufficiency, community. We saw people healing from trauma and loss at work crafting their own futures with the help of many "Wave of Hope" volunteers, an NGO that Warner established, and of other humanitarian groups.

We were in El Salvador in 2002, working on numerous microcredit projects with village banks that had been in operation for several years. We heard stories from the microentrepreneurs about how their lives had changed for the better. They were moving toward economic stability, self-reliance, and independence. All because of a tiny community bank that Warner had formed to provide microloans with training on how to be a successful microentrepreneur. These strategies for social change have generated life-changing impacts on his and other volunteers. They have become social entrepreneurs who look for opportunities to serve others in productive ways for the rest of their lives. They continue to exemplify the values of their Christian beliefs throughout their ongoing faith journeys. Read this book! Take the messages into your heart. Find ways to manifest your values and your faith by serving others.

International management consultant; Adjunct Professor at Southern Methodist University, Lyle School of Engineering; Board President of Socio-Technical Roundtable; author

Readers who wish to learn more can communicate with the author at:
warnerwoodworth.com

DEDICATION

This humble little volume is dedicated to my amazing brother and parents. Mark is a professional with decades of editorial achievements since earning a master's in journalism from Columbia University. Also, it's dedicated to our loving parents—my father, Arthur Joy Woodworth, a Methodist from Ohio, and my mother, Ruth Lazelle Peay, a descendant of Mormon pioneers, who taught me about people's suffering, empathy, and how collectively we can address societal problems.

CONTENTS

PREFACE

This book draws on my Christian life as both a believer in God and a global change agent, as well as a practicing academic. At multiple times, I have also been an influencer, social innovator, disruptor, renegade, catalyst, mover, and shaker. While consulting with Fortune 500 corporations, founding or working with nonprofit humanitarian organizations, advising labor leaders and government officials across the United States and in a number of other countries, as well as while teaching MBAs, law students, and undergraduates from multiple disciplines, I have always sought to engage others in applying their very best abilities to serve the world's "have-nots." Doing so over decades has given me the sense of having a spiritual calling, not only in my heart, but also in my very genes. My life has been a significant platform from which I personally could launch efforts against poverty, so as to foster humanitarian outreach and to instill in other people a vision of their own potential…to have them look again at their own comfortable lifestyles and blessings…to perhaps reflect on their global travels, the poverty they saw, the suffering they witnessed, and the sense of helplessness they felt from time to time about what they could actually do to respond. Growing out of my biblical beliefs, I have sought to share valuable gospel principles that would help my students to retain and even grow their faith, as well as then to *use* their faith in God to make a real difference in society. I fervently believe they can apply their skills and formulate some personal strategies in such a manner that they could become, in effect, *Christians Without Borders.*

ACKNOWLEDGMENTS

First, I want to thank my Savior Jesus Christ, for his life, atonement, and resurrection that promises us all eternity. His teachings are spread throughout this practical book for Christians as biblical quotes are used to share ways in which our efforts to reduce human suffering and poverty may be implemented. Two things make the book even more relevant today than several years ago. First is the ugly scourge of war occurring since Russia invaded Ukraine recently, with the resulting slaughter of innocent women, men, and children; the war has shown how much we need the "Prince of Peace" today. Equally, the terrible past two years of the COVID-19 pandemic has wreaked havoc with the world. Whether referring to millions of deaths and a whopping 85 million people sickened in the United States, the health crisis has spread much disease, as well as caused an economic decline. This has, of course, been outdone by worldwide statistics, totaling over six million dead and an astounding 529 million people made ill by the virus.

I also want to acknowledge the support and collaboration I've enjoyed over the decades from Dr. Muhammad Yunus, the Nobel Peace Prize Laureate who founded the Grameen Bank to serve poor women in impoverished Bangladesh. He has been my partner in many of these efforts. Although he was relatively unknown decades ago, I personally funded him to come out to my university, for his very first visit. He came and spoke to my students, and after that, feeling impressed with our work and the dedication of the hundreds of students I was mobilizing, he remarked, "I want to come back!" So, I persuaded the university to fund him, and he has returned eleven additional times. Eventually, officials at my university decided to award him an honorary doctorate—the first Muslim so honored at my home school. He and I have been hanging out together, off and on, since 1993, and his two nephews also came to study at Brigham Young University and later earned undergraduate or MBA degrees.

I also must acknowledge the thousands of students I've had the privilege to teach in a range of college courses (Management, Ethics, Social Entrepreneurship, Organizational Behavior, Latin American Studies, Consulting, Microfinance, Psychology, Nonprofit and NGO Management, and Leadership). They have all blessed both my own my life as well as the lives of tens of thousands of God's struggling children, as we labored together to design innovative nongovernmental organizations (NGOs) and to engage as volunteers in the villages of many developing nations. Beyond my university base, where I've had tenure and served as a full professor for decades, I've also enjoyed lecturing, doing research, and teaching for a time at other universities. I have worked with faculty and students literally around the globe, including the University of Michigan, in Ann Arbor; the International Labor Office of the United Nations, in Geneva, Switzerland; the University of Rio de Janeiro, in Brazil; Claremont University, in Los Angeles; and other schools in Hawaii, Cambodia, the United Kingdom, Lithuania, Hong Kong, and Russia. I've also served as a visiting faculty member at Wayne State University, in Detroit, and the University of Utah, in Salt Lake City, near my home base.

This volume is a labor of love, derived from some 48 years of my work in villages of the global poor to reduce poverty, hunger, and the stress and strain of challenges in the developing world. I have been blessed to enjoy the benefits of a comfortable life, an amazing wife, and ten special children, including triplets and two adopted kids (one Mexican and the other Brazilian). I owe an enormous debt of gratitude to them, most of whom have accompanied me at various times to volunteer for weeks combating poverty along with a number of NGOs that function as nonprofit enterprises seeking to aid the "poorest of the poor." Over the decades, we have labored together in Mali (in West Africa), Honduras, Thailand, Haiti, Chile, Brazil, Kenya, Peru, Fiji, Guatemala, and other countries—paying our own way, becoming trained, and raising money for village projects.

ABOUT THE AUTHOR

For readers of my new book, *NGO Strategies by Christians to Change the World*, I want to share a bit of biographical information as to my Christian background, experiences, and motives for drafting this humble little volume, as well as my religious convictions that form its foundation. I have lived a life of Christian devotion for my 80 years of existence on this planet. My personal association and collaboration with other believers in practicing the teachings of Jesus have been greatly enriched by my association in learning from those of other faiths. Many like you, dear reader, and like me, accept Jesus Christ as our Savior and Redeemer. Here are just a few of those experiences:

I first started reading the Bible in the 1940s at age six or seven and recall that I had completed the entire book of scripture before my twelfth birthday when I was ordained a deacon in my church. When a teenager, I attended religious classes six days a week as a youth. Beginning in my twenties, I have led religious congregations and organizations as one of the top two or three leaders for some 30 years of my lifetime, ministering to those in need, whether Christians, Jews, Muslims, or people of no religious belief. Like President Jimmy Carter, I was also a Sunday School gospel doctrine teacher for over a decade. I've given biblical sermons in a variety of multifaith Sunday services for many years.

As a kid I grew up and attended public schools with friends of multiple Christian faiths. In 1961, at age 19, I began serving God as a missionary in Brazil for 30 months as a young man, volunteering 100 percent of my time and paying my own way. During my service there, I volunteered with leaders of Protestant and largely Catholic communities, including ministers who were evangelicals, Lutherans, Baptists, Presbyterians, Methodists, or members of other Christian churches.

In the mid-1960s after college and back in the US, I began teaching in a Christian seminary full-time for six years in the western United States, helping young people learn and live the values of Jesus Christ. Later, I moved to Ann Arbor, Michigan, where I became the director of religious education while getting a PhD. During five years there I was heavily involved with other ministers in the community, collaborating with them on community projects to serve the disenfranchised. At an institute in 1971, I directed and guided religious teachings for several hundred graduate students. Later I was invited to teach the early history of my own church as a University of Michigan academic, three-credit course in the highly regarded Religious Studies Department of the university for students from across campus. I labored ecumenically to work with ministers and priests of multiple faiths to build a grassroots movement that would ultimately generate $5 million to recruit, prepare, and then educate young Blacks from Detroit and other cities where racism was so extensive. A new Black Studies program was initiated, and expert faculty from across America were hired to teach. Our interfaith efforts would ultimately give young minorities opportunities for a first-class education at one of the most highly ranked public universities in the world, the University of Michigan. A significant initiative that I worked on as a consultant arose in 1972 through the Detroit Industrial Mission, wherein my colleagues and I, mostly former or current pastors and religious priests, labored to empower poor young minorities and single mothers with kids, in inner-city locations like Detroit, Muskegon, and Grand Rapids, by building innovative strategies to give them a more sustainable future.

Upon completing my PhD in Ann Arbor in 1974, I spent a year and a half as a young professor working full-time at the Catholic University of Rio de Janeiro (Pontifícia Universidade Católica do Rio de Janeiro), which was led by a priest serving as the institution's rector, whom I got to know and learn from. Living in Rio allowed me to collaborate with a number of spiritual leaders at the school, as well as at other Protestant churches in the area.

Eventually, I felt inspired to move to Utah and become a Marriott School of Business management professor at Brigham Young University. That was in 1976. After several decades, beginning in the 1990s, I also served voluntarily on the board of the Utah Valley Ministerial Association in Utah County. I worked alongside ministers from the Congregational Church of Christ, the Catholic Church, Southern Baptist, St. Mary's, and the area's other major Christian congregations, such as Methodist, Presbyterian, Seventh Day Adventists, Latter-day Saints (Mormons), and others. I became strong friends with various faith leaders representing churches, plus various nondenominational chaplains.

Internationally, over many years as a global business consultant to corporations and nonprofit agencies combating poverty, I enjoyed building strong relationships with officials of other faiths. Over four decades I consulted, advised, collaborated with, and learned from leaders of multiple spiritual traditions, including the following: Catholic nuns in a convent in Bethlehem, Israel; meeting with padres of Catholicism in Brazil, plus nuns and monks, where I adopted an abandoned Brazilian baby boy 50 years ago, as well as also adopting a Mexican baby girl. I've led seminars with Catholic priests throughout Latin America and Europe, including liberation theology advocates in Central America and conservative priests and Protestant ministers in African countries such as Kenya, Uganda, and Ghana. In 2017 I spent a week in an Irish abbey in rural Ireland communing with monks and other scholars exploring the meaning of mortal happiness. For a time, I supported a Catholic priest and an Anglican leader in Rwanda as they sought to help parishioners overcome the horrors of mass genocide in that nation. I also worked for six years in the 1980s with collaborators of Catholic Church leaders in Gdansk, Poland, whose earlier bishop and later archbishop had become Pope John Paul II. That experience was a privilege for me in my efforts to support the country's fledgling democracy and free elections, including advising *Solidarność* (the Solidarity

Union organization) and its struggle for Polish freedom, alongside its great trade-union leader, whom I got to know personally, Lech Walesa.

Since 2010, I've volunteered on the board of the Coalition of Religious Communities (CORC), based in Salt Lake City, Utah, as an interfaith or multifaith religious organization. It operates out of the historic Methodist Episcopal Church, built in 1905, in which today's Crossroads Urban Center provides a community food pantry, homeless shelters, drug rehabilitation, and other services. As believers in Christ, the CORC ministry works with state and city officials to address concerns such as child poverty, low-income housing, minority issues, exploitative wages, citizen power, and disability rights in our state. These and other agenda items are the focus of much lobbying with the Utah legislature and other policymakers.

Ever since the early 1980s, during four decades of humanitarian service globally, I have collaborated with ADRA, the wonderful Adventist humanitarian organization; worked with the Southern Baptists; volunteered in evangelical refugee camps in Greece; and partnered with Catholic Relief Services in various nations during times of floods, earthquakes, droughts, wars, and other natural disasters. In all those cases, I learned much from faithful leaders about Christ, service to the poor, and love itself. Living a life of religious purity and service to others has helped me to fulfill the sacred counsel of the Savior, expressed not only in the Ten Commandments and in God's other major teachings, but also in the very Beatitudes of Christ's counsel to true disciples in his powerful Sermon on the Mount.

Finally, readers of this volume, *NGO Strategies by Christians to Change the World,* may be interested to know that my life through decades of a wonderful, Christian-based marriage has been one of devotion to God. My amazing wife, Kaye, and I started having a daily devotional to strengthen our love immediately after our wedding. We began the practice of scripture reading and daily family prayer when we married. Over the years, we have enjoyed a growing family that ultimately consisted of ten children of our own, plus six others who lived with us while going to college at nearby universities. Our daily ritual? Each day, we would start with the oldest children awaking at six in the morning for our daily devotional, consisting of ten minutes of scripture reading aloud, several minutes of discussion about understanding God's meaning in the day's verses, and then all kneeling in humble, family prayer. The kids would then do their chores, eat breakfast, and head off to junior high or high school. An hour later, the younger children would be awakened, and we would repeat the process: reading scripture out loud as a family, praying to God vocally as family prayer, doing chores, and then they would head off to their elementary school. Those were the rituals and values practiced in our lives as we sought to serve God and Jesus Christ, His Son. That practice continues to date in our children, their spouses, and our grandkids' lives, as well as in the life my wife and I enjoy, even in the late years of our 70s.

These kinds of experiences have framed the moral fiber of my personal life. They have helped prepare me and have greatly inspired me to write this book on how Christians can actually change the world.

GLOSSARY

Here are a few definitions of methodologies cited in this book that are often used for changing the world and empowering poor people. They are described in the chapters, case studies, and appendixes as innovative ways to help reduce people's suffering.

civil society—Sectors of a country's social problems and challenges, sometimes referred to as its "social sector" or "third sector," or by other terms. This is in contrast to the traditional arenas of the private sector, such as business and for-profit enterprises, or public sector systems like federal, state, regional, and city governments; schools; and so forth.

humanitarianism—The belief and practice of regarding others' lives, as individuals perform benevolent treatment of those in need and offer assistance to them, so as to improve their living conditions.

INGO—International nongovernmental organization.

international development—Usually means large-scale government programs focused on alleviating poverty, fostering economic expansion, and improving living conditions in poor nations around the globe.

MFI—Microfinance institution, a term as well as an acronym used herein for all financial services for the poor.

micro-bank—A village or communal bank group.

microcredit—Tiny loans or microloans made to the very poor.

microenterprise—A very small, income-generating activity or family business.

microentrepreneur—Recipient of a microloan with which one can start or expand a small business.

microfinance institution—A more-inclusive term for the above five *micro-* terms, sometimes also including programs such as client savings, health insurance for the poor, education loans, and others.

NGO—A nongovernmental organization or nonprofit that may provide a range of humanitarian and development services, such as literacy, health care, education and schools, crisis response and aid, computer skills, village progress aid, agricultural help, and women's empowerment, as well as microcredit itself.

social entrepreneur—A person who seeks to design programs to improve society, using business methods, not simply charity.

social impact—The seeking of funding that leads to major economic results, not merely charity but also long-term innovation.

CHAPTER 1

How to Change the World: An Introduction to New Christian Global Innovations

I believe this book is an exciting new volume on how believers in Christ can reduce human suffering, uplift the poor, and improve society. The approach is not what the institutional church may do. Nor is it about the things that government programs, the World Bank, USAID, the United Nations, Big Business, and others can accomplish. Instead, it focuses on what Jesus taught—that we, like him, should "go about doing good." In this book on practical Christianity, I will primarily address private humanitarian initiatives as we collectively see social needs around the globe and respond by reaching out with both faith *and* action to "lift up the hands that hang down," as the prophet Isaiah declared.

As I see it, we believers in the Bible can provide humanitarian service in three principal ways. First are the *traditional church programs*, such as paying donations, making personal offerings, or going abroad as a group or even serving as international missionaries in a needy African country, for example. I've come to believe that this kind of service should be our top priority—offerings that we give to bless the poor.

Of course, a second area of outreach and humanitarian assistance can be provided through *partnering with other institutions*. Examples are numerous, including religious groups like the Adventists' ADRA, the Baptist Global Response (BGR) organization, Catholic Relief, and the Muslim Relief Society, as well as various other outreach efforts that can help us bless our neighbors in need.

The third category, and the one I will describe in these pages, is that of our *engaging in individual acts of consecration and stewardship* as contemporary Christians. These are what we might refer to as personal initiatives—not our own church's programmatic initiatives as an organization, but rather the inspiration that comes when we pray about how we might help those around us or when we see on the nightly news the devastation impacting a community or a region or a country or even our own neighbors right next door and others who might suffer and struggle in our community. I might add that I believe it is crucially important that we engage in these kinds of activities locally, not merely globally, because those suffering in circumstances around us typically affect our own lives, and thus we can affect *their lives* much more easily, more rapidly, and with fewer costs, than we can affect people globally. However, in this volume I will specifically emphasize international humanitarian initiatives.

Practical Christianity

I believe that individual acts of consecration and stewardship are the kind that show we can go beyond simply depending on large organizations or the institutional services even of a church, but rather that we can also engage in noninstitutionalized acts of service to the poor.

We may consider types of believers to be unsung heroes—individuals doing wonderful work to bless the lives of others while not demanding recognition for their work. Such faithful Christian disciples are individuals having characteristics such as being self-starters who don't wait to be commanded. They take action when they see a problem. They are authentic individuals. They are real. They are true to themselves. They are not motivated by external rewards, or pressure, or recognition. Rather, their services come from pure and authentic motives.

So, in this book I will build off these general themes and talk about a number of global humanitarian Christians whom I have had the great blessing of having worked with. In some cases we started projects together. In other cases, they were students in my university courses who took the initiative to use their advanced education to go out into the world and bless others less fortunate. In some instances, they felt motivated by events and saw people's suffering, and felt determined to lessen the pain of those in this world of toil and trouble. I would characterize these as mostly people who are largely unknown. They are engaging in unofficial religious actions. Quite frequently they go unappreciated or unremarked-on. Instead, they make quiet commitments to design and carry out humanitarian efforts, often in far-flung corners of the world, and they are going to go ahead and *do* them whether the UN is part of it or whether the Red Cross or USAID are involved. At bottom, they are simply seeking to do acts for good.

The capacity for us followers of Christ to change the world is limitless, I truly believe. Yet far too often in our society we do not fully appreciate those who live their faith. I reflect on the inspiring words of the Apostle Paul: *"Be on your guard; stand firm in the faith; be courageous; be strong. Do everything in love."* (1 Corinthians 16:13–14).

Over my years of working, teaching, and consulting in my chosen vineyard, I've met any faithful Christians who have developed what I refer to as *social entrepreneurial acumen*—the capacity to see problems and then take action. Many draw on business and other training to establish nonprofit start-ups of what we might call nongovernmental organizations, or NGOs. And as I have been privileged to be a part of growing that movement, I see a powerful trend that, in some ways, I would argue is far more important and ultimately will give us better recognition as Christians than would the typical for-profit business start-up or other means of wealth generation.

Instead, I think what we are seeing now is the flourishing of means for building up civil society. These include private voluntary organizations (PVOs), nongovernmental organizations, and third-sector institutions that are having an enormous impact in benefiting the lives of the poor around the globe. Most have been launched in the past several decades as social enterprises by what we might call "social entrepreneurs" who are Christians drawing on their faith, relying on their values, harnessing their educations, and calling forth their business skills in designing and launching effective humanitarian services strategies. We see growing efforts by Christians beyond the U.S., outside the U.S., and across the world in Latin America, in Africa, in Asia, who are starting their own similar programs, drawing on that same faith, and as a result achieving significant impacts for good.

Some of the cases I relate in the chapters that follow have drawn on my own experience and may best be illustrated by the mobilization of my college students in spinoffs: that is, ways in which together we use the university as an incubator for NGO creation. For example, we go above and beyond the official university programs we have at the business school I've taught in for 40 years at Brigham Young University (BYU, 2022), as well as in the social sciences, international studies, or colleges like engineering or nursing that have begun to promote international internships and programs to study abroad. In the past decade or two, many such programs around the country have begun moving into more action, not just research and study; not just theory and concepts, but instead practical implementation of concepts.

The work that I do has primarily been with students, most of them Christians who may be alumni of own university (BYU) or alumni of other schools where I've mobilized volunteers to work with our NGOs—institutions such as Emory, Baylor, Notre Dame, Texas Christian University, Duke, Southern Methodist, St. Olaf College, and American University in Washington, D.C. Also and my colleagues have reached out for volunteers beyond academia, such as home makers, retirees, businesspeople, school teachers, CPAs, artists and musicians, and lawyers. In all that work, I try to use biblical principles, defining" charity" (the very term comes from old words for "Christian love") as helping the poor and elevating them in such a way that they may help themselves and in turn can begin to help others. So, it's this notion of a beneficial ripple effect. It's not a hand out, it's a hand-up. It's not a building of dependency and giving out things and goods. It's not a form of creating a culture of wanting more and living passively while charity and relief simply continues to flow to them. Rather, the Christian labor that my friends and I seek consists of helping people learn principles and develop systems so that they may empower themselves and in turn reach out and empower others.

I now will briefly highlight the global context for this work. The reality is that a great many people on the face of this earth are suffering. Over two and a half billion of them—or almost half the world's entire population—lives on less than $2 a day. And over one billion live on less than a single dollar a day. It is clear to experts that critical needs are not being met by the "Big Boys," by the enormous systems, by the large institutions, whether they be governments or the UN or the International Red Cross. And the reality is that, even if we gave away all the money we have as a country through USAID, that still wouldn't solve the problems of the billions of poor people. Churches could give away all of their billions; that too wouldn't solve the problem. The challenge is to learn how we can use capital—whether financial, human, or organizational—to build a better world and to address these terrible problems that the poor face around the globe and, by doing so, help them lift themselves up.

I believe that the reason most people are not able to develop the talents and abilities that are within them is just the lack of opportunity. This is the condition of most of the peoples on earth. And Jesus requires us to take these people who have been named through conversion to Christ and teach them how to live and how to become healthy, wealthy, and wise. I fully believe this is our duty.

The major chapters of this volume describe inspiring stories of far-reaching Christian efforts to combat poverty. They include cases of serving leper colonies through Rising Star Outreach, in India; the case of Grameen Danone Foods in Bangladesh, for maximizing social benefits of ethical business rather than profits alone through the Grameen Bank; Wave of Hope, for rebuilding Thailand after the horrendous 2004 Asian tsunami; Care for Life's Family Preservation Program, in Mozambique, using the Bible as a guide; Native American microfinancing for poor Indigenous communities; Christian microfranchise and other development tools to combat poverty; and several approaches for Christian as well as Muslim microfinance programs in East Africa.

This book will also examine core tools and concepts of international development, including theoretical and conceptual ideas as well as practical designs and implementation of social change approaches. It will assess such methods, both their strengths and weaknesses, along with innovations for a better future, such as global Appropriate Technology approaches using low-cost innovations in developing societies. Finally, a concluding chapter will integrate my core themes and describe the potential social impacts.

Brief Highlights of Other Programs

The above descriptions will serve as cases offering in-depth focuses on this book's agenda. Each following chapter will detail how good Christians have succeeded in empowering the poor in various corners of the globe. However, in this initial chapter, I want to introduce readers to a handful of related efforts by simply scanning other initiatives. I won't dig into the what, how, why, and where of these organizations, which I have more fully published as case studies elsewhere. Instead, here I'll offer some "helicopter-view" visions of such work. I hope each of the following paragraphs will give readers a look at a particular humanitarian outreach effort, so as to lay the groundwork for the more in-depth stories that make up the essence of this book. Here are but a few mini-examples, some with a paragraph of explanation, others with more information of a page or two.

CHOICE Humanitarian: Emerging from the Andean Children's Foundation in 1988 was the Center for Humanitarian Outreach and Intercultural Exchange, launched by Christian missionaries to help Indigenous communities, especially in Bolivia and Peru. It evolved into the acronym-name "CHOICE" as a nonprofit, nonsectarian organization that sponsors what they term "volunteer expeditions" in which families, organizations, groups of associates, or even single persons (whether trained or previously untrained) can "work side by side with the rural poor to develop projects that the villagers request and will be able to sustain after the expedition departs." CHOICE volunteers have expanded their projects into Mexico, Nepal, Guatemala, Kenya, Ecuador, and the Navajo Nation. With Indigenous staff hired to manage each program, this NGO develops water supply systems, greenhouses, and schools and literacy, and has provided health and medical assistance (CHOICE, 2020).

Unitus: This nonprofit organization was established by a few of my wealthy business colleagues and me, to accelerate the global expansion of microfinance. Raising tens of millions of dollars in its first several years, it has continued to make great impacts. Unitus works to find permanent solutions to poverty among millions of the poor. It is called Unitus (pronounced *Unite-Us*) because of a belief that unity is a key to eliminating poverty. Its founders believe that greater global unity among people will motivate and enable more people to get involved in helping their sisters and brothers in lasting ways. Unitus (2021) fulfills its mission by various means, including primarily a comprehensive sponsorship of innovative new MFIs (microfinance institutions).

HELP International: This organization was established in 1999, in the aftermath of Hurricane Mitch, which essentially set back the nation of Honduras for 50 years, according to the United Nations. At my university, I began teaching MBAs (masters of business administration) in a new semester and asked the question whether a big American university such as ours was relevant to the destruction and suffering in Central America. In response, we mobilized more students as volunteers, spent a semester training them to practice Christianity as social entrepreneurs, and had them devote their summer in laboring to rebuild the small nation of Honduras. The mission of HELP was to assist the poor of the developing world to improve their quality of life while developing competent U.S. student and community leaders for tomorrow's continued fight against poverty. By working in conjunction with other microfinance institutions, HELP continues to grow while providing students a hands-on experience working with microcredit. Volunteers are also given the opportunity to create, implement, and sustain their own humanitarian service projects, microcredit programs, and other development projects in the developing world (HELP International 2020).

We ended up deciding to go to Honduras, because it was the country hardest hit by the hurricane, whose damaging results were just incredible. We ended up with 46 volunteers from my school, Brigham Young University, as well as from the University of Utah, Stanford, and others, who joined us in that venture. Instead of just a few thousand dollars, we were able to raise $116,000. With that money we were able to start 47 communal banks (also called micro-banks)—mostly groups of women who gathered together and whom we trained how to become self-reliant, how to be social entrepreneurs, and how to be microentrepreneurs. Many of them had lost husbands and jobs. Roughly speaking, we helped to create new micro-businesses, which we nicknamed "microenterprises," consisting of about 800 jobs benefiting on average five people per family; that resulted in some 4,000 family members being blessed with the loans that we were able to provide to them as we started these communal banks.

In addition to microcredit and microfinance and microenterprise, our volunteers throughout the summer of 1999 performed about 20,000 hours of community service. They even delivered babies out in rural medical facilities. They shoveled mud out of schools and rebuilt the schools, plastered the walls, disinfected the damaged areas, sanded and painted the walls, rebuilt houses, mentored street children, started family gardens, and trained families on how to become square-foot-garden experts and how to grow enough produce to feed themselves nutritious vegetables throughout the year. Other volunteers taught in schools after we got them fixed up and reopened. Still others provided computer training skills. We took down supplies from religious congregations in six U.S. states that donated materials for newborn kits for babies and their mothers, hygiene kits for refugee families that had lost everything, school kit supplies, and basic materials for children. We took these items down in extra suitcases and organized the kits in-country. We also brought supplies we needed with our own that cash we took to Honduras, and so were able to bless the lives of many schoolchildren. From those humble beginnings, HELP has continued to grow and thrive. We've expanded throughout our beginnings in Honduras to serve all of Central America, plus much of South America, Africa, and even Asia.

First Hope: Founded in 1986 by Cecile Pelous when she was president of a Christian women's association in Paris, First Hope supports an orphanage and school in Nepal (Woodworth, 2016). The founder started taking summer vacations to Nepal, leaving her prestigious job with the high-fashion industry in France, to volunteer by helping abandoned children high in the Himalaya. Later she had the first orphanage built, and eventually left her job of luxury to operate a home and school in order to develop a better future for the local children. Some 20 years later, Cecile Pelous is still dedicated to this simple yet amazing program.

Eagle Condor Humanitarian: Formerly named Chasqui Humanitarian, this is a 501(c)(3) nonprofit corporation working mostly in Peru and Bolivia. The foundation works with local civic and religious leaders through projects that will empower impoverished villagers to acquire for themselves what they need, and even want, so that they will raise their own standard of living and have a more fulfilling life. With a variety of projects, volunteers work in several areas including agro-industry, education, health, hygiene, housing, water, family gardens, small enterprises, microcredit, job and vocational training, and English and computer classes.

Eagle Condor was launched in one of my courses I taught when earning a master's degree in public administration in the late 1990s. I and my volunteers started doing humanitarian work in the Sacred Valley of the Inca between Cusco, which was the ancient Inca capital, and Machu Pichu, which is the site of the Peru's most historic ruins. Down in the valley between the historic Inca valley sites we began to work with several villages, as well as some located higher in the mountains.

One of my students returned to his homeland and lived there for a number of years, setting up schools, providing microcredit, establishing health care systems and anti-HIV AIDs training, agriculture projects, and so on. In years that followed, hundreds of Christian volunteers spent weeks or months there as community volunteers.

The mission of Eagle Condor is to enrich family life and to empower people and build self-reliance. Its purposes include to offer employment opportunities, to work out ways of raising the standard of living, to offer basic humanitarian charity, and to build an ongoing organization that would improve the lives of the meek and the humble in Peru. Eagle Condor drew for its value statement on religious teachings that remind us we are all sons and daughters of God and must reach out to one another with love and concern. Lifting the sorrow and suffering of those who are in distress is made possible by U.S. followers of Jesus who give financial and other resources such as skills and talents that rise out of people's generosity.

These values became the driving motif of Eagle Condor Humanitarian. The structure of this NGO is basically that of having a board here in the U.S. with 22 board members and two paid employees here, plus a board of six in Peru with four paid employees working up in the urban areas of northern Peru, along with a number of volunteers.

Eagle Condor organizes expeditions of North Americans as humanitarian tour groups whose members pay their own way, take donated goods such as tools or books or clothing or medicine and computers, and spend 10 to 14 days laboring among the poor. They provide labor and skills in building houses and schools, in offering teaching, in doing microenterprise training, in stocking libraries, helping with agricultural tasks, and sometimes even providing professional services such as medical or dental.

Eagle Condor is much different from most microfinance institutions in Peru because it offers training and consulting and credit (meaning loans), as well as workshops and libraries. It has even created a microenterprise incubator by which groups of impoverished Peruvian microentrepreneurs can gather to help each other and share best practices in a region where some 60 percent of the population is unemployed. Eagle Condor takes its clients through a series of training opportunities, including extensive workshops based on business idea generation and evaluation. It also introduces other topics, like how to design a business plan, ways to obtain funding to implement one's business plan, or how to learn rudimentary skills for regeneration, refixing, and redesigning. Altogether, it helps the microenterprises get up and running, with a maximum possibility of being successful.

The consequences of our work in Peru have led to considerable financial support from American Christians, as well as many news stories, leading to yet more attention, which in turn has attracted many fresh recruits as volunteers, and more.

MicroBusiness Mentors: This enterprise was founded in the Marriott School at BYU to address economic challenges, mostly of refugees and immigrants from Latin America entering the U.S. Operated by graduate as well as undergraduate students from several university campuses in the region, MBM, as it is known, offers business training, mentoring, and microloans starting at $500 to individuals seeking to become economically self-reliant. It provides tools and skills to assist Latino families, primarily, in achieving a better quality of life.

An important implication for me, in this mini-case, is that we don't have to go overseas to do this kind of work. I've had the great opportunity of collaborating with many of my students, who during each semester in the courses they take with me are required to do a literature search so they can come to understand microfinance and social entrepreneurship rules and methods. Then, as they get the theory and the concepts and the literature under their belt, they design some form of field project, some kind of either hypothetical or realistic case.

One group of students in a course I taught called "NGO Management" in the Marriott School came to me in 2002 and said, "Warner [I always asked students to call me by my first name], we want to do something locally. Your classes are doing some marvelous work around the world. We're interested in local impacts where it doesn't cost as much to travel there and where we can achieve a result that addresses a problem in our own community that's not really being addressed by community officials." Out of that grew a "little" organization that started as a class project called MicroBusiness Mentors (Woodworth, 2017).

And that little effort has been thriving and growing now for more than two decades. The guts of it are the following. First, we put together a plan based on surveys of the communities or subcultures in Provo, Utah—the home of Brigham Young University and several other colleges— whose needs were not being met very well. For us as a university community, for people in the business community and the education community and others, we felt we had pretty good lives. But the very poor, especially immigrants, and primarily those in the local Hispanic community, had a very tough time. A number of studies conducted at several universities over the years revealed that that this community, in particular, experienced an extremely high rate of unemployment. Its people had troublesome financial stresses. They weren't able to qualify for bank loans so they could start their own businesses. They couldn't land jobs with lots of companies because their immigrant status was uncertain. They often didn't speak English well. They couldn't get welfare benefits. They had no access to medical assistance when the need arose.

So this group of my very impressive students in their master's in public administration (MPA) program decided to launch a project to address some of these concerns. We saw many of these families moving two or three or four times a year from one rental unit to another, from one barely livable apartment to another, from one neighborhood to another. Their kids had no stability in school so many of them struggled to stay afloat academically. The parents lived under tremendous amounts of stress. Their neighborhoods among the poorer sections of the community were challenged by much higher crime rates. Many of the older kids failed to graduate from high school, and even if they did few of them could go on to college. Responding to all these important findings, my students and I designed a four-pronged approach for helping to generate economic sustainability within our local Hispanic community.

The first pillar we erected, so to speak, was to provide a series of training programs for folks as we could recruit them, which would help teach them business skills; *and* we'd do this all in Spanish. We would next help form groups that would work together and share ideas and plans with each other. For the second pillar, we would find trainers to do the training, and then ask experienced facilitators to teach and practice group processes so that our impoverished clients could design new business start-ups here in the Utah area.

For the third pillar, after they graduated from the training, our volunteer teams assisted folks to develop a solid business plan while simultaneously gaining support from their peers. Then we helped our clients form "solidarity groups," what we might call "social collateral groups," to which we would offer small, $500 loans. In the U.S., $500 seemed to be the minimum. Of course, many non-Latinos laughed at our plan and said a $500 loan wouldn't get a person anything in America. But that's all we had.

For the fourth and final pillar, as they graduated from our programs, received the initial loan, and started their business, each client would be assigned a mentor from the community. Often, she or he was a local businessperson who spoke Spanish, and perhaps had even lived a while in Latin America—someone who loved the people, who would be patient, who also was an entrepreneur and had their own business in Utah Valley. With that background, they could really help coach Latino clients while at the same time providing their own real-world experience as these immigrants tried to set up their own little start-up enterprises.

This MBM program of ours has grown to be enormously successful. For many years it has been operating as a kind of classroom laboratory for many of my students in which, as part of their regular coursework, they will labor on this project. They volunteer for one semester and provide training, they help design the training materials and then translate them, they prepare the video slideshows and charts, they provide many types of group support, they help us raise money, and they do all things necessary. And little by little this effort has grown. It's been amazing to me to see our clients as we recruited from all over the community, ranging from Latino food markets and their *mercados;* from their courses in English as a second language; and from their Catholic, evangelical, and Mormon (now called Latter-day Saint) congregations. MBM has seen a tremendous response from these people. They come to this country hoping for a better life, and yet they struggle so tremendously and with such faith in their own future.

Public perceptions about MicroBusiness Mentors have been impressive. The organization even had the great honor of bringing on our advisory board Professor Muhammed Yunus, the recipient of the Nobel Peace Prize and our great friend from the Grameen Bank of Bangladesh. Muhammed, whom I later often hosted in my own home when he came to visit Utah, often talked about this work in inner-city United States in a number of his speeches around the globe. Eventually he also established Grameen America to principally serve refugee women coming to the U.S. from places around the world.

Ouelessebougou Alliance: This alliance, often simply called "OA," was begun in 1985 by a Utah group of Catholics, Mormons, and Muslims. Their goal was to develop a long-term socioeconomic relationship with people living in a group of villages in Mali, a West African country that at the time was the third-poorest nation in the world. OA undertakes projects requested by the villagers, who define their own needs, contribute labor to projects, and provide leadership from their own ranks. Projects include constructing wells, fencing off gardens, providing basic health care training, teaching literacy, and establishing a village bank, along with various microenterprises and producer cooperatives (Woodworth, 2008).

Charity Anywhere Foundation: This Christian nonprofit, based in Idaho, has the goal of arranging service projects to anyone, anywhere, who has a real need for charitable relief. CAF offers a variety of projects, including service trips to Mexico and Nicaragua, as well as domestic service opportunities. It is always looking for people among Christian congregations who have promising ideas for service projects but don't know how to get started, and it welcomes a variety of volunteers for its current projects projects (Charity Anywhere, 2022).

Mentors International: Founded in 1990 by a group of Christian business executives, a few of my BYU students, and myself, Mentors International (2022) is a human development foundation designed, as its mission statement proclaims, "to build self-reliance and entrepreneurial spirit within those who struggle for sufficiency in developing countries." Working first in the Philippines and now having expanded to nine countries in Latin America, Africa, and Asia, Mentors works with Indigenous staff, building increased self-reliance among the recipients of its aid. Efforts are made to charge for consulting services based on ability to pay, which transforms the typical donor–receiver dependency relationship into a more effective character-building, consultant–client relationship. Mentors is set up as a nonprofit, tax-exempt organization whose primary interventions include training, consulting, walk-in services, professional referrals, and access to microcredit loans. Mentors depends on individual, foundation, and corporate donations to achieve its goals. As of early 2022, it has raised more than $172 million to train people and to provide them with loans that in turn can establish more than one million new jobs, thus benefiting some five million poor people in the developing world.

Sustain Haiti: This student-managed NGO arose after a massive 10.1 earthquake wreaked havoc on the island nation of Haiti, in the Caribbean Ocean, in 2010. From my social entrepreneurship course, dozens of students in programs such as master's of business administration, accounting, social science, economics, and others volunteered to be trained so they could travel to Haiti as volunteers, beginning in spring 2010. Their goal was to help rebuild destroyed communities with construction skills, microfinance programs, business plans, family agriculture, environmental strategies, water purification technologies, orphanage support, and much more. The volunteers taught health and hygiene, assisted in providing education in schools, helped rebuild damaged orphanages, and conducted other vital programs (Woodworth, 2010). U.S. teams raised funding in the states and sent summer volunteers to Haiti, while the Indigenous staff on-site managed multiple programs on the ground. This organization has collaborated for a decade with other NGO partners to assist the people of Haiti in regaining their lives and rebuilding their livelihoods.

Implications

As I have offered each of these brief illustrations of my many initiatives, and thinking back on the challenges and successes achieved over the years as I designed and launched projects with my students, friends, and even family, I fondly remember talking with some university administrators. One of them remarked that I'd be lucky to get even *five* students to go volunteer in the developing world for a summer. Others warned me that with my students receiving zero compensation, doing physical labor in the hot tropics or foreign deserts, and not even earning college credit hours, my little projects had no viable future. As one business school dean averred: "These are *students*. They don't have time and money and energy to go do something. They need internships in corporate America!" When I first tried raising some project funding, one of my business department colleagues counseled that I should focus on academic research and journal publications, otherwise I was simply wasting my time. One department chair advised me: "You'll be fortunate if you get $5,000, because these are poor kids, and middle-class kids. They don't have the skills to fund-raise, and they certainly don't have the capability of really making a difference."

Navala Village elders in community meeting hut in Fiji, with
the author and members of his HELP team.

Despite all such warnings, I drew on my faith in God and the potential I always felt that our amazing young people have. I believed that such criticisms were just not true. I knew we could do a great deal. We could probably even exceed our own expectations. Happily, several months ago, in early 2022, one of those doubting deans came up to me to express thanks and even congratulations. He said my faith, hope, and charity had yielded much more than he or other bureaucrats ever anticipated! Thankfully, I've received multiple awards and enjoyed academic admiration not only from my own university base, but also from other schools, as well as from scholarly and humanitarian institutions such as a Maria Montessori Award for Education in 2022 from the EURASIA Institute. Our NGOs have been recognized by the Acton Institute for the Study of Religion and Liberty; *Fast Company Magazine;* the Society for the Scientific Study of Religion; the Skoll Award at the World Forum; Oxford University; the Red Cross Global Award; and dozens more.

I believe these mini-cases offer the reader glimpses of the many ways in which believers in Jesus can utilize their God-given talents to carry out what the Bible teaches. The scriptures range from Christ's own words: *"Give to the one who asks you, and do not turn away from the one who wants to borrow from you"* (Matthew 5:42). Or, as James 1:27 says: *"Religion that God our Father accepts as pure and faultless is this: to look after orphans and widows in their distress and to keep oneself from being polluted by the world."* Likewise, the Apostle Paul declared, *"Be on your guard against all kinds of greed; a man's life does not consist in the abundance of his possessions."* (I Corinthians 6:10). Such counsel is in vivid contrast from the Oliver Stone's 1987 movie *Wall Street,* in which the corporate raider Gordon Gekko proclaims that "greed is good!"

Concise Orientation to This Book

As I begin to describe some of these cases and strategies in the following chapters, I want to highlight my colleague Professor Muhammad Yunus, who has been a mentor and partner with me in a number of these efforts. He has often served as an influential adviser to us in the projects we have launched out of my university here, as well as among private groups of citizens off campus in Utah Valley and in Salt Lake City. I will again note that he was granted the prestigious Nobel Peace Prize in 2006, partly for the work he has done over the decades with global microcredit efforts, as well as for the formation of Bangladesh's Grameen Bank. Muhammad made an intriguing comment to me once, after seeing my students in action serving the poor. He has seen us volunteering not only in his native Bangladesh, but also in various parts of Africa and Latin America and Asia where he was consulting or speaking. He has witnessed us attending global conferences, doing presentations, and launching numerous microcredit organizations, and he has reviewed some of the reports written by these young Christian students and noted the kind of work they are doing and the impacts they are achieving. Several times he's essentially said to me, *"Warner, your students are incredible."* The first time I brought him to my business school, he was greatly interested in the fact that we began his momentous lecture presentation by offering a Christian prayer to the God of the Bible. To me, it illustrated the way in which our collective good works can strengthen and improve the perceptions around the globe that people have of our religion, our faith, our beliefs, and even our lives.

Nobel Peace Prize Laureate Muhammad Yunus and global social entrepreneur
Warner Woodworth, hanging out at a worldwide Microcredit Summit.

To summarize this big-picture introduction, I must mention that my students, alumni, and I myself, having have worked together since the mid-1980s, now have created and conducted some 42 international projects! Readers interested in greater detail about ways in which they can engage with the NGOs described in this chapter or the rest of the book can refer to *Appendix I* to find extensive information, lists of books and videos, and other links to a variety of sources of information.

All have become legally incorporated NGOs that now operate in dozens of nations. Last year, in 2021 alone, we trained more than 340,000 microcredit clients. We grew our microentrepreneur base to over seven million families, meaning we now have impacted more than 28 million clients to whom we have given loans with our partners from the funds that we've raised. And the fundraising itself has been tremendously significant. Starting with just a few hundred thousand dollars two decades ago, the total amount these projects and these NGOs have raised comes to over *$1.3 billion*. This strongly suggests to me that there's no limit to what we can do, above and beyond the typical programs of Christian churches and other religious institutions. There is so much possibility, and there are so many great individuals out there, who want to make a difference, ranging from the most humble students to the most wealthy and successful believers.

But to make these changes, we must adopt a fresh mind-set. One way to look at this is my simple attempt to describe how we in our present state need to get a vision. We need to imagine a better future. We need to visualize a richer, more fulfilling alternative. I call it *"Imaginization"*— pulling together words such as "visualization" and "imagination" as terms meaning to explore and to dream, not from the status quo of many of us on this planet, but rather from the point we can imagine some ideal future state. When we get that vision, if we can imagine a world without poverty, then we can begin to backtrack and build steps to help us collectively move from our current lowly situation of suffering, of unemployment, of illness, of disease, of poverty ravaging millions and millions of people in dozens of countries that are worse off now than they were even a decade ago. We can thus begin to develop a vision for a future, for an ideal state to come that will be an entirely different world.

Throughout my life, I've always drawn from the great humanitarian Albert Schweitzer, who was a deacon at Strasbourg's Lutheran church of Saint Nicholas and later became the leader of the Saint Thomas Theological College. Among his notions that I've always appreciated are these words: *"I don't know what your destiny will be, but one thing I do know: the only ones among you who will be really happy are those who have sought and found out how to serve."* That amazing humanitarian to Africa inspires me even today. As believers in Jesus, we are building through these various programs in Latin America, Asia, and Africa. Our NGOs are changing the world one family at a time, building self-reliance, creating sustainability, setting up education systems, establishing economic and microenterprise programs, launching agricultural initiatives, specifying in some cases how one's faith can be used for humanitarian services. Often, our efforts initially occurred because of a particular global crisis, such as the devastating earthquakes in Nepal and Haiti. The enormously generous people who help fund our NGOs are doing more than merely writing checks to other organizations. They are designing innovative projects. They are seeking to build awareness. They are creating new projects, new NGOs, and they are also partnering with other NGOs around the globe.

I've been greatly impressed with numerous Christian families around the United States, over the last 20 years, as they have contacted me and said they wanted to make a difference. They've inquired: "What can we *do?* Where's a project for us? We have time, we have money, we feel a sense of stewardship. What can *we* do?" I'm thinking of families like the Ponds of Denver, who for four years have traveled with some of their friends and neighbors and church members, collaborating to assist a poor rural village in the highlands of Guatemala. Or the Pope family of Utah, who started a little project to do microenterprise with a small group of women in Mombasa, Southern Kenya, and have now assisted an amazing total of some 20,000 borrowers, as well as setting up a factory to produce coconut oil for U.S. consumption, thereby creating jobs. These and other generous families they have witnessed, either from afar or on-site, multiple thousands of borrowers starting businesses and working toward independence and dignity.

I'm thinking of Robert and Lynette Gay, from Connecticut, who have given so much of their money and expertise to work on projects in Latin America, India, Ethiopia, and Ghana.

I'm also thinking of the Shepherd family and their friends, who served as Christian missionaries some 30 years ago to Peru and Bolivia, after which they got some of their former mission friends together, motivated and inspired them, and started a wonderful effort to help the poor in the Andes.

And I think of the Williams family, of Sacramento, some of whom attended one of our microcredit conferences and then went with us down to El Salvador to see the situation for themselves. They came home from that experience, inspired to start what they later called the Elk Grove Action Group. It became a collection of fellow workers and managers at their businesses, as well as friends, neighbors, and educators, who collaborated for some seven years to raise donations from their own businesses and friends. The goal was to support several Salvadorian village banks that were working with their partner, the Organization of Women's Economics (OEF). Together they have been helping to spread multiple methodologies to help impoverished women in El Salvador.

These families, together with many others over the decades of my work, are true followers of Jesus. They study poverty together, donate to the relief of the poor, travel to countries in the developing world, volunteer to serve in poor communities, and conduct humanitarian expeditions at their own expense and time. Then, after working in the villages and getting to know local needs, they typically return home and form action groups, share their experiences, tell their stories, recruit others, and in some cases even set up their own wonderful (and generous) family foundations.The results of these sorts of private initiatives by committed Christians have had marvelous impacts, as my friends and I work voluntarily from love. We seek God's Spirit. We start at the bottom and move out and move up. There's no pride involved, there's no control involved, there are no political goals involved. Rather, there's this simple, humble desire among followers of the Savior who find a purpose in their lives and who go well beyond their traditional church services to figure out ways of saving the living, and of saving and blessing the Lord's children around the globe.

Readers who wish to learn more about my work for the globe's poor can review my biographical details in *Appendix III*. It contains links to sources of useful information on social entrepreneurship organizations that I have created or developed over my long life.

Conclusion

I devoutly hope that this book will inspire many more Christian initiatives for believers everywhere to offer increased and heartfelt service to those who struggle—especially people in developing countries who suffer from abject poverty, illness, hunger, and even war. *Let us begin!*

References

BYU. (2022). Website of Brigham Young University. https://www.byu.edu/.

Charity Anywhere Foundation (2022). https://www.charityanywhere.org/.

CHOICE Humanitarian. (2020). https://choicehumanitarian.org/annual-report/.

I Corinthians 6:10; 16:13–14.

HELP International. (2020). *Journal of Research in Business and Management* (JRBM). http://www.questjournals.org/jrbm/papers/vol8-issue5/A08050108.pdf.

James 1:27.

Matthew 5:42.

Mentors International. (2022). https://mentorsinternational.org/.

Unitus. (2021). *Noble International Journal of Social Sciences Research,* vol. 6, no. 4, pp. 48–55.

Woodworth, W. (2008). Development from Below: Strengthening Rural Village Families Through Core Capacity-Building Methods. *Conference Proceedings.* Association of Third World Studies, October 12.

Woodworth, W. (2010). Laboring in the Trenches with the Poor of Haiti. *Meridian Magazine*, December 28, pp. 1–10.

Woodworth, W. (2016). "The Work of First Hope Programs in Nepal." An analysis by the author of school and orphanage, 2002–2015.

Woodworth, W. (2017). Engaged Learning in MBA Programs: Hands-on Microfinance, International Institute of Social & Economic Sciences. *Proceedings of Annual International Academic Conference,* http://www.ISBN 978-80-87927-31-1, IISES, pp. 53–160.

Woodworth, W. (2019). Disruptive Innovation from the Base of the Pyramid: Cases in Peru, the Philippines, and Honduras. *International Institute of Social and Economic Sciences Research Series,* pp. 53–56.

Serving Leper Colonies: Rising Star Outreach in India

Jesus heals a leper in Luke 8:2–4: *"When He had come down from the mountain, great multitudes followed Him. And behold, a leper came and worshipped Him, saying, 'Lord, if You are willing, You can make me clean.' Then Jesus put out His hand and touched him, saying, 'I am willing; be cleansed.' Immediately his leprosy was cleansed. And Jesus said to him, 'See that you tell no one....'"*

The plague of leprosy has afflicted millions of people before and long after the Savior's earthly ministry. This chapter explores in depth the processes and outcomes of a Christian woman from Atlanta, Georgia, a dear friend of mine, who through faith and love established an American-based organization seeking to generate positive social impacts in India. Her nonprofit/nongovernmental organization (NGO), named Rising Star Outreach (RSO, 2021), operates in India. Established in the U.S. it seeks to reduce the suffering of leper communities in the state of Tamil Nadu (2017), in southern India, as well as to provide education and other services to lepers' children. As a facilitator of this NGO, I have been closely involved by serving as an informal adviser to it over the years. This chapter integrates some of my academic research and my gospel values, drawing on interviews, annual reports, group discussions, and even direct observation at RSO meetings. After analyzing the entrepreneurial start-up of this organization and assessing its public policy features, I will present a brief critique of pluses and minuses, along with suggestions for future management and social policy as to how believers in Christ can *"go and do likewise."*

Introduction to RSO

In this chapter I seek to elucidate the difficulties of external intervention by using a case I have been intimately involved with as a management adviser. I will describe the highlights, motivations, and systems used, and will summarize various challenges we met in rolling out RSO's programs. These include barriers to entering the nation of India, difficulties in design and implementation, and mixed outcomes. I hope that this case will shed light on similar programs that might be pursued by foreign organizations to help the wonderful people of India, especially those marginalized by disease, poverty, and other dimensions of human suffering, so that they may enjoy greater benefits and more satisfying lives in the future.

Rising Star Outreach's Leper Relief: A woman named Rebeca Douglas (Becky) founded Rising Star Outreach (RSO) after she felt God inspired her to help Tamil Nadu's leper colonies during a visit to the region. Her trip occurred after the tragic suicide of her daughter, Amber, who was a young college student in the northeast United States. After her daughter's death, Becky learned that Amber had been mailing some of her parents' money for her monthly college expenses to an orphanage in India known as the Belmont Children's Home. Becky felt so shocked, because she had never heard anything about this. So she invited several Christian neighbor women to take money raised at her daughter's funeral and visit the orphanage in person, donating the $10,000 in contributions to it. Initially she learned that the facility was caring for children whose parents had succumbed to leprosy. It was a shocking discovery for this group of naive, well-off Americans.

But Becky's journey soon began to turn her response from tragedy to joy. While in India, after visiting the orphanage and making their very generous donation, Becky and her friends went by taxi through the streets as beggars rushed to the car windows seeking a handout. Such suffering people flock through India's congested cities, a fact unknown to the American women. The experience shocked them so deeply that they inquired of the taxi driver. He explained that India is overrun with lepers, and remarked that they are both dirty and dangerous. Becky recalled how in the New Testament, beggars were condemned and called names such as "unclean." Later, when I hosted her in my home for a fundraiser, she confessed how naive she felt. "I thought Jesus had healed all the lepers in his day," she said (Woodworth, 2018). However, after learning the wide existence of leprosy in India, she didn't bemoan the plight of its victims. Nor did she turn away. Instead, Becky plunged into the situation. She studied, consulted doctors back home in the U.S., and returned to India to learn more. Then she moved forward in launching ways that she proposed to help change the world.

I now turn to examine how this Christian woman used her faith, family values, brains, and even her life's tragedy, to design and roll out her nonprofit so as to bless and help leprosy sufferers. To frame her work, I begin with the counsel of Mahatma Gandhi as he surveyed modern society and felt concerned (Gandhi, 1925). In the late 1990s, I met Arun Gandhi, a grandson of that great philosopher and liberator, who was with him just before he was assassinated in January 1948. Soon after we met, I invited several academic associates to join me in drafting an article on what I learned. Arun referred to seven specific practices or habits as Gandhi's "Seven Blunders of the Modern World," which became the title of an article I wrote for a publication at my business school at BYU (Woodworth, et al., 1998). These are things that will destroy us, often referred to as "The Seven Social Sins":

1. Wealth without work
2. Pleasure without conscience
3. Knowledge without character

4. Commerce without morality
5. Science without humanity
6. Religion without sacrifice
7. Politics without principle

And, of course, in the case of Rising Star Outreach, we see the opposites, the very things that give life and love to the world: Wealth from the work of our labors; Pleasure with a conscience; Knowledge that comes from character and values; Commerce (or Business) built on ethics and morality; Science connected to humanity; Religion and worship with sacrifice; and finally, Politics that grows from moral principles. These seven beneficial practices and skills don't come merely from Jesus's sacrifice on the cross, but also from sacrifices that we Christians make almost every day, offering some of our time, money, skills, and energy to improve the plight of other of God's children on earth. As I analyze Rising Star Outreach's work in India, I will identify some elements of these principles.

India's leprosy colonies have tragically emerged as "refugee camps" for people forced to leave their homes, and often even their families, after being diagnosed with leprosy. In the recent words of one patient: "Even our own parents and siblings despise us." Seeking relief from the bitter social stigma, lepers gather together in remote places where they do their best to cobble out a meager living. Even today, India's caste system—which, tragically, is still very much alive—stigmatizes leper families at the very bottom of society: no education, no jobs, no health care, no chance of marriage so no children, and not much of a future.

Thus, RSO became an NGO providing schools and education, medical services, microenterprises, infrastructure projects like clean water, and development programs to increase the dignity and self-reliance of colony members. The founders came to fully appreciate the words of the great Apostle Paul, who decreed: *"Love never fails"* (I Corinthians 13:8).

What does Rising Star do? Basically, it's a school for lepers and any offspring they may have, including children, grandchildren, and even people from neighboring area villages. Beginning in 2002, but dramatically expanding in 2004, RSO has had three main objectives: (1) reduce suffering from leprosy, (2) empower victims to move toward self-sufficiency, and (3) help children of India's lepers become healthy, productive citizens of their country (Woodworth, 2009–2017)

Below are some numbers of achievements made in its first decade (2021–2011) to frame RSO's initial mission. Briefly sketched, they include such facts as the following:

- Served 340 students grades K–12
- Also sent 67 students to universities
- The Rising Star Campus included:
  - Safe living quarters
  - Marriott School for Boys

- Amber Douglas School for Girls
- Peery Matriculation School Volunteer quarters
- Dining hall
- Meditation hall
- Staff of over 60
- In contrast to leprosy as suffering, lifelong pain, and amputation, RSO became a place of peace, learning, and beauty

- Areas of impact:
  - RSO helps facilitate infrastructure, growth, and community development within India's leprosy colonies.
  - RSO staff and volunteers operate through mobile clinics and partnerships with those few hospitals that provide critical medical treatment for leprosy patients.
  - The fastest, most effective ways to overcome fear and the stigma of leprosy is education.

Leprosy Facts as Important Background

To appreciate the true value of the economic, medical, and educational services that RSO offers the leper colonies surrounding the city of Chennai, in the state of Tamil Nadu, it will be helpful first to overview various historical efforts that have been made to eradicate leprosy, to analyze ensuing social legacies of stigma and social separation, and finally to deconstruct the unfolding, motivation, and methodology in implementing various programs.

The Disease of Leprosy: An important, more-educated term for leprosy is Hansen's Disease (HD), named for a Norwegian researcher who worked in the 1870s. India, in particular, has had a long and grim relationship with endemic HD; most historical estimates put nationwide prevalence rates in the high 50s (per 10,000 persons). In 2001, India's leprosy statistics 69 percent of global prevalence, and 81 percent of globally detected new cases. In 2002s National Health Policy, the National Leprosy Elimination Program (NLEP 2002–2015) declared India's goal of eliminating leprosy as a public health threat by the end of 2015. Through increased political will (including the 1983 repeal of the oppressive Lepers Act of 1898), augmented technology, improved information (through the amplifying effect of mass media), and enhanced cooperation efforts (offering free and in-home care for the duration of treatment), that elimination goal was met, remarkably, by 12 of India's 35 states and territories.

The 2005 prevalence rate of 0.95 cases per 10,000 residents may have qualified India to eliminate HD as a public threat, but the immense size of the country still managed to allow for over 168,000 new infections that year alone. Nonetheless, India's Health Ministry chose to withdraw funding from actively searching out new cases through surveillance, instead shifting the responsibility for eradication from states to high- and medium-endemic districts and blocks. By 2007, 80 percent of the 611 districts and 75 percent of the 6,239 blocks had managed to achieve elimination goals, logging steady declines each year of over 15 percent. Although the national rate did drop down to 0.72 cases per 10,000 residents, the official detection of 137,000 new cases that year still placed 54 percent of global prevalence within India's border (Ministry of Health, 2004–2019).

Tamil Nadu itself had been the second-most endemic state in all of India's 32 states in 1981, back when Prime Minister Indira Gandhi first challenged her country's scientists to develop an action plan for eradicating leprosy. Today it is home to only 4 percent of the country's HD infected, thanks largely in part to the stimulating effect of regional specialization. World Bank and World Health Organization (WHO, 2021) funding, for example, helped the country establish and implement programs that increased the effectiveness of NLEP guidelines. Mobile Leprosy Treatment Units (MLTUs) and Voluntary Reporting Centers (VRCs) allowed for near-complete urban and rural house-to-house surveillance, as well as for the integration of leprosy diagnosis and treatment in health care staff training. Urban Leprosy Centers (ULCs), attached to hospitals, were also created to help facilitate MDT treatment and the sometimes-necessary reconstructive surgery after bodies have been ravaged by leprosy.

As a result of the NLEP Final Push strategy of "detect and treat," rates of disability and deformity among the newly infected has fallen to a minuscule 2 percent of cases; and its other nonquantitative goals of increasing awareness and reducing stigma are generally assumed to have been achieved by project coordinators. Subsequent analysis of impacted communities does support reduced incidence of measurable social stigma, but only in locations where HD treatment has been sufficiently integrated into existing health care systems (University of Pennsylvania, 2016).

Sadly, 20 percent of India's health facilities still have not made the successful transition of incorporating HD diagnosis and treatment into their primary or even hospital care services. This absence has been positively linked to the continued preservation of negative social stereotypes and harsh treatment of newly detected cases by the general public. Tamil Nadu, however, is one of the top five states (out of 32) with a higher proportion of health facilities offering HD treatment; irrespective of rank, other studies highlight that district disparities can exist between hospitals throughout states. Other studies shed light on the persistent practice of health systems in larger cities overlooking and underserving rural areas they deem as too inaccessible and difficult to reach.

Site and Situation: RSO began to focus in Tamil Nadu, a province that sits at the very bottom of the Asian continent. Its economy is the fifth largest in the country, and 40 percent of its population lives in urban centers, of which the city of Chennai is the largest (ranking as the fourth largest city in all of India). The average daily wage is about 80 rupees (about $1.07 US) per day, and per capita income ranks it sixth of the top 15 most wealthy. The total fertility rate is 1.43 (children per mother), the second lowest in the country; infant mortality is 48 (deaths per 1,000 live births), versus a national average of 67.6; child immunization rates top 93 percent. On a national level, when ranked using the UN Human Development Index, Tamil Nadu is India's third highest achieving state (2017).

The population is predominantly of the Tamil ethnicity, and Hinduism is the prevailing religion. As such, cultural legacies of the caste system continue to be vital predictors for social organization and classification, and little possibility exists for social mobility or economic improvement. Those on the underbelly of society never historically had enough economic worth to be assigned a class of their own by Hindu thought, and throughout the course of history they have been called many unsavory names—including Untouchables, Dalits Harijans, and (more recently) Scheduled Castes and Scheduled Tribes. Approximately 19 percent of the state of Tamil Nadu is inhabited by this social underclass. At the bottom of this base group lie those with signs of leprosy infection, or HD.

Social Burden: People living in and around the city of Chennai who find themselves plagued with Hansen's Disease come from all levels of social strata, but nationally 33 percent come from "Scheduled Tribes/Castes," formerly branded as "Untouchables." Similar to other communicable disease burdens, women and children share a vulnerability to HD, as just over 34 percent and 10 percent of new cases come from these populations, respectively. One analyst reported: "In Tamil Nadu alone there are 15,000 people who have leprosy. They are kept in government run homes, each of which can accommodate around 400 people. Here they are provided with food, shelter and medical care. There are ten such homes, one in each district of the state. Those with families are put up in leprosy colonies located far away from the general population. In Tamil Nadu there are 45 leprosy colonies, each of which has around 20 to 130 families" (Mujtaba, 2007). Absorbing these statistics, Becky Douglas's RSO began to see that it could perhaps counter this crisis.

Most people who go on to encounter HD realize they are infected with "something" during the early stages of infection when skin becomes blotched. Many can confuse that with other dermatological disorders, attempt to continue on with life as usual, and neglect to seek out medical attention or advice out of fear of receiving some disconcerting news. Most sufferers are not even aware that HD is reversible if detected early enough. Only when people spot visible signs of infection do they realize that they are soon likely to suffer the full brunt of social stigma by their peers and even their loved ones.

Families of HD-infected people will unfailingly sever ties with them (including all social and economic ties), in an effort to avoid public exposure, shame, and dishonor on the family name. Families that include young and unmarried men or women realize that the entire family is especially vulnerable to the negative stigma attached to HD, since arranged marriages continue to be the preferred and predominant method of wedding in Tamil Nadu. In the unfortunate event that rumors of infection reach the ears of any influential member of the opposite family, a child's matrimonial value is often completely destroyed, and decades of goodwill, friendships, and even business relationships are likely to be eroded.

The local Hindu religious and Tamil cultural traditions relating to leprosy infection continue to consider people suffering from HD as being cursed. This stance is not at all unique to the region, as evidenced by centuries of harsh treatment. Infected people throughout greater India have been customarily shunned and outcast from their homes, clans, villages, and cities. HD sufferers were once corralled into certain areas outside city limits, but over time the government allowed for the formation of leper colonies, which nevertheless remained geographically isolated and distant from old city–centers. Recent urban growth has resulted in the expansion of city boundaries, the inevitable encompassing of these segregated colonies, and eventually their incorporation into a greater cityscape. Despite leprosy sufferers' being much more integrated geographically, antileprosy social norms continue to allow them to suffer.

Leper Colonies: The quality of life for those residing in leper colonies still falls short of local averages, which are routinely some of the lowest in the country. The persistent absence of local and regional government involvement has only further exacerbated the dire infrastructure, health, and social problems. Those affected by HD continue to be publicly feared and openly discriminated against, as evidenced by the public's negligent withholding of employment, health care, education, and even adequate clean water and sanitation. The failure to provision these essentials basic to HD sufferers' human rights relegates them to lives of extreme poverty and humiliation. Most are perpetually sick, many are also homeless, and all are jobless; and as a consequence they find themselves obliged to resort to street-begging in order to generate even a submeager income with which to provide for survival.

Many HD sufferers enter the leper colonies as younger single adults, and over time they tend to partner up with other individuals in the community who find themselves in the same situation, and thus form families in the midst of the colonies' squalor. Offspring, if they come, are born into a most ill-fated situation, despite being free of disease, but because of familial proximity to HD they still suffer a social brunt as if they themselves had leprosy. The unfortunate coinciding of push/pull factors (the lack of primary education in the leper communities *and* the ability of young children to garner ever-increasing wages while street-begging in the city) affects children especially hard. Their parents primarily see them, while in their formative years, as capital-generating devices that must be exploited as early and often as possible.

The use of children for begging may provide a resource that parents can use to generate income, but it also serves to alienate HD-affected families from each other. Through the physical separation of young children from their parents (and parents from their children) for extended hours during the day, and for even several days in a row, the family as a unit of colony organization suffers enormous strain. Such an extensive lack of familial contact threatens to obliterate many of the unique linguistic, social, and even culinary customs and values that HD-affected parents have learned and practiced. If parents cannot teach their children what it means to be Indian, or Tamil, or the son or daughter of a person with HD, then these concepts of self-worth can, at best, only be intuited by children from their miserable occupation. This overt use of children for eliciting monetary donations both upholds and contributes more flame to the fire of negative stereotypes associated with those who suffer from leprosy as being lazy, ignorant, and altogether lacking in family values.

Sadly, many of such parents are the byproduct of the very same legacy of begging that they continue to perpetrate with their own children. Having been born in a leper colony though without HD, they were confined by social stigma to being able to live only there, close to their parents who actually were infected with HD. Because they were both genetically predisposed to HD infection and then subsequently exposed to the untreated bacteria for long periods, it is typically only a matter of time before they too contract the contagion. This inevitable eventuality therefore serves to accomplish the "family curse" prediction aspect of the social stereotype, and reinforces its self-fulfilling characteristic.

Purpose: The situation described above has remained fairly unchanged for generations, and continues down to the present. Who can place a finger on why? Maybe the primary cause was inadequate public policies. Perhaps other causes were scientific ignorance, technological inability, infrastructural malice, or even the inability of the HD-affected people themselves or their families. The simple fact remains that no one and no state or private agency has been adequately addressing the basic human rights, needs, and wants of those living in the leper colonies.

Rising Star Outreach Emerges as a Strategy

The first few RSO attempts that Becky Douglas and her American friends group made in their initial years of 2001–2002 to address the vulnerability of Tamil Nadu's leprosy-affected people could be described as small and as insignificant. The folk-wisdom equivalent might have been "give a man a fish, and you will feed him for a day." The dispersal of rice, beans, and saris to wear, one day served no other purpose than to create a need for those very services and commodities the next day, thereby inculcating an unhealthy dependency of the local population on continued, ever-growing humanitarian aid. As genuine and kind-hearted as this kind of help might have been at the time, Becky and her volunteering colleagues came to see it as ultimately detrimental to the overall well-being of those whom it was originally intended to benefit. After a few years of dealing with the ebb and flow of the humanitarian aid field, Becky struggled to find a more efficient, progressive, and sustainable way to tackle the host of economic problems that always seemed to be undermining her temporary relief efforts. Years ago, she never would have imagined that she would one day become the face of a vital NGO serving a community thousands of miles away from where RSO was headquartered (Woodworth, 2009–2017).

Transformation: Unbeknownst to her at the time, this same dilemma that she was wrangling with in Tamil Nadu—the establishment of a viable and self-sustainable program—was emerging as an actual impediment to long-term success across the entire humanitarian aid industry of India.

Many aid organizations were aware that they indeed possessed the expertise and capacity to provide large amounts of relief to needy populations in some of the most isolated of locales. For decades, the guiding principle in their aid allocation required that they focus efforts on short-term interventions, targeted at satisfying clear-cut and narrowly defined goals of tackling hunger, health crises, or poor sanitation. The end-result of the post-aid process always included the passing of the baton back to governments and local entities, which ordinarily should have then assumed ownership of the humanitarian crisis and worked toward its resolution.

Intrinsic in this transfer was a reliance on the ability of India's national and local governments to have the political will, resources, and determination to pick up where support endeavors ended. Unfortunately, the reality on the ground was that in the majority of cases the situation for those in need persisted, either in a similar or an even worse state than before. More and more agencies were beginning to realize that before the dust from their Jeeps could settle, the source causes of the incendiary economic, health, and infrastructural deficiencies would undoubtedly creep back in the mix and ultimately would undo any progress achieved. It became increasingly apparent to those in both provider and recipient camps that no amount of freely donated and distributed foodstuffs, medical services, or survival supplies could undo the centuries of social inequality, subservience, and political alienation that continued to give nourishment to the roots of these "emergencies."

Activists and aid agencies alike began to realize that if the source causes of crises remained unrecognized, untreated, and unresolved, they would continue to unravel other efforts. Thus, traditional humanitarian aid was time and again faced with a daunting reality: that they simply lacked the right set of tools to generate the kind of measurable and enduring societal change that could break the cycle of unstable and precarious situations that necessitated their involvement. This being the case, a multitude of pioneering development attempts were undertaken to try to counteract the bittersweet end-products of conventional aid, over a diversity of geographic regions and organizational specializations.

Microcredit: By the close of the millennium in the year 2000, the novel concept of "village banking" was the methodology that had risen to the top of the heap of competing development tactics. Finding its foundation in the early 1980s, the term comes from Muhammad Yunus's (2006) Nobel Peace Prize–winning Grameen Bank model (2018). Interestingly, "grameen" simply means village in the Bangla language (Grameen Bank, 2018). Subsequent related methodologies took on many different names, including "community banking," "microcredit," "microlending," "microloans," and "micro-financing" (Woodworth, 1997). By providing small amounts of credit to ever-larger numbers of people in economically vulnerable positions, practitioners began to garner more and more success toward undermining the diverse, deep-seated, and wide-ranging causes of poverty while at the same time alleviating its often-extreme side effects.

Although Becky Douglas may not have been explicitly aware of the existence of village banking and other tools before she started her original endeavors, after a few years of practice she intuitively felt the need in her Rising Star Outreach nonprofit for exactly the kind of multipronged intervention it actually espoused. From her experience on the ground, she saw that before landing in their current condition, many of the colony's residents had considerable amounts of experience living and working in cities. HD only took them away from their lifelong professions and imposed on them unforgiving physical limitations. Most of the sufferers retained unique knowledge of outside markets, or specialized technical abilities, or even a latent but keen entrepreneurial spirit. It was only the harsh application of HD's social stigma that managed to block their access to and utilization of traditional clan relationships for financial help. This, of course, only exacerbated the consequences of having lost employment, which then caused a chain reaction of overreliance on savings, and the acceleration of the eventual implosion of their individual money-making capacities (Shao, 2010).

It began to appear that most, if not all, of the economic damage suffered as a result of the negative effects of HD could be reversed through the adoption of village banking principles—if only RSO could help residents tap into the latent industrial capacity already available in their own colonies. Becky merely lacked access to a relatively small amount of start-up capital, a proven organizational system for implementation, and a recognizable and trusted local champion for the cause. All these factors came into focus upon her meeting Padma Venkataramen (2013) who, together with the Danish charity called Danida, already had gleaned more than a decade of experience using village banking to influence the lives of those affected by leprosy.

Champion: Venkataramen's personally-held values hold an admittedly particular potency, as she believes that anything given without charge lacks any importance at all. To a certain extent, she adamantly feels that nothing of value ought to be given away for free, lest those on the receiving end should consequently come to depend on its provision as a given, and subsequently will fail to recognize the inherent worth of the good or service. She also strongly believes that many HD-affected individuals continued to possess the fundamental abilities of identifying niche markets with opportunities for progress, coalescing into borrowing groups, and using modest quantities of capital to create small businesses that address the identified market failures. Through the formation of manageable ventures, built incrementally from the ground up, Venkataramen strongly believes that those with HD are just as capable as anyone else, living anywhere else, to facilitate the jumpstarting of their own local economies without having to rely endlessly on humanitarian aid.

This mentality perfectly meshes with village banking's emphasis on group formation, community participation, and interpersonal accountability. The conventional banking sector throughout the world requires a minimum of collateral to get involved with and utilize traditional forms of credit as a rule. The lowest segment of society has none of the many items that can be used as forms of a security deposit—whether large household consumer goods, forms of transportation, or deeds to land, structures, or businesses. The one thing they do have is each other, and that is the very same commodity that village banking is designed to allow them to take advantage of. The provision of loan guarantees likewise has shifted from a reliance on personally owned goods to the stability of this intrapersonal network among borrowing groups. Loans are allocated to groups, then is divided up among them according to their own predetermined needs. Payment for the entire loan is received by the group as a whole on the entire loan amount.

The emphasis on group payment allows individual members a certain flexibility that is often necessary in the extremely underdeveloped settings in which borrowers must work. Most colonial environments are relatively lacking in basic infrastructural elements, such as paved roads, adequate housing and sanitation, universal education facilities, and most other government-funded projects that are typically to be expected in cities of comparative size and scope. Far from the ideal environment from which to launch a business venture, borrowers then must persevere in overcoming obstacles that are uniquely difficult, even when viewed under local standards. As such, the enhanced ability for them to rely on other members of the loan group to cover payments during periods of less or nonproductive time provides a sort of breathing room in the inevitable event that something doesn't go quite right.

Microfinance Critique: Other social benefits exist that extend far beyond the fiscal responsibilities of loan repayment. Because each borrower is aware that the group will take responsibility for their individual part if they fail in their endeavors, this decreases the significant anxiety they may feel toward starting up their own business. This can consequently increase their confidence in trying something a little more risky, a little more foreign to them, and with a commensurately larger possibility for reward. The social stability also provided by the interpersonal network of borrowers can create a positive notion of dependency between individuals as well, as members eventually begin to worry about and care for the well-being of others in the group.

Assuring the success of the group as a whole is in every individual member's self-interest, in both the short and the long run. As the importance of this external result gets internalized, the true power of village banking as a sustainable "community builder" in the leper colonies emerges as another triumphant result. It fills a niche by providing credit to this underserved population, thereby allowing them the necessary seed money with which to grow their current business efforts. They feel free to start completely new companies or even to use preexisting and proven plans provided to them by RSO, similar to the idea of franchising. It also replaces the former familial connections, which had been severed as a consequence of negative social stigma, with new relationships of commonality and trust among loan group members.

It remains a matter of speculation whether the increased economic prosperity of HD sufferers in certain regions of India can potentially overcome the negative social stigma associated with the disease. Anecdotal evidence at the individual level leaves room for hope, as stories continue to grow of former street beggars having turned themselves into vendors of the same shops in front of which they previously used to petition. Using the same logic, whether the aggregate success of microbusinesses can translate into colonial improvements also remains to be demonstrated, as evidenced by RSO's reliance on the regular inflow of American volunteers to build housing and improve sanitation facilities in the colonies.

The priorities and goals of a typical leper colony's population, on the whole, have yet to be evidenced by official referendum. The political authority, responsibility, and capacity to extract taxable funds that would prove indispensable in infrastructural development have not yet surfaced. Overall, social organization that would provide for the implementation of any plans, also remains a matter of conjecture. If a given leper colony continues to grow economically, a subsequent shift in strategy and scope will necessarily need to follow, transitioning from an emphasis on small-group lending to some other more-conventional form of development aid that would be given to the newly formed colonial government. It may only be a matter of time until those in the colonies have squeezed all they can out of what "village banking" has to offer, and at that time an ever-more-versatile financial solution may have to be applied (or perhaps devised) that would better suit their new needs. If this becomes the case, then surely the economic intervention of "village banking" can rightly consider itself a success.

On a more general note, despite worldwide applicability, I find that the microcredit industry offers few suggestions as to its owns limitations with regard to long-term appropriateness. If it was meant to substitute for the service-delivery failures of conventional banking, its higher interest rates and increased need for social dependence may not be able maintain potency if access to traditional lending resources is eventually restored. In addition, despite proving that microcredit programs can be scaled up to include millions of people (so long as all of them are intricately managed at the small-group level), it may not be reasonable to expect it alone to transform economies, writ large.

Rising Star Outreach's Programs, Structure, and Budget: After the above review of RSO within the context of India's leprosy challenges, poor communities of those nationally (and especially in Tamil Nadu State), along with the potential applications of microcredit to help victims of HD to improve their lives, I will now summarize its extensive programs. Although RSO was founded in Atlanta, Georgia, in 2002, it is now headquartered in Provo, Utah. It has a board of 26 fairly wealthy members who each donate at least $25,000 annually to support RSO activities. All told, its yearly budget is about $1.5 million. It operates abroad with a native staff of 30 or more Indians, and additionally has 3 paid staffers at its headquarters in the U.S., who each receive a modest salary.

Volunteerism: The bulk of RSO's productivity derives from trained volunteers. They include retired American married couples who live at the RSO complex in villages near Chennai for one to two years of volunteering. In addition, all board members and top managers frequently serve as volunteers. Some 220 college students are annually trained as volunteers and take one or two semesters' leave from their educational pursuits to help run the programs in India, raising their own funds for international travel, and also covering their on-the-ground expenses while in India.

Indian workers rebuilding houses and thatched roofs for leper families.

Expeditions of shorter duration are planned that take U.S. families seeking to make a difference who spend 10 to 15 days at the operations doing volunteer work. This may include doing such things as the following: teaching math, English, and other basic subjects to the children of lepers; constructing new schools or organizational facilities; cooking meals for the leper children or outside volunteers; teaching singing, dancing, water painting, or other skills to those in the school programs; providing microloan capital and start-up entrepreneurial training to those seeking to establish microenterprises; evaluating existing RSO programs for their impacts and problems; assessing needs and launching new interventions as approved by the board—and so on. Each year a number of well-trained volunteers plan and carry out an Annual Science Fair day at the Peery Matriculation School. They work with lepers' children to prepare them for demonstrations and diagrams of complex scientific topics and projects like nuclear power plants, solar power, herbal medicines, and much more.

Throughout the U.S., Rising Star Outreach mobilizes groups such as Rotary International, Kiwanis, and others, to plan, raise funding for and implement programs to benefit leper colonies within the RSO network. Many groups of American mothers devise projects, such as making children's clothing, sewing pillow cases, knitting winter caps, and creating various other products for schoolchildren. Some volunteers raise funds to purchase sewing machines so that teens in the colonies may gain the skills to become tailors. Or they ship raw materials for vocational training in jewelry-making skills. Groups of U.S. schoolchildren gather supplies to make a hygiene kit (typically, a backpack filled with soaps, towels, washcloths, shampoo, bandages, ointments, toothbrushes and paste, feminine hygiene products, and the like), or to make school kits (carrying-bags with pens and pencils, writing paper, crayons, art paper, chalk, erasers, and more), all to be transported and delivered to each child in a leper colony.

Other forms of volunteerism are such activities as RSO's celebrity golf challenge, which is highlighted by participation by major sports heroes in the U.S., coming from the NBA, major league baseball, the NFL, and other sports. Wealthy players are drawn to tournaments at attractive Utah resorts on a given weekend. Rubbing shoulders with well-known U.S. athletes often yields collective donations of $100,000 or more in just a weekend golf match. In addition, large-event gala dinners and breakfasts, which feature auctions of donated art and other fine things, will at times generate $200,000 or more annually. For instance, the *American Idol* TV singing sensation David Archuleta has headed several RSO gala dinners that each generated over half a million dollars.

RSO Facilities: Its campus in Tamil consists of six buildings spread across 14 acres, which are a safe haven for up to 400 leper children at a time. The U.S. Peery Foundation, a California philanthropic nonprofit group, has played a key role in RSO's education of its targeted children (Goodman, 2011). Built in the Kerala style, the Peery Matriculation School offers a high standard of education from kindergarten through 10th grade. That high school was completed and dedicated in 2010; it houses a library science lab, along with upper-curriculum classrooms for older kids. Energy conservation was built into the design, with bricks used in construction specifically designed to use air as natural insulation, keeping the school cool without air conditioning, even during the hot summer months. The Secondary School is connected to the Elementary School, forming a right angle. Inside the angle are a playground and a quarter-mile track.

The Marriott Children's homes (donated by the large U.S. family that founded the Marriott hotel chain worldwide) are family-style dormitories in which children live, divided into small groups under the care of a housemother or housefather. In their small "families," they learn values of character, cleanliness, health, and service. The homes are safe places for the children to live and grow.

The RSO kitchen and dining hall make for an impressive building. It seats some 400 people comfortably to dine or gather for assemblies. It has an industrial-size kitchen with an entire staff of cooks providing three meals a day to all the students, as well as to staff and volunteers.

The Elephant House is a "home away from home" facility for volunteers. The building was designed as a volunteer dormitory and a community center. Providing most of the comforts of home, it has the ability to provide lodging for up to 60 visitors at a time.

Microfinance Model: A unique feature of Rising Star Outreach's microcredit program is its difference when compared to traditional, Grameen-type lending. Instead of providing loans to solidarity groups that are responsible to support each other by paying the loans back with interest, RSO "gives" loan capital to groups of lepers who can either keep the funds for themselves or use the money for enterprise creation. A colony establishes a "welfare committee" consisting of five to seven members, at least two of whom must be women. The committee is formed to conduct the colony's microlending system, creating a self-policing mechanism within the colony where capital is lent out, repaid, and reloaned in ongoing fashion. The committee scrutinizes and decides on loan applications, collects repayments, and deposits funds. The moneys, plus interest, are held in a revolving fund that stays within the colony so that the system becomes a kind of perpetual microlending fund. Thus, when the money is revolving in a colony, if borrowers fail to repay, they won't be able to grow their firms. Once a month, each colony sends a representative to a larger meeting with others to provide updates, present bank statements, and discuss common problems or issues.

With microloans ranging from $20 to over $1,000, individual lepers are able to create microenterprises such as small-scale gardening, haircutting, tool repair services, raising small farm animals, woodworking, tea selling, and so forth. By 2010 RSO operated a microloan program in 46 colonies, and that number now exceeds 100. It plans to ultimately be operating such programs in more than 700 Indian leper colonies by 2025—a truly ambitious goal.

Medical Care: Lepers and other impoverished community members suffered much, due to a lack of adequate and affordable health care. The problems were mostly due to society's social stigma as well as logistic access, travel challenges, and so on. So in 2005 RSO launched a Mobile Medical Unit to serve area patients in need. Operated by a team of local Indian MDs and staff, the unit traverses the region, providing medicine, leprosy screening, and ulcer care, as well as treating other diseases such as typhoid fever, diabetes, and tuberculosis.

Rising Star's medical team not only visits the colonies each week, but also travels to mountain villages in remote parts of Tamil Nadu. Much-needed medications, vaccinations, and the tender act of washing wounds and changing bandages are supplied. These acts continue to give hope to those affected by leprosy.

The author washing the feet of a leper in his 70s, in the colony.

Colony Services: In seeking to help lepers in their colonies, RSO provides a number of items to those living in leper colonies. These include a variety of things, ranging from nutritional drinks that offer improved health, mosquito nets for all individuals, housing improvement materials (such as a tin roof rather than thatch), a cement floor inside instead of dirt or mud floors, hygiene and sanitation supplies for victims of leprosy, and many more services.

During my trips to India, I've rejoiced when visiting with some of my former graduate students. One who served in the colonies was my dear friend Sylvia, whom I recommended that Becky hire. She spent three years there in the beginning, laboring to set everything up. On a more recent trip, I met Dr. Susan, the chief medical manager running all of RSO's health services for hundreds of people. I was so impressed by new, simple inventions being used to make life somewhat easier for the lepers, including a wooden hand scooter so a person could physically slide around the village using her hands in the dirt on a board with roller-skate wheels to help her move.

Colony members in certain cases received microloans to purchase art paper, oils, charcoal, acrylics, and watercolor products to paint Indigenous or folk art that could be sold in the tourist markets. The art was often impressive, and the loan recipients were able to repay their microloans, thus becoming somewhat economically independent. Others bought seed and grew vegetables or fruits to sell as village street vendors. Yet others, if they still had hands and fingers that worked, crafted various stitchery products—pillowcases, crocheted table covers, place mats, and more—to sell as microentrepreneurs in local street markets.

When I last visited RSO, it was good to see improvements. I met new volunteers from firms like E-Bay, who took a year's unpaid leave from their careers in the San Francisco Bay Area to offer unpaid support services at RSO. I slept in the recently constructed Elephant House and ate with several other foreign volunteers staying there. The staff dressed me in their native Tamil Nadu Veshti robes for ceremonial purposes. I enjoyed walking along village paths alongside roaming sacred cows going in the same direction. I felt humbled by the invitation to wash and anoint the feet of aged leper males, some as old as I. In fact, one of them, Abdul, was older than me, even age 80! He'd been a leper for over half a century. Rubbing the special oils into their tough, leathery skin, whether on their feet or backs and shoulders, was both uncomfortable and also gratifying. I got a glimpse as to how the Savior may have felt, millennia ago, to serve the downtrodden, the rejected, the outcasts. I came to at least glimpse a bit of how Jesus himself felt serving the "unclean" of his time.

Frankly, there are probably many limitations about the work of Becky Douglas and her NGO, Rising Star Outreach. In India, the current premiere, Narendra Modi, wants "foreign" nongovernmental organizations out so as to build India's reputation as a country that can solve its own difficulties, not needing any foreign assistance. In other words, he's putting pressure on nonprofits like RSO, showing a high degree of worldly pride rather than continuing to collaborate with outside governments and religions.

An additional matter of concern is that some may doubt RSO's replicability throughout India, thinking it may be too dependent on the energy and vision of Becky Douglas herself. Still, it has continued to grow and deepen its effects, even when she was serving a Latter-day Saints (LDS) church mission with her husband in the Dominican Republic for three years without taking time to lead RSO or to travel to assess its efforts in India. Overall, through bringing on new board members and hiring new staff to manager the organization, RSO has enjoyed continued growth and been able to deepen its impacts.

How, one wonders, does RSO compare and contrast with other private NGOs as they all wrestle with the horror of leprosy throughout India? One may conclude that RSO's scale is still too small to have a significant impact in reducing leprosy, even just in the state of Tamil Nadu. At least, so far. But its impacts are, in fact, growing. The frequent political instability in certain areas of India may at some point become a point of tension or even opposition to RSO's work, an issue about which its managers are concerned.

Additional questions might be asked about this NGO, as well. Is the RSO model viable for the long haul? Can hundreds of volunteers continue its ability to operate on a fairly limited financial budget of $1.5 million annually? Will the organization be able to attract big-name popular media stars to bring in the attention and funding that are necessary? Will the Indian staff be willing to remain employed by RSO if and when their skills grow and other new jobs come along? If something were to happen to the founder, the social entrepreneur Becky Douglas, could RSO continue to operate without her far into the future? Does it have a deep-enough bench within its staff and board to continue walking the path of combating leprosy while providing microenterprise strategies to create employment?

Observers might conclude that this NGO has frankly enjoyed much luck and good fortune in its early years. Clearly, most such nonprofits do not swiftly arise to benefit hundreds, then thousands of clients, among the developing world (which we formerly termed the "Third World"). Nor are the social, health, and financial impacts generally so easy to achieve as they clearly have been for RSO to have accomplished. How well, then, may outside evaluators assess the organization's sustainability to continue on its quite remarkable journey?

The ultimate end of the Rising Star Outreach NGO in India is yet to be written. But the evidence so far is quite convincing to me, just one researcher. It's clear that an individual Christian woman, admittedly naive as she perceived herself, motivated by the shocking ugliness of leprosy, coupled with love for those who suffer, can foster significant impacts. Becky Douglas seems to have mobilized many others with a great mix of skills and persuasive abilities in order to compensate for her own lack of understanding about how NGOs work. This is impressive. To collect research data about the organization's past and present, along with future prospects for RSO, suggests inspiring impacts as well as a promising future. I would not be at all surprised to observe, two or three decades from now, that Rising Star Outreach in India has become hugely expansive in its state of Tamil Nadu. Indeed, it may appropriately be concluded that RSO amounts to a "disruptive organization," in the sense of one Harvard Business School theory about innovative leaders (Christensen, 1997). Becky Douglas truly seems to fit the idea of being a genuine, global social entrepreneur. And we may well discover, in time, that RSO will serve as a model for other NGOs and Indian government entities by providing a viable methodology for empowering leper colonies to gain control of their own destiny. They will then look forward to a destiny of dignity, not dependency.

Our understanding of the scourge of leprosy that has devastated millions of lives over thousands of years continues to vex individuals and families as well as entire communities. In India, even having sufficient health care workers is proving difficult. A recent Indian news story reports that Mumbai's century-old leprosy hospital goes woefully understaffed. Partly due to the Coronavirus pandemic, as well as longer-term financial problems, it seeks to limp along with merely half its necessary employees (Chakraborty, 2021). However, occasional good news about the disease itself comes forth, as reported from Canada recently, as researchers now are suggesting that leprosy's effects may not be as debilitating as once thought (McGill University, 2021).

Rising Star schoolgirls with the author, whom they laughingly called "Dada" (Grandpa).

Children's Education: RSO believes that one of the best ways to help India's lepers is to assist in educating their children so they will eventually be able to secure employment and have a better future than their diseased parents. From the beginning, the organization has focused on channeling education to kids, initially paying their tuition to attend local schools. It soon became apparent, though, that even getting admitted was difficult because the children lacked basic math and reading, and that when these issues were combined with the stigma of leprosy, such educational opportunities were extremely rare. So Rising Star launched two small informal schools for lepers' children, along with free housing so the kids could escape the depressing realities of colony life, attend classes, and gain an education. Gradually, funds were raised and nice, modern schools were constructed, along with dormitories for the students to live in five days a week, where they received good nutritional meals and health care. Then on weekends they are transported back to spend time with their families in the home village. Finally, as they grow through their teen years, those who want to go on to achieve a university education can receive an RSO Scholarship to move to the next level and ensure that they will have realistic career opportunities after graduation.

Conclusion

As I finish writing this chapter, the calendar reads November 29, 2021. Rising Star Outreach was established exactly 20 years ago today—on November 29, 2001! Here's an update from back then until now: Initially, the number of leprosy colonies in India that RSO started working in was 1, but *94* is the number of such communities where its programs are making a difference now. The number of students who began being helped in 2001 was a mere 27; currently, the number of K–12 students attending top-rated schools for children from leprosy colonies has reached *640*. All told, the number of lives impacted in the past 20 years by Rising Star Outreach is tens of thousands—and they are not just schoolchildren, but also their leper parents and grandparents throughout India. RSO started out by housing just a handful of toddlers and orphans and has since become so much more. It currently runs three schools—the Peery Matriculation School in Tamil Nadu, the Little Flower School in Bihar, and a preschool in Pune—with 600-plus children, as well as many more students whose education is supported so they can attend a school in their various villages in Indian states (Cook 2021).

I conclude this chapter, as I began it, with the words of Mahatma Gandhi (2021), that great Indian liberator who believed in his native Hinduism, as well as in being a believer in Jesus: "Leprosy work is not merely medical relief. It is transforming the frustration in life into the joy of dedication, personal ambition into selfless service. If you can transform the life of a patient or change his values of life, you can change the village and the country."

References

Chakraborty, R. (2021). "At Mumbai's only specialized leprosy hospital, half of medical staff posts vacant." *Indian Express*. November 18.

Christensen, C. M. (1997). *The Innovator's Dilemma*. Harvard Business School Press.

Cook, E. (2021). *Rising Start Outreach Newsletter*, vol. 21, November 29.

1 Corinthians 6:10; 16:13–14.

Gandhi, M. (1925). Original words in his weekly newspaper *Young India,* October 22, 1925. Later it appears in *The Collected Works of Mahatma Gandhi* (electronic edition), vol. 33, pp. 133–34. ISBN 8123007353, ISBN 9788123007359 OCLC 655798065.

Gandhi, M. (2021). Gandhi Memorial Leprosy Foundation, (LEPRA). https://leprosyhistory.org/database/person7.

Goodman, M. (2011). "Rising Star Outreach: Becky Douglas Works to Secure a Future for Children from India's Leprosy Colonies." *The Huffington Post.* January 5.

Grameen Bank. (2018). http://www.grameen.com/.

Hansen's Disease. (2020). Centers for Disease Control & Prevention, U.S. https://www.cdc.gov/leprosy/.

Luke 8:2–4.

McGill University. (2021). "Leprosy and Its Stigma Are Both Curable: One of the most feared diseases, leprosy, is not quite what we think it is." Office for Science and Society. November 6. https://www.mcgill.ca/oss/article/health-and-nutrition-history/leprosy-and-its-stigma-are-both-curable.

Ministry of Health. (2004–2019). Central Leprosy Teaching & Research Institute. General of Health Services. Government of India. http://cltri.gov.in/.

Mujtaba, S. A. (2007). "Microcredit Help to Leprosy-affected Persons." *Indian Muslim Relief & Charities.* May 13.

National Leprosy Eradication Programme (NLEP). (2002–2015). India. http://nlep.nic.in/

RSO. Rising Star Outreach. (2021). http://risingstaroutreach.org/.

Shao, Maria. 2010. "Microlending Gives Dignity to People with Leprosy." *Stanford Knowledgebase,* May 8. http://www.gsb.stanford.edu/news/knowledgebase.html?tr=forbesIndia.

Tamil Nadu. (2017). State Government Portal. http://www.tn.gov.in/

University of Pennsylvania. (2016). "Model in Practice: The Comprehensive Rural Health Project (CRHP) – Jamkhed, India." https://www.impact.upenn.edu/wp-content/uploads/2016/2015/03/121206_Jamkhed-FINAL.pdf.

Venkataramen, P. (2013). http://www.gnanodaya.in/President_popUp.html.

Woodworth, W. (1997). *Small Really Is Beautiful: Micro Approaches to Third World Development— Microentrepreneurship, Microenterprise, and Microfinance.* Third World Think Tank.

Woodworth, W. (2009–2017). Author's Rising Star Outreach India interviews, group discussions, fundraising events, speeches, meeting observations, and more, in both India and the US.

Woodworth, W. (2018). Conversation with Becky Douglas and others at fundraiser in author's home with friends and neighbors. Provo, Utah.

Woodworth, W., et al. (1998). "The Seven Blunders of the Modern World." *Exchange Magazine*, Spring, pp. 4–9. chrome-extension://efaidnbmnnnibpcajpcglclefindmkaj/https://marriott.byu.edu/magazine/00000177-da0c-dfa9-a7ff-dece652d0000/1998-spring-exchange-pdf.

World Health Organization. (2021). On leprosy, its causes, campaigns to eradicate, and so on. United Nations. https://www.who.int/news-room/fact-sheets/detail/leprosy.

Yunus, M. (2006). http://www.nobelprize.org/nobel_prizes/peace/laureates/2006/yunus-bio.html/.

Note: For their invaluable help, I express my gratitude to several research assistants at the Kennedy Center for International Studies at Brigham Young University. I also appreciate the university's providing of small funding amounts for such support.

CHAPTER 3

Wave of Hope: The Faith to Rebuild Thailand after the 2004 Asian Tsunami

This is a story that I call "The Tsunami Rescue Brigade of 2005." In that year, As a professor at Brigham Young University's Marriott School, I rallied my students to travel to Thailand and help rescue and rebuild the lives affected by the terrible Asian tsunami. This chapter is dedicated to the hundreds of thousands who lost their lives in the tsunami that year, and to the millions more who survived but struggled in terrible poverty. The story is also dedicated to the hundreds of students who responded to my call to action, giving of their time, money, and skills to help Thai survivors of a devastating earthquake and the destructive tsunami that followed. May we never forget!

In 2005, I participated in numerous conferences and seminars about the crisis in Thailand. I also gave no fewer than 26 speeches on my organizational behavior and leadership research, presenting at institutions such as Harvard, the Wharton Business School, and Stanford. In 12 months, I spoke at many BYU events and seminars.

This chapter relates the story of a number of students from all around the United States who actually dared to practice what religious leaders have long taught by selflessly serving those who suffer. But it was not done for big crowds or public relations purposes. Rather, we did our work quietly, drawing on the biblical injunction that we were inspired by in Proverbs 19:17: *"Whoever is kind to the poor lends to the Lord, and he will reward them for what they have done."* And we did it devotedly, as an act of personal and collective consecration, as described in an article I wrote that became the cover story of *Meridian Magazine* (Woodworth, 2005).

Most of the world faces challenges over time. Crises in the home, the community, and occasionally in an entire nation are common. Over the centuries, leaders of various faiths have often called for their followers and believers to assist others. Becoming self-reliant, they have affirmed, is a core value that we are to internalize, thus becoming able to reach out and assist others.

This chapter details an applied research case of mobilizing many young people attending university to change the world. It's a retrospective looking at 15 years since the disastrous Asian earthquake in the Indian Ocean caused a massive tsunami that wreaked havoc when it slammed into the coastlines of 14 countries, killing some 230,000 people, injuring over a million more, and destroying or badly damaging hundreds of towns and coastal villages. The quake struck on December 26, 2004, and he regions hit the hardest included Indonesia, Sri Lanka, India, and Thailand. The shocking incident quickly inspired many people globally to desire to help, leading to financial contributions of some $14 billion. Yet the human capital donated by volunteers from around the world was perhaps valued even more in the years afterward. The case below is but one example involving college students.

As a faculty member whose role is to "profess" something, after the earthquake and tsunami, I challenged my students to take action. As members of the BYU community who make covenants to serve others, we wondered whether we could offer assistance, even living some 8,600 miles from the Asian tragedy, particularly in Thailand. In this chapter I provide a summary of the Asian tsunami disaster and give it a comparative context, analyze how some students mostly in Utah initiated a social entrepreneurial plan in college and implemented it in Thailand, articulate strategies and systems they used that generated impacts that were rolled out, both in the short term and over subsequent years, and draw on our private humanitarian legacy in articulating a call to action. They wished to challenge older members and also young millennials of their faith, to address new potential global crises in the coming decades.

Overview of the Horrific Asian Tsunami Crisis

The damage from the Asian tsunami began on December 26, 2004, starting off the coast of Sumatra, Indonesia, as an unprecedented 9.3 magnitude earthquake exploded some 20 miles below the earth's surface—the third-largest quake ever recorded. It generated a 500-mile-an-hour powerful tsunami with waves of up to 60 feet high, creating a disaster of epic proportions. The region of Banda Aceh, Indonesia, was turned into a massive junkyard of twisted steel and cement, uprooted yards, rubble from numerous cars, and thousands of human corpses strewn over the area. It quickly became a large breeding ground for terrible diseases, such as dengue and malaria.

The waves rushed to engulf everything in their path, sucking up bodies on land and violently smashing debris with massive waves three yards high, going as far as six miles inland. In Sri Lanka, the death toll was estimated at 24,000, with another 7,000 missing. Over 1.5 million people in that country alone were forced to flee their neighborhoods, including 880,000 who no longer had houses to return to (Jayasuriya and McCawley, 2010).

To put this crisis in context, we can reflect on the horrific toll that the terrorist attacks of 9/11 exacted on the World Trade Center in New York, the Pentagon in Washington, D.C., and a plane crashing in a field in Pennsylvania. These were truly terrible events. Yet in the 2004–2005 tsunami, many Asian coastal villages lost more than *half* their people and infrastructure. When New York City was struck by terrorists, it lost some 3,000 people, much less than 1 percent, and was set back a few months after the airliner attacks, though over time it recovered.

I make the following comparison not to minimize the tragedy of 9/11, but simply to show the scale of the Asian tsunami. The extent of waves rushing inland in Indonesia would be equivalent to destroying Manhattan from the tip of the island at South Street, taking down everything in its path clear up to 85th Street. Gone would be the Statue of Liberty, all of the Wall Street financial district, landmark buildings such as the Empire State and Chrysler, all the big retail giants, Greenwich Village, Broadway and its immense theater district, the train and subway stations, and half of Central Park. The percentage of those killed in the destruction of the Indonesian city of Banda Aceh was 60 percent, according to UNICEF officials. Its equivalent, if applied to New York City, would total a staggering 4.8 million people.

The countries that were affected ranged from Asia even to Africa. Official death rates were 270,000 dead or missing; many bodies never were recovered. But the unofficial toll may have been higher, since it could never be counted. For example, in Thailand, government estimates were that 8,500 were killed, though that number did not include some 10,000 missing aliens, mostly Burmese laborers who, because of desperate conditions in their own country, had been doing menial jobs in Thailand's tourist areas. The same occurred elsewhere as well. Thus, it may be assumed that the overall region's total death toll in the December 2004 quake was closer to 300,000 people. That was from the first incident alone, but in addition a large 8.7 quake followed in March that killed many more. Hundreds of aftershocks kept many people on edge for months and years afterward, as many have apparently been both scared and scarred for life.

Beyond the death toll, some 1.7 million individuals were displaced in the region. With so many severely injured, and lacking houses, jobs, schools, or even minimal medical care, the overall need was unfathomable. Experts estimate that some places like Sumatra and Sri Lanka were set back decades. Towns and villages were utterly demolished, industries destroyed, education systems decimated, and transportation in shambles. Infrastructure like roads, bridges, and rail lines were obliterated. Wonderful beaches and upscale tourist amenities disappeared. Tens of thousands of families lost their loved ones. The so-called "survivors" lacked food, water, shelter, and security.

Beyond Thailand itself, many countries bordering the Indian Ocean were affected, to varying degrees. In addition to the four major affected nations, Indonesia, Sri Lanka, India, and Thailand, tsunami waves reached other Asian regions, such as the Maldives, Myanmar, Bangladesh, and Malaysia. They even extended to African locations of Tanzania, South Africa, Kenya, and Somalia, many thousands of miles distant. Government relief from nations around the globe was quick and helpful, and groups such as the Red Cross and United Nations were soon on the scene. However, some of those large multilateral organizations soon withdrew from damaged areas. The Red Cross halted even taking donations. Much of the promised cash from world governments never did materialize.

How Students Became Social Entrepreneurs

As I began a new winter semester of my courses at BYU in January 2005, I reacted viscerally to the extraordinary far-off crisis, as did many of my students. I felt the time was ripe for mobilizing my classes to see whether the concepts and theories we would be exploring could be helpful in tackling cases of human suffering and economic disintegration. So I and my students raised these questions in the very first class session: Are we people living in relative comfort, safe and sound in Utah, actually relevant to societal suffering on the other side of the globe? Or are we only about leadership and power and money? As believers in Christ, who himself always served the poor, could we too try to somehow embrace those who were suffering throughout Asia, even to empower those who had just lost their loved ones, their homes, and their very communities?

Final class of students in the author's global change course at BYU, anticipating their overseas volunteer work in Thailand.

My course on that occasion was named Organizational Behavior 490: "Becoming a Global Change Agent/Social Entrepreneur." So I felt that perhaps a small group of my students right there in Utah might be interested in taking action on the other side of the globe. If they showed a degree of willingness, maybe together we could organize an intervention model to help tsunami victims begin to recover a bit.

So I adjusted the course requirements to include considerable reading on the disaster. I asked students to write short "thought papers" about its ramifications, and to pass a final examination. Additionally, all of them were to design and execute a personal action project, either during or following the semester, which would be a significant part of their final grade. The class included 33 registered students, and at first only perhaps a dozen of them expressed interest in my query about the Asian tsunami crisis. About half of them were undergraduates focusing on sociology, international development, pre-med, business, the sciences, and humanities. The other half were seeking master's degrees in programs including MPA, MBA, accounting, neuroscience, law, education, social work, international studies, and so forth.

During the semester's initial two weeks that January, more students joined the cause, as several planning teams began to form. Even from a world away, the teams investigated locations of tsunami destruction to determine where services could be provided while at the same time maintaining a degree of student safety, which I emphasized heavily as a professor concerned with deep learning but also security for all volunteers.

In addition, over a dozen other students from across the Provo campus came to sit in on the class, which they heard about from their friends and families. Unregistered, either they couldn't carry the extra credit hours because their course load was too heavy, or they only learned about the course after the enrollment deadline had passed. One person even drove an hour from Salt Lake City each class session to participate, a distance of 40 miles each way. But these attendees all joined in, read the material, took the tests, and participated in a service-learning team. No one received grade credit. We decided to call the project "Wave of Hope." And we agreed that individuals would be assessed according to their rigorous academic performance: heavy reading; taking quizzes and tests; writing research papers on self-reliance, social entrepreneurship, project design and implementation, and team research and planning strategies; as well as giving in-class presentations.

As we discussed what we might do, we came to believe that traveling to the hardest-hit area of Banda Aceh, in Indonesia, or to Sri Lanka, would be too chaotic and stressful (not to mention too expensive for most). We also realized that the massive amount of death and destruction would likely overwhelm our little group, some of whom had lived relatively sheltered lives. The students' health and safety played a major factor in ruling those countries out. Trying to communicate in a foreign language or absorbing even a little of the culture seemed too complex, as well. Thus, we soon decided to target the coastal area of Khao Lak, Thailand, about an hour north of the heavily traveled tourist resort island of Phuket. Several students had at least vacationed there, so we had a bit of firsthand experience. It was located in southeast Thailand, in Phung Gna Province, a long nine hours by bus from the capital, Bangkok. We imagined that, laboring there as Americans, we would be around a number of English-speaking resort staffers (both locals and foreign nationals) who understood "Western ways." We figured there was more development there than in the hardest-hit area, as well as a more stable government situation and perhaps also better infrastructure.

In the first month after we resolved to try to launch our own small disaster recovery efforts, we knew we needed to train our potential volunteers about the realities of traveling to Thailand after the tsunami's destruction. We wanted to make them aware that they would face hardships and difficulties, not just reveling in "sweetness and light" in that beautiful part of Asia. A realistic orientation would be critical so as to weed out anyone expecting just a "fun summer" at area beaches. In our preparation meetings, we stressed such concepts as the following, explaining that most volunteers initially go through several stages when working in a new environment: "First: *Rejection*. Second: Trying to change the 'system' because they are wrong and I'm right. *My way is best*. Third: Take a step back, try to understand, *figure things out*. Fourth: *Work with 'it.'* Accept the difficult reality and chill out. Fifth: *Keep learning*. In doing so you will be taking a BIG step forward" (Wave Training, 2005). Conducting orientation sessions along these lines, we began to determine which students could likely handle the stress and complexities of helping rebuild Thailand's coastal villages. Also, we started to identify a few individuals who probably were not going to handle the pressure well or be very productive, so they were encouraged to withdraw from the effort.

Inventing a New NGO

Within the first month of the new semester in 2005, we had developed five teams operating as self-organizing groups, studying not only management and social entrepreneurship, but also Thai history and culture, suggesting programs that we could offer to help rebuild the region, brainstorming about fundraising, estimating costs for volunteers willing to spend their summer in Khao Lak, and much more. After the initial meetings and planning, groups reported what things they were learning, what challenges they saw, and next steps needed. Several proposals offered a name for the project—which was necessary for us to begin developing marketing materials, recruiting more student volunteers, and raising money.

Eventually the class project was named "Wave of Hope"—a bright contrast to the tsunami's waves of destruction and sorrow. Would-be student volunteers began to talk more seriously about traveling to Thailand to help. Many felt that we should focus on the tough and complex work of doing small-scale programs, helping to jump-start Thai village economies that were stressed, and assisting in rebuilding some destroyed villages from the bottom up.

We knew we were not a big, rich, government institution, nor a major nongovernmental organization with millions of dollars and donors. Rather, we were just a small group of volunteers who felt we possessed the moral energy and college-age skills to make a modest impact. We couldn't do *everything*, but we could each do *something*. Through Wave of Hope, we developed or adopted useful tools to rescue the poor among the tsunami victims. The surviving Thai people, we knew, felt desperate for jobs. They needed incomes sufficient to buy rice and beans just to survive. They also wanted education to continue for their children, and their houses would obviously need to be rebuilt. We gradually realized that what was most essential, what we were in a position to do, would be to help build those people's own capacity—to help them increase their resilience in the face of disaster.

So our teams planned how to launch microcredit projects, how to initiate simple school experiences in rural areas, and how to establish modest construction projects for low-cost, self-made homes with simple new wooden furniture. We began communicating with aid groups already in the Kao Lak area to learn what was occurring and how we might help further their cause.

Well, when we stopped to think about it, designing and rolling out a humanitarian strategy for a disaster zone a world away, from a little college course in far-way Utah, was certainly audacious. As students informed their parents back home, worries were mentioned, but also admiration. As well, BYU bureaucrats were doubtful about the plan, if not outright critical. Yet, having successfully launched two other social ventures in my courses earlier in 1989 and 1999, I myself was confident that we could succeed in 2005. A new dean and a department chair who knew little about those successes didn't make things easy. However, I sought to share with administrators some of the social and economic impacts of my earlier projects that were proving increasingly successful in the Philippines and Honduras. Over the course of that winter semester, those facts gave me a growing degree of credibility with administrators and parents alike, supported by my having done similar, impactful work elsewhere (Woodworth, 1996).

In the two weeks before our class first met, I'd observed friends, extended family members, and neighbors sitting, stunned, in front of television screens, shocked at the horrendous devastation of the Asian tsunami. Some wrote out checks to provide emergency aid, as did people from various other nations. However, four months later, the flow of money had stopped, and media attention shifted to "important" new events such as spring baseball, a royal wedding in England, the coronation of a new Pope, TV's *American Idol* and the trial of pop superstar Michael Jackson. Despite all these distractions, my sincere hope—and that of my students—was to do something more important to alleviate the Asian suffering.

As Wave of Hope began to take shape, my focus remained on tsunami orphans who were suffering alone. Thousands of broken-down, desperate families were trying, with limited success, to eke out an existence as refugees in tent camps. Day-to-day survival became the norm for millions of individuals. Our projected team members felt that, being young, energetic, smart, and generous religious folks with a sincere belief in the call to help others, we needed to take action. Our many prayers inspired us to not waver.

Wave of Hope, then, was launched as a response by a few individuals to see how much we could actually do. Our venture operated from the faith that we were our "brother's (and sister's) keeper." We became a kind of "Students Without Borders" project. Over a thousand hours of collective volunteer group project work occurred outside regular class periods. Plus, students attended four training meetings during certain evenings: a devotional session, a new volunteer orientation and project management session, a Khao Lak logistics briefing session, and a final send-off meeting beginning in April 2005. Some of my academic colleagues, campus bureaucrats, and students' parents likely thought we were foolish, because our tasks and hopes seemed impossible to them.

Yet I cdrew on the words of that great woman anthropologist Margaret Mead, who wrote about such ventures in these powerful words: "Never doubt that a small group of thoughtful, committed citizens can change the world. Indeed, it's the only thing that ever has."

In my earlier experiences with global change agentry, recruiting volunteers, and teaching efforts that established previous projects, I had learned that engaging in *doing good* also helps students build a sense of stewardship. So, as volunteers, whether joining the Thai humanitarian effort for four weeks or for the entire summer, my students would become part of a work in which we as human beings learn to go beyond ourselves. I felt confident that these Wave of Hope global change agents were able to think more consciously and broadly than merely of themselves, so they could respond to the suffering of others. Social entrepreneurs associated with Wave of Hope would look beyond the here-and-now to working to achieve greater social justice in a better future. Over time, Wave of Hope efforts were picked up by various media outlets in Utah, resulting in additional contributions streaming in to secure more and new potential volunteers, beyond my BYU class members (Brown, 2005). As I pondered our efforts, I liked thinking about our Christian faith's commitment to God regarding helping tsunami victims as an act of generosity.

My original goal for that summer of 2005 had been to take my wonderful wife—my amazing humanitarian partner of more than four decades—on an around-the-globe tour for two months of service in Indigenous villages, as a kind of warm-up tour. We planned to first work with the poor in Latin American *barrios,* where we had earlier created several NGOs. Next, we would move on to labor with rural villagers through our partner organization in Mali, West Africa. Then we would fly to Manila, where we planned to serve the poor of urban Philippine cities. Last, we planned to head further on to the South Pacific to work on collaborative projects with Polynesian islanders. But after the shocking devastation of the December 2004 tsunami, my wife and I changed our plans in order to launch this new strategy, specifically focused on Thailand's coastal villages. I later came to appreciate that our focused mission to the Khao Lak region in summer 2005 actually did as much good as our circling the earth to labor in multiple locations.

So we began various efforts to generate moneys for the students' travel and living expenses in Thailand. Soon after the Wave of Hope start-up, we realized we could attract more charitable donations if we were actually registered as an NGO with the I.R.S., so that interested donors could receive a "motivating" tax benefit by giving to our charity. It so happened that three of my students had worked with me to launch another nonprofit a year earlier. We had planned to launch a project in Somalia, Africa, in several villages, because of a request from a Somali student I had mentored years earlier. But just before our departure, serious terrorism attacks occurred there, so I halted everything. However, we'd already incorporated as a 501(c)(3) nonprofit registered with the I.R.S. as a United States charity, named Empowering Nations. So we decided to fold Wave of Hope into Empowering Nations, which would perhaps give us greater legitimacy, boost financial contributions, and enable the larger and more-inclusive NGO to move forward, albeit in different directions (Empowering Nations, 2010).

Design of Strategies and Systems for Wave of Hope

What were some of our plans to produce short-term impacts in Thailand, as well as longer-term outcomes? Below are but a few of the results during the first couple of intense years.

We had cobbled together a lead team of the brightest, most organized BYU students to initiate Wave of Hope in-country. The first three students arrived in Thailand by early May 2005, and within two short days they had made food, housing, and service arrangements so that the larger group of 20 volunteers flying in within the next few days could be quickly put to work.

From 35 individuals in my original class, the group had exploded over the semester to about 60. Eventually some 100 volunteered to work for a month or more, rebuilding villages and devastated lives along the hard-hit coast of Khao Lak. Students came from seven countries, from universities across the states between Cambridge, Massachusetts, and Berkeley, California, along with a few of my older friends and neighbors. Some were homemakers and busy mothers, entrepreneurs, CPAs, or consultants, along with a few of their own spouses. We all labored together to assist the earthquake and tsunami survivors along the Indian Ocean's coastline. Collectively, as we expected, we had many ups and downs. We felt horrified by the scenes of destruction. We all shed tears at the nearby Buddhist temple where thousands of bodies waited in large refrigerated trucks to be identified (when possible), buried, or cremated during the long months of our time in Thailand.

The in-country leader of our Wave of Hope team in Thailand was Sarah Carmichael, a Canadian graduate student at BYU who was studying neuroscience, which of course has nothing to do with disaster relief. While her fiancé was fighting as an American soldier in Iraq, she decided that helping the poor of Thailand would be a meaningful way to manage her life while he was in harm's way in the Middle East. Her leadership was superb, and much of the credit for our team's success was certainly due to Sarah. The balance of the lead team consisted of both undergrads and graduate students from various disciplines.

Managing our efforts from within the U.S. was Enoc Velazquez, a graduate student from Panama who had served as an American Peace Corps manager in Kenya for several years before returning to college. Having a wife and children, Enoc made the wise decision to remain in Provo, but agreed to oversee the efforts in Thailand. The leadership and dedication of these two individuals, along with various other students, all helped make Wave of Hope a genuine success.

The facts that our group was well-trained, and that we developed and insisted on high expectations for all volunteers, ensured that our overall experience was positive. We had strict ground rules: Everyone up, eat, pack a lunch, and be ready to go by 7:00 a.m. No alcohol, no drugs other than prescribed medicines, no dating or sex. While a number of other young volunteers (not members of Wave of Hope) from Europe eventually arrived in Khao Lak, they were often perceived as partygoers who danced and played at night, slept in late each morning, and rarely had a coherent plan or commitment to the effort. In contrast, the Wave of Hope folk were all seen as hard-working, honest, and committed. The result was our enjoying a good deal of community credibility and appreciation.

Below is a selective list of the ongoing projects we carried out that first summer, as highlighted in an article I wrote for a Scottish journal (Woodworth, 2013):

- Constructing permanent housing for displaced victims
- Setting up a "Thaikea" furniture shop to create income
- Teaching English in classrooms
- Doing basic flooding cleanup
- Staffing the Tsunami Volunteer Center
- Distributing donated hygiene kits and clothing
- Building and repairing long-tail fishing boats
- Assisting the women's pearl cooperative
- Repairing damaged buildings and other structures
- Providing nursery care for victims' children
- Offering microenterprise training and microloans to create jobs and jump-start the damaged economy
- Providing assistance in local schools
- Supporting other community reconstruction efforts

We were also able to secure many used clothing items in our American home states before we traveled to Thailand. We took them as extra paid baggage on our flights, along with suitcases full of children's toys and simple school supplies. Since we knew how great the people of Thailand's needs were, we were better able to secure donations that filled the hundreds of boxes and suitcases we took.

The Wave of Hope team launched its own small initiatives to begin in Thailand, but as the number of our volunteers continued to grow and more projects seemed necessary to give everyone meaningful experiences, we began partnering with other groups in Khao Lak. One was the Tsunami Volunteer Center (TVC). Another was the Mirror Art Group Foundation, consisting of university students in Bangkok who used art, drama, music, and dance to promote social good. A third group that generated a good deal of involvement was, surprisingly, the Thai Army, units of which had been sent to manage the government's programs and oversee its use of federal funds.

I should mention that Wave of Hope not only had a large team on the ground in Thailand. We also needed a small support group back in Utah to help manage logistics, visas, travel, and money. They could assist in coordinating with both me, as the professor and group leader, and the donors whom we wanted to inform and work with so as to raise more funding. Not all students in the Social Entrepreneurship course were able to volunteer in Thailand, because of jobs, graduation deadlines, marriages, babies due, and so forth. So Wave of Hope leaders in the states recruited applicants who, if they desired, could qualify for college credit or earn internship hours while in the U.S.

Students stateside could offer any of seven types of support: (1) *General Management:* Providing management to aid the project team, communicating between team leads, web updates, coordinating training meetings for new volunteers, fundraising, and public relations; (2) *Volunteer Coordination*: Responding to emails from interested volunteers, communicating important information regarding training meetings, departure dates; keeping track of volunteer information, accounting and budget efforts, managing large volumes of information, providing training materials for volunteers departing to Thailand; (3) *Logistics:* Making travel arrangements for volunteers departing to Thailand, purchasing tickets, and tracking donations; (4) *Providing* guidance and direction to volunteers; (5) *Developing* budgets, submitting, and managing the approved budget; (6) *Speaking* to the media and making public events presentations; and (7) *Participating* in planning and weekly meetings. The desired skills and qualifications for most of these support positions included: project administration, volunteer management, administrative, multitasking, and follow-up skills; at a minimum, some college or university or equivalent combination of education and experience; a good sense of humor, flexibility, and the ability to work in a BYU team environment.

Using creative personal and group fundraising strategies, we secured an amazing initial total of $118,000 in donations to cover our travel, housing, and meals while in Thailand, as well as for the purchase of tools, wood, cement, and more for our projects in-country. We also felt blessed to receive small donations from local Utah businesses that we approached. Grocery owners, hardware store managers, and many other types of enterprises each gave us much-appreciated money to help roll out our plans.

We also boldly convinced other NGOs to help us fund larger, more expensive projects. For example, we helped native boat builders in-country repair badly damaged vessels they needed for their work, even though the motors were destroyed or lost during the destruction. So we asked a large American church for funding to pay for about 40 needed motors for fishing boats, so that Thai fishermen could get back to work on the seas to harvest their needed catches.

A people known as the Moken, also called the "sea gypsies," dwell with their families in ramshackle houses along the Thai coast. The ground is usually waterlogged and the air extremely humid, accompanied by a nauseating stench. Masses of mosquitoes are always biting, and all these factors make life there unpleasant and people's health problematic. Still, villagers along the country's coastline had survived for centuries because of their own work ethic, and after the quake and tsunami, with new boats and motors provided, we believed he Moken could continue caring for their families far into the future.

As a professor teaching social innovation, and seeking to inspire students to help those who suffer and to change lives around the globe, I felt tremendously gratified about my students' achievements arising in my little class on the Provo campus in 2005. But not only theirs alone. For many had recruited siblings back home and friends of their own faith who had already graduated from BYU. One was a construction worker in Los Angeles. Another was employed by the federal government in Washington, D.C. Two young British men who had learned about us in the U.K. even flew to Thailand to volunteer with us. Even a television producer with Channel 5 (KSDK) in St. Louis, Missouri, went with his son to build houses in Laem Pom village for four weeks—and ended by making an effective documentary film about our collective work. In my own case, I convinced several neighbors and friends to join our efforts, including a local banker, the owner of a real estate firm, and a consulting associate from Dallas whom I'd worked with.

In that summer of 2005, working on-site in far-off Thailand, we collaborated with numerous village families in repairing or building small, new houses for them along the Khao Lak coastline. We laid foundations, installed water and sewer lines, made family garden areas, and helped the individuals build simple wooden furniture, such as a kitchen table, wooden chairs, a few simple beds, perhaps a couch, thatched walls that would let the breezes through or plastered walls in some cases. All the furnishings were hand made in our somewhat primitive wood shop, which we named "Thaikea" (yes, a play on words linking Ikea, the gigantic Swedish corporation, with Thailand, where we were laboring with simple materials). We purchased considerable amounts of woodworking tools and taught the village women how to make humble household furniture they wanted or needed.

As we assembled a mix of power tools (jigsaws, drills, circular saws, sanders, and the like), along with hammers, nails, measuring tapes, wrenches, and more, we were gradually able to help local folks develop new hands-on skills, as well as to simultaneously serve one another. For instance, the Wave of Hope teams made basic desks, chairs, and bookcases, which we then delivered to newly built rural schools. There the schoolchildren were invited to help by picking out their favorite bright colors and painting their own little wooden desks and chairs. A favorite memory of mine from those times is the day that Condoleezza Rice, the U.S. Secretary of State, arrived to survey the flood damage and learn how the American government could be of assistance. She came to a new little school we had just helped complete in Bang Sak. Thai government officials were present, to bask in the glory, as were of course teachers and school kids. So was Wave of Hope, shining brightly! After learning what our small team had been doing there as volunteers to aid in the region's recovery, Rice gave a public speech. Among other things, she pointed out that while she held the title of Secretary of State, she was merely a government official. She declared that young Americans like our small group from BYU "were the 'real' secretaries of state." It was a poignant experience for some of our volunteers.

Wave of Hope volunteers after Asian tsunami doing rebuild. BYU volunteers thanked
by U.S. Secretary of State Condoleezza Rice (center), with student Kate Kelly (R).
In background: Thailand's General Lertrat Ratanavanich and Wave volunteers.

During the first several years of Wave of Hope's operations in Thailand and several other countries, the managers held strategy meetings to assess our effectiveness. One of the methodologies they used is a technique known as *SWOT Analysis* (standing for *Strengths, Weaknesses, Opportunities, and Threats*). This enables organizations to evaluate what they're doing well and ways in which they can plan for the future. (See *Appendix II* for details on this process.)

Legacy of Social and Economic Impacts

In framing the methodologies used in our Wave of Hope enterprise, I must mention six distinct but interdependent roles that were carried out to ensure long-term success. Essentially, the students were trained and evolved from "mere people" in a university classroom to becoming social entrepreneurs—that is, actual change agents engaged as on-the-ground consultants following the tragic natural disaster in Asia. They worked to develop various roles throughout the semester at university, and then carried out those roles while serving tsunami survivors in Thailand, managing various projects, and much more. Their core responsibilities included specifically: (1) acquiring knowledge, (2) applying knowledge, (3) creating knowledge, (4) sharing knowledge, (5) leveraging knowledge, and (6) challenging knowledge. Previous to our travel, we had spent much of the semester in the U.S., seeking to cultivate these various kinds of expertise and knowledge. Then, after we started rolling out programs on the ground in Khao Lak, our emphasis shifted to application, experimentation, and utilization of both old and new types of information.

As justifiably proud founders of a new NGO, our Wave of Hope team learned a great deal during the winter semester of 2005, then during a long, hot summer laboring in devastated areas of Thailand, and even during the years that followed. Together we continued learning through various iterations of education and the acquisition of new skills. Our skill set in the design and implementation of our efforts consisted of the following major core competencies:

- Project management
- Understanding Thai culture
- Volunteer logistics
- Cross-cultural awareness and effectiveness
- Team-building
- Microfinance
- Leadership and managerial competencies
- Public relations
- Business training
- Fundraising
- Teaching English (English as a second language)
- Travel planning
- Refugee needs
- Conflict management

Our efforts that first summer with Wave of Hope inspired many students participating to continue doing humanitarian work even years after 2005. In fact, four new nongovernmental organizations were launched by students who had first volunteered with us in Thailand! A number of young people from those first few years engaged in subsequent summer projects in Latin America and Africa, drawing on those sweltering, hard months in 2005 when we spent our time in Khao Lak. Many learned how much they still didn't know, so after earning their bachelor's degree, they went on to graduate studies for an MBA, a law degree, an MD degree, or even a PhD. Some of us have kept in touch over the 15 years since, sharing stories, feeling pride in our work, and remembering the challenges we met and the sheer joy of serving other people, whatever their religion.

Based on survey feedback we gleaned from all our volunteers at the end of each summer, several key themes emerged, either shortly after concluding our efforts in late 2005, or over the years and based on participants' reflections that came later. These themes included such issues and action research as the following: the need for *visions of empowerment and change*; the *passion* to dedicate oneself to a great cause; a willingness to shake things up, or, in other words, *"If it ain't broke, break it"*; the importance of taking *radical steps*, not accepting passivity or conformity; a *commitment to experiment* and try new things; and employing *positive deviance* in resisting the status quo and mere safety. In retrospect, each of these themes appeared central to big, seemingly extreme interventions that promise a better future for all.

Each year, after returning from their global ventures, many of the volunteers and team members and leaders continued to further develop Wave of Hope, from being just a project in 2005 toward becoming incorporated as an ongoing, significant NGO with real results and long-term staying power. We accomplished this by doing several things: debriefing and documenting the summer's experience and learning; taking a realistic look at pluses and minuses so as to be more effective in the future; and devoting considerable time to read reports from our volunteers who oversaw the financial aspects so that we could become confident of properly handling budgetary matters. Deeply knowing the sources of income, how the money was handled, and identifying all expenses down to the tiniest details helped us be good stewards with the contributions of all donors, whether large or small. Each year after we debriefed about that year's accomplishments and outputs, our follow-up discussions would help those of us on the management team debate organizational options for the future. After becoming legally organized as a new social enterprise, we knew we had promising pathways for moving forward. Finally, these kinds of deliberations facilitated our beginning to plan for the coming year. This cycle was more or less repeated every subsequent year.

We discovered that, from small, humble beginnings, long-term sustainable results may be achieved by dedicated Christians, whatever their particular denomination, who show that they "have a heart." For instance, while I was in Khao Lak, I was invited to meet with a group of craftswomen whose for years had designed and sold simple, native-style jewelry. But with the collapse of the tourist market after the tsunami, they had few or no business opportunities, nor did they have adequate income to even feed their precious children. So I proposed that they shift from being individual creators to forming a women's worker-owned cooperative in which they would work together, share designs, and support each other. Based on my consulting work with companies large and small around the globe, I felt sure that if they aligned themselves as an artisan co-op, they would become empowered for a better future. Ultimately they did so, and several of our student team, including a woman and her husband, remained in Thailand for many months, helping them flesh out their new business model. Thus, when they experienced success, they all shared in the fruits of their labor. When they had rough times, instead of excluding or laying anyone off, they would collectively sacrifice a bit to keep everyone productive and their families fed. Upon returning to Utah after that first summer, I met with a local friend whose pearl jewelry business, called Pearls with Purpose, was supporting women in faraway Philippines. I encouraged her to visit Khao Lak as a potential new source of fine products. She did so, and their new business relationship began—a genuine success, and a win-win for both sides.

Among additional key lessons and insights I and my team members drew from our labors in Thailand are these, each of which may be relevant to this book's readers in the future:

- Rapid design and implementation are quite complex and time-pressured.
- Shifting from humanitarian aid to longer-term development requires new models.
- University as well as community-college students, whatever their age, *can* become empowered to make a difference in the world.
- Wave of Hope showed that life-changing volunteers may enjoy experiences that have potential long-term applications in their future roles of education, work, and family.

I'm gratified to report that Wave of Hope expanded in Thailand over the next several years, as our Khao Lak projects continued in sustainable ways. Likewise, our "parent" NGO, called Empowering Nations, also grew elsewhere around the globe. Through its additional outreach efforts, we grew to attract some 38 volunteers who spent subsequent summers in northern Ghana, in Africa, laboring alongside rural women's organizations as well as providing health care and teaching English (Espinosa, 2006). Another team began working with Indigenous villages along the coast of Panama, and as the cofounder of both these NGOs, I was invited to spend a month in that Central American country working to facilitate the small start-ups there. Two more from our original class traveled to Paraguay and began providing technical assistance to rural farming villages outside Asunción. Subsequently, I took some students there to help foster an innovative program in which agricultural families integrate their farms with a network of local schools. They all collaborated in transforming the schools into ones that pay for themselves—now a movement throughout the developing world. My good friend Martin Burt, the former mayor of Paraguay's capital, Asunción, launched both an NGO, named "Schools That Pay for Themselves," and Fundación Paraguaya, which now promotes what is called a Self-Sufficient School Model connecting underprivileged kids with quality education in various nations (Burt, 2013). He is cofounder of "Teach a Man to Fish," a London-based global network that promotes "education that pays for itself" in order to develop schools, mostly in rural areas.

After a few years, leaders of both Wave of Hope and Empowering Nations realized that their efforts were paralleling the mission and purposes of another NGO launched from my courses back in 1999. In their respective cases, each was, of course, a response to a different crisis, not an earthquake or a tsunami in the Indian Ocean. Instead, my NGO named HELP Honduras arose after Hurricane Maria destroyed much of that country, as well as damaging other Central American countries. We launched that NGO in my microfinance course at BYU in 1999, mobilizing no fewer than 86 of my students to learn how and what they could do that very spring. After many of them spent an intense summer volunteering in Central America, the NGO continued to grow in social and economic impact in subsequent semesters, expanding beyond Honduras to Brazil,

Venezuela, and El Salvador in 2000. As we integrated Wave of Hope's programs into those of HELP International, we were soon generating greater financial resources and attracting college students from Stanford, Virginia Tech, UCLA, Yale, and the University of Oregon (HELP International, 2019).

Conclusion

Today, several decades since our merger of strategies, synergies, and staffing, I and my colleagues and students have recruited, trained, and sent out teams of student volunteers to many places around the globe, including impoverished areas of the South Pacific, Africa, and Asia, and even to Middle Eastern refugee camps.

Finally, by synthesizing the social and economic impacts analyzed above, I hope this type of action research project articulates a "call to action" for many future volunteers of Christian and other faiths, who are seeking to address global crises that will surely arise in coming years.

Our brains, energy, and hearts were dedicated to the survivors of the Asian tsunami, beginning in the spring of 2004 and also over subsequent years. We literally embraced Jesus'ss admonition to *"Give to the one who asks you, and do not turn away from the one who wants to borrow from you"* (Matthew 5:42). The coastal Thais *needed* us, and we felt *blessed* to respond and to serve.

As I remarked to a campus newspaper reporter, "I think there's this great, expansive, global spirit of humanitarianism that I personally believe is tied to the light of Christ" (Espinosa, 2006).

We all know the world will continue to be hammered by natural as well as human-made disasters. It may accurately be said that, back in 2005, Wave of Hope effectively served the poorest of the Khao Lak poor after the disastrous Asian tsunami, helping them pick up the pieces of their devastated lives—one family, one house, one boat, one shop, one village at a time. That legacy continues through various iterations of our individual labors until today. In the future, if Christian students, professors, and families of many faiths feel committed to making authentic social change, they can join numerous efforts so as to become incubators in reducing human suffering in small yet powerful ways. Those developments may, over time, and if carefully cultivated, generate sustainable results for years to come.

I conclude this story of how Wave of Hope embraced and collaborated with thousands of victims of the earthquake and tsunami in Thailand, by remembering advice from other cases of suffering and death. In particular, I recall the poignant words that the teenage Anne Frank wrote in her journal in an Amsterdam attic while hiding from the Nazis during Germany's terrible catastrophe: "How wonderful it is that no one need wait a single moment to improve the world."

References

Brown, J. (2005). *Wave of Hope*. ABC News, Channel 4 TV, Salt Lake City, Utah, news story.

Burt, M. (2013). "The 'Poverty Stoplight' Approach to Eliminating Multidimensional Poverty: Business, Civil Society, and Government Working Together in Paraguay." *Innovations: Technology, Governance, Globalization*, vol. 8, no. 1–2 (January 1: 47–67). doi:10.1162/INOV_a_00165.

Empowering Nations. (2010). Wave of Hope projects in Thailand, plus in Paraguay, Ghana, Panama, and other nations. http://empoweringnations.org.

Espinosa, J. (2006). LDS humanitarian efforts on the rise. BYU *Daily Universe*. May 5. https://universe.byu.edu/2006/05/05/youth-develop-through-global-service/.

HELP International. (2019). *Fighting Poverty, Empowering People*. Overview of HELP's ongoing commitment to social innovation. https://help-international.org/. August 22.

Jayasuriya, S., and McCawley, P. (2010). *The Asian Tsunami: Aid and Reconstruction after a Disaster*. Edward Elgar Publishing.

Matthew 5:42.

Wave Training. (2005). *A Handbook for Preparing Volunteers in Thailand*, unpublished materials, 49 pp.

Woodworth, W. (1996). Indigenous Management: Microentrepreneurship in the Philippines. *Exchange Magazine*, Spring, pp. 1–13.

Woodworth, W. (2005). The Joseph Smith Tsunami Rescue Brigade of 2005. *Meridian Magazine*, 11 pp.

Woodworth, W. (2013). Social Business in Times of Crisis: Microcredit Strategies During Social Unrest and/or Natural Disaster. *Journal of Social Business*, Glasgow University, vol. 3, no. 1, April, pp. 70–88.

CHAPTER 4

Grameen Danone Foods and Christian Business: Transforming Capitalism to Maximize Social Benefits Rather than Profits, with Grameen Bank in Bangladesh

The scriptures call on us to use our skills and resources by serving God and aiding those in need. In the book of Luke, Jesus offers the parable of the rich man preparing a great banquet. Eventually, instead of offering a sumptuous feast to his proud and wealthy friends, Jesus commands: *"Go out to the roads and country lanes and compel them [the poor, crippled, blind, and lame] to come in, so that my house will be full"* (Luke 14:23).

This chapter tells the story of a large, powerful corporation shifting some of its considerable wealth and resources from its coffers to the world's have-nots. Grameen Danone Foods (GDF) is a genius social business enterprise conceived by Dr. Muhammad Yunus, who was the founder and managing director of Grameen Bank in Bangladesh, in partnership with the France-based Danone. Apparently, some wealthy Catholics and Protestants deign to assist impoverished Muslim women in a country like Bangladesh where every day is a struggle to survive. Globally, 10 percent of the world is living on less than $2 a day. Over 700 million people try to eke out an existence on less than $1.90 a day, defined by the World Bank as extreme poverty. Moreover, a third of the globe's entire urban population dwells in a slum wherein unsafe, unhealthy homes crowd city streets. Much of Bangladesh consists of rural villages where slums may not proliferate but good jobs in the formal economy are scarce.

Hence, in the 1980s, Dr. Yunus had a vision of giving tiny loans to poor women so they could work themselves out of extreme poverty. After various experiments while a professor of economics, he launched the Grameen Bank of Bangladesh. He realized that regular banks in that country wouldn't lend to the poor, citing their lack of creditworthiness, so he started offering small, collateral-free loans from his own pocket to villagers near his campus at Chittagong University. in Bangladesh (Businessweek, 2005). Recipients repaid their loans, on time, every time, through their hard work. Yunus began giving loans to the poor without requiring collateral, credit history, or the signing of any legal paperwork. Eventually, the concept he called "microcredit" took off and has since spread globally.

This radical idea to integrate Grameen's and Danone's efforts is but one of several innovations that Dr. Yunus envisioned In this case, the new social business is jointly owned and operated by Groupe Danone (a France-based world corporate giant in dairy products) and by subsidiaries of the Grameen Family of Companies (a group of companies founded by Yunus that are dedicated to eradicating poverty and other social ills in Bangladesh). The business was first established in the Bogra district in Bangladesh, later spreading to other locations. The joint venture's primary aim was to optimize social good rather than to make corporate profits. Its mission was to fight hunger by bringing daily health nutrition primarily to poor, malnourished Bangladeshi children through its fortified nutrient-rich yogurt. Its first state-of-the-art small yogurt factory went into operation in 2007. The venture also hoped to reduce poverty by stimulating the local economy through the plant's operation that would create more jobs for additional people. About 50 small yogurt factories are being built throughout Bangladesh, primarily from profits earned from the first plant. It was hoped that this business enterprise would spark a new movement called "Social Business" throughout the world, by shifting the current conventional focus of traditional capitalism from maximizing profits that usually channel financial benefits to only a few individuals, to realizing social and moral benefits for the entire society. In other words, by using ethical and religious values it could improve societies in developing nations.

Scott Leckman, M.D. (left) and Danone Vice President Emmanuel Faber meeting the author after their speeches at an international microfinance conference.

GDF's Conception

On October 12, 2005, across a lunch table of French cuisine at the fashionable Fontaine Gaillon restaurant in Paris, Muhammad Yunus (founder and managing director of Grameen Bank) and Franck Riboud (chair and CEO of Groupe Danone) explored a new partnership. Then they arose and shook hands. "Let's do it," Riboud affirmed. They had reached at a deal. In partnership with the Grameen Family of Companies, Groupe Danone would create the world's first multinational, consciously designed "social business"—a dream that Yunus had contemplated for some time and even tried to implement to a certain extent, by establishing a few forms of social businesses. Now, under this joint venture, the two partners would set up a yogurt manufacturing enterprise in Bangladesh, with the primary objective of offering nutrition to malnourished Bangladeshi children, rather than maximizing corporate profits. The venture would be named Grameen Danone Foods (GDF). Its products would be sold at a low price that would be affordable to the poorest population of Bangladesh. This case of highly ethical human efforts suggests three main ideas: (1) closing the gap between the concepts of traditional "capitalism" and "social business"; (2) building a role for GDF in Bangladesh as an example of the concept of a "social business"; and (3) building a future for social business in the global society, thereby suggesting (at least to me) possible ways that Christian business women and men may better practice what Jesus preached—the ideal of doing good and serving others.

In explaining this case, I'll describe the premise of such action by delineating the contrast between traditional capitalism and this new ideal known as "social business." Conventional economic theories and practices hold that capitalism and its associated free markets breed wealth creators and competitors who spread money by creating jobs and opportunities for the good of societies (Prasso, 2007). However, extreme wealth disparities and other social ills that are associated with capitalism challenge the viability of capitalism as a solution to the world's social problems. For example, of the world's over 6 billion people, the richest 1 percent of adults owned a staggering 40 percent of all global wealth back in early 2000 when the Grameen/Danone venture was conceived. At that time, the richest 10 percent of adults owned 8 percent of the entire world's wealth, while the bottom half combined owned a meager 1 percent (UNU-WIDER, 2006). By 2018, just three years ago, *Forbes Magazine* (Kirdahy, 2018) declared that three men at the top of America's wealthiest class—Amazon's Jeff Bezos, Microsoft founder Bill Gates, and investor Warren Buffett—held combined fortunes worth more than the total wealth of the poorest half of all Americans! As of my crafting this chapter in 2021, startling new statistics reveal that during the first two devastating years of the COVID-19 pandemic, America's billionaires greatly increased their economic power, as reported in analyses of economic data that showed the combined wealth of all U.S. billionaires grew by $2.071 trillion (70.3 percent) between March 18, 2020, and October 15, 2021, from approximately $2.947 trillion to $5.019 trillion (Inequality, 2021). Of the more than 700 U.S. billionaires, the richest five (Jeff Bezos, Bill Gates, Mark Zuckerberg of Facebook, Google cofounder Larry Page, and Tesla's Elon Musk) saw a 123 percent increase in their combined wealth during this period, from $349 billion to $779 billion (Collins et al., 2020).

It is often said by those justifying extreme amounts of financial holdings that "Rising tides lift all boats." But is this reality or mere rhetoric? Can such extremes between the haves and the have-nots really improve the world? On this matter, the *New Testament* declares the following: *"Then Jesus said to His disciples, 'Truly I tell you, it is hard for someone who is rich to enter the kingdom of heaven.*

Again I tell you, it is easier for a camel to go through the eye of a needle than for someone who is rich to enter the kingdom of God.' When the disciples heard this, they were greatly astonished and asked, 'Who then can be saved?'" (Matthew 19: 23–25).

To me, rather than solve social problems, greed derived from unregulated markets has actually exacerbated poverty, disease, pollution, corruption, crime, inequality, exploitation of the poor, and child labor, and further has created deceptive marketing and advertising campaigns to promote harmful and even unnecessary products. Thus, this new ideal of social business stands as a viable alternative to economic disparity and social ills. In this case-discussion, companies whose primary objective is to maximize profits will be referred to as "Profit-Maximizing Businesses" (PMBs), while those whose principal objective is to optimize social and moral benefits will be referred to as "Social Business Enterprises" (SBEs). Illustrative examples of social business, social enterprise, and microfinance in countries such as the Philippines, Honduras, Peru, and other nations can be found in the *Global Journal of Economics and Finance* (Woodworth, 2020).

What is a "social business?" It's an organizational form that is created by shifting the focus of traditional capitalism from maximizing profits that usually benefit only a few individuals, to realizing social benefits for the entire society. This new form of a more-humane, even Christian, type of capitalism, is an SBE. While PMBs and SBEs may operate and compete in the same market, they will always try to outmaneuver each other for the greater market share. SBEs also compete among themselves for market shares and push each other to improve the quality of their products and services. Examples of social benefits that can be created by social businesses include poverty alleviation, social justice, housing for the homeless, environmental cleanup, domestic violence control, crime prevention, and change of political environment of given societies, among others.

In its organizational structure, operation, and overall management, a social business differs from PMBs primarily in its objectives. It is cause-driven rather than profit-driven. It is designed to meet social and moral goals. It pays no dividends, and it should incur no losses (Grameen Trust, 2006 April). A social business is designed and operated as a business enterprise with a business plan and strategy, products, services, workers, customers, markets, expenses, revenues, and performance metrics—but with the profit maximization principle replaced by the social-benefit principle. Such a business provides its goods and services to its customers consistent with its social objective. It sells products or services at prices that make it self-sustaining. It enjoys the potential for almost unlimited growth and expansion. And as the social business grows, so do the benefits it provides to society.

The owners of SBE companies can get back the amount they have invested in the company over a period of time, but no profit is paid to investors in the form of dividends. Any profit made is plowed back into the business to finance expansion, create new and affordable products or services, acquire new technology, and spread the SBE's social benefits to the wider society. Once the initial investment funds are recouped, investors might choose to reinvest their funds in the same social business, invest in another social business, or even use the money for personal purposes. If investors reinvest their recouped money in the same or a different social business, the same money can bring even more social benefits. Investors remain owners of the business, have considerable control over it, hold its management accountable for its operation, and decide its future course. A social business may be owned as a sole proprietorship, or as a partnership, or by one or more investors who pool their money to fund the social business and hire professional managers to run it. It may also be owned by a government or a charity, or by any combination of different kinds of owners. A social business will avoid causing more social problems while solving a given social problem. For example, a manufacturing plant dedicated to a social course will avoid causing any form of environmental degradation.

Forms of Social Businesses

At the moment, three forms of social business are being played out in the world economy, and increasingly practiced by Christian executives. The first involves companies that focus on providing a social benefit rather than on maximizing profit for the owners. The second kind involve PMBs that are fully or mostly owned by the poor or disadvantaged, in which dividends and equity growth go to benefit the poor, thereby helping them to escape poverty. Grameen Bank, founded by Yunus, falls under this category, since 94 percent of its shares are held by its borrowers, who are mostly poor Bangladeshi women. The borrowers earn annual dividends from the bank's profits. The third kind is a hybrid version, which combines the characteristics of a PMB with those of a SBE. For example, a company may be driven by 70 percent social-benefit objectives and 30 percent personal-benefit objectives, or vice versa. It is hoped by humanitarians that in the future, as the concept of social business becomes embraced by society, more social businesses will begin to spring up around the globe, and that new features and forms will emerge (Yunus, 2007, 28).

What Social Business Is Not

Traditional Humanitarian Aid: What is known as traditional humanitarian aid encompasses volunteer, charitable, and nongovernmental sectors. These sectors devote a great deal of resources, time, and energy to dealing with various social problems. Charity is very important and usually appropriate in disaster situations and also when helping those who are so seriously disabled that they cannot help themselves. However, in cases where people can help themselves, overreliance on charity in the form of giveaways and handouts takes away initiative and responsibility from the recipients. Also, handouts encourage dependence and laziness rather than self-reliance, hard work, and self-confidence. Handouts also encourage corruption. When aid is donated to help the poor, the officials who are in charge of distributing the free goods and services often turn themselves and their favored friends into recipients. Finally, charity creates a one-sided power relationship. The beneficiaries of charity are favor-seekers rather than claimants of something they deserve. Such one-way relationships only make the poor more vulnerable to exploitation and manipulation by donors (Yunus, 2007, 115–16).

Charitable Organization: A social business is *not* a charitable organization. While a charitable organization creates social benefits by partly or fully relying on donations, foundation grants, or governmental support to implement its programs, a social business must recover its full costs from its operation, on a sustained basis, while achieving its social objectives. Once it is set up, a social business should be self-propelling, self-perpetuating, and self-expanding. Donors or investors do not need to pump any more money into this business. Any social business that has to rely on subsidies and donations to cover its losses remains a charitable organization.

Corporate Social Responsibility: Unlike a social business, which devotes its efforts toward creating maximum social benefits for the society, corporate social responsibility, in some cases, tends to primarily pursue the selfish interests of PMBs while achieving fewer social benefits for the society at large. Although the concept of corporate social responsibility is built on good intentions, some corporate leaders misuse the concept to produce selfish benefits for their companies. Some of these selfish benefits might include supporting the personal goals or values of a powerful or respected corporate leader, earning favorable publicity for the company, deflecting criticism over the company's past ethical and business lapses, attracting customers who may prefer to do business with a company they perceive as socially responsible, wining the friendship and support of government regulators or legislators who are considering laws that might affect the company, and gaining a foothold in a new market that holds promise for the future but is currently unprofitable (Yunus, 2007, 36). Every year, many companies spend tens or even hundreds of millions of dollars on corporate social responsibility efforts, most of which primarily support selfish interests and achieve less social good.

Overview of Bangladesh, Grameen, and Danone Collaboration

With the above definitions and explanations, I will now turn back to the case of Grameen Danone Foods (Grameen Danone Foods Ltd., 2018) in Bangladesh and detail how this new ethical-business venture was rolled out, as well as describe some key features and complexities.

First I will parse the national context for a partnership in Bangladesh. The nation of Bangladesh is located in southern Asia, in the northeastern portion of the Indian subcontinent. It covers an area of 56,977 square miles, about the size of the state of Wisconsin. Dhaka, its capital and largest city, has about 5.4 million people. Prior to the 1940s, present-day Bangladesh was part of British India. In 1947, the region was partitioned into two independent states: India and Pakistan. Pakistan was initially composed of two wings separated by a 1,000-mile stretch of eastern India territory that became present-day Bangladesh, and a west wing that is present-day Pakistan. Due to the west wing's marginalizing the east wing politically, economically, and culturally, the east wing revolted though a civil war and became the sovereign nation of Bangladesh in 1971. For administrative purposes, Bangladesh is divided into six divisions. Each division consists of districts (zillas), which are the largest and most important units of the local government. The country's 64 zillas consist of subdistricts, which are further divided into unions (or groups of villages) with popularly elected councils (Bin Sakhawat, 2009). The principal unit of currency in Bangladesh is the taka. Currently in 2021, one $US equals approximately 85 taka.

Bangladesh is one of the ten most-populous countries in the world, with an estimated population of 165 million people. Its overall population density is over 3,000 persons per square mile, one of the highest in the world. About 75 percent of the population lives in rural areas, where life expectancy at birth is roughly 63 years. The country has a relatively young population with some 60 percent around age 25 or younger. Islam is the state religion, with 88 percent of the people identifying themselves as Muslims (Bin Sakhawat, 2009).

Poverty and Malnutrition in Bangladesh

With Grameen Danone Foods' new agenda beginning in the first decade of the twenty-first century, we hope that life for the masses will improve significantly. Although Bangladesh has made great strides in reducing its poverty levels, it remains one of the poorest countries in the world, with about half of its population living below the national poverty line (Hunger Project, 2009). Malnutrition (meaning improper or inadequate diet and nutrition), waterborne diseases (such as cholera), diarrhea, and other illnesses remain serious public health threats in the country. About 45 percent of Bangladeshi children under age five are chronically malnourished. They suffer from deficiencies in calories, iron, vitamin A, calcium, iodine, and other important nutrients and elements. Malnutrition impedes the growing children's body metabolism and retards the immune system, causing them to become stunted in their growth, to be more susceptible to all forms of severe infections throughout their life, and to have higher mortality rates. Lower family incomes and higher illiteracy levels among mothers significantly contribute to the malnutrition menace in the country (Rayhan and Khan, 2006). Also, regular heavy rains coupled with the country's proximity to sea level altitudes make the country more prone to frequent devastating floods and hurricanes (Van Schendel, 2009, 4–7).

Grameen Danone Foods

The October 12, 2005, handshake deal between the two leaders had culminated from an invitation that CEO Franck Riboud had send Dr. Yunus earlier, before Yunus's arrival in France for a major microcredit global engagement. Riboud was fully aware of Yunus's and Grameen's landmark achievements of enabling millions of poor Bangladeshis to escape poverty through microcredit. At their luncheon, Riboud had wanted Yunus to advise him regarding how Groupe Danone could participate in the poverty and hunger alleviation efforts. Yunus then proposed the concept of a "social business" to fight malnutrition in Bangladesh, an idea that Riboud immediately accepted with keen interest and enthusiasm.

Following the lunch meeting, Riboud assigned Emmanuel Faber, the then-president of Danone's Asia-Pacific operation, who at the time was stationed in Shanghai, China, to be the logical person to direct the implementation and operation of the joint venture. While Yunus was still in France, he received a call from Faber, who wanted to find out how Danone could immediately begin rolling out the project. Danone's team, with the backing of its board of directors, quickly committed to the venture and enthusiastically started working with Grameen to implement the project over the next few months (Woodworth, 2009; Yunus, 2007).

During the initial planning meetings in 2005 for the joint venture, Faber and his team traveled to Bangladeshi and worked with Grameen managers and other parties of interest to gather information to create a business plan, framework, and operational strategy for the venture. The information gathered covered the products to be produced by the venture, market information (marketing channels, pricing, existing substitutes, and so on), current data and studies on malnutrition in Bangladesh, plant size and location, supply of raw material for yogurt manufacturing, governance structure for the venture, and even the kind of talent needed to operate the venture (Yunus, 2007, 131).

Grameen Danone Foods yogurt lady selling her products to area villages in Bangladesh.

By early 2006, Grameen and Groupe Danone had reached a Memorandum of Understanding (MOU) to enter into a 50:50 venture to form a company called "Grameen Danone Foods (GDF), A Social Business Enterprise." The MOU specified that the initial funding for the project, a total of 75 million taka (about US$1.1 million), would be provided on a 50:50 basis—half by Danone and half by Grameen. The partners planned to take out their initial investments after three years of the plant's operation. Nonetheless, they would remain owners of the joint venture on equal basis. Also, virtually all the profits would be reinvested in expanding and improving the business, rather than rewarding shareholders. In addition, the MOU made it clear that GDF was not a "corporate social responsibility" project of Danone, but rather an example of social business (Yunus, 2007, 144—45).

Business Model

GDF adopted what was referred to as a "Unique Proximity Business Model" to enable it to achieve the highest level of operational efficiency. The model would bring the supply of raw materials, food production, storage, distribution, retailing, and consumption as close to one another as possible (Ghalib and Hossain, 2008). Besides providing daily healthy nutrition to malnourished Bangladeshis, this model would reduce poverty by stimulating the local economy through involving local farmers to supply milk to the plant, by involving local villagers via a low-cost and labor-intensive manufacturing model that minimizes the use of machinery and maximizes job opportunities for villagers, and by helping to create local jobs through the distribution chain that involves local vendors. Other ingredients of yogurt, mainly sugar and date molasses, would also come from poor rural areas close to the plant.

By situating food production, retailing, and consumption as close to one another as possible, elements that would be eliminated included expensive refrigeration required for cold chains of distribution, trucks required for long-distance shipping, and other costly distribution measures that Danone utilizes in its plants throughout the world. Thus, the strategy would provide a quick turnaround of the product from the factory to the consumer, in order to maintain the product's fresh taste, flavor, texture, and acid content. It was projected that daily yogurt products could be sold conveniently by local distributors in the plant's neighborhood within 48 hours of their manufacture. In addition, the model would require the venture to make the plant as small as technically possible, as well as economically feasible, in order to create other "community-based" plants throughout the villages in the country (Yunus, 2007, 133).

Key Venture Partners

There were to be several main entities involved in rolling out this new business strategy from both France and Bangladesh. One was *Groupe Danone*, the giant food products corporation and world leader in dairy products. It also produces bottled water, baby foods, and medical nutrition products. The Danone brand yogurt (known as Dannon in the U.S.) is popular throughout Europe, North America, and other countries. More than 40 percent of Groupe Danone's business takes place in developing markets. In 2008, the company's annual revenues stood at US$21 billion (Danone, 2009), and its success has only increased over the past decade. Besides providing funding for research, planning, and the establishment of Bangladeshi factories, Groupe Danone provides business expertise in food manufacture and leadership in its various operations.

Another critical role player was, of course, Professor *Muhammad Yunus* himself. He was born in 1940 in Chittagong, Bangladesh. After attending Dhaka University, he studied economics as a Fulbright scholar at Vanderbilt University in Tennessee, United States. He became chair of the Economics Department at Chittagong University in Bangladesh. The devastating Bangladeshi famine of 1974–1975 that claimed countless lives compelled Yunus to abandon trying to solve Bangladeshi's poverty and hunger merely through teaching Adam Smith's and other renowned economists' elegant theories of profit-motivated free-market capitalism; instead, he decided he must look for viable alternative solutions.

As noted, Yunus eventually conceived of the radical method known as "microcredit." His humble initial venture, which began with giving tiny microloans to just a few peasant women making simple reed baskets near his university, gradually grew to assisting millions of Bangladeshi women with microfinancing in an astonishing 78,000-plus villages around Bangladesh. Since its founding, it has given out US$9 billion in loans. The loan repayment rate for the poor borrowers is 98.6 percent—significantly higher than that for well-off borrowers with collateral at regular banks in both that country and all other nations.

Yunus with his Grameen Bank helped launch the global movement called microcredit, which helps poor people escape poverty by offering them small, collateral-free loans to use in starting tiny businesses. The early years resulted in $9 billion for the microlending global industry and gradually drew the participation of giant institutions, including Citigroup, Deutsche Bank, and the Bill & Melinda Gates Foundation (Woodworth, 2014). More-recent data analyzed in a World Bank book by Shahidur Khandker and others (2016), *titled Beyond Ending Poverty*, found that all Bangladeshi microfinance institutions collectively have booked sustained benefits over two decades in reducing poverty and increasing incomes. Microcredit accounted for a 10 percent reduction in rural poverty in Bangladesh over that time. This means that MFIs have lifted some 2.5 million Bangladeshis from the ranks of the extreme poor.

The movement continues to grow, not only in Bangladesh, but worldwide as well. As of late 2021, the efforts to take access to capital for the poorest throughout the entire planet has mushroomed to more than 140 million borrowers receiving microloans with a total loan portfolio estimated at $124 billion (Thunstrom, 2021).

In Bangladesh itself, some 80 percent of poor families have been reached with microcredit. Yunus and the Grameen Bank were eventually jointly awarded the Nobel Peace Prize of 2006 for their pioneering efforts to create economic and social development, and ultimately to benefit peace worldwide by utilizing microcredit initiatives (Yunus, 2007, pp. 51, 66, 237). Yunus has provided decades of valuable guidance and remarkable leadership to the global movement, as well as, in particular, the Grameen team's partnering with Groupe Danone to ensure that GDF would succeed as a social business.

Besides Grameen Bank itself, Yunus labored to initiate the founding of some 24 other organizations, all of which are involved in various activities dedicated to fighting poverty and other social ills in Bangladesh. Collectively, these enterprises are described as "The Grameen Family of Companies." Seven are involved in enhancing the operation of GDF, which became the 25th company. Of these, four of them (Grameen Byabosa Bikash, Grameen Kalyan, Grameen Shakti, and Grameen Telecom) provided half of the $1.1 million that was required for the initial funding of the Bogra plant (Yunus, 2007, 144). They became joint owners of the new venture with Groupe Danone (Ghalib and Hossain, 2008). In addition, Grameen Shakti has been involved in installing bio-digesters for producing organic fertilizer as well as biogas facilities for cooking and lighting, to help the small dairy farmers who mainly supply milk to GDF. The Grameen Agricultural Foundation began organizing and improving milk production in the Bogra district, in collaboration with Danone experts. The foundation uses a comprehensive design for farm improvement that involves cattle development, milk-quality enhancement, organic fertilizer, and biogas production. Grameen Fisheries and Livestock provided training, vaccination, veterinary care, and other support to poor dairy farmers to enable them to provide sufficient milk to the yogurt plant. And Grameen Bank continues to provide loans to micro borrowers so they may buy cows, and later can produce and sell the milk to the GDF yogurt plants.

Yet another entity aiding this project early on was the Global Alliance for Improved Nutrition (GAIN). It is a Geneva, Switzerland–based United Nations affiliate alliance of governments, international organizations, the private sector, and elements of civil society, whose mission is to reduce malnutrition worldwide through food fortification and other strategies aimed at improving the health and nutrition of populations at risk (GAIN, 2009). The organization supports the GDF joint venture in a number of areas. First, its experts conduct detailed, follow-up efficacy studies according to the best scientific protocols, to measure the health benefits enjoyed by the venture's yogurt. Second, it defines the nutritional benefit message to consumers so as to make the message accurate, easily understandable, and appealing. Third, it helps design the "nutritional marketing" tools, such as leaflets and posters, used by the venture to optimize its reach to malnourished customers. Last, it supports and assists in creating training materials and then training local poor women—those referred to as "Grameen ladies" below—who dispense the finished yogurt product to malnourished fellow villagers (Yunus, 2007, 146).

Facilities and Factories

The basic entity for facilitating the creation of GDF was the new Green Plant at Bogra, a location chosen to build its first plant located just outside the town, which lies 140 miles northwest of the national capital of Dhaka. The Bogra area was selected as an ideal location because it is connected with other key areas with properly constructed and well-maintained roads, which are a vital aspect of future success. The region also has reliable power, and is less prone to flooding. In addition, the immediate vicinity contains a large population of some three million potential customers. When built, the factory occupied 7,500 square feet and featured state-of-the art yogurt manufacturing equipment that included a cold storage room for the manufactured yogurt. Initially, the facility was operated by 35 employees (Ghalib and Hossain, 2008), but has expanded continually in that facility and beyond.

Premium-quality, full-cream milk used to manufacture the yogurt was, and still is, collected from poor dairy farmers by especially refrigerated vehicles that operate across various collection centers. The centers are strategically located to maximize the venture's reach to all dairy farmers in the plant's area of operation. Farmers supply these centers with the milk. GDF's staff tests the quality of milk with lactometers at the centers, and if the minimum quality standards are met, payments are made at a pre-agreed stable price, roughly at 20 taka/liter. The milk is then transported to the plant to manufacture the yogurt (Ghalib and Hossain, 2008).

Many features have made the factory genuinely "green" and environmentally friendly. Rainwater collection vats were installed to collect rainwater for the plant's operation and minimize the use ground water, ultimately reducing the depletion of ground water (Prasso, 2007). There is equipment for treating the incoming and outgoing water, to ensure that all the water used at the plant meets safety standards, as well as that all the water returned to the environment is clean and safe. The venture has even installed solar panels that generate renewable energy to heat water used for the plant's operation. To eliminate the use of plastic cups, which are not biodegradable and thus pose a trash-disposal environmental problem and that also are expensive to recycle, the venture utilizes biodegradable cornstarch containers for its yogurt. The plant has an especially prepared recycling facility to convert the used cups into fertilizer. Also, to encourage the reuse of yogurt cups, the factory offers 90 grams of yogurt (instead of the regular 80 grams) for the 5-taka price, to customers who bring their own cups to the factory to buy yogurt-refills. The venture researched ways to develop nutritious edible cups that are analogous to edible ice cream cones. Also, although the GDF ventures use natural gas to supplement solar energy, special efforts were made to use biogas to minimize or completely replace the use of natural gas (*Daily Star*, 2009). It also is used to illuminate the perimeter fencing of the factory (Ghalib and Hossain, 2008).

Target Market

Yunus had initially proposed that GDF introduce "weaning food," to target for babies in order to help them receive proper nutrition after passing the breast-feeding stage. From mother's milk, Bangladeshi babies traditionally have moved straight to rice gruel, which gives them inadequate nutrition necessary for healthy growth and development. However, since babies particularly are vulnerable to disease, and because baby food requires a very strict standard of hygiene, GDF chose to target primarily small children. However, the venture made its product also appealing to the general population, including adults. Over time, the GDF venture began manufacturing baby food as well as bottled water businesses in later stages of its operation in Bangladesh.

Marketing Mix

Product: GDF chose yogurt as the initial product to enter the Bangladeshi market, for several reasons. First, as a dairy product, yogurt contains many healthful nutrients necessary to fight malnutrition. Second, the active cultures in yogurt promote good intestinal health and help reduce the incidence and seriousness of diarrhea among children. Third, additional micronutrients were added to the yogurt in the form of supplements to create a more-fortified yogurt. Fourth, it was hoped that yogurt would become a popular food among Bangladeshi children as well as their parents, since it is creamy and slightly sweet, a kind of food that children enjoy eating. Last, there emerged a local popular tradition of eating and enjoying yogurt as a snack as well as a dessert in Bangladesh. Under the name of *Mishit Doi* (sweet yogurt), it gradually became sold in clay pots at local shops and roadside stalls throughout the country.

Initially, GDF made a one-flavor sweet, creamy yogurt in a small, easy-to-handle package, to make the product tasty and attractive for children. The product was promoted as a snack rather than as a medicine, and it encouraged "self-feeding" by children. It became a product made from pure, full-cream milk, containing an average of 3.5 percent fat. Fortified with vitamin A (beneficial for the eyes), it also offered iron, calcium, zinc, protein, iodine (to help maintain thyroid function), and other micronutrients. To ensure adherence to premium quality standards, these micronutrients were imported by Groupe Danone. The end product is moderately sweetened with molasses made from dates from local palm trees, a favorite flavor enhancement in Bangladeshi desserts. The formula mix is so rich that a single 80g cup provides 30 percent of a child's daily requirements of vitamins, iron, zinc, and iodine.

Pricing: GDF decided to make the price for its yogurt product low, for two reasons. First, to enable the poorest parents and children to afford the yogurt, the venture decided to keep the price within the price point for any snack-food purchase aimed at the poorest Bangladeshis, at a maximum of 10 taka, or about 15 U.S.cents (Yunus, 2007, 134). Second, given that the existing *Mishit Doi* is usually sold for around 20 taka (30 U.S.cents), which is beyond the reach of most poor children, the price of less than 10 taka would make the venture's yogurt more competitive in the poor Bangladeshi market. Thus, the venture decided to position its 80-gram cup of yogurt at just 6 taka, or about 7 U.S.cents (Grameen Trust, 2006 November).

Product Placement: The marketing methods were designed to ensure that the yogurt would be sold mainly to poor, rural families who needed the fortified yogurt the most. Since the original yogurt factory was adjacent to it consumers in Bogra, the distribution system emphasized a quick turnaround from the factory to the consumer. In addition, this proximity eliminated as many "middlemen" as possible in order to keep the price for yogurt low for poor customers. To ensure the consistency of the yogurt's flavor, taste, texture, and acid content, the product was usually produced and consumed within 48 hours of production. The venture provided vendors with plastic spoons, which were sold for half a taka each, for customers who wish to eat their purchased yogurt on the spot.

The distribution system and sales program involved "Grameen ladies" who were local borrowers of Grameen Bank microloans. They directly sold cups of yogurt door to door, among their friends and neighbors, and across the counters of small grocery and sundry shops that exist throughout Bangladesh. These women were clearly ideal for the marketing, selling, promoting, and publicizing of GDF's yogurt. Why? First, they themselves are part of the target customer base of village families, especially as parents of small children. Second, they are known and trusted members of the community. Third, they know potential customers and what is likely to appeal to them. Last, they are already in daily touch with customers for their other businesses, such as poultry or dairy farming, craft production, services, food sales, and so forth.

To ensure that the distribution of the yogurt would be fast and efficient, detailed plans for local distribution of yogurt were set in place early on. Sales and marketing managers would map their areas within a radius of about 15 miles in terms of local village consumption markets, selecting about a hundred depot locations for delivery of yogurt supplies. They would determine shops for yogurt sales and prepare for recruiting of the "Grameen ladies" who would distribute the product. The company provided insulated blue bags to such ladies to keep the yogurt cool and chilled while dispensing it around the neighborhoods. The bags were meant to only carry each day's supply of yogurt, thus ensuring that fresh yogurt is picked up from nearby yogurt depots and sold on a daily basis. The "Grameen ladies" make a commission of one-half taka per cup sold, which would increase their family's monthly income by a few hundred taka. On average, each vendor could sell perhaps 60 to 70 cups of yogurt per day. Through experience, these vendors have established how much stock they can turn over every day, and thus they order accordingly, to minimize wastage.

Promotion: Introducing the first yogurt factory near Bogra made good promotion and marketing sense for GDF. The town was well known in Bangladesh for the yogurt it had already been producing for years—a sweet, thick mixture usually taken as a dessert (Mishti Doi). Thus, by utilizing this already existing marketing factor, GDF hoped to establish a similar promotion pattern to roll out its own yogurt product. Hence, the joint venture positioned its product to be easily promoted among potential customers throughout the local region first, and later throughout the entire country. GDF also adapted its packaging concept to the target market. Since, it wanted to name its yogurt Shokti Doi ("Yogurt for Power"), it picked the figure of a lion as the ideal symbol to use in promoting the fortified yogurt. The lion is very popular among Bangladeshi youngsters, and thus was well suited to represent the "power" that the yogurt provides to children through its health benefits. The venture's attractive plastic cups for dispensing the yogurt were decorated with a picture of a cartoon lion, showing off its muscles. The cups also bear the GDF logo, which was composed of the globally known blue lettering of Groupe Danone, surrounded by the Grameen Bank's red-and-green house-shaped symbol (Yunus, 2007, 143).

The official launch of Grameen Danone Food yogurt occurred in March 2006 when Danone CEO Franck Riboud went to Dhaka to cosign and publicize the Memorandum of Understanding (MOU) with Yunus and officially roll out the GDF joint venture (Ahmad, 2006). Later the same year he made a second visit to Bangladesh to officially inaugurate the first completed GDF yogurt factory in Bogra. Accompanying him this time was Zinédini Zidane, popularly known as "Zizou," the world-famous French football player. He became a world hero, having been selected by FIFA as the best footballer on the planet three times. He was and still is extremely popular among most Bangladeshis. Zizou was the brand ambassador for the Danone Foods (Grameen Trust, 2006 Nov.). He made a spectacular GDF brand launch by signing his autograph on the foundation stone of the first GDF plant in Bogra (Daily Star, 2006). Soon after, in January 2007, the first commercial batches of yogurt rolled off the manufacturing line and entered the malnourished Bangladeshi market (Yunus, 2007, pp. 144, 154, 156). The venture expanded gradually with a strategy of eventually creating more yogurt factories throughout the country over time (Grameen Trust, 2006 Apr.). Its primary goal was— and still is—to reach many malnourished children in Bangladesh with its fortified yogurt. Within GDF's first several years, its managers hoped their business would grow rapidly after the Bangladeshi government announced its increased support for milk products to improve people's health, especially children's, but the results seem to have been negligible (Daily Star, 2009).

Early Risks and Challenges Faced by Grameen Danone Foods

Despite significant successes in getting the fortified yogurt to many malnourished Bangladeshis and improving the local economy of Bogra district, GDF was immediately faced with risks and challenges that threatened its efforts back then, and continue to partly do still today in 2021. Of course, in most business start-ups, whether PMBs or SBEs, there are complex factors in realizing a firm's objectives. In this case of GDF, reaching the desired maximum *social* benefits for consumers and achieving optimal and sustainable financial *revenues* was, and remains, a challenge.

In the case of GDF, the risks and challenges include the following:

Dwindling number of trained distributors: The venture invested significantly in time and resources to train more than 1,000 "Grameen ladies" for its yogurt distribution campaign. However, this figure gradually dwindled, mostly because early vendors made a low profit margin of only 0.5 taka per cup. Given that the turnover rates of the product average from only 60 to 70 cups per day, there was less overall daily monetary incentive for the female microentrepreneurs to stay in the distribution business. Thus, a large number of vendors were not committed enough to go out and sell the yogurt on a daily basis. Rather, they used distribution as a part-time source of extra income. Consequently, the venture struggled to realize optimal returns on its investment.

Reaching a limited number of target consumers: Advertising was initially done primarily by word of mouth, through local village meetings and social networks. However, unlike mass media campaigns such as television and radio, which may have reached mass audiences, GDF's word-of-mouth campaigns were only reaching limited numbers of potential consumers. Thus, it faced the challenge of maximizing its social benefits to all its targeted consumers.

Easily perishable yogurt product: The yogurt product also proved difficult to distribute and market to consumers, due to its quick and perishable nature. It had a thick consistency when cooled but would become runny as it was removed from a chilled environment and distributed around. Since many consumers dislike yogurt in a runny state, the "Grameen ladies" found it difficult to sell the yogurt, despite the nutritional content of the yogurt's remaining intact.

After its first year of operations, the venture was still struggling to make enough profits to cover its costs. Essentially, its revenues came only from the sale of yogurt, so its profit margins were low. Management debated increasing the 5 taka/80-gram cup price, but worried that doing so might make the fortified yogurt unaffordable for the intended poor consumers. To overcome this challenge, the venture considered replacing its limited rural-focused marketing strategy with a larger, more encompassing one that would cover a much wider area and target a larger population. It also planned to enter urban markets by offering the product in larger packs at a higher price, much like Costco and Walmart do in their massive stores in the developed world. It was hoped that the ensuing higher profits might subsidize the prices of smaller packs that were being offered to the poor rural markets. These and other debates have continued to be explored and tried over the past decade.

The Broader Challenges of Social Business Enterprises (SBEs)

The social business movement will need to overcome a number of significant challenges in order to succeed in creating massive social and ethical benefits for society. Some of these challenges include the following:

Wrong Delivery of Products and Services: Poor delivery occurs when a service or material good, meant to help the people at the bottom of the social and economic pyramid, instead ends up among those of middle-class or affluent status. One way to address this challenge involves flooding the product to all segments of the society, to ensure that it reaches the target consumers. Another approach is to adopt innovative and creative social business models designed to reach target consumers with a laser focus. For example, a social business might need to keep its multiple markets effectively separated through innovative packaging and pricing, product or service differentiation for each economic class of consumers, geographic location, and marketing methodology. Making the product look different for each economic class may thus make most affluent people feel uncomfortable about buying products that are clearly packaged and designed for the poor. They might sense that they are unfairly benefiting from goods and services intended to help the unfortunate, and they might also fear lowering their own status by utilizing such goods and services.

GDF initially chose to ensure that its fortified yogurt would reach malnourished poor villagers by choosing to separate its market by geographic location and marketing methodology. The joint venture located its first yogurt factory and afterward other factories were established in remote rural areas so that *Shokti Doi* would reach the poor first, rather than be available to the affluent population in the capital city of Dhaka. Also, local, poor, Grameen borrowers were selected to serve as distributors of the product to their friends and neighbors, who were—and are—also poor.

Dishonest Social Businesses: Dishonest individuals and groups in some situations globally, including in developing nations, may try to deceive investors as well as the general society by creating social businesses marred with deception, false reporting, inflated claims, and disguised PMBs. Thus, some social businesses might claim social benefits, while they actually produce less-good things, or none at all. For example, a company that does nothing to help the environment may create its image as a champion for green business through clever and deceitful media campaigns, thereby misleading innocent investors to fund it. Having a set of clear, government-enforced definitions of social business tends to help prevent unscrupulous businesspeople from creating such deceitful social businesses. Also, developing institutions, methodologies, and defined conventional metrics for credible impact evaluation of social businesses are critical to the success of the growing social business ideal.

Conflicts of Interests Especially for Hybrid SBEs: Some corporations might find it difficult to convert their businesses into hybrid social businesses, due to potential conflicts between their for-profit pursuits, not to mention social and moral causes. For instance, a major American food company may find it difficult to maximize profits while at the same time making sure that poor children benefit nutritionally by being provided with high-quality meals at the lowest possible price. Thus, for hybrid models to be adopted, as in the case of Groupe Danone operating GDF, most firms need to rewrite their organizational missions and philosophies to incorporate and embrace the concepts of social business. Groupe Danone has done exactly that, and as a result shows a strong commitment to supporting the success of its yogurt plants throughout Bangladesh. The company's commitment has always been inspired by its philosophical and emotional stakes, rather than any financial or other ulterior motives. As a result, the company has committed massive resources and expert talent to the Bangladeshi market, where its financial stake is quite insignificant.

The Future Growth of SBEs

The growing world of social business remains largely unexploited, with their combined assets remaining a small component of the global economy, yet I firmly believe that its future remains bright (Woodworth, 2021). Muhammad Yunus concurs, as revealed in his books and speeches.

As societies increasingly recognize the viability and impacts for good arising from the Grameen Danone Food results, some will begin to adopt social business as a valid economic structure, and revolutionary changes will expand. Noticeable trends will emerge in the growth, funding, and much-needed government regulation of social businesses, as well.

Creativity, innovation, supportive institutions, policies, regulations, norms, and rules will all come into being to help social businesses grow, thrive, and become part of the expansive mainstream economy. Unique forms of SBEs that turn existing problems into opportunities will also rise rapidly. For example, social businesses that may recycle garbage and other waste products that would otherwise generate pollution in poor neighborhoods will be established to support local economies. Companies will choose to launch their own social businesses rather than simply donate moneys to philanthropy, corporate social responsibility efforts, or foundations.

Academic Institutional Support for Social Business

Increasingly, social business will be part of academic curricula, with a number of schools beginning to offer Social MBA degrees as alternatives to traditional, capitalist-oriented MBAs. My own 30-plus years of work to build huge SBE pioneering efforts as a full professor at BYU (Brigham Young University, 2021) has spread beyond its campus to those of Stanford, Wharton, Yale, Harvard, and more. Seeing the parallels between solid Christian values and biblical teachings helped me raise an initial $3 million in 2003 to design and launch what was initially called the Marriott School of Business's Center for Economic Self-Reliance (CESR). Ultimately, the organization was renamed the Ballard Center for Social Impacts, to honor a prominent Christian leader, Melvin J. Ballard, whose faith that he developed in the 1930s inspired him to promote, scale up, and implement major self-reliance initiatives during the Great Depression (Ballard Center, 2021). It is now the world's largest university program focused on social impacts that help students learn to solve the world's most pressing social problems. Mobilizing thousands of students and hundreds of professors annually, its programs are vetted by leading independent organizations such as the Skoll Foundation, Ashoka, the Schwab Foundation, the Mulago Foundation, and more. It offers numerous social business programs, including the Peery Social Entrepreneurship Program, the Impact Investing Program, and the Corporate Social Impact program, which advises leading companies globally how to improve society. Its motto: "Doing Good. Better."

As for myself, after having designed and taught one of the first courses on SBEs in the world, I have sought to foster such courses throughout the United States, including at Notre Dame University, Southern Methodist University, Georgetown, Cornell, University of Southern California, Yale, Liberty University, University of Michigan, University of California at Berkeley, New York University, Duke, the American Jewish University, Boston College, and Oxford. Today, courses and academic programs are being implemented at hundreds more institutions of higher learning. By design, their core curricular concepts challenge some of the traditional theories that are inherently held by free-market capitalism. Students pursuing social MBAs now master many of the same skills as their classmates in traditional MBA programs. A number of these schools also have established centers to focus on social business, social entrepreneurship, and innovation, and are increasingly devising and offering related curricula. Gradually, we are seeing a reformation—or even a rejection—of traditional Profit-Maximizing Businesses (PMBs) as today's ethical young people want newer, better, more-humane corporations.

Innovative New Funding of Social Businesses

A range of commercial lending institutions and venture capitalists are increasingly following in Danone's path by financing social businesses, since these will generate profits that will easily allow borrowers to make loan repayments. Some investors may even choose to fund social businesses in consideration of social benefits achieved, rather than sustainable profit optimization alone. Governments are creating funding and other measures, and enacting tax regulations to support and encourage social businesses. Major international and bilateral development donors, including the World Bank, are choosing to create funds to support social business initiatives in recipient countries. Foundations are investing in social business, since their endowment funds are being recycled endlessly to produce even more social good (Yunus, 2008, 1–2).

Social businesses may choose to create their own new type of capital market simply to raise financing for doing good. Investors in greater numbers are buying and selling shares on emerging social business stock markets, just as they used to do on traditional PMB stock markets. The prices of shares on the social stock market may even be measured in terms of social benefits produced, rather than simply profit expectations (Yunus, 2007, 181, 244). High-impact social businesses will accrue more stock value that low-impact ones. Investors who wish to withdraw their investments from given social businesses at any point will do so by selling their shares to other shareholders who accept the philosophy, practice, and conventions of those social businesses (Ghalib and Hossain, 2008).

Future Regulation of Social Businesses

Certification companies and audit firms will be created to monitor the claims of social benefits put forth by social businesses. In addition, other specialized rating agencies will be created to certify various aspects of social businesses—for example, adherence to labor standards, use of renewable energy sources, and fair practices in selecting suppliers that represent local communities. Media will pay an equally great deal of attention to social business, just as they do to PMBs. For example, magazines devoted to social business will appear on newsstands, television programs featuring leading experts on social business will pop up on the news networks, and executives of the world's top social businesses will become as famous as those running conventional PMBs (Yunus, 2007, 183). Social businesses will self-regulate through competing both among themselves and with PMBs, in terms of their products' or services' prices, quality, convenience, availability, brand image, and all other traditional factors that influence consumer choices today. Also, rather than compete, certain social businesses will choose to collaborate or even merge, to achieve maximum social benefits.

Key Lessons and Opportunities from the Grameen Danone Food Case

The success of the concept of social business in Bangladesh is creating a small but emerging global revolution in the worlds of conventional capitalism and charity. Success may well prove that capitalism, if it accepts a social conscience out of self-preservation, can more significantly eradicate poverty throughout the worldwide in the coming decades (Yunus, 2007). It is hoped that once poverty is eradicated, "museums of poverty" will spring up around the globe to display its horrors to future generations. People will then wonder why human society ever countenanced contemporary capitalism's selfishness, which provided luxurious conditions to merely a few individuals while billions of people struggled throughout their entire lives in misery, deprivation, and despair.

The GDF social business in Bangladesh may be part of the beginning of such a revolution. GDF so far is only serving malnourished poor villagers in Bangladesh. Importantly, many are vulnerable children. It also provides local villagers with incomes, along with jobs in sales and distribution to. Hundreds of trained "Grameen ladies" add to their meager incomes by dispensing yogurt door to door within a dozen or two kilometers' radius of the area yogurt factory. Hundreds of Grameen Bank–supported local dairy farmers herd their milk cows, earning higher incomes by supplying milk to the plant. The factory also provides direct jobs to local villagers who are involved in the manufacture of the yogurt. Besides improved nutrition and local jobs, direct and indirect, another key social benefit realized by these plants is the environmental conservation that is achieved through its green factory. Some dairy farmers are being mostly financed with microloans provided by Grameen Bank so that they can gradually achieve their agriculture dreams.

Over time, GDF has continued to evolve. In 2018 it became a B-Corp, which is an innovative, unique, and more-humane type of business organization that increasingly is being recognized by leading firms globally. The following year, GDF was designated as "Best for the World" in the Community category. This recognizes the positive impact toward creating a shared, sustainable prosperity for all (B-Corp, 2018–2019). An important aspect of GDF's agenda seeks to support the United Nation's Sustainable Development Goals (SDGs) that had been officially announced earlier (UN, 2015). In particular, the enterprise highlights key items in this ranking: No. 1 is No

Poverty, No. 2 is Zero Hunger, No. 3 is Good Health and Well-Being, and No. 8 is Decent Work and Economic Growth.

Groupe Danone now measures its value though social benefits rather than profit maximization alone. The company annually reports the social benefits that accrue from the Bogra plant in Bangladesh, stating them on its bottom line, along with monetary revenues from its annual operations (Danone, 2009). Employees at the company discuss the joint venture with pride when discussing their company in public. It is truly impressive that a US$1 million business arising out of a $21.31 billion enormous French corporation can achieve such good results for poor Bangladeshis. Perhaps GDF offers positive impact like those achieved by the billions of dollars given out annually by foundations, corporations, and other donors. For example, between 1996 and 2006, foundation giving in the United States skyrocketed from $13.8 billion to $40.7 billion (Lawrence, 2007). In 2007 (Kirdahy, 2008), the top 10 most generous corporations in the United States made a total of US$1.526 billion in cash donations alone (excluding "in-kind" donations) to charity through corporate social responsibility efforts). However, because this money went directly to charity rather than to social business programs, it was most likely depleted and hence created minimal rather than perpetual maximum social benefits for the society. Thus, with Grameen Danone Foods' example, perhaps other PMB corporations and donors will come to realize that the social business euro or dollar can mean more than the charity dollar, which will incentivize them to invest in social business efforts to tackle some of the world's most serious social problems.

Through the years, GDF has grown, held the required annual shareholder meetings (Grameen Danone Holds Annual Company Convention, 2011), and maintained stable operations. However, there has not yet been the significant growth originally that Muhammad Yunus and Franck Riboud dreamed of even after some 15 years. The most recent data reports annual revenues of US$2.4 million. It has 238 employees, who collaborate with 313 rural farmers supplying milk to make the healthy yogurt that benefits some 130,000 Bangladeshi children (Fondation Grameen Crédit Agricole, 2021).

Today, just like the microcredit movement that sprang from Bangladesh and has now become a worldwide movement, the social business practice that started in the same country may equally spread to become a worldwide movement. Asad Kamran Ghalib and Farhad Hossain (2008) predicted in the early 2000s that it would be refined, replicated, and adapted in various forms throughout the world, thus creating innovative social and moral benefits for diverse many societies. Once this concept becomes a recognized part of the mainstream economy, then capitalism and free-market concepts will need to be redefined so as to incorporate the goals and objectives of pursuing not only maximum profitability, but also social and ethical causes.

I want to share a few other Danone ventures that Christian business leaders and entrepreneurs throughout the world may be interested in learning about. The early partnership continues to expand. Today, the following list shows a wide range of social business innovations inspired or created by GDF that may help to serve the biblical mandate to be our *"brother's keeper"* (Danone Partnerships, 2019).

- Danone Ecosystem Fund: "Madre Tierra," a Regenerative Agriculture Project with Mexican Strawberry Producers
- La Laiterie Du Berger: Proving Lasting Social Impact and Economic Success Go Hand in Hand!
- Danone Ecosystem Fund: "Les 2 Pieds sur Terre," Helping French Dairy Farmers to Reduce their Environmental Footprint
- Livelihoods Fund for Family Farming—Aguascalientes, Paving the way for a large-scale solution to mitigate an aquifer's deficit in Mexico
- Danone Communities—Drinkwell: Bringing Safe Drinking Water to the Most Populated Areas of Bangladeshhttps://www.danone.com/integrated-annual-reports/integrated-annual-report-2019/sustainable-projects/livelihoods-carbon-fund-araku-2.html
- Danone Ecosystem Fund: "Stand by Mums," Supporting Motherhood in Romania
- Livelihoods Carbon Fund: "Araku 2," Ranging from degraded lands to a biodiverse terroir for premium coffee and food forests: the journey of 40,000 Araku farmers in India
- Danone Ecosystem Fund: "H'Lib Dzair," Improving sustainable milk production in Algeria
- Livelihoods Fund for Family Farming: Building a Resilient Vanilla Supply Chain with 3,000 Smallholder Farmers in Madagascar
- Danone Ecosystem Fund: "'Cartoneros," Doing inclusive Recycling in Argentina
- Livelihoods Carbon Fund: Restoring mangroves in Senegal to sequester carbon and improve the lives of the local communities
- Danone Ecosystem Fund: "Rejoso Kita," Protecting Indonesia's Rejoso Watershed
- Danone Ecosystem Fund: "Warung Anak Sehat," Improving child nutrition in Indonesia through female entrepreneurs

https://www.danone.com/integrated-annual-reports/integrated-annual-report-2019/sustainable-projects/livelihoods-fund-for-family-farming-building-resilient-vanilla-supply-chain-in-madagascar.html

Conclusion

All these are examples of how Christians, Muslims, Jews, social businesses, microfinance nonprofits, and nongovernmental organizations alike can build alliances that promise a better quality of life for those oppressed by hunger, unemployment, a lack of education, and more. "Profit-Maximizing Businesses" (PMBs) need to apply alternative models of economic development whose principal objectives are to optimize social and ethical benefits known as "Social Business Enterprises" (SBEs). Citing Nobel Prizewinner Muhammad Yunus once more, he declared GDF's importance thus: "We need a new type of business that pursues goals other than making personal profit—a business that is totally dedicated to solving social and environmental problems" (Yunus, 2021). While Grameen Danone Foods and SBEs alone are not literally building the Kingdom of God on earth, nevertheless it made manifest that innovative and ethical structures promise movement toward a better planet for more of God's children.

References

Ahmad, R. (2006). "Grameen Teams Up with Groupe Danone to Set Up Food Plant," *The Daily Star* (web edition), March 13; vol. 5, no. 636. Accessed June 13, 2020. http://thedailystar.net/2006/03/13/d60313011410.htm.

B-Corp. (2018–2019). Accessed August 17, 2020. https://www.bcorporation.net/en-us/find-a-b-corp/company/grameen-danone-foods-ltd/.

Ballard Center for Social Impact. (2021). Brigham Young University, Marriott School. Accessed November 5, 2021. https://marriott.byu.edu/ballard/about/overview/.

Bin Sakhawat, F.. (2009). "Bangladesh," photo by Fahad, Dhaka, Bangladesh. Accessed June 17, 2020. http://photobyfahad.com/fahadnew/index.php?option=com_content&view=article&id=31&Itemid=20&651051b9366bfd3dff599ebba23b3635=qxxtwocpms.

Brigham Young University. (2021). Accessed November 2, 2021. https://www.byu.edu/.

Business Week. (2005). "Nobel Winner Yunus: Microcredit Missionary," *Businessweek*, December 26. Accessed July 13, 2020. http://www.businessweek.com/magazine/content/05_52/b3965024.htm.

Collins, C., et al. (2020). "Billionaire Bonanza," Institute for Policy Studies, April 23. Accessed December 27, 2021. https://ips-dc.org/wp-content/uploads/2020/04/Billionaire-Bonanza-2020.pdf.

Daily Star. (2006). "Grameen Danone Foods Opens Wednesday," *The Daily Star* (web edition), November 6; vol. 5, no. 868. Accessed June 13, 2019. http://www.thedailystar.net/2006/11/06/d61106050257.htm.

Daily Star Bangladesh. (2009). "Declaration of Milk Sector as a Thrust One Soon." August 11. Accessed August 27, 2021. http://www.thedailystar.net/newDesign/news-details.php?nid=101026.

Danone. (2009). *2008 Annual Report, Groupe Danone.* March 20. http://www.danone08.com/catalogue/index.htm. English version accessed June 13, 2021, from http://media.corporate-ir.net/media_files/irol/95/95168/press/RegistrationDocument2008.pdf.

Danone Partnerships. (2019). *Annual Report.* https://www.danone.com/integrated-annual-reports/integrated-annual-report-2019/sustainable-projects/social-innovation.html.

Fondation Grameen Crédit Agricole. (2021). Accessed December 9, 2021. https://www.gca-foundation.org/en/organisation/grameen-danone-foods-ltd/.

GAIN. (2009). "Investing in Partnerships to Fight Malnutrition," The Global Alliance for Improved Nutrition (GAIN), Geneva. Accessed November 18, 2021. http://www.gainhealth.org/about-gain.

Ghalib, A., and F. Hossain. (2008). "Social Business Enterprises—Maximising Social Benefits or Maximising Profits? The Case of Grameen-Danone Foods Limited," Institute for Development Policy and Management, School of Environment and Development, University of Manchester, UK; *BWPI Working Paper 51*, July. Accessed June 18, 2021. http://www.bwpi.manchester.ac.uk/resources/Working-Papers/bwpi-wp-5108.pdf.

Grameen Danone Holds Annual Company Convention. (2011). *The New Nation,* Dhaka. September 21. Accessed November 30, 2021. http://www.highbeam.com/doc/1P3-2463963531.html.

Grameen Danone Foods Ltd. (2018). GDF Became a Certified B-Corporation in 2018. Accessed May 13, 2021. https://www.bcorporation.net/en-us/find-a-b-corp/company/grameen-danone-foods-ltd/.

Grameen Trust. (2006). "Grameen Danone Foods Launched," *Grameen Dialogue*, Grameen Trust, Bangladesh; April, Issue 63. Accessed May 13, 2020. http://www.grameen-info.org/dialogue/dialogue63/regularfl2.html.

Grameen Trust. (2006). "Zidane Inaugurates First Grameen Danone Dairy Plant**,"** *Grameen Dialogue*, Grameen Trust, Bangladesh; November, Issue 64. Accessed August 13, 2015. http://www.grameen-info.org/dialogue/dialogue64/specialfeature3.html.

Groupe Danone. (2009). "The Danone Groupe." The Dannon Company, Inc. Accessed June 13, 2017. http://www.dannon.com/about.aspx.

Hunger Project. (2009). "Bangladesh," New York. Accessed June 18, 2021. http://www.thp.org/where_we_work/south_asia/bangladesh/overview?gclid=CPv1zfjtlJsCFRBbagodS1skoA.

Inequality.org. (2021). October 18. Accessed November 5, 2021. https://inequality.org/facts/wealth-inequality.

Khandker, S., et al. (2016). *Beyond Ending Poverty.* World Bank Publications.

Kirdahy, M. (2008). "America's Most Generous Corporations," *Forbes Magazine*, October 16. Accessed December 12, 2021. http://www.forbes.com/2008/10/16/most-generous-corporations-corprespons08-lead-cx_mk_1016charity.html.

Lawrence, S., et al. (2007). "Foundation Growth and Giving Estimates: Current Outlook," The Foundation Center. Retrieved June 18, 2021. http://foundationcenter.org/gainknowledge/research/pdf/fgge07.pdf.

Luke 14:23.

Matthew 19:23–25.

Prasso, S. (2007). "Saving the World One Cup of Yogurt at a Time," *Fortune*, February 19; vol. 155 (Issue 3), pp. 96–98, 100, 102.

Rayhan, M. I., and M. S. H. Khan. (2006). "Factors Causing Malnutrition Among Under Five Children in Bangladesh," *Pakistan Journal of Nutrition* 5 (6): 558–62. Accessed June 18, 2021. http://www.pjbs. org/pjnonline/fin488.pdf.

Thunstrom, T. (2021). "21 Microfinance Statistics You Need to Know in 2021." *Fit Small Business*, September 15.

UN. (2015). The United Nation's 18 Sustainable Development Goals (SDGs). Accessed July 17, 2021. https:// sdgs.un.org/goals.

UNU-WIDER. (2006). "Pioneering Study Shows Richest Two Percent Own Half World Wealth," The World Distribution of Household Wealth Study. December 5; United Nations University–World Institute for Development Economics Research. Helsinki. Accessed June 18, 2021. http://www.wider.unu.edu/ events/past-events/2006-events/en_GB/05-12-2006.

Van Schendel, W. (2009). *A History of Bangladesh.* Cambridge University Press.

Woodworth, W. (2009). Interview and co-presentation with Grameen Danone Foods CEO Emmanuel Faber at a microfinance conference in Denver, February 26.

Woodworth, W. (2014). "Financing for Social Enterprise: Third World Impact Strategies for 'Necessity Entrepreneurs.'" *Academy of Management Annual Meeting Proceedings.* Accessed November 22, 2021. (1):16605-16605, 10.5465/AMBPP.2014, October.

Woodworth, W. (2020). "Microfinance, Economics, and Business Collaboration: Subsistence Entrepreneurship for the World" (Cases from Eagle Condor in Peru, Enterprise Mentors in the Philippines, HELP International Global). *Global Journal of Economics and Finance,* vol. 4, no. 2, pp. 1–7. Accessed October 30, 2021. http://gjefnet.com/images/Vol4No2/1.pdf.

Woodworth, W. (2021). "Big, Bad, Audacious Unitus: Building a $1.2 Billion Social Business for Microcredit." *Noble International Journal of Social Sciences Research.* Vol. 6, no. 4, pp. 48–55. https://napublisher.org/ pdf-files/NIJSSR-6(4)-48-55.pdf.

Yunus, M. (2007). *Creating a World Without Poverty: Social Business and the Future of Capitalism.* Public Affairs.

Yunus, M. (2008). "How Social Business Can Create a World without Poverty." *Christian Science Monitor,* February 15, pp. 1–2.

Yunus, M. (2021). "Yunus Quotes." Accessed December 30, 2020. https://quotefancy.com/ muhammad-yunus-quotes.

I acknowledge the invaluable assistance of several of my research students, in particular John Oirya, who was pursuing an MBA degree at the Marriott School of Business, BYU, when we began coauthoring several drafts of what is now this chapter.

CHAPTER

5

Care for Life: The Family Preservation Program in Mozambique, Using the Bible

In the early 2000s, several Christians in Arizona who seek to practice their religion in untraditional ways launched a nongovernmental organization that they named Care for Life (CFL). This chapter draws on my decade of fieldwork helping CFL's volunteers to improve the quality of life among villagers in the nation of Mozambique, in southern Africa. With one of my MPA graduate students from Brazil, João Bueno, along with other students, friends, and neighbors, we have sought to lift the poor, drawing on Jesus's words in Mark 10:43–44 when one of his disciples wanted recognition and perhaps even to obtain high church positions: *"whoever wants to become great among you must be your servant, and whoever wants to be first must be servant of all."* Collectively, these American social entrepreneurs have labored for years to make the world better by empowering some of the very poorest people on earth. We have viewed our work as truly a call from God.

Care for Life (CFL) was set up as an Arizona-based nonprofit foundation and a 501(c)(3) charitable organization registered in the U.S. that has NGO status in Mozambique. It works to relieve suffering by offering programs to orphans, vulnerable children, and families to assist them with meeting immediate basic needs and finding long-term solutions.

I'll begin this story by relating a few personal experiences in Mozambique as a CFL board member and also as an academic adviser to various leaders driving this cause to do good in that faraway place. This case is about strengthening the African informal economy and includes results from NGO records, data, interviews, charts, and field studies in Mozambique from 2007 to 2022. the organization established what they called the Family Preservation Program (FPP), a unique, family-based program whose main objective was to overcome poverty by preserving and empowering families (whatever structure a given family might have). FPP's sustained success in its initial few years was impressive, relative to peer programs. The number of people it helped grew from 534 in 2005 to over 11,000 by summer of 2009.

Mozambique

The population of Mozambique in 2022 is approximately 31.2 million inhabitants (World Population Review, 2022).. However, it is important to note that this estimate took into account the effects of excess mortality due to AIDS and COVID-19, which can cause lower life expectancy, higher infant mortality, lower population growth rates, and higher death rates. Infant mortality rates in the country reached an alarming 105.8 deaths per 1,000 live births, while life expectancy floats around a staggering 41.18 years. These statistics also help explain the high total fertility rate estimate of 5.29 children born per woman in Mozambique (World Bank, 2019).

Mozambique is slightly less than twice the size of California and consists of tropical ranging to subtropical terrain. The Zambezi River flows through the north-central and most-fertile part of the country. Some of its natural hazards are severe droughts, devastating cyclones, and floods in the central and southern provinces. However, there are more dangers than natural hazards that natives of Mozambique must face in their daily lives.

The country experienced the ravages of a civil war for over 15 years of conflict, pain, and death. It lasted from the late 1970s to the early 1990s, causing millions there to suffer hunger and be displaced, and many even to die. As with other parts of the world, including much of Africa, such wars emerged from the Cold War dynamics between East and West. In Mozambique, it occurred between the nation's USSR-backed ruling Marxist Front for the Liberation of Mozambique (FRELIMO) against the right-wing, anticommunist insurgency known as the Mozambican National Resistance (RENAMO). Tragically, over one million Mozambicans were killed and some five million people were displaced during that tumultuous time. The fighting absorbed much of the region's blood and treasure, making most citizens' well-being suffer for more than a decade.

An eventual peace agreement, made in 1992, fell apart from 2013 until 2019 when a new reconciliation pact was agreed to. Sadly, nearly two million people were made refugees, becoming displaced victims even in their own nation. Still today, deep divisions remain within families and in neighborhoods, caused by the competing political agendas of the previous era. On my first visit to work with Care for Life, I was somewhat shocked to see that the national flag continues to feature an AK-47 rifle! As if a Soviet-inspired assault weapon weren't enough, there is a bayonet attached to the barrel, and it's crossed with a hoe. I think it's the only such symbol of any national flag in the world.

In today's Mozambique, some 2 million people face severe food insecurity due to the recent security situation, as well as a long drought and the socioeconomic impact of COVID-19. The fragile humanitarian situation there continues to deteriorate. Escalating violence has so far displaced more than 700,000 people, while some 1.3 million require immediate humanitarian assistance and protection in certain provinces.

The professional health care needs of this country are extremely sobering. According to the Human Development Report, Mozambique has only about three physicians for every 100,000 people. Deficiencies in other key health care providers (nurses, pharmacists, lab technicians, and the like) are comparable. Community-based initiatives and volunteers end up being largely responsible for health care needs, as well as for the multisector HIV/AIDS response, because a severe HIV/AIDS epidemic is still under way in Mozambique. In 2005 the prevalence of HIV infections among adults ages 15–49 was estimated to be 16.1 percent. The most common method of transmission continues to be heterosexual contact. Ever since movement within and outside Mozambique became unrestricted in 1992, HIV prevalence has dramatically increased, and it nearly reached the high HIV levels found in neighboring African countries. In addition to HIV/AIDS, Mozambique suffers from co-epidemics of tuberculosis and malaria, as well as outbreaks of seasonal cholera. These diseases and sicknesses all exacerbate the HIV/AIDS epidemic.

An African minister and his spouse, with the author holding their baby.

On a related note, Mozambique is a destination country for men, women, and even children trafficked for the purposes of forced labor and sexual exploitation. For the second consecutive year, it is on the Tier 2 Watch List for its failure to provide evidence of increasing efforts to combat human trafficking in 2007. High levels of stigma and discrimination also disadvantage the country.

Some financial improvements have been made in Mozambique, though the country still faces significant economic challenges. As of 2016, it was the seventh poorest country on the planet (World Bank, 2016), with some 46 percent of residents living below the official poverty line. Portuguese is the official Mozambican language (also spoken by 27 percent of the people as a second language). However, languages used to communicate across the country are generally fragmented tribal languages such as Emakhuwa (26.1 percent) and Xichangana (11.3 percent).

Obtaining basic education is another struggle most Mozambicans must face in their lives. In terms of literacy (defined by those persons 15 years of age and over who can read and write), only approximately 47.8 percent are literate. Among this literate segment of the population, 63.5 percent are males, while only 32.7 percent are females. This low literacy rate is strongly correlated with the low school life expectancy of eight years (primary to tertiary education) in which males receive more education than females on average. One of the major factors hindering young natives from obtaining education is the fact that individual and family daily survival needs take priority over education.

In the past several years, Mozambique has suffered dangerous new crises. As if HIV-AIDS and civil wars were not enough, its people have been afflicted by some 23 epidemics since the 1980s. Making matters even worse, more than 70 natural disasters have occurred during the last three decades: 25 major floods, 13 drought events, and 14 tropical cyclones. The regional El Niño–induced drought emergency of 2015–2016 was the worst in many years. But things became even more fraught in March 2019 when Cyclone Idai made landfall on the country's central coast. Its heavy winds and torrential rains brought devastation to much of central Mozambique, as well as to parts of eastern Zimbabwe and southern Malawi. Around three million people were affected, including several hundred thousand who were internally displaced. Nearly two million acres of crops were destroyed. Just over a month later, in April, Cyclone Kenneth hit northern Mozambique with sustained winds of up to 140 miles per hour, affecting another 300,000 people. More recently, in December 2020 and early 2021, tropical storm Chalane and tropical Cyclone Eloise wreaked yet more havoc. Many Mozambicans felt perhaps God had forsaken them, but through it all Care for Life donors gave more funding, while its NGO staffers on the ground in Africa labored more furiously than ever to reduce the suffering and help keep Indigenous people alive.

Then came COVID-19 as the global pandemic struck the entire world, including much of Africa. Mozambique suffered over a hundred thousand cases and 1,100 deaths as of July 2021. Experts worry that many more cases may be identified and have to be treated, but they are undercounted for various reasons. So the challenges in combating Mozambique's many ills continue even today.

The Development Dependency Dilemma

An old phrase from folklore, supposedly a Chinese proverb, says: "Give a man a fish and you feed him for a day. Teach a man to fish and you feed him for a lifetime." Over the last five decades, the West has given more than $2.3 trillion in aid to address the poverty that prevails in many developing w world countries. Unfortunately, there is shockingly little to show for it. Humanitarian aid and handouts are commonly given to the poor and suffering found in these countries. While such efforts help provide short-term relief to these people,, providing welfare almost always addresses merely the symptoms and not the cause, the pain and not the problem.

In his book *The White Man's Burden,* William Easterly, a New York University professor and a former World Bank economist, describes this development dilemma in a helpful manner that simplifies development players into two groups: planners and searchers. Planners are the well-meaning but often actually injurious folks who sit far away from the crisis at vast institutions dreaming up large-scale solutions. Searchers, by contrast, work in the trenches among those in need, by designing tailored solutions and teaching self-reliance on the ground. Easterly outlines this stark contrast:

> In foreign aid, Planners announce good intentions but don't motivate anyone to carry them out; Searchers find things that work and get some reward. Planners raise expectations but take no responsibility for meeting them; Searchers accept responsibility for their actions. Planners determine what to supply; Searchers find out what is in demand. Planners apply global blueprints; Searchers adapt to local conditions. Planners at the top lack knowledge of the bottom; Searchers find out what the reality is at the bottom. Planners never hear whether the planned got what it needed; Searchers find out whether the customer is satisfied (Easterly, 2007, p. 163).

In his own Mozambique field research, João Bueno, my Brazilian student hired by Care for Life, had made similar observations. Based on his experience, João believed that approximately 95–98 percent of the nonprofit organizations present in Mozambique were focusing solely on short-term results and were not concerned with achieving any kind of behavior change. The goal of this large group of organizations seemed to be to *provide*, not to *train*; to *give* the people fish, not *teach* them how to fish. The motives of those controlling these organizations are often the cause of this "providing mentality," which frequently yields results that end up debilitating the very people it seeks to help. João explained his views in the following way:

> There are several reasons why these organizations do this. For starters, the Communist mentality of Mozambique's past government encouraged this type of central planning. Also, providing in this way makes it much easier to have a feeling that you did something good, and nearly all the donors of these organizations want to see immediate results. A child was starving before and now has milk; an orphan was homeless and now has shelter; and so on. But these organizations don't seem to understand the dependency created and the associated long-term consequences of these actions (Bueno, 2006).

The dependency that is inadvertently fostered often drives the poor further down the economic ladder instead of up. This concept can be seen in the following account that took place in Mozambique. The government itself had used NGOs to build an orphanage called ASEM. At one point, several NGOs were providing multiple resources to ASEM. One day, the government mandated that any child in the orphanage with some type of family connection would have to return to their families.

Out of 600 orphans, only 29 remained who were considered true "orphans." In other words, almost every child had someone in the family who was able to help provide their *own* independent solution. Orphanages such as ASEM can end up becoming places where parents can "give away" their children and bear no accountability or responsibility for them. This illustrates what happens all over the African continent, and offers a vivid example of the negative impact of dependency.

Most donors have a concrete image of what an orphanage looks like. It is a physical place that can be seen, touched, and visited. In contrast, most donors are not familiar with the programs that help keep children in families. These preventive programs are harder to immediately see and describe, though their benefits can be far greater and are able to reach many more children (Firelight Foundation, 2006, p. 17).

Similarly, rewarding special groups with handouts and supplies can warp the people's focus and bring out their worst side. When João first went to Mozambique, he was part of a team in charge of determining who most deserved to receive scarce supplies, such as rice, medicine, school supplies, and clothing. One day in a new village, João encountered a man with HIV who convinced him that he was dying claimed that he lacked sufficient food to take his HIV medicine. Without food, the man said, he would die soon. Later, after João and his colleague insisted on seeing this man's home, he reluctantly let them in. What they found was startling. This man and two others had hoarded over 100 kilos of rice by deceiving and lying to organizations about their conditions. These natives apparently found this deception and creation of false conditions to be highly rewarding. Instead of directing their efforts toward working, planting crops, selling goods, or learning, these three—and many others—spent their time deceiving and scheming up ways to obtain free handouts.

Woman pounding millet with her mortar and pestle in her village in Africa.

In addition to creating dependency, giving handouts to special groups can fragment communities and families. For example, when an organization only provides supplies to a special group, such as those infected with HIV and widows and orphans, then the rest of the neighborhood that is equally poor sees this and gets jealous. Instead of unity, this aid selectivity creates division in the community and among families. What's, the sick or wounded child who belongs to the selected special group being aided often tries to stay "sick," or the parents even keep the child's wounds open. In some cases, mothers desperate for supplies and survival wish that one of their children had HIV so the child would belong to one special group and so be chosen to receive food, clothing, and other fundamental provisions that he or she could share with the family. Sadly, it often seems much easier for parents to scheme this way than to invest in their children's future and in overcoming their situation on their own.

The Framework, a document prepared for UNAIDS/UNICEF, argues that families and communities should be the basis for effective, scaled-up responses to child orphans, due to HIV or AIDS, as well as to address the wider range of poverty and suffering. Help through multiple interventions should be directed to all vulnerable children as well as their communities. Such programs need to be integrated with other services so as to promote child welfare and reduce poverty. Targeting children living with HIV or AIDS, or children orphaned as a result of either affliction, will only serve to exacerbate the stigma and discrimination against them (UNAIDS, 2008).

While the situation portrayed above seems utterly bleak, deep down most families want to improve their own situations. They wish to grow, live better lives, build better homes, create better habits, become independent, and generate their own income. However, many people have a hard time focusing on the future because they must concentrate almost entirely on their daily needs and survival. Goals and dreams can be far from their thoughts. Some 95 percent of organizations in Mozambique deliver tangible goods that the poor need, but unfortunately this often inhibits people's self-reliance and even limits vision. As João Bueno and others at Care for Life pondered their field experiences, they adamantly believed that something else needed to be done to help these people help themselves.

Care for Life

Our work at Care for Life to bless Africa's poor was featured in The Christian Science Monitor, which opined that "Care for Life is at the forefront of what has become a new trend in foreign aid to Africa" (Hanes, 2007). It's also consistent with my own evaluation of João Bueno's work in Mozambique: "I love what CFL does because it's grassroots, strategic, bottom-up, and it builds the poor's capacity for solving their own problems, rather than breeding a handout mind-set. CFL creates dignity, not dependency" (CFL documentary film, 2011).

Care for Life was founded in 2000 by Blair and Cindy Packard of Arizona, born out of their desire to help those in need. Their first fact-finding trip to Mozambique took place in 2000. "We saw the dire poverty of Mozambique and realized that even small efforts could make a difference," Blair Packard recalled (2011). The Packards and a few others knew they had both resources and knowledge to share, as well as friends who could do the same.

The couple were determined to create a more effective type of organization that would truly help the people help themselves. To do this, they recognized the need to work alongside the people. "Our guiding philosophy is: Go to the people; live with them; love them; learn from them; work with them; start with what they have; build on what they know. We want to help the people help themselves," said Linda Harper, CFL's Operations Director in the U.S. (2006). To realize this philosophy, to understand the primary problems, and to achieve sustainable results, CFL meets with and listens carefully to government leaders, educators, local agents, religious leaders, and, vitally, the people themselves. This practice helps CFL understand what kind of solutions the people and their local leadership see and desire.

The guiding principles of Care for Life may be summarized as follows:

1. We believe that all people on this earth are children of God, making us literal brothers and sisters. Accordingly, the people we serve inherently deserve our love and respect. Because of this relationship, we have a familial and moral obligation to help those in need.
2. We actively seek to help the poorest of the poor.
3. The mission of Care for Life is to instill hope, alleviate suffering, and foster self-reliance. CFL is focused on providing education and medical assistance in pursuit of that mission. Other projects (however worthy) outside of this focus must have proper approval to be considered a part of Care for Life, such as our farm at Marocanhe.
4. Care for Life is not affiliated with or sponsored by any religious, political, or social organization.
5. While CFL is not affiliated with any specific religion, we acknowledge God's hand in our labors and see His divine approval of guidance in all we do.
6. While there is poverty and need across the globe, Care for Life has found its current mission in Safala Province, Mozambique. We hope to be seen as a trusted friend of, and partner with, the leaders there and work along with them. As long as we are welcome, safe, and making a difference, we are committed to continue our efforts. We realize long-term, sustainable results can often take 20 years or more.
7. We recognize that we are not alone in this labor. Many other groups and individuals are working to sustain similar endeavors. We do not see them as competitors, rather as fellow laborers.
8. CFL employees and volunteers recognize the privilege and blessing that it is to work and serve for the betterment of others. Our goal is not to enhance our own financial standing, or to achieve public recognition, but to make a difference in the lives of others. All CFL

staff should clearly exemplify characteristics of honesty, integrity, respect, and kindness in all areas of their work.

9. We believe any labor, no matter how small, can make a difference in the life of the beneficiary. These small successes can, over time, change countless lives (the Starfish Principle).

10. The greatest gift we can provide is knowledge leading toward self-sufficiency. Our focus is education, combined with practical application that will enable individuals to adequately care for themselves and their families (the Teach a Man to Fish Principle).

11. We understand that, in many cases, alleviation of suffering must come before issues of self-reliance are applicable.

12. Care for Life does not exist to serve as a mouthpiece to showcase the individual views, politics, or beliefs of its individual participants. CFL is a community of many different players, but with one unified voice.

13. We regard the time, money, and materials donated to Care for Life as sacred contributions, requiring our care and trust. CFL funds are to be used in accordance with CFL goals, policies, and approval.

14. Care for Life does not have the means, nor the desire, to administer short-term, high-cost solutions to the problems it encounters.

15. We recognize the authority of our respective governments, both local and national. We strive to follow the laws of the land. If we disagree with them, we work through the proper channels to see them changed.

16. Before we attempt to effect solutions, we first try to understand the primary issues causing or creating the problems. We prefer our "treatment" to be cause-specific, not simply symptom-specific.

17. Our programs are designed wherever possible to have an exit strategy, so that at some future point projects will be able to carry on without continued dependence upon CFL.

18. We strive to train teachers and leaders and not just teach students. We want to grow future leaders and give them experiences that will enable them to become the teachers and mentors for the future.

Over the past 20 years, CFL has evolved from a charitable organization to an organization that focuses primarily on helping people help themselves out of poverty. This focus didn't come all at once, because finding long-term solutions at local levels that produce sustained results can be hard to envision, capture, and repeat. "We don't do for people what they can do for themselves. This concept can sometimes seem counterintuitive. For example, when you see an old African lady raising eight grandchildren alone, your instinct may be to help them by giving them some type of welfare. However, the best thing to do is to teach them to help themselves," said Sylvia Finlayson, former CFL Executive Director (2009).

Clearly understanding the importance of self-reliance in the fight against poverty, the leadership of CFL has endeavored to create a truly innovative program that, instead of targeting individuals and rewarding special groups, targeted *families*. The creation of this family-based program would rely on myriad observations that CFL leaders and others had made in the field. Rather than counting on just the organization for leadership and help, communities would partner with CFL. Going beyond providing cement, seeds, mosquito nets, and other valuable provisions to families and communities, these materials would be *earned* by their reaching clearly defined goals and milestones.

The Family Preservation Program (FPP)

One of João Bueno's greatest contributions as a young leader was to design and implement the Family Preservation Program (FPP). Its work primarily rests on *families*, whatever structure they might have. FPP utilizes an integrated approach that is centered on seven crucial areas of improvement: education, food/security/nutrition, community mentoring, housing, health, income generation, and psychosocial well-being, as depicted in figure 5.1.

Figure 5.1

Many NGOs fail, in part, they focus on negative problems in communities. In contrast, FPP concentrates on the positives, by creating meaningful opportunities for its people to encourage others in building on their own strengths. Leaders from the community teach and train others in their path to success.. In short, FPP is implemented and administered by local women and men who have found a way to achieve a higher quality of both life *and* health, despite living their far-too-familiar conditions of poverty

As its main objective, FPP seeks " to overcome poverty by preserving and empowering families. Children are the main victims of family failure; they will naturally be the main beneficiaries of healthier and happier families. Sickness, hunger, and ignorance are both the cause and consequence of family disintegration, describing a continued downward cycle. Family Preservation Program breaks this cycle by creating a sustainable community environment that fosters behavior change, instills hope, and promotes self-reliance" (Family Preservation Program, 2015). It accomplishes this through the following steps.

Step One—Understand Partnership: Preparing a forward-looking culture of trust, accountability, and goal setting is the first step of implementing FPP. However, it can take time for villages to trust CFL field-workers and understand the long-term benefits of their family-focused program. As João Bueno described it (2007), "Interestingly, there is not a long-term view of things there. They spent three days with the people working on goal setting because of how strong their focus was on living for today." Sylvia Finlayson (2009) added, "When CFL approaches new villages offering the value of their FPP program, something interesting often happens. Villages that have grown accustomed to receiving handouts initially turn away CFL representatives. The vision and concept of self-reliance must be carefully explained to and eventually understood by village leaders before CFL can bring in the FPP program."

Frequently, the initial reaction of villagers is one of disappointment. This occurs, in part, because villages become accustomed to unkept promises from the government and other organizations that drop off supplies and leave shortly thereafter. However, it doesn't take long for villagers to catch the vision and understand that it is better that CFL and FPP will not do for them what they can do for themselves. This program is a partnership that requires community participation and local leadership. In fact, local workers who help teach are volunteers who are not paid.

Step Two—Develop Trust: Once the concept of partnership is understood, trust begins to develop. This is most prevalent once the goals program is rolled out. For example, when families achieve ten goals, they receive materials such as bags of cement, roofing material, mosquito nets, and so forth. Families are taught on the front end how to prepare the ground for their garden, but the work must be completed by the families and not the FPP instructors. Once the ground is prepared, they will receive seeds to plant. Allowing family participation and following through with FPP commitments fosters trust among the native Mozambicans. Whereas before, local families and communities felt excluded from decisions and work, they now feel empowered and begin to trust and believe in one another. Becoming productive and beginning to solve one's own problems yields individual dignity.

Step Three—Realize Choice and Consequence: Understanding choice and consequence helps individuals become accountable. If families don't follow through on their end, they will not receive the desired incentive. Essentially, only work leads to reward. If the garden ground isn't prepared, for example, they won't receive seeds. If the seeds aren't planted, they won't reap valuable fruits and vegetables and will go without. Thorough comprehension of this concept usually occurs after 9 to 10 months in the FPP program.

Step Four—Witness Change: Change is another opportunity that becomes very apparent in the lives of families and communities after 12 to 15 months of consistent FPP participation. For instance, deaths resulting from diarrhea have decreased by an average of 80 percent. This staggering statistic comes from building and using family latrines and then burning or burying garbage. Keeping yards clean also improves hygiene and increases community dignity.

Step Five—Take Ownership: As a natural next step, families begin to take ownership for their problems and situations. Embracing complete ownership is most common around two years into the FPP program. Some of the benefits associated with ownership are feelings of unity, solidarity, and self-reliance. As villages progress in this program, CFL leaders increase delegation to local leaders. As additional time passes, families decrease their need of learning from volunteers and local leaders.

Step Six—Create Self-Reliance: Creating self-reliance is the final step of the FPP program. It is also a crucial part of CFL goals that are focused on being "sustainable now and in the future, meeting basic human needs, providing long-term benefits, and creating self-reliance so they can teach others."

Two Decades of Care for Life Results

The core tenets of CFL have always been its projects, its goals, and its focus on self-reliance. Over the years, it has identified clear issues that were addressed in each community project. They include: working toward sustainability now and in the future, with the right people in leadership and without political repercussions or compromise of safety; making everything relatively simple so that projects can be easily duplicated; making deliverables easily portable to other villages. Other goals are to make the program suit basic human needs, and over the long term. CFL's core strategy is to support a "Center of Strength" approach, rather than being spread too thinly (or widely), with disparate results. Other key issues are to ensure that each new project meets the current budget, and that it is designed for future financial sustainability. These elements of each intervention by Care for Life form its basic criteria for ensuring success.

CFL works with each village for a fixed three years—not promising "forever care." The final year places great emphasis on teaching families basic economic principles, through the FPP Income Generation Program. Participants are taught lessons on major themes:

1. *Planning* – Needs, Wants, Priorities, and Goals
2. *Business Plan* – What, When, Where, and How
3. Understanding Costs
4. Pricing – Supply and Demand
5. Quality Control and Customer Care
6. Bookkeeping
7. Cash Flows
8. Business Ethics
9. Savings and Business Growth (Loan Opportunities and Partnerships)
10. The classes are based on traditional microenterprise principles
11. No one will do it for you or help you succeed
12. In our business, we must always live the "Law of the Harvest"
13. Without making a profit, we will have no business
14. We must always guard those profits that we save ("Protect our Capital")
15. We must maintain strict separation between our business finances and our personal money
16. Plan your business
17. Visualize the business (Look for opportunities)
18. Plan the business
19. Do the business
20. Work with wisdom — Work with self-discipline
21. Be completely honest on all occasions
22. Keep accurate records, without which you will never achieve long-term success; no true growth will happen
23. Never confuse your business's cash flow with its profit

Once families learn these principles and are trained to use them, they start selling something they themselves produce. Because employment opportunities in most villages in Mozambique are limited, the best chances for income generation come through private enterprise. Generally, families either start and manage a small business, or they generate income from their own farming and agriculture. In addition to taking classes and absorbing principles taught, families have access to FPP consultants *and* CFL staff, who help them make key decisions and get them started in the right direction.

Since resources are scarce and savings often nonexistent, microcredit loans are extended by local banks that partner with CFL. As stated in the Income Generation Program Guidelines, "For many families, receiving micro loans would represent the best, and many times the only, possibility to start or to develop an income-generation activity. CFL does not give loans, but works in partnership with microcredit institutions to provide the service to FPP families."

Synergies and Success: Positive synergies have played a large part in the success of FPP. Care for Life works with *every* family in the area, thus avoiding jealousy and instead fostering unity and cooperation. This unity is multiplied by the fact that families need each other to earn and reach program incentives. Also, their use of local leadership throughout the program gives them a sense that it is *their program*. Families have already begun to successfully graduate from the FPP program, with many villages committed to remain self-reliant. Key statistics and community morale indicate that FPP has made a significant difference in the lives of over 21,000 individuals in Mozambique. As Romana Mussa João (2010) of the Mbatwe village put it: "Most of the families are now planting gardens and drinking clean water. We are learning many important things that we didn't know before! We have fewer diarrheas and everybody is more clean and happy."

Twenty Years of Care for Life Success

Through the years, João Bueno and his NGO compatriots from the United States and our staff in Africa have dreamed big, have designed projects as they turned into long-term programs, and have greatly improved the quality of life for impoverished rural Mozambicans. For some two decades they and others who followed in their footsteps have witnessed what I consider amazing results. They labored hard after dreaming bi, and by doing so thousands of African lives have been improved. Clearly, CFL has not yet established a utopia. But hard data show significant results.

A detailed analysis is beyond the scope of this chapter, but what follows are illustrative changes in several communities of CFL's impacts for good among impoverished Mozambicans through the years, beginning in the early 2000s when the NGO began its work (Care for Life, 2009):

Mungassa: During 2006–2008 this village had CFL staff assessments of well-being growing from 177 families to 243, which totaled 951 individuals. Deaths dropped from 68 down to only 4 people in that period. Healthier practices after training rose from only 49 families' making and using a pit latrine on their rural property, up to 194 families. Those using only treated, healthy drinking water expanded from just 56 families before CFL training to 224, virtually the entire community.

Casa Banana: This community saw its individual use of mosquito nets to avoid the scourge of malaria jump from a mere 174 to 634 people practicing safety. Those being tested for the scourge of HIV-AIDS rose dramatically over the two years from a mere 3 to 106 adults.

Ndunda: After community adults received basic training on how to collect and dispose of its household garbage instead of just tossing matter out one's door or window into the jungle (thus attracting insects and developing diseases), this new, healthier practice jumped from 158 families to 249. Equally important, adult literacy classes led to a 61 percent growth from 369 to 609 people who achieved rudimentary reading and writing skills.

Similar trends upward occurred among *all* the village populations among the seven early villages in northern Mozambique.

By 2014, CFL had expanded to serve 17 villages. Rounded statistical results showed that some 73 percent of children ages 6 to 17 in Care for Life villages were attending school (compared to 50 percent in all Mozambique). Approximately 1,043 adults participated in village literacy classes, while 73 percent of family members over 15 year were deemed literate in Care for Life villages as a result of classes taught by staffers (compared to only 56 percent in outside areas). Additional community classes covered such things as health and hygiene, nutrition, sanitation, family gardening, income generation, women's and children's rights, home improvement, disease prevention, and many more self-reliant skills. Food security, along with planting a family garden for better nutrition, rose significantly from 6 to 38 percent. Most individuals were also able to sell their excess produce for an income-generation activity. More than 90 percent of families grew a vegetable garden and enjoyed protein daily. Some 124 agricultural kits (rake, hoe, watering can) were earned by families completing their development goals, and 14,000 packets of seeds were distributed, along with 903 watering cans and 22 rakes and hoes (Care for Life, 2014).

Six years later, as of 2020, CFL updates showed improved lives as the Coronavirus pandemic began around the world. That year's annual report showed that 23 villages had recently participated in the Family Preservation Program. A total of 4,431 families had been helped, amounting to 26,312 individuals who completed the Family Preservation Program training and developed lifestyle improvements. Although the efforts of our entire CFL team became more complicated as COVID-19 proliferated, in the year 2020 alone Care for Life worked with about 1,200 families in five villages (Macharote 1, 2, and 3; Ilha Marfarinha; and Nazare).

Other improvements that CFL fostered included infant deaths greatly reduced; new kitchens built and roofs added; family income rose for those starting a microenterprise; credit and savings increased a whopping 535 percent; most families registered their children for school, and 80 percent of adults achieved literacy; home sanitation and trash disposal improved; 91 percent of families now drink treated water, and even more now sleep under mosquito nets; family diets and regular meals improved; because of increased feelings of well-being, families use less alcohol and feel more optimistic about their futures; and more families participated in community activities through FPP. Many families started setting, and achieving, social-change goals, and even won CFL rewards for reaching them—not handouts that breed dependency, but NGO rewards for making things better.

Challenges

The lifeblood of both Care for Life and the Family Preservation Program is capital. Like most nonprofits, CFL is continually seeking to raise the needed funds to perpetuate the FPP program in Mozambique, as well as to fuel expansion. Although it only costs $30 to support an individual for a full year, CFL continues to have fundraising challenges.

While CFL thrives on creating sustainability in poor villages, it still struggles with marketing to sustain its own organization. "CFL is great at achieving sustained results, but has challenges in the area of marketing. Funding is the number one challenge for CFL to move FPP into another country," reports Sylvia Finlayson, former CFL Executive Director (2009). CFL Vice President Randall Voss said it another way: "CFL has the best program in the world to do good, but has a mediocre marketing program and is operating on a shoestring budget all the time" (2009). This lack of capital has negative implications on CFL in more than one area.

In addition to expansion implications, fundraising challenges also have important personnel implications for CFL. The leadership and implementation of FPP may suffer if CFL lacks sufficient capital to pay for high-quality employees. Some organizations that are more successful in marketing and fundraising can afford to pay their personnel higher salaries. Although our valuable field-workers feel passionately about their work and continue making a tremendous difference, staff income remains an important component of their retention, performance, and even quality of life.

Conclusion

A recent formal study of both CFL and FPP has been published by my colleagues from several other universities in Utah (Panos and others, 2020), showing that data accumulated from the last five years of their efforts are quite impressive. Clearly, neither the Family Preservation Program, Care for Life, nor the nation of Mozambique are becoming utopias. Yet on a small scale, at least, a growing group of historically impoverished native communities in the region are well on the path to a better future. Family self-reliance and strengthened practices of healthy living are on the increase.

Reflecting on the extensive labors of Care for Life, I recall the teaching of Jesus: *"For I was hungry and you gave me something to eat, I was thirsty and you gave me something to drink, I was a stranger and you invited me in, I needed clothes and you clothed me, I was sick and you looked after me, I was in prison and you came to visit me"* (Matthew 25: 35–36). Care for Life has designed and implemented the great Christian values espoused in the New Testament, thereby aiding many Mozambicans to grow and consume better food, improve their nutrition, enable more-solid house construction in a dozen rural villages, start enterprises, foster greater women's literacy and empowerment in village decisions, and give people greater access to rural health care services. All this portends a better future for some of Africa's poorest people.

References

Bueno, J. (2007). From a personal interview.

Care for Life. (2009). https://careforlife.org/.

Care for Life. (2014). https://careforlife.org/.

Care for Life Solutions. (2022). https://careforlife.org/our-solution/.

CFL. (2011). Documentary film.

Easterly, W. (2007). *The* White Man's Burden: *Why the* West's Efforts *to* Aid *the* Rest Have Done So Much Ill *and* So Little Good. Oxford University Press.

Family Preservation Program. (2015). https://careforlife.org/our-solution/.

Finlayson, S. (2009). Former CFL Executive Director to this author's social entrepreneurship class.

Firelight Foundation. (2006). *From Faith to Action.*

Hanes, S. (2007). In Africa, lives are improved without handouts. *Christian Science Monitor.* September 5. https://www.csmonitor.com/2007/0905/p13s02-lign.html.

Harper, L. (2006). Interview with CFL's Operations Director in Arizona.

João, R. M. (2010). This author's field research in Mozambique villages. (Unpublished.)

Packard, B. (2011). Personal interview.

Panos, A., et al. (2020). *Research on Social Work Practice,*vol. 30 (1), 84–96.

UNAIDS/UNICEF. (2008). July.

Voss, R. (2007). Woodworth interviews with CFL's vice president, in Beira, Mozambique, regarding CFL and FPP challenges. May.

Woodworth, W. (2010). Unpublished interview notes while consulting in Beira, Mozambique.

World Bank. (2016). *Accelerating Poverty Reduction in Mozambique: Challenges and Opportunities.*

World Bank. (2019). https://data.worldbank.org/indicator/SP.DYN.TFRT.IN?locations=MZ.

Native People's Microfinancing: Serving the Poorest of the Indigenous Poor as Jesus Would Do

Many people throughout the United States face socioeconomic challenges: Blacks, Asians, rural southerners, inner-city minorities, immigrant groups, Latinos, and more. Among the toughest struggles of people are those of Native Americans, including people living on reservations and in rural agriculture areas, as well as those trying to eke out an existence in large urban settings. In spite of a century of federal government efforts, including enormous amounts of money, educational programs, and various policy efforts, many such people still live hand-to-mouth. The lack of education and adequate housing, as well as endemic cases of alcoholism and violence toward women, are grievous problems for Native Americans. All such factors combine to "keep our people down," as a Paiute tribal elder told me, and all are relevant to Native Americans' economic well-being. This chapter describes a potential innovation known as microenterprise development, and describes why or how it has great potential to benefit tribal groups. After defining its basic ideas and tools, the chapter reports on several intriguing applications in contemporary Native American communities.

Poverty Seems Inescapable

In the Bible, we read in Deuteronomy 15:4: *"However, there need be no poor people among you, for in the land the Lord your God is giving you to possess as your inheritance, he will richly bless you."* On the other hand, read Jesus's words: *"The poor you will always have with you"* (Matthew 26:11). A well-known Catholic priest offers another perspective admonishing us to take action: "Poverty is not inevitable. Poverty is the worst scourge ever created by human beings; it is up to human beings to end it," declared Father Joseph Wresinski, a Christian born to immigrant parents in a poor neighborhood of Angers, France (ATD Fourth World, 2022).

Not only among tribal peoples of North America, but also in much of the developing world, economic conditions have been getting both better for some and worse for others over recent decades. During the past half century, some 1.2 billion people suffered from chronic poverty, trying to subsist on less than $365 per year, which worked out to only $7 per week (Daley-Harris, 2002). Glancing back at the last 60 years, the wealthiest 20 percent of the world consumed some 70 percent of all income. By the beginning of the twenty-first century, that share had mushroomed further to over 80 percent. Simultaneously, the poorest 20 percent of the world's population saw decreases in their meager share, from 2.3 percent of all wealth dissipating to a mere 1.4 percent (Brown, 2000). Among females in the developing world, absolute poverty had grown by 50 percent in those two decades (UNIFEM, 2001).

The author using microfinance tools and social investing as he works with and supports Native American cultures and their economies; photo taken at a powwow.

However, beginning in the year 2000, gradually the good news was that, thanks to massive allocation of capital and various programs by the World Bank, United Nations, USAID, and other organizations and programs, things improved for two decades. But after several decades of poverty worldwide being reduced, sadly the problem is now significantly worsened due to the 2020–2022 COVID-19 pandemic. It has been the worst increase in a quarter of a century. Today, "Of the 736 million people living in extreme poverty worldwide, half live in just five countries: India, Nigeria, Democratic Republic of the Congo, Ethiopia, and Bangladesh" (World Bank, 2022). The most recent data from the World Bank suggest a bifurcation. On the one hand, millions who were in extreme poverty began to climb out of their economic hole. On the other hand, a significant portion still remain, or have become even worse off. The global pandemic has exacerbated this phenomenon. It has caused been the worst increase in the numbers of poor people in a quarter century. "Global extreme poverty rose in 2020 for the first time in over 20 years as the disruption of the COVID-19 pandemic compounded the forces of conflict and climate change, which were already slowing poverty reduction progress. About 100 million additional people are living in poverty as a result of the pandemic" (World Bank, 2022).

Among the world's more than 7 billion people, as of early 2000 the richest 1 percent of adults essentially owned a staggering 40 percent of all global wealth. At that time, the richest 10 percent of adults owned 8 percent of the entire world's wealth, while the bottom half combined owned a meager 1 percent (UNU-WIDER, 2006). The past two decades have apparently showered even more money from heaven on the upper classes: in dollars, euros, yens, francs, pounds, renmimbi, and rands.

While Indigenous families attempt to manage to stay alive in broken-down shacks on coast-to-coast reservations, America's elites grow ever more wealthy. Just a few years ago, *Forbes Magazine* (2017) declared that three men at the top of America's wealthiest class—Amazon's Jeff Bezos, Microsoft founder Bill Gates, and investor Warren Buffett—held combined fortunes worth more than the total wealth of the poorest half of all Americans! Recent diseases always make matters even worse. Startling new statistics reveal that during the first two devastating years of the 2020–21 COVID-19 pandemic, America's billionaires greatly increased their economic power, as reported in analyses of economic data that showed the combined wealth of all U.S. billionaires growing by $2.07 trillion (70.3 percent) from March to October 2021—from approximately $2.9 trillion to $5 trillion (Inequality, 2021). Of the more than 700 U.S. billionaires, the richest five (Jeff Bezos, Bill Gates, Mark Zuckerberg of Facebook, Google cofounder Larry Page, and Tesla's Elon Musk) aw a 123 percent increase in their combined wealth during this period, from $349 billion to $779 billion. Meanwhile, Native Americans struggled mightily against both the Coronavirus pandemic and declining personal incomes.

Unemployment is a major aspect of poverty creation, but underemployment is perhaps equally significant. It refers to the condition in which people do not hold jobs equivalent to their abilities and training. In the Philippines, for instance, it is widely known that although many people are literate and well-educated, good jobs are hard to find, resulting in underemployment well above 50 percent during recent years. Projections for the future of the world's poor suggest that poverty may only worsen in the coming decades. For example, an International Labor Organization (ILO) study predicts that during the next quarter of a century, 1.5 billion new jobs will be needed to provide incomes for the growing global population. It assumes that if present rates continue, there will be some 3.6 billion working-age people on the face of the earth, and that possibly a third of them will be unemployed. Is it really feasible to create 40 to 50 million new jobs annually throughout the coming decades? Not if history is any indicator. Over the last three decades, the world's workforce increased by nearly a billion people needing work. But tens of millions failed to obtain jobs. To make matters worse, only 10 percent of future jobs will arise from the industrialized nations, meaning that 90 percent will be needed for the Least Developed Countries (LDCs)—in other words, for the developing world where population is growing, and where poverty is booming.

Traditionally, social scientists have conceptually divided a society's economic activities into the formal sector, such as labor at a factory or work as a government employee in an office, and the informal sector—where a person survives on the street as a vendor or provider of small services. Informal or underground economy workers are essentially considered to be problems themselves by some experts. These are small, clandestine, unregistered individuals performing family-based economic activities that do not produce taxes to the state. Typically, such people can be observed in developing nation cities living in shantytowns or functioning as street vendors. Often marginalized, they subsist by "hustling" (also called "sweat equity"), making up for the shortcomings of not landing formal jobs, such as factory employment or government positions. While traditional economists have often viewed the informal economy as a minor phenomenon, or even as a temporary reaction to natural or financial disasters, reality suggests the opposite. The informal economy of the developing world is in fact growing. It is here to stay, and it makes up a significant percentage of many LDC cultures (de Soto, 1989; Webb, et al., 2013), especially among Indigenous people.

Microenterprise

Models for economic development among Indigenous people in the past have tended to consist of large-scale, top-down approaches like the Green Revolution, through which huge multinational agribusinesses attempted to overcome world hunger by selling John Deere tractors and Monsanto seeds. Today, there are many new, small, grassroots methods like microenterprise that function as alternatives for fighting poverty from below.

This new tool—the creation of small, street-hustling microbusinesses emerging with funding known as microcredit, and innovation referred to as microentrepreneurship—has yielded impressive results. My groundbreaking book *Small Really Is Beautiful: Micro Approaches to Third World Development—Microentrepreneurship, Microenterprise, and Microfinance* (1997) describes and analyzes the basics of these early approaches from the bottom up in a dozen nations.

Such a strategy consists of developing technical assistance centers that provide microenterprise start-up training and microloans as well as savings programs, often with consulting, to create self-employment and income-generating activities. Such workers bootstrap themselves, essentially creating their own jobs. Most of this type of work requires one's own sweat and equity, perhaps including that of one's family. It is a bottom-up method for building an income and becoming self-reliant, and it is currently enjoying considerable success in certain countries as an innovative path to earning a living and caring for one's own. Often, training is provided, along with access to capital (microcredit), so that the small entrepreneur is able to acquire raw materials, equipment, or whatever else is needed in order to grow the business.

Global microenterprise may be classified as small-scale loans of $30 to $100 that are accessible to the very poor, primarily in the developing world. With even a small amount of such capital, microenterprises may be started, or perhaps expanded. In the mid-1990s, the World Bank conducted an analysis of microentrepreneurial schemes, finding that there were in excess of 900 institutions in some 101 nations that offered microcredit to the poor (Paxton, 1995). The organizations studied had been in existence at least three years and each had over a thousand clients. They included banks, credit unions, and numerous nongovernmental organizations (NGOs). Today there are many thousands more of newer, smaller such programs that did not figure in the World Bank's original analysis. A sample of 206 of the 900 institutions studied in 1995 enjoyed an aggregate loan portfolio of almost $7 billion, totaling over 14 million small loans to poor people to support their tiny enterprises. Approximately 53 percent of loan recipients resided in rural regions around the globe. By extending microfinance capital to the poorest of the poor, millions of new jobs have been created among those languishing in extreme circumstances, thereby empowering individuals and families to gain a greater degree of control over their destinies in the move toward sustainability (World Bank, 2022).

Today the numbers are far in excess of those from the 1990s. According to research as of late 2021, the efforts to establish microenterprises and to provide access to microlending services for the poorest individuals around the entire planet has mushroomed to more than 140 million borrowers who enjoy a total loan portfolio estimated at $124 billion (Thunstrom, 2021).

Several institutions helped accelerate this global effort. Early in 1997, the first worldwide Microcredit Summit was held in Washington, D.C., to launch an ambitious plan for empowering a hundred million of the world's poorest families through microloans and job creation. Some 27 heads of state and thousands of NGO representatives participated in this global organizing effort. The method advocated at the summit for obtaining credit is sometimes referred to as group banking, also "village banking" (Woodworth, 1997). The typical operations of such programs are quite simple: The NGO essentially offers programs to give mostly impoverished women access to some microenterprise education, that is, small business training. In most cases, five to ten villagers are helped so as to receive small or "micro" loans pegged at market interest rates. They need no collateral, nor are they required to have a strong credit history. Instead, the borrowers as a group are jointly organized into "Solidarity Groups" of others whom they trust, and collectively they become liable for paying off both the interest and principal. Social pressure and trust thus become powerful incentives for assuming one's own financial responsibility and personal accountability. This strategy to help ensure that loans are repaid is often called "Social Collateral," in business English. The payback rates range from 94 percent to an amazing 100 percent—*much* better performance than that of most regular bank loans. In 2002, the Microcredit Summit + 5 conference was held to assess progress since 1997. It was reported that the movement had grown to 5,225 NGOs providing microloans to over 50 million poor borrowers and their families (Microcredit Summit, 2002). As mentioned earlier, today the number is more than 140 million microentrepreneurs.

With the preceding introduction, we now briefly document a case of Indigenous microcredit, that of Grameen Bank in Bangladesh.

Bangladesh's Grameen Bank for Poor Women

This case began with the innovative financing scheme developed by Dr. Muhammad Yunus, a U.S.-trained economist who started experimenting with tiny loans in the 1970s, each totaling only $27, to help the poor in rural Bangladesh. It has since grown to become an impressive illustration of a bottom-up approach, a capacity-building mechanism known as the Grameen Bank of Bangladesh (Wahid, 1993; Yunus, 1997). Gaining global recognition for his amazing efforts, in 2006 Yunus was the recipient of the prestigious Nobel Peace Prize (Nobel, 2006).

Bangladesh, a country in Southeast Asia with some 164 million people, is today among the poorest of all nations, with the bulk of its citizens still in rural areas, young, and living well below the poverty line. Many babies there die before attaining age one, and the country's mortality rate is dismal. Waterborne diseases, diarrhea and other illnesses remain serious public health threats, as is malnutrition, especially for the children. Lower family incomes and higher illiteracy levels among mothers significantly contribute to the malnutrition menace in the country (Rayhan and Khan, 2006).

The low status of poor rural women in Bangladesh, combined with their informal economic activities, made it difficult in the past for them to receive credit from traditional banking systems to support the development and growth of their small income-generating efforts. Banks perceive poor women, as well as poor men, to be high-risk groups with limited ability to pay back their loans (Mayoux, 1995). Furthermore, the poor generally desire loans that are not even of sufficient size to cover the bank's transaction costs (Berger, 1989), so financial institutions have largely ignored the poor, at least until the last few years. In some systems, a husband's approval and signature are required in order for a loan to be approved for a woman (Tomasevski, 1996; Berger, 1989). When banks are located in urban centers, sufficient time and geographic mobility are necessary so that applicants can make multiple trips to the bank to complete the lengthy application and approval process. These become major constraints for women, particularly because of traditional property and seclusion norms (Berger, 1989; Mayoux, 1995). Illiterate women are also often unable to read and fill out the required multiple, written, legalistic forms. The entire process of applying for a loan tends to be forbidding to a rural, uneducated, poor woman without previous experience in dealing with the formal lending sector. Collateral requirements are especially difficult for women, since property in Bangladesh is typically registered in the names of the male household members and passed from father to son (Berger, 1989; Todd, 1996; Woodworth, 2000).

After a number of years, however, through Dr. Yunus's leadership, financial organizations in Bangladesh, such as the Grameen Bank, BRAC, ASA, and Proshika, have sought to overcome these barriers women encounter when accessing credit. Collateral requirements are replaced by loans to a cluster of women who act as peer groups to give support and exert social pressure, if needed, for repayment. Bank workers go to the villages to meet with the women and disburse loans, thus eliminating the need for women to travel to unfamiliar urban areas. Furthermore, women are specifically targeted and sought after by Grameen. This motivation to lend to females stems from the desire not only to help poor, rural women but also to help their families. When women have their own income or control over the household income, they are more likely to spend money for food, health, and education for their children (Sebstad and Chen, 1996; Tomasevski, 1996). Thus, by targeting poor women, initiators of development programs such as these feel they have tapped into a way to help the family as a whole.

The results have been impressive since the time Dr. Yunus was inspired to create the first village bank in the mid-1970s among landless Bangladeshi peasants. After starting very small, he gradually grew his Grameen Bank, which helped launch the new global movement, enabling thousands of poor people to escape poverty by offering them small, collateral-free loans to use in starting tiny businesses. The early years resulted in $9 billion for the microlending global industry and gradually drew the participation of giant institutions, including Citigroup, Deutsche Bank, and the Bill & Melinda Gates Foundation (Woodworth, 2014). More-recent data analyzed in a World Bank book by Khandker (2016), Beyond Ending Poverty, found that all Bangladeshi microfinance institutions collectively have had sustained benefits over two decades in reducing poverty and increasing incomes. Microcredit accounted for a 10 percent reduction in rural poverty in Bangladesh over that time. This means that MFIs have lifted some 2.5 million Bangladeshis from the ranks of the extreme poor! For this chapter, the basic question is whether such an approach could help Native Americans in the United States.

The microfinance movement continues to grow, not only in Bangladesh, but worldwide. As of late 2021, the efforts to take access to capital for the poorest throughout the entire planet has mushroomed to more than 140 million borrowers receiving microloans with a total loan portfolio estimated at $124 billion (Thunstrom, 2021).

In Bangladesh itself, some 80 percent of poor families have been reached with microloans through microenterprise methodologies. Yunus and the Grameen Bank were eventually jointly awarded the Nobel Peace Prize of 2006 for their pioneering efforts to create economic and social development, and ultimately enhancing peace worldwide, by utilizing microcredit initiatives.

Based on my visits and interviews with managers in Bangladesh at Grameen headquarters some years ago (Woodworth, 2000), and other published data (GF-USA, 2004) as well, the following picture emerges about Grameen after its first two decades:

- Millions of tiny enterprises have been launched by impoverished Bangladeshis.
- More than 3.1 million people became Grameen borrowers.
- Collectively over $4 billion was loaned to the poor.
- Some 5 million family members benefited from these credit and savings programs.
- 37,000 village economies had benefited from the added flow of new capital.
- Total savings, including individual and group funds, exceeded U.S. $100 million.
- The percentage of overdue loans not repaid after two years was a mere 1.32 percent.
- 1,094 village bank branches now exist throughout Bangladesh.
- The bank employed a staff of over 12,600 persons. Only 583 staffers work at the big bank headquarters, while about half of the rest conduct banking in villages. The remaining 6,000 staff were engaged in technical projects, such as developing projects like wells and shrimp farms.

These numbers illustrate a dramatic change from the paltry $27 in capital that Dr. Yunus first loaned to 42 poor women over two decades earlier (Fuglesang, 1995; Yunus, 1990). Since 2000, Grameen has expanded even more significantly. The institution's last published data (Grameen Bank Annual Report, 2019) shows important numbers, as follows: distribution of $2.99 billion in microloans to clients; establishing 2,568 bank branches in 81,678 villages; an overall growth of 13 percent; more than 175,000 new members joined the organization, resulting in a countrywide bank membership of 9.26 million active members. Additional results of Grameen's impacts included funding for children's education, better housing, and more. The impacts continue to be rather amazing, even for a strong advocate like me.

While I believe that microenterprise as a strategy holds much promise of improving the lives of many of the world's poor, it seems a particularly relevant benefit for Native Americans and other Indigenous groups. I now turn to such relevance.

Indigenous Well-Being Around the Globe

At the United Nations, from years 1995 through 2004, celebrations occurred to mark the "International Decade of the World's Indigenous People" (United Nations, 2004). Events culminated at a global forum of 1,500 participants from some 500 tribes and groups meeting at UN headquarters in New York City. "Partnership in Action" was the motto of the ten-year effort to address the hopes and aspirations of those in poverty, to exchange best practices, and to broaden the participation of Indigenous communities in decisions that affect them. The state of Indigenous people was one of social exclusion, suffering, illiteracy, and poverty. Some 5,000 groups totaling over 300 million Indigenous people live on five continents within approximately 70 countries. They include designations from various global areas, including Native Americans (USA), Indigenous peoples or *povos indígenas* (Brazil's roughly 2,000 tribes), First Nations (Canada), and/or Aboriginals (Australia and regional island nations), plus other classifications. They may be rural, jungle, or in some cases urban dwellers (WSIE, 2003).

To address these problems, leading experts, well-meaning politicians, and large multilateral institutions such as the World Bank and the International Monetary Fund have argued that globalization itself will improve conditions for the poor. Their rhetoric has been that programs like the United States' NAFTA (the North American Free Trade Agreement) will bring jobs and better incomes to Indigenous people, and that free-market, top-down capitalism, operating as a "rising tide," will "lift all boats." In 2020 NAFTA was replaced with a new cross-border program dubbed the USMCA (standing for "the United States–Mexico–Canada Agreement").

Yet few poverty-stricken Indigenous groups around the globe believe that their economic boats have in fact risen. Under NAFTA, for example, Mexican official poverty has grown, instead of declining as predicted. Even worse, many *maquiladoras,* the foreign firms that invested in new factories along the U.S.–Mexico border in the 1990s, have shut down as capital and production shifted to lower-cost nations, such as Vietnam, India, and China. Mexican buying power ultimately dropped by 40 percent (Salgado, 2000). Such worsening conditions fueled the 1990s Zapatista rebellion in Mexico's state of Chiapas, where armed conflicts exposed the degree of the people's economic suffering.

Likewise, in Ecuador a group of Indians took control of the presidential palace for a few weeks back in 2000, precisely at the time of the World Economic Forum, which was held by the rich countries in Davos, Switzerland. The Indians' revolt was called to protest the globalization process, a strategy that has consisted of harsh economic reforms that lead to Native stress and strain. Indigenous Ecuadorians struggled to survive on a monthly income of only about $40 per person, and as a result 39 percent of those living in rural areas became chronically undernourished (Coffey, 2001). The uprising grew to over 15,000 people in the capital city of Quito alone. Such protests have continued annually at Davos, as well as at the United Nations and other such meetings.

In 2003, many Bolivian Indians organized a national strike that effectually shut down transportation, retail activities, and factory production, eventually forcing the country's president out of office. Militants complained of closed mines and unemployment, high gas prices, government corruption, and other extremely painful economic conditions. Massive demonstrations called for more jobs and less inequality between the haves and the have-nots. Similar Indigenous upheavals have also occurred in nations in Africa and Asia since 2000.

Traditional strategies for global economic development during the past century were often limited to just two options: state-run Marxist economics, in which big industries were controlled by government bureaucrats; or, the other option, "trickle-down" capitalism in which private, market-based logic promised economic well-being to all, but often failed to deliver. Among dozens of other countries, Nepal has had long-term Maoist and socialist political movements in its Congress that have been strongly supported by Indigenous communities.

The author working with volunteers to rebuild a village school in
Nepal after it had been destroyed in an earthquake.

With the collapse of the now-discredited dictatorship of the proletariat in countries of the former USSR and the Eastern Bloc, many observers assumed that unfettered free trade strategies would quickly dominate world politics. However, leftist elections continue to occur around the globe, including movements in India in 2004, actions by socialists in both Spain and Argentina, political advances made by Indigenous groups in Ecuador, Peru, Bolivia, Paraguay, Chile, and dozens more.

An alternative model, called the "Third Way," has emerged as another vision that combines some of the values of the other two paradigms that prevailed throughout most of the twentieth century. This Third Way attempts to integrate economic markets with the values of socioeconomic justice. According to a former U.S. Secretary of Labor, Robert Reich (1999), the new paradigm requires "that the economically displaced must be brought along," not dropped along the side of the road to so-called progress. Reich's argument is that "Third Way leaders will have to broker a new social contract between those who have been winning and those who have been losing."

For Robert Reich, as well as former president Bill Clinton and many others, microfinance is one vehicle moving toward an expanding Third Way. In fact, Bill and Hillary Clinton even advocated the creation of U.S. microenterprise back during their governorship era in Arkansas. The two of them collaborated in the creation of the Good Faith Fund for the poor in 1988—one of the first microcredit programs in the United States. Likewise, during their eight presidential years of the 1990s, they each labored to accelerate microcredit both domestically and internationally, through speeches, legislative advocacy, and otherwise.

The viability of the Third Way approach to development around the globe, as well as within the United States, may or may not endure long term, yet at least it is being experimented with. Let me now turn to an analysis of the Native American experience with microcredit as being a partial solution to tribal economic pain.

Tribal Realities of Poverty and Development

The picture of Native American life is often hidden from white America. Today there are 574 federally recognized Native tribes, with over 1.9 million American Indians and Alaska Natives in the United States. Their poverty is not unlike that of Indigenous peoples in the developing world. Huge gaps separate the white majority and the Native minority in education, health care, employment, decent housing, and income. On the positive side, some observers justify this by pointing out that at least Indigenous Americans enjoy government payments for "reservation abuses," as well as welfare and unemployment benefits, oil reserves from multinational corporations, growing tourism, and, in recent years, increasing revenues from the casino economy on many reservations that function independently from state regulations.

On the negative side are factors such as centuries of exploitation, forced relocations to lands with few natural resources or arable land, a brutal history of genocide, and today's often-contentious relationships between the tribes and local Anglo government entities. Add to these, frequently inept Bureau of Indian Affairs (BIA) officials, mismanagement, and corruption, along with ongoing questions about tribal sovereignty and inter-clan conflicts. Other negative factors include rampant alcoholism and drug use, domestic abuse of women, general poor health, high mortality rates, and feelings of dependency and helplessness in the lives of many. Of course, a 28 percent unemployment level, as revealed by the Brookings Institution, only exacerbates many of these problems (Sanchez, 2021) revealing that Native Americans are "the most economically stressed of any racial/ethnic group" in the United States.

While a more extensive picture of the plight of poor American and Canadian Indians, as well as Alaskan Natives, is beyond the scope of this chapter, suffice it to say that much needs to change. Various roads to economic improvement are advocated by Native leaders, government advisers, business consultants, and academic researchers. These include the following: expanding tourism and developing the hot, new phenomenon of ecotourism; increasing educational access for greater numbers of Indian children; turning parts of reservation land over to toxic waste-management firms so as to generate new sources of income; creating "healing funds," such as the $350 million account established in Canada to compensate for systemic abuses committed in the past; and mobilizing Native activists to achieve greater political clout in the electoral process of selecting delegates and participating in candidate races, conventions, and so forth.

Fortunately, a notable Native woman, a single mother named Deb Haaland, eventually rose up through the political ranks of her state, New Mexico, and then became a Democratic Representative in the U.S. Congress. Her tribe, the Laguna Pueblo, with nearly 8,000 members, is her Indigenous affiliation. As a small business advocate, she quickly expanded her credentials with progressives by advocating for the Green New Deal climate proposal, single-payer health care, and other "left-wing" policy priorities. As reported in the BBC, she was perceived to possess important Indigenous values regarding American wildlands, nature, women's rights, and the environment, as well as restoring social issues (S. Cabral, 2021). Her credibility as a new member of the House of Representatives who succeeded in getting more bills passed than any other freshman soon led to President Joe Biden's appointing her to his cabinet as Secretary of the Interior. To me, it seems a curious twist of fate that after some 500 years of the White Man taking away Indian lands, now one of their own will manage future policies for over 500 million acres of public land. Will "Red Power" now have a greater voice?

Sadly, a number of studies suggest that past government-led initiatives have tended to preserve the status quo rather than fuel change. For example, William Lawrence, a Red Lake Band Indian and publisher of *The Native American Press/Ojibwe News,* wrote a provocative piece titled "Do Indian Reservations Equal Apartheid?" (2003). He argues that the United States established the reservation system much like whites created Black townships in South Africa to racially divide groups of people, resulting in a two-tiered system. In spite of billions of dollars spent over the years, supposedly to benefit Lawrence's neighboring tribes in Minnesota alone, massive socioeconomic difficulties still exist there today. He argues that the current system simply perpetuates the problem, and, therefore, needs to be demolished.

While such a proposal may seem extreme, a 15-year series of studies by Harvard University's Project on American Indian Economic Development suggests that federal bureaucratic controls, along with a unwillingness to relinquish bureaucrat's power, coupled with tribal mismanagement and politics, tend to suffocate Indigenous autonomy. A basic premise is that "sovereignty matters. When tribes make their own decisions about what approaches to take and what resources to develop, they consistently outperform non-tribal decision-makers" (Harvard Project, 2004). Researchers Cornell and Kalt (1998) make a cogent argument promoting self-determination as perhaps the single most important factor in effective tribal economic development. They and their associates point out that Indians who obtain government grants to start companies usually do not enjoy long-lasting firms. Hiring is often compromised by patronage, profits go to a few favored people rather than being reinvested for enterprise growth, and eventually the money disappears.

One Humanitarian NGO

So, what is to be done? This chapter suggests a different method: Rather than giving large grants to tribal corporations that only last short term and that typically suffer from accompanying governmental bureaucracies and inefficiencies. Smaller, more nimble programs may be more effective. For instance, there is an organization called American Indian Services (AIS) that a group of Christian professors, farmers, and cultural experts rolled out beginning in 1971 as part of an innovative Brigham Young University strategy to educate, and empower tribes beginning in the West. It was envisioned by Dale Tingey who had lived and served as a missionary on the large Navajo Reservation where poverty, a lack of formal schooling, and malnutrition abounded. Tingey, a friend of mine, formed a board of advisers and gradually raised moneys to assist elderly Natives with better food and nutrition, and more. He would round up produce, including crops from wheat and potato farmers, to distribute in distant hogans. Each Christmas, his charity would solicit children's gifts from thousands of white families around Idaho, Arizona, Utah, Nevada, and New Mexico and would fly the goods in small, privately owned planes so that thousands of Native kids would enjoy at least several treats, as well as kids' socks, shoes, dresses, and pants. It also donated blankets for sleeping and coal for cooking and heating to parents and grandparents as the desert snows of another winter set in. Over time, AIS spread across the U.S. and on into Mexico and even Guatemala, where I trained and sent students to help construct simple A-frame houses in rural areas alike Chemaltenango, Guatemala.

Tingey created a Native service mission that would be the cornerstone of his life's work—that of aiding Native Americans by using effective humanitarian methods, yet while also maintaining their tribal cultures and honoring their heritage. Multiple programs were implemented over the years, but education was always seen as the path out of suffering and poverty. Over the years, BYU eventually shifted AIS away from being a university program and chose to discontinue it. With the encouragement of a group of donors, American Indian Services became set up as a 501(c)(3) nonprofit charity. Tingey took up the role of volunteer director and established an office with donated office space near campus to expand AIS programs, turning more heavily toward accelerating Native American education. The AIS board of trustees and staff became fully Indigenous with members from multiple tribes, not just Navajo, but also Oneida, Zuni Pueblo, Shoshone, Ute, Sioux, Hopi, Iroquois, and even Pacific Islanders. Today hundreds of thousands of dollars are generated through private contributions to provide scholarships to young Natives. So far, college scholarships from AIS through the decades have gone to young people in over 350 registered Indian tribes from coast to coast.

More recently, AIS has placed emphasis on recruiting high schoolers from multiple reservations, allowing them to enjoy all-expense-paid weeks of training in new leading-edge technologies. For example, at the University of Utah, a Pre-Freshman Engineering Program called "AIS PREP" began several years ago, cohosted by the College of Science. It's a free program that allows Native Americans to take advanced science, technology, engineering, and mathematics (STEM) courses for six weeks, for three consecutive summers. Programs like these are especially significant when students are able to leave their normal circumstances on a distant reservation and have expense-paid travel to Salt Lake City to immerse themselves in new tech experiences that will motivate them to work toward a college degree, often as the first in their families. It's also a shift away from living in an adobe hogan in a rural desert in which there is no running water or electricity. Other programs offer exciting innovations for students to begin exploring careers that include solar energy development, chemistry, and new solutions for Native respiratory health.

AIS also arranges additional learning opportunities, including an annual three-week Native American program for youth through the Idaho National Laboratory (in partnership with its Engineering Program), and a Utah State University experience in such careers as aviation, genetics, and more. The fact that the majority of Native students recruited are female is an additional plus for the future of reservation life as new generations come along. Today, the American Indian Services board and staff continue leading and growing the organization to success, continuing its values of caring, and generosity. Other programs beyond AIS exist, which I turn to next. They seek to establish independent Native American microenterprise development as a viable alternative.

Cases of Native Microenterprises

Small, grassroots-operated microenterprise strategies may become effective catalysts for tribes to achieve greater self-sufficiency. One example of such microenterprise was developed in New Mexico. A public service project, called Finance New Mexico, connects Native people to resources that help their microbusinesses expand. It draws on private as well as public entities that endorse the goal of increasing economic activity and building development among Native communities. Native Americans as small business owners may be linked to a range of resource opportunities that exclusively focus on tribal members' enterprises, both on and off the area's reservations (Finance New Mexico, 2021). The project channels potential clients to a variety of services having a Native-owned agenda. The following are a few such opportunities that collaborate with Finance New Mexico:

NEIR (Native Entrepreneur In Residence) program is intended for eligible entrepreneurs, managed by New Mexico Community Capital. It's an intensive six-month one-on-one training focusing on business idea development, start-ups, and growth. All of it is tailored to each Native entrepreneur's needs. Participants are paired with an experienced entrepreneur or mentor to lay the foundation for successful business growth. New Mexico Community Capital has graduated 46 entrepreneurs since the NEIR program started in 2014. This nonprofit offers a range of services through partners to identify, develop, and implement household and community asset-building strategies that empower Native people. It values center on the slogan "Strengthening Native American Communities and Economies." Working with community partners in tribal colleges and community development financial institutions (CDFIs), NEIR shares ideas through peer learning and financial developments through grantmaking. It conveys information about household asset-building programs that improves people's lives, such as Individual Development Accounts and Children's Savings Accounts. The organization conducts research on predatory lending in Native communities and seeks to raise awareness of the problem so that more families can move toward financial security. It also works with Native communities to develop new businesses and services and to reclaim direct control of assets.

- Another innovation is New Mexico State University's American Indian Business Enterprise Center (AIBEC). With offices at the campus Arrowhead Center, it provides a suite of services designed to build Native entrepreneurship in the region. It relies on the collaboration and input from Native leaders—Native business owners and organizations, plus tribal community members—to provide equitable and inclusive delivery of culturally representative services. Student internships and business acceleration are among its programs. Its services range from funding opportunities, free online business training, and one-on-one business advising to providing access to more than 50 professional advisers, including accountants, intellectual property lawyers, and business attorneys who specialize in Native American services.

- The Tribal Economic Diversity Fund is another source of assistance. It provides $1,000 to $8,000 in grants to Native microenterprises operated by a federally recognized Indian tribe or businesses that is owned by an enrolled member or members. An example is Bison Star Naturals, a Native firm that received funding from the program. Applications are accepted once a year from one of the many federally recognized tribes in northern New Mexico, an area specifically established to serve as the Regional Development Corporation.

Below are several other microenterprise support institutions. In particular I highlight the programs of Capacity Builders, Inc. (2021), which for two decades has provided financial support to Diné (Navajo) and other Native American communities. Its N.A.T.I.V.E Project (standing for "Navajo Artists Technology Innovation and Vision Enterprise") offers financial and consulting assistance to Native Americans in the Four Corners region of Utah, Arizona, New Mexico, and Colorado, where several tribal organizations come together geographically. The project offers both mentoring and microloans to start or expand Indigenous microenterprises that engage in various business dimensions. They include Native crafts, art and culture, wood carving, pottery, weaving, jewelry-making, silversmithing, fashion design, film, sand painting, crafts, and more.

Elsewhere, several Hopi tribal microenterprise institutions have been offering financial support services to small businesses. One back in the early 2000s was affiliated with a Protestant church group, though it collapsed. In contrast, the Hopi Credit Association (2021), with its motto of "For Hopi, By Hopi," has built a 60-year track record of providing financial support for microenterprise and additional small business ventures as a certified Native Community Development Financial Institution (CDFI).

Yet another institution I might briefly highlight is the Native business hub called Change Labs, based on the Navajo Nation in Arizona, that grants interest-free loans of up to $5,000, with no credit check, to Native entrepreneurs and small business owners. A news article in the Navajo-Hopi Observer discusses how its financing grew out of the Navajo (Diné) Kinship Lending program to support business owners and vendors who sell products, whether on the shoulders of a reservation highway or at an area flea market (Locke, 2020). Recipients can qualify by getting several friends to vouch for their character—no credit history required. By early 2021 the program had assisted some 30 applicants who collectively had received a total of over $100,000 in microloans, thereby helping existing microentrepreneurs as well as new ones to deal with the rise of the Coronavirus pandemic, which hit Native communities so hard. The example given was of one particular Navajo maker of beaded jewelry who had been badly affected by the loss of business during the pandemic. Getting a loan, along with mentoring by Change Labs, kept him going during the economic downturn (Locke, 2020).

Perhaps one of the most important sources of Native American microenterprise development is the Lakota Funds, which I will describe and analyze in more detail next.

The Oglala Lakota Nation Case

One of the best Native American tribe-initiated small business efforts has been the Lakota Funds, which in 1986 became the first microenterprise financing program explicitly established for Native Americans. This effort, on the Pine Ridge Indian Reservation, was launched because the region in South Dakota was among the poorest within the United States. When I first visited there in the early 1980s, tribal members' unemployment tended to range between an astonishing 70 and 85 percent.

In previous years, the roughly 22,000 Native Americans at Pine Ridge had largely survived on federal funds to support their schools, health care systems, and tribal government. Otherwise, agriculture had been the only source of income, except for a few small private firms. Thus, the Lakota Funds was established in Kyle, a central village on the reservation. Over the past several decades, hundreds of tiny loans have been accessed by tribal members who launched new microenterprises.

It all began as a 1986 project of the First Nations Development Institute, originally founded in Virginia, but now based in Colorado, an organization to which I have donated for years. The Institute was the idea of Rebecca Adamson, a daughter of a Cherokee mother in the southern states. Taught Indian ways by her maternal grandparents, she had become involved with the Lakota people during the 1970s. Shocked at learning of the massacre of hundreds of tribe members a century earlier in the Battle at Wounded Knee, Adamson became an activist for Native children's education at Little Wound School. She taught kids, organized protests, was even arrested, and always fought for the inclusion of Indigenous languages and traditions in reservation schools. She ultimately helped push through Congress the Indian Education Self-Determination Act, which began to give tribes local control of their own children's education.

But Rebecca Adamson saw that genuine power would require economic clout, as well. She began to search for alternatives to large-scale Bureau of Indian Affairs (BIA) corporate projects, which she viewed as "boondoggles." Often encouraged by outside business experts, such ventures frequently failed, exemplified on many reservations today by desolate industrial parks and tourist motels that stand deteriorating and empty. The only way to overcome dependency, she felt, would be to apply strategies that meshed with Native culture. Thus, small-scale enterprise development seemed to her a better Indigenous path to a brighter future (Ridley, 1997).

So, Adamson incorporated First Nations in 1980 and shopped her ideas to the biggest U.S. foundations. Eventually, the Ford Foundation liked her proposal enough to give a $25,000 grant for planning the start-up as she overcame doubt from the outside world, as well as from her own Native community. Since 1980, First Nations has offered technical assistance to nearly 12,000 Native American entrepreneurs and tribal organizations. Its $46 million in tribal grants have assisted hundreds of tribes in 42 states. Among them, it helped the Oregon-based Umatilla Tribe get back its former land; secured $10 million in trust funds for Michigan's Saginaw Chippewa Tribe that the federal government had entangled in a bureaucratic morass; and during 2020–2021 of the COVID pandemic distributed $5.4 million that provided vaccines and other medicines, as well as food and water, to tribes across America (First Nations, 2021).

But channeling loan capital to Lakota Funds was only one of First Nation's, and Adamson's, greatest successes. In the start-up years, loans totaling about a million dollars had been given to would-be microentrepreneurs at Pine Ridge. As a result, *Ms. Magazine* awarded her its "Woman of the Year" designation. Gloria Steinem, the founder of *Ms.*, said of Adamson, "When Rebecca speaks about Indigenous economics she calls it economics with values added... It's just a broader and deeper measure of things" (E. Cabral, 1997).

First Nations also labors to foster entrepreneurship and business development projects targeted at both the tribal (macro) and individual (micro) levels. It also seeks to aid Native families in accessing healthy food, a challenge for many reservation children and families. Without access to healthy food, a nutritious diet and good health are out of reach. To increase access to healthy food, it supports tribes in building sustainable food systems that improve health, strengthen food security and increase their control over Native agriculture and food systems. This is achieved through financial and technical support, training programs and materials. Other development services are adapted and used as well.

Lakota Circle Banking

Two different programs within the Lakota Funds operate with their respective financial services. One is that of "Circle Banking," based on the group lending model of the Grameen Bank. Small peer groups of 4 to 10 individuals form their own group and participate in five microentrepreneurial training sessions. Most participants would not be considered "credit worthy," according to traditional U.S. banking criteria.

Upon completion of the Circle business education, the group is "certified" and its members may then determine who will receive what amount of loans, usually ranging from $400 to $1,000, with which to start. Like other microcredit programs, Lakota uses the social collateral of others in the Circle to guarantee that each loan is repaid. As co-debtors, this practice ensures a high loan repayment rate of about 90 percent. As loans are repaid, another loan for a larger amount may be borrowed to expand one's microenterprise.

The Lakota Funds project began by following the Grameen approach to microenterprise development in Bangladesh as a microlender. It thus began helping microentrepreneurs on the Pine Ridge Reservation realize their dreams through minimal $500 loans. Back then there were only two Native American–owned businesses on the Pine Ridge. Some 85 percent of people had never had a checking or savings account; 75 percent never had a loan; and 95 percent had zero business experience. Regular financial institutions in the area deemed tribe members to be "unbankable," so they languished for decades in a broken-down environment.

From its website today, happily we learn the following: "Lakota Funds continues to play a vital role in improving life for the Oglala Lakota people by placing capital with new and growing businesses on the Pine Ridge Reservation. Our loan portfolio now exceeds $4 million, and our maximum loan size has grown to $300,000. Since 1986, we have deployed over 1,250 loans totaling over $17.5 million, helped establish or expand nearly 850 businesses, [and] created nearly 2,050 permanent jobs" (Lakota Funds, 2022). It has moved beyond tiny microloans to offering needed financing to improve residents' homes, grow a business, and obtain financing for agricultural projects like Native cattle ranching, as well as to offer training in financial literacy, entrepreneurship, and more.

From my trips to and interviews with folks on the reservation, early on, I learned of several interesting cases as microenterprises were established, step by step. These illustrate the type of borrowers and businesses financed through microlending. For example, Roselyn Spotted Eagle was an older woman who lived on the Pine Ridge Reservation in a two-room house without running water or decent heating. She supported not only herself, but also a grandson who was afflicted with fetal alcohol syndrome. Ms. Spotted Eagle made beautiful, beaded crafts for the tourist market, and through microcredit she was able to purchase new tools and a greater inventory of beads and other materials to expand her microenterprise. Other microentrepreneurs obtained loans for agricultural projects. Bamm Brewer owned a piece of tribal land for starting a buffalo herd; with a Lakota Funds loan, he was able to construct a strong fence to contain his animals (PBS, 2000). Robert Hornbeck and his sister, Connie Two Crow, established a floral shop and video store (E. Cabral, 1997). While Indigenous artisans like them made up the bulk of borrowers, others have included a caterer, a pig-farmer, a musician, and a tire-repairman who needed new tools.

Keys to Circle Success

What features help to explain Lakota Circle banking success? Several factors seem critical. First, it is not just about money, but it involves training and education. The course modules include basic business skills, such as budgeting, marketing and sales, quality, tax and licensing, and so forth. Borrowers also may participate in life-skills education that covers topics such as problem-solving, goal setting, and drug abuse as well as alcoholism issues. In its early years, Elsie Meeks, the executive director, reports: "If I were to identify the one most valuable aspect of Circle Banking, I would have to say that learning to deal with and solve problems is more important than even the loans" (SCN, 1997, p. 91). She cites the example of a mother of five children, a recovering alcoholic who underwent Lakota Funds training and received a $250 microloan. With that she launched her own craft microenterprise, became the team leader of her Banking Circle, made on-time payments, and qualified for larger loans after each was repaid. With a new sense of dignity and self-worth, she successfully won her battle over alcoholism and moved from dependency to self-sufficiency and off government welfare. The business grew and other Native Americans became inspired by her success (SCN, 1997, p. 91).

A second important factor in Lakota Funds' achievements has always been its Native control. Rather than be operated by Anglos or other outside "experts," the fund is managed by a staff of four members from the tribe. They are overseen by a nine-person board of directors who, with one exception, also live on the reservation as tribal members. The ninth slot is reserved as a rotating seat for an outside professional. At times it has been filled by a white person, or by an expert from another tribe who is skilled in banking. Thus, Indigenous values and culturally appropriate policies were embedded and maintained over the years (Meeks, 2000).

Another facet that ensured the Lakota Fund's achievements was strict adherence to the Grameen Bank model, not a break-off U.S. variation that some white organizations used, thinking they needed to "Americanize" their microlending programs. In the early 1980s when the Lakota Fund was launched, it was simply a small business program giving individual loans to tribal members. It experienced a number of failed start-ups and very high delinquency rates. So, its staff flew around the world all the way to Bangladesh to see firsthand how Grameen had succeeded so well. According to a Lakota loan officer at the time, named Dani Not Help Him, "We didn't go to [any] model... [but] went to the real one...in Bangladesh" (Garr, 1996). Upon returning to what locals call "the

Rez," the leaders decided to revamp the fund's operations so that its staff would rigorously adhere to principles of Grameen's own group lending program. This effort dramatically turned around a troubled system. The Lakota Fund also insisted that borrowers deposit at least $5 every two weeks as a nest egg of personal savings, also a replication of the Grameen system. Thus, members invested in the process personally and, along the way, learned important financial practices like savings and long-term planning.

Small Business Loans

The second mechanism for building entrepreneurial start-up was the Lakota Funds' Small Business Loan (SBL) program. In contrast to microcredit for Circle Banking enterprises, SBL started by giving initial loans for up to $25,000—quite a bit more money than that of the microenterprise level. However, candidates had to first participate in a seven-week training program where they learned and practiced the basics of small business success and then developed a feasibility plan. Lakota Fund staffers conducted the training and provided hands-on technical assistance in writing business plans and helping with marketing studies.

These early in-depth training and performance demands helped to screen applicants so that only the most sincere, hard-working candidates survived. The grueling requirements of preparation thus became an additional factor in ensuring both success and high loan repayments at Lakota. Back then, the interest rates on SBL's loans was around 11 percent for large amounts, to be repaid over five years. Examples of successful enterprises needing more capital than Circle Banking included such businesses as construction, electronic repairs, gravel hauling, restaurants, and hair salons (Garr, 1996).

SBL also added another ingredient that helped Native Americans in their business achievement. That was the synergy that developed from small firms working together, the Indian way, rather than individualistic competition, the Anglo way. To illustrate, in 1995, the Lakota Funds acquired commercial land and started to construct a new Lakota Trade Center. It had 13,000 square feet, large enough to house not only the fund itself but also seven start-up service or retail firms. As those firms grew and succeeded early on, they could then afford to move out on their own, freeing up space for other new start-ups. The $1.2 million construction project also helped a number of small firms get started as a kind of incubator, and it continues to pay for itself with revenue from leasing fees.

At its inception the Trade Center had grown to include a craft shop, an art gallery, a Tribal Business Information Center that partners with the U.S. Small Business Administration, the Oglala-Sioux Parks and Recreation Agency, a fundraising business, and even a hospice. The fund also launched a pilot project to build a ten-unit housing development, called "Eagle Nest Homes," in Wanblee, South Dakota. This strategy was all about ways to develop the community, and how to impact family life positively by strengthening and stabilizing residential services. But it has done much more, since it has also generated employment, empowered Native Americans, and produced revenue for the creation of more small enterprises early on (Lakota Funds, 1998).

Four teams of HELP International volunteers at BYU, who trained and headed out in early 2001 to serve Indigenous communities in Honduras, El Salvador, Peru, and Venezuela.

Basic Principles and Values for Personal Success Using Microenterprise Methods

As I conclude this chapter about Native American tiny business start-ups that promise people better economic lives, I wish to describe an important and effective Grameen method that the institution uses to help its clients succeed in life itself. As far as I'm aware, this method is not yet used by any Native American microenterprise institution. But because of its power and promise, I include here an adaptation I've used in microcredit consulting with many organizations since the 1980s. It's designed not only to help small microenterprises succeed and or even just to encourage repayment of Indigenous microloans. Rather, it's a set of guidelines that enable poor women (in particular) to enjoy a higher quality of life—a huge challenge facing Native Americans throughout the United States. These are the "Sixteen Decisions" that Yunus and his early female Bangladesh borrowers established to use in training them for building character and creating a better future. The great decisions are recited by all groups of microentrepreneurs at the beginning of every Grameen Center meetings (local bank group gatherings) for training, for reporting good results, and more. Whether a woman is achieving considerable success with her small family business, or is facing her initial efforts as a newcomer to start a tiny enterprise, the principles are the same. Starting and staying on the pathway to a bit of success, they are iron-clad values that require a public commitment along with routine assessments. With my personal edits from notes made at such meetings and my interviews over time, I summarize the essence of Grameen microenterprise and living as consisting of the following principles (Woodworth, 2019):

1. *We shall follow and advance the four principles of Grameen Bank: Discipline, Unity, Courage, and Hard work—in all walks of our lives.*
2. *We shall bring prosperity to our families.*
3. *We shall not live in dilapidated houses. We shall repair our houses and work toward constructing new homes at the earliest.*
4. *We shall grow vegetables all the year round. We shall eat plenty of them and sell the surplus.*
5. *We shall plant as many seedlings as possible during the planting season.*
6. *We shall plan to keep our families small. We shall minimize our expenditures. We shall look after our health.*
7. *We shall educate our children and ensure that they can earn to pay for their education.*
8. *We shall always keep our children and the environment clean.*
9. *We shall build and use pit latrines [since in rural Bangladesh most houses don't have bathrooms, toilets, or even running water].*
10. *We shall drink water from wells safe for drinking. If it is not available, we shall boil our water.*
11. *We shall not have nor give any dowry at our sons' and daughters' weddings. Instead, we shall keep our community free from the curse of dowry. We shall not practice child marriage.*
12. *We shall not inflict any injustice on anyone, neither shall we allow anyone to do so against another person.*
13. *We shall collectively undertake bigger investments for higher incomes over time.*
14. *We shall always be ready to help each other. If anyone is in difficulty, we shall all help him or her.*
15. *If we come to know of any breach of discipline in any Grameen Center, we shall all go there and help restore discipline.*
16. *We shall take part in all social activities collectively.*

My own sense is that if Native American microenterprise efforts instituted something akin to Grameen's remarkable Sixteen Decisions, it would bring important values, internal discipline, and other strengths to both existing and future programs.

Conclusion

Can Native American self-help strategies for building economic sustainability survive? Are they replicable elsewhere? I think the answer to both questions is a resounding "Yes!"

The Lakota Funds (LF) continues to grow, and it increasingly is recognized and rewarded as a viable model. For instance, in 1999, Women of Vision International selected the LF as one of its collaborative partnerships, by providing seed money for expansion (Women of Vision, 1999). The Hewlett-Packard Development Company established a Microenterprise Development Fund, and in 2003 gave over $100,000 as a grant to the Pine Ridge program (Hewlett-Packard, 2003). The U.S. Senate Committee on Banking, Housing and Urban Affairs (2002) received written testimony about the Lakota Funds' success at its hearing on "Capital Investment in Indian Country," specifically regarding the role of Native Community Development Financial Institutions (NCDFIs). Its final report suggested that lack of business experience and access to capital are both major barriers to tribal economic development. When the Lakota Funds began, 85 percent of its borrowers had never had a savings or checking account, 95 percent had zero business experience, and 75 percent hadn't received a loan in their lives. A new tribal ecosystem has been growing and strengthening over the decades for Sioux tribal families.

LF now is transforming individuals like these examples above into business entrepreneurs. The fund operates the center, gives out loans of up to $200,000 currently, and has expanded its available loan capital to $3.5 million with backing from government, private donors, and foundations. As the center has grown, a Pine Ridge Area Chamber of Commerce was started, and the number of housing units has risen from 10 to 30. Admittedly, the number of homes is still too few. But, perhaps most of all, Native Americans have developed new capacities perhaps never before envisioned by the participants. Gradually, with financial literacy training on "the Rez," a new, more sustainable culture of Indigenous economics has emerged.

The Lakota Funds also began to have ripple effects that spread far beyond Pine Ridge. For instance, a Four Bands Community Fund has been established on the Cheyenne Reservation in Wyoming. The Lakota housing unit project has been studied by the Navajo Partnership for Housing, Inc., in New Mexico to provide homebuyer education and to develop small loans to fund the gap in its housing market. New NCDFI start-ups recently include the Hochunk Community Development Corporation of the Winnebago tribe in Nebraska; the Affiliated Tribes of the Northwest Indians Revolving Loan Fund in the state of Washington; the Four Directions Development Corporation launched by several tribes in Maine; and the Hopi Credit Association in Arizona. Thanks to the early example of the Lakota Funds as a role model, these other organizations have created their own promising new ventures to build Native American self-reliance from the ground up.

Hence, quite a microenterprise track record of expanding impacts and applications seems to be occurring, from just a small, simple idea. The Lakota Funds program is clearly becoming a model for other tribal entities around the nation. And, like much of the global developing world, several tribal elements in Native American culture seem to facilitate microcredit's becoming a viable, innovative movement. Strong Indigenous communities within U.S. reservations tend to have a high degree of trust, collective norms, and interpersonal networks. All these factors may be more fully integrated thorough the pursuit of shared tools for economic betterment. Collectively, they make up what I call "social capital"—the availability one has in times of hardship to draw upon support and concern from other people, to be able to "count" on them when needed.

It just may be that Native American social capital is the most critical factor in expanding the access to financial capital among U.S. tribes. In the future, microcredit may become an even more constructive and widely used strategy in achieving that objective. It holds much promise for empowering "the poorest of the poor" among Native American families. Once-proud tribal members who today suffer from a lack of self-worth may again become confident warriors as they move from dependency to dignity.

In emphasizing the responsibilities that we as Christians have toward Native peoples, as I lay out in this brief chapter, let us recall the prophetic action and subsequent promise from the great Old Testament prophet Isaiah, who declared: *"If you do away with the yoke of oppression, with the pointing finger and malicious talk, and if you spend yourselves in behalf of the hungry and satisfy the needs of the oppressed, then your light will rise in the darkness, and your night will become like the noonday. The Lord will guide you always; he will satisfy your needs in a sun-scorched land and will strengthen your frame. You will be like a well-watered garden, like a spring whose waters never fail"* (Isaiah 58:9–11).

References

ATD Fourth World. (2022). Accessed January 14, 2022. https://www.atd-fourthworld.org/who-we-are/overcome-poverty/.

Berger, M. (1989). Giving Women Credit: The Strengths and Limitations of Credit as a Tool for Alleviating Poverty. *World Development, 17*, 1017–32.

Brown, L. (2000). *State of the World*. Worldwatch Institute.

Cabral, E. (1997). Building Entrepreneurship and Hope Among Native Americans. Ford Foundation Report, profile.

Cabral, S. (2021). "Deb Haaland: America's First Native Cabinet Secretary." BBC News, Washington, March 16. Accessed November 14, 2021. https://www.bbc.com/news/world-us-canada-56421097.

Capacity Builders. (2021). Accessed November 5, 2021. https://capacitybuilders.info/.

Coffey, G. *The Established Order*. Accessed February 6, 2003. http://www.focusweb.org/popups/articleswindow.php.

Cornell, S. and Kalt, J.P. (1998). Sovereignty and Nation-Building: The Development Challenge in Indian Country. John F. Kennedy School of Government, Harvard University, Paper #PRS 98-25.

Daley-Harris, S. (2002). *Pathways Out of Poverty: Innovations in Microfinance for the Poorest Families*. Kumarian Press.

De Soto, H. (1989). *The Other Path: The Invisible Revolution in the Third World*. Harper & Row.

Deuteronomy 15:4.

Finance New Mexico. (2021). "Specialized Assistance for Native American Entrepreneurs." Accessed February 3, 2022. https://financenewmexico.org/?s=native+american+small+businesses&submit=Search.

First Nations. (2021). COVID19 Emergency Response Fund. Accessed December 30, 2021. https://www.firstnations.org/covid-19-emergency-response-fund/?gclid=CjwKCAiAxJSPBhAoEiwAeO_fP7CeMxetwVwPz3iqAYAUegpPptcZLViSSJAgc9X-XhZbm93imgL-ahoCZWIQAvD_BwE.

Forbes Magazine. (2017). The 3 Richest Americans Hold More Wealth Than Bottom 50% of the Country, Study Finds. November 9.

Fuglesang, A. (1995). *Participation as Process—Process as Growth*. The Grameen Trust.

Garr, R. (1996). *Groups That Change Communities: The Lakota Fund*. @ grass-roots.org. Accessed May 1, 2004. http://www.grass-roots.org/USA/LAKOTAFUND.shtml.

GF-USA. (2004). *Grameen Connections*, vol. 7, issue 1, Spring.

Grameen Bank. (2019). *Annual Report*. Accessed January 17, 2021. https://grameenbank.org/wp-content/uploads/bsk-pdf-manager/AnnualReportPDF_2019.pdf.

Harvard Project: American Indian Economic Development. (2004). John F. Kennedy School of Government. Project home page. Accessed May 6, 2004. http://www.ksg.harvard.edu/hpaied/overview.htm.

Hewlett-Packard Development Company. (2003). Microenterprise Development Program. Accessed June 12, 2004. http://grants.hp.com/us/programs/micro/index.html.

Hopi Credit Association. (2021). Accessed January 4, 2022. https://hopicredit.us/.

Inequality. (2021). October 18. Accessed January 7, 2022. https://inequality.org/facts/wealth- inequality.

Khandker, S. R., et al. (2016). *Beyond Ending Poverty: The Dynamics of Microfinance in Bangladesh*. World Bank Publications.

Lakota Funds. (1998). About the Fund. Accessed May 14, 2004. http://www.lakotafund.org/about/htm.

Lakota Funds. (2022). Accessed January 16, 2022. https://lakotafunds.org/about/.

Lawrence, William. (2003). "Do Indian Reservations Equal Apartheid?" *The Native American Press / Ojibwe News*, June 6.

Locke. K. (2020). "Change Labs Offers Zero Interest Loans up to $5K." *Navajo-Hopi Observer*.

Matthew 26:11.

Mayoux, L. (1995). From Vicious to Virtuous Circles? Gender and Microenterprise Development. *Occasional Papers 3*, United Nations Research Institute for Social Development.

Meeks, Elsie. (2000). A Conversation. *Community Dividend*. Federal Reserve Bank of Minneapolis, Issue No. 2.

Microcredit Summit, 2002. (2002). Accessed March 27, 2003. http://www.microcreditsummit.org.

Nobel. (2006). Accessed December 30, 2021. https://www.nobelprize.org/prizes/peace/2006/summary.

Paxton, J. (1995). *Sustainable Banking with the Poor: A Worldwide Inventory of Microfinance Institutions*. World Bank.

PBS. (2000). To Our Credit: Bootstrap Banking in America. Video documentary on U.S. cases of microcredit. Accessed April 26, 2004. http://www.pbs.org/tourcredit/stories_tmo.htm.

Rayhan, M. I., and M. S. H. Khan. (2006). "Factors Causing Malnutrition Among Under Five Children in Bangladesh," *Pakistan Journal of Nutrition* 5 (6): 558–62. Accessed June 18, 2021. http://www.pjbs.org/pjnonline/fin488.pdf.

Reich, R. (1999). We Are All Third Wayers Now. Accessed March 12, 2004. http://www.prospect.org/print/V10/43/reich-r.html.

Ridley, Kimberly. (1997). Indian Giver. *Hope Magazine*, pp. 5–6.

Salgado, A. G. (December 26, 2000). *El Financiero*. Accessed February 11, 2003. http://www.elfinaciero.com.

Sanchez, G. R., and Others (2021). "The Monthly Jobs Report Ignores Native Americans. How Are They Faring Economically?" November 10. Accessed January 4, 2022. www.brookings.edu/blog/the-avenue/2021/11/10/the-monthly-jobs-report-ignores-native-americans-how-are-they-faring-economically/.

SCN. (1997). Sustainable Communities Network. The Lakota Funds, pp. 91–92. Accessed May 1, 2013. http://www.sustainable.org/casestudies/SIA_PDFs/SIA_South_Dakota.pdf.

Sebstad J., and Chen, G. (1996). Overview of Studies on the Impact of Microenterprise Credit. *Assessing the Impact of Microenterprise Services (AIMS)*. Management Systems International.

Thunstrom, T. (2021). 21 Microfinance Statistics You Need to Know in 2021. https://fitsmallbusiness.com/microfinance-statistics/. September 15.

Todd, H. (1996). *Women at the Center*. Westview Press.

Tomasevski, K. (1996). *Women and Human Rights*. Zed Books.

UNIFEM. (2001). United Nations Development Fund for Women. Accessed March 4, 2003. http://www.unifam.undp.org/ec_pov.html.

United Nations. (1995). *The World's Women 1995: Trends and Statistics*. United Nations.

United Nations. (2004). The Rights of Indigenous Peoples, Fact Sheet No. 9 (Rev. 1). Accessed April 30, 2016. http://www.unhchr.ch/html/menu6/2/fs9.htm.

UNU-WIDER. (2006). The Global Distribution of Household Wealth UNUWIDER project on Personal Assets from a Global Perspective. https://www.wider.unu.edu/publication/global-distribution-household-wealth.

U.S. Senate Committee on Banking, Housing and Urban Affairs. (2002). Hearing on Capital Investment in Indian Country. Accessed June 6, 2015. http://banking.senate.gov/02_06hrg/060602/meeks.htm.

Wahid, A. N. M. (1993). *The Grameen Bank: Poverty Relief in Bangladesh*. Westview Press.

Webb, J. W., et al. (2013). Research on Entrepreneurship in the Informal Economy: Framing a Research Agenda. *Journal of Business Venturing,* vol. 28, 598–614.

Women of Vision. (1999.) Accessed June 1, 2021. http://www.womenvision.org/history.htm.

Woodworth, W. (1997). *Small Really Is Beautiful: Micro Approaches to Third World Development—Microentrepreneurship, Microenterprise, and Microfinance*. Third World Think Tank.

Woodworth, W. (2000). Notes from personal interviews with Grameen Bank executives, middle level managers, field staff, and village female microentrepreneurs in Dhaka, Bangladesh.

Woodworth, W. (2014). Unpublished research study.

Woodworth, W. (2019). Grameen's Sixteen Decisions. Various iterations of these principles for a better future be independent women borrowers. Notes from multiple trips to Bangladesh as well as discussions with Grameen officials through the years in various other countries.

World Bank. (2022). January 15. Accessed January 17, 2022. https://www.worldbank.org/en/topic/poverty/overview#1.

WSIE. (2003). World Summit of Indigenous Entrepreneurs. Accessed December 23, 2003. http://wsie.wtuglobal.org/intro.php?page=introduction.

Yunus, M. (1990). Credit as a Human Right: A Bangladesh Bank Helps Poor Women. *New York Times*, April 2, A17.

Yunus, M. (1997). The Grameen Bank Story. *Dollars and Sense*, July–August, 27–29.

CHAPTER 7

Alternative Technologies for Reducing Human Suffering: From "Biblical Tech" to Our Day

Technology was occasionally used or at least mentioned throughout the Bible. For example, in Genesis 6 we learn that Noah used various technological skills to build a viable ark that saved the chosen ones. In Genesis 4:2 we learn that Tubal-Cain made things out of bronze and iron. In I Kings, we read that King Solomon built an enormous and sophisticatedly designed temple (I Kings 6). Jesus learned simple technology as a carpenter's apprentice working for his earthly father, Joseph. Unbelievers also possessed various technical competencies, including designing and erecting a high tower known as Babel (Genesis 11:1–9), and Adam's son Cain even built an entire city (Genesis 4:17), as did prophets such as Enoch. The technology of languages proliferated in ancient scripture, including the fact that Hebrew, Greek, and Aramaic were used to write the Bible itself. Paul used letters, as did others. And Luke was a physician, therefore knowing much about the technology of ancient medicine. Of course, other civilizations also used a degree of scientific technology, including the Babylonians' development of sophisticated weapons, and the Egyptians' skills in astronomy, while also engineering the construction of gigantic pyramids.

This chapter reports on several low-tech solutions designed and applied in rural settings of the developing world in which Christian university students from the United States have developed various, simple prototype projects in their college courses on social entrepreneurship. Drawing on scriptural passages to become our *"brothers' keepers,"* (Genesis 4:9), we learn we are to not reject caring for others, as Cain complained. In Romans 12:10, the Apostle Paul exhorts us: *"Love one another with brotherly affection. Outdo one another in showing honor."* Galatians 6:2 admonishes us to *"Bear one another's burdens, and so fulfill the law of Christ."*

Thus, in the following pages, I will describe various tech interventions designed, tested, refined, and then implemented by student nongovernmental organization (NGO) teams that I have organized or worked with as they spread around the world to build capacity and to empower impoverished villagers in recent years. The settings include Guatemala, Honduras, and Haiti in the western hemisphere and India, Thailand, and Ghana in the eastern hemisphere. To orient the reader, let me say that some key words that I define and describe in this chapter (some of which have been used in previous chapters) include terms such as Socio-Technology, International Development, NGOs, Appropriate Technologies, Social Entrepreneurship, and Grassroots Innovation.

The author with volunteers, training survivors of Haiti's disastrous earthquake, as they installed new water systems in damaged villages.

Introduction

The great Mahatma Gandhi, who admired and believed in most of what Jesus himself taught, once said, "You must be the change you wish to see in the world." I examine several innovative start-ups using simple, low-cost engineering methods to invent, produce, and sell solutions to enhance village living in various parts of the globe so as to improve the quality of life among struggling families, especially women and children. The academic settings in which these innovations were created are described by my summaries of course designs, teaching methods, and the mix of students on campus. Then I turn to their specific inventions and tell how such technologies were developed. Finally, I highlight the processes used and the resulting outcomes, as well as detail ongoing outcomes reported over the years.

The Academic Context

My career has been that of an academic activist, social innovator, disruptor, change agent, renegade, catalyst, and even mover and shaker. I've always sought to work with students, faculty colleagues, and researchers in doing applied work that empowers workers with organizational democracy tools, and also to utilize our collective academic efforts to reduce human suffering. My professional and personal questions in much of this book center on how we, as interested and willing global citizens, may tap into concepts theories as well as the application of management science to serve the interests and needs of the global poor.

Thus, the context for this paper is related to my work as a Professor of Organizational Behavior in the Marriott School of Business (2022), Brigham Young University (BYU, 2022), in Provo, Utah. I've invented and taught new courses on Microfinance, Social Entrepreneurship, and Appropriate Technology, as well as other more-traditional courses such as Leadership, Management Consulting, Teamwork, and Organizational Development. Collectively, they have led to the establishment of a variety of social enterprises emerging from my action research courses over some 40 years, impacting literally thousands of students. For many of these young people, their lives were changed as they evolved into more-caring and more-competent social entrepreneurs and changemakers (Smith and Woodworth, 2012).

My first start-up emerged in a little microfinance course I developed over 30 years ago, in 1988. It was the first of its kind taught in the United States, and at the time the concept of providing tiny microloans so poor women could start their own microenterprise was a radical new idea. The course began with a small group of students I recruited for gathering data on poverty and unemployment in the Philippines. We then collaborated with Filipino managers and academics there, to plan and roll out a microcredit nonprofit organization in that country. In spite of criticisms from academic colleagues, a few deans, and other campus administrators, our little start-up survived, growing to have some 600 employees operating a dozen offices throughout the Philippines, as well as in Peru, Mexico, Guatemala, and El Salvador. Thus far, in the Philippines alone we have raised some $171 million, trained, mentored, and given microloans to over a million microentrepreneurs, creating hundreds of thousands of new jobs through self-employed microenterprises that have benefited some five million Filipinos. Our success over 30 years has confirmed that I and my fellow Christian academics can actually change the world, not just teach theoretical courses, do research, and publish.

A second the case is an NGO launched from my social entrepreneurship course in 1999 that has operated in 17 nations, from Fiji to Tanzania, in which some 3,400 university students from 15 or so schools across the United States have been implementing programs such as appropriate technology, social entrepreneurship, sustainable development, literacy and computer skills, microentrepreneurship training, and many others. I recruited management students from MBA and

MPA programs, engineering students from across campus, and computer and other tech students, and we began sharing tools and methods to empower rural people around the globe.

A third example is of local college students and me, starting in 2003, using our large university as an incubator to recruit, train, mentor, and give $500 microloans to Latino immigrants in our Utah Valley, located high in the Rocky Mountains where the school is located. We later recruited students from other Utah institutions, including the University of Utah and Westminster College in Salt Lake City, as well as Utah Valley University in Orem, next door to Provo. Growing ever stronger even today, with financing from banks and credit unions, this experiment has convinced me that we can generate changemakers and empower poor refugees and migrants locally, as well as globally.

Finally, I mention a major microfinance institution (MFI) accelerator that I cofounded with students, several engineers, and a number of successful entrepreneurs. I served as the first board chair, showing others how like-minded Christians can come together, share their best practices, and become integrated in assisting small MFIs around the world to rapidly scale up, with a leg up from our financial backing. We learned how to be laser-focused, bring together a mix of management competencies with young students' energies, and become a major player around the world in growing the global field of microfinance. Over 15 years, we garnered loan capital for some 20 MFIs, achieving a total of more than $1.2 billion in loans and investments in Africa, Latin America, and Asia. With the financing we could then draw on, these once-MFIs rapidly ramped up from their early years when they had a total of fewer than 300,000 clients until today, when they serve an astounding 20-plus-million borrowers.

Having briefly highlighted basic facts about these social enterprises, I turn to summarize some founding theories and wisdom from a few early books about what is called Appropriate Technology, also Intermediate Technology, that I will draw upon in the rest of this chapter.

Appropriate Technology Resources

Major concepts and themes about these interventions, their founders, and a few key books include the following literature. First is the work of E. F. Schumacher and the Intermediate Technology Development Group (ITDG) that he founded in the United Kingdom. He authored the worldwide classic *Small Is Beautiful: Economics As If People Mattered* (1973), as well as subsequent volumes. A German by birth, Schumacher went to England and became a Rhodes Scholar at Oxford University, and over time developed a career working in what seemed a strange mix of science, agriculture, academics, and business. In his long career, he came to prefer making cogent proposals for human-scale enterprises instead of aiding giant corporations. Gandhi became an intellectual and moral hero of Schumacher, who also studied and then advocated for decentralized economic ventures and "appropriate" technologies that would be clean, less costly, more efficient, and available

NGO Strategies by Christians to Change the World

to the world's masses. While working in Burma, Schumacher developed his ideas of "Buddhist Economics," a set of principles adopted "as if people mattered." In his early years he was a self-declared atheist, but became fascinated with Zen Buddhism. In his middle years he gradually was drawn to Christianity, being moved especially by the words of Pope John Paul XXIII. Other sources of Christian influence included Thomas Merton and G. K. Chesterton, and late in life he finally converted to the Catholic faith. Schumacher eventually became known as a pioneer of what is now called "appropriate technology," advocating for the creation of self-reliant economies that are user friendly and ecologically suitable for technology that would foster a sustainable, cleaner, and ultimately better world.

A second influencer, living at roughly the same time as Schumacher, was Ivan Illich, a European-born Catholic priest who traveled throughout the continent as an intellectual and theologian, was educated in seven languages, and became a top administrator at several Catholic universities, including (and finally) in Puerto Rico. Over the decades, he was developing his own views about a kind of humanistic technology, as a matter of philosophical inquiry. Eventually, after serving as vice rector of the Catholic University of Puerto Rico, Illich left it to live and work in Cuernavaca, Mexico, an ancient city dating from the colonial years of the conqueror of Latin America, Hernán Cortés in the 1500s. There Illich crafted a little volume, titled *Tools for Conviviality* (Illich, 1973), describing and advancing the proper use of technology, which became celebrated as a book that was both highly innovative and useful, much like Schumacher's books. Illich published his book only two years after his *Deschooling Society* became a classic in 1971. Both his books emerged from the think tank where he founded the Center of Intercultural Formation (CIF) in Mexico, a place that hosted significant thinkers, tech giants, global politicians, and religious leaders over decades. Illich often referred to himself as "a wandering Jew and a Christian pilgrim" (his mother was Jewish until Naziism overtook his family's lives), and also called himself "an errant pilgrim." With respect to this chapter, I can safely say that Ivan Illich was an original thinker who challenged the dominant paradigms of modern scientific output. Instead, he sought a different paradigm in which people—not systems—mattered most. He opposed the institutionalism of modern culture, whether in the fields of medicine, religion, politics, education, law, or science itself. Mass consumption diminishes our humanity, according to him, leading to the dehumanization of all things near and dear to the human heart. He sought to establish a free-thinking perspective on life, championing forms of education that are liberate rather than demean. He advocated for both hardware and software technologies that open us up, rather than control our thinking and activity as human beings. Ivan Illich published a dozen or more provocative books advocating for liberating ideologies, ecological economics, and a more-critical pedagogy. He constantly labored to counter what he called the radical control of technology by elites who held sway as technocrats, monopolizing many aspects of modernized society. In the end he argued for more caring and sharing, and less controlling, manipulating, and wealth-hoarding.

A third major voice that I admire for advocating more-humane technologies and international development strategies came several decades later, in the work of Paul Polak. He was born in what was then Czechoslovakia. His parents escaped the Nazis in World War II, eventually moving the family to Canada where Paul grew up and graduated from medical school as an MD, later earning a degree in psychiatry. Eventually working in Denver, Colorado, Polak rebelled against traditional "straitjacket" hospitalization methods for treating and controlling patients. Gradually, he developed bottom-up innovations that won global recognition for their humane approaches to helping patients in crisis. His fame grew globally, and his alternative approach to top-down psychiatric control of patients became adopted across the United States, as well as throughout parts of Europe and Asia. From the medical services he developed in rural India and elsewhere with peasant communities, where a kind of humility-centered practice emerged, Polak developed simple business principles that formed the foundation for what became iDE, which he established in 1982. The organization, originally called International Development Enterprises, is said to have helped some 27 million people to gradually move from abject poverty into a more-viable existence. Progressing from living on just a dollar (or less) per day, they have gradually grown toward experiencing a better quality of life—not enjoying great wealth, but not suffering in base poverty, either. In other words, they have become free from extreme poverty. In the U.S., Polak has advocated for a more-freemarket-centric view in his principal book, titled *Out of Poverty: What Works When Traditional Approaches Fail* (Polak, 2008). Since launching his movement on behalf of the poor four decades ago, this social innovator combined new, simple technologies to empower the "poorest of the poor." Since the early 1980s, Polak has collaborated with rural peasants in inventing a new type of donkey cart in Somalia, treadle pumps to pump water in Bangladesh, sanitation innovations in Vietnam and Cambodia, and other services in Mozambique and Nepal. At base, Polak's iDE organization has literally revolutionized life for millions of the poorest of the poor, in dozens of developing nations (IDE, 2022).

Other key groups that I have come to admire and learn from are America's Engineers Without Borders, and the IEEE (Institute of Electrical and Electronics Engineers), both of which have begun cooperating to produce Engineering for Change. That effort supports the development of affordable, locally appropriate, and sustainable solutions to the most pressing of humanitarian challenges. I could name numerous other institutions and movements here, but I wanted to give short introductions to the three that I have used, more than others, for purposes of the cases in this chapter. So with these quick introductions to our efforts and early sources of inspiration, I will turn to highlight a few practical examples of hands-on engineering with NGO and innovative financing strategies designed and rolled out from a number of my college classrooms to serve the global poor. I should emphasize that most of these efforts were designed not just to provide new engineering methods for efficiency, but also to actually create jobs by building devices that would enhance production and reduce global suffering. Two centuries ago, history tells us, some 90 percent of the world lived in abject poverty. While the picture is improving year by year, far too many people still struggle to make ends meet. Today's gap between rich and poor is enormous. In 1800, the ratio between haves and have-nots was roughly 4:1. Today, for instance, the gap between people living in Switzerland and those in Mozambique is roughly 400:1. These innovations seek to change this reality in many nations.

Next, I highlight a few examples of appropriate technology innovations, to these ends.

Electricity-Generating Merry-Go-Round Project

Through the decades, our work in rural parts of Africa have not enjoyed the benefit of any electricity. In some cases, my science and engineering colleagues have assisted our team by bringing light to places like Uganda, by helping us install solar panels on school buildings that would aid local teachers and students better read, see the chalk writings by their teachers, and recharge their mobile phones so farmers could get up-to-date changes in prices for selling their cotton or coffee. About a decade ago, several students taking my NGO courses in the Marriott School of Business, BYU, decided to utilize their tech skills in developing a rather unusual and fun machine to generate African village electricity. They proposed the idea to several engineering professors and an outside professional engineer, and began to draft their unconventional yet potentially quite delightful ideas. By semester's end, they had their first prototype: a simple merry-go-round for turning children's play into electricity.

Designing a product to be first used in rural Ghana in West Africa, their merry-go-round used a direct-current generator system to turn the rambunctious energy of kids into electricity that would light schoolhouses. Students labored on the project to make a device complicated enough to capture and translate human energy into electricity, but simple enough to incorporate old car-parts that could be found on abandoned vehicles along country roads in the region. This would be a low-cost way not only to build merry-go-rounds but also to replace parts when problems arise.

So, the BYU project itself used car-parts from a local scrap yard to ensure that they would work. This technology promoted sustainable development, because it was more than just lighting a schoolhouse; it also provided self-sustained education to Ghanian kids who might eventually want to pursue further college schooling so as to become engineers and entrepreneurs themselves.

After a year or so, the result was the incorporation of a small Utah enterprise (Empower Playgrounds, 2022). It became a senior capstone project funded by one of my major NGO donors who himself had been an engineering student in BYU's Mechanical Engineering Department when younger. Meshing their undergraduate work with humanitarian values motivated them to do better at every stage. They succeeded in applying course concepts to ensure that the product would operate as designed. Their outside, older adviser was himself a former BYU engineering student with a career in the tech field. In addition, he had recently spent a year-plus with his wife on a church mission in Ghana, so he understood well the poverty, school needs, and struggles of impoverished children.

The product was eventually refined sufficiently that the team could box up its parts and travel to Ghana's capital city, Accra, and later drive out to a rural village, called Essam, where the clever machine device was reassembled and began operating. The group was greeted with enthusiastic African dances and music from crowds of smiling schoolchildren. Even the village chief happily took a ride on the contraption. Several villagers mentioned how long they had tried to obtain government funding for a village generator, but to no avail. Even if they had one, such equipment is costly to transport, repair parts are hard to get, and diesel fuel is very expensive. Having a piece of simple, cheap playground equipment was an ideal solution, they said. That first day, several hundred children took their new toy for a joyous, dizzy spin, and also rejoiced because their school was lit up on the inside for the first time—and it was all done with "kid power!" Child's play, when combined with simple technology, demonstrated that much can be done to improve planet earth.

The first product produced some 300-plus watts of electricity, enough to light three or four classrooms. Villagers from distant areas around walked for miles, curious to see the "miracle," as one later told me. It soon became several things: a fun piece of equipment as a toy, but also a means of electric light, a power source for other purposes, and even a school science lesson. Merry-go-round power was stored in a car battery that recharges 20 to 30 portable LED lights for use both in simple village houses as well as in classrooms. After the school day, students were able to take a charged-up lamp home with them to light their houses. Before the new BYU technology arrived, Ghanian families had to sit around in the dark at night with little or no light. Maybe they could rely on an outside fire for cooking meals under a mango tree, candles, kerosene lamps, or open flame "bobo" lights. Now they would have opportunities for greater education, literacy, and productivity for families.

Officials from Ghana's Ministry of Education declared they would like a half dozen more merry-go-rounds to install in neighboring villages, thereby providing a viable power option for some 10,000 Ghanaian public schools that currently had no power source at the time. It should be added that in such regions of Africa, playgrounds and public parks are virtually nonexistent. As I've observed over the decades, most children there also have no toys, unless they craft some rudimentary "toy" from mud along a river, or weave a "doll" from tall grasses, or make a "car" with bark from a tree. Having a merry-go-round for the first time in their lives was true a miracle for kids, regardless of generating electric light.

Ultimately, several BYU students and faculty in future want to extend their innovative system to include power for windmills that would move water to the rows of rural crops, instead of having to carry cheap plastic buckets of water by hand to grow better crops. They also would like to make solar panels and so be able to charge larger batteries, using their generator for lots of additional, human-powered projects that would ease life for such impoverished people.

More recently, as cheap mobile phones have become increasingly accessible in Africa, this merry-go-round power has also begun to recharge cell phones and laptop computers. Ghanaian leaders over time have also seen how science and engineering lessons are becoming more popular, being sought by kids and teachers who felt inspired by the innovative merry-go-round technology. In Africa, there has historically been little interest by either teachers or students in hands-on education, as they prefer getting a white-collar job as, say, a bank teller. But now, with this new low-tech methodology, maybe there will be more interest in science. As one official told me, "You never know, there might be a young Thomas Edison waiting to be discovered."

H2O for Humanity: Clean Water in India

In 2009, several engineering students were taking my course Organizational Behavior 682: "How to Change the World," when one BYU alumnus, Kevin Cluff, came to Utah from the Chicago corporation where he worked. He informed me about his dream to begin providing clean drinking water to areas of India where children were dying because of contaminated water. He, along with his engineering brother and their father in Texas, were all successful researchers at various firms, but they wanted to invent new solutions for the masses in the hot, dry regions of India. They decided to stop talking about social change and *do* something. They enlisted several graduate engineering students in my course to help achieve this, as their required course project for the semester. With water purification technology developed by the father, Dr. Brent Cluff, the group created a new NGO, which they named "H2O for Humanity." The father and both his sons had served as volunteer Christian missionaries as young men, each in a different nation—an experience that instilled in them a great love for the world's poor.

Why water? There are some 800 million children, women, and men in developing countries who get their drinking water from unsafe sources. They suffer from more than a billion episodes of gastroenteritis annually, due to poor water quality. Approximately 1.7 million human beings die every year from waterborne illnesses, including 5,000 children *per day* who tragically die from diarrhea. Within India itself, some 38 million people annually get sick from contaminated water, and over 450 Indian children die each day from this sad reality. So the Cluff brothers, both trained engineers, decided to take action.

To do this, they decided to establish H2O as a "social business"—a relatively new business entity, according to U.S. law. It was set up as a hybrid organization using business techniques and solutions, but without seeking profits as most American companies do. Within this model, the owners participate primarily for social reasons and may only be reimbursed for expenses and compensated time, not for achieving business profits. Instead, the financial returns are plowed back into the company so as to develop further technologies and other new products, having the required capital to create more engineering innovations and further grow the business. Dr. Muhammad

Yunus, Nobel Peace Prize Laureate in 2006 and founder of the Grameen Bank in Bangladesh, coined this concept. As my own partner in other NGO ventures, Yunus established the term "social business" in a post-Nobel book by that name, *Building Social Business: The New Kind of Capitalism That Serves Humanity's Most Pressing Needs* (2010), which offers a vision of the ideal social business.

Technically, according to legal regulations, H2O is thus incorporated as an L3C firm (Low-Profit Limited Liability Company). L3Cs are a new form of business entity in only some U.S. states, and operate as hybrids between a nonprofit and a for-profit organization. L3Cs have been structured to take loans and equity investments from U.S. nonprofit foundations. By providing a financial return, the company can become a sustainable business that strives for the social good. Kevin and Eric Cluff initially funded their project with personal savings, a home refinancing, and a seed grant from the Deshpande Foundation in America, launching H2O for Humanity in five villages in Karnataka, India—and a sustainable social business was born!

The engineering model that the firm uses is "reverse osmosis" technology to tailor the system to the local water quality. The water is softened as harmful bacteria and excess fluoride are removed, making healthy tasty water. H2O hires and trains an all-Indian staff who understand the local culture and values of rural communities. It creates partnerships with NGOs and establishes operations to also provide jobs and minimize capital requirements. The business is sustainable through a tiny 0.2 U.S. cent per liter charge to the water customers—making water affordable by even the poorest households. These funds are then used to capitalize and maintain the installations.

In 2010 the Americans launched H2O to some 13,000 customers in five villages within the state of Karnataka, India. Early on, H2O partnered with the Shri Kshethra Dharmasthala Rural Development Project, popularly known as SKDRDP (2019), a charitable trust. SKDRDP concentrates on the empowerment of people by organizing Self-Help Groups (SHGs) on the lines of Joint Liability Groups (JLGs), and further provides infrastructure and finance through microcredit for rural people. SKDRDP takes H2O's water purification strategy to increasingly larger areas where the need is great.

The business model is rolled out as follows: Either the NGO partner or a village finances and builds a water store. The store serves as a convenient location where villagers can collect their daily clean water. H2O for Humanity provides the equipment, technical support, and expertise for a small monthly charge and no up-front capital costs. Customers bring their 20 liter containers and fill them at the store. Production water is tested for Total Dissolved Solids (TDS) three times daily to ensure that the system is working properly. H2O for Humanity technicians replace the pre-filters and wash the membranes regularly. They also test the water for other key parameters.

Within India, the firm began using the name "AquaSafi" to designate its brand and water stores to dozens of villages. They continue to expand clean water possibilities into as many villages as possible. SKDRDP is involved in many additional sustainable development projects across India.

By 2014 they grew to over 70 water systems serving more than 20,000 families throughout western India.

Depending on the village size and available electrical power, three sizes of AquaSafi Water Systems may be installed. For example, the AquaSafi-200 can typically purify 1,300 liters per hour. Village employees are trained to operate and perform daily maintenance on the system. The footprint is less than 250 square centimeters (98 square inches), making it easy to transport and install.

The operational systems use only top-quality membranes and filters from a leading manufacturer. Many systems have been sold commercially, and so far customers have been pleased with their high reliability and performance. Recent advances in SMS-based technology have allowed H2O to remotely monitor its water purification systems. By providing real-time updates regarding water usage, contamination levels, and system diagnostics, this new technology allows the social business to collect useful data as well as monitor equipment in remote locations.

The latest evolution of the business model is that AquaSafi sells equipment to a local NGO, which then either owns the store or gives it to a village. Then it is installed and maintained by the local organization, along with H2O ongoing support. The NGO goes on to staff and manage the store. In many instances, villages provide the store or building, and by being the water source the village leaders have a direct incentive to make the enterprise successful.

To summarize the enablers that enable H2O to achieve success as an innovative engineering enterprise, I must note that several factors are operating: (1) a large, untapped market that is well understood, knowing such facts as that less than 3 percent of people in the region have affordable, safe drinking water; (2) this allows H2O/AquaSafi to cluster operations and select villages, targeting appropriate communities based on their needs; (3) benefits accrue, such as lower-cost operations due to lean design, local manufacturing, and remote maintenance; (4) driving down costs enables direct model and revenue sharing; (5) revenue sharing strengthens relationships with H2O partner villages; and finally (6) machine operation and water distribution will keep building barriers against any future competitors that may try to enter the region and poach on H2O's successes.

Of course, many challenges still remain, including the fact that H2O's financial debt for more equipment has grown to approximately $1.9 million. But it is assumed this can be reduced as more customers emerge. From its small start-up in 2010–2011 in just two villages with some 3,400 people, over half a million people are being served today. Cumulatively, approximately two million Indians have benefited from access to clean, good-tasting, inexpensive water for their pleasure and—more importantly—for their health.

Over the past several years, AquaSafi units have served on average 300 households with 1,200 to 1,500 individuals. This means increasingly more villages served, while at the same time reducing a family's cost for health care, since some 70 percent of diseases are waterborne. In terms of economics, the system actually creates entrepreneurs and offers local employment for operators. Then there are the jobs of servicing, maintaining, and operating each unit, using strong processes and a good training program. Additionally, there is the work of daily online performance monitoring of water quality (TDS), unit performance (pressure, product, reject), flow volume, and tracking the number of customers. All these elements offer decent jobs in communities where work is scarce and wages are low. All told, AquaSafi promises a better future for its employees and their families.

In terms of business strategy, today in many areas of the state of Karnataka there is a 30 to 35 percent market penetration by H2O, which now operates to serve literally hundreds of thousands of impoverished customers every day. There were over 210 stores serving customers in 2017, but the number increased to over 500 in 2019, before the Coronavirus pandemic hit. Expansion continues to slowly increase in order to serve more Indians. Plans are now in the works for H2O to expand resources for clean water to other parts of the world. The business has already launched in Mexico, with a few stores starting to offer clean water to local folks. Africa is next on H2O's horizon, and the plan is to go beyond these nations in 2022.

Other Appropriate Technology Cases

With the detailed H2O clean water campaign described above, I now turn to briefly highlight additional engineering examples in which BYU students taking my "How to Change the World" course have designed other innovative start-ups. Several are high tech, while some are based on agricultural innovations as well as other technologies. In each case, students researched possibilities, debated with each other on their team, and then put together a project that could be experimented with during the summer. They then ventured out to areas in the developing world the following summer, to roll out their projects on behalf of struggling village families, usually in rural regions of Asia, Latin America, or Africa. They often sought advice and feedback from faculty of BYU's College of Engineering, as well as at times seeking input from professors in the Accounting School or the Kennedy Center for International Studies.

Peruvian Projects—Libraries, Greenhouse Design, and Construction: In my master's of public administration class, some of my students devised an NGO called Eagle Condor Humanitarian. They intended it to assist in building huge log-and-stone greenhouses up in the Urubamba mountain range of the Peruvian Andes, where we worked as volunteers in villages such as Patancancha, some 14,000 feet high, so as to double the growing season for descendants of the ancient Inca civilization. They also built schools and libraries in rural communities and brought Spanish books contributed by US donors. In addition, teams of Utah computer experts raised the necessary funding to take numerous laptops and other tech devices to rural communities. For the first time they linked villages to government power grids and achieved Internet connections to open up the region to new sources of information, including weather forecasts, agricultural services, educational programs on the web, and, later, mobile phone access.

Eagle Condor volunteers present US educational materials to
rural Indigenous children high in the Andes.

Kenyan Interventions: Affordable Housing, Lumber Mill, and Coconut Oil: Appropriate technologies in Kenya were developed through the Asante Foundation, which was launched by some of my graduate students, in collaboration with local engineers and executives of the first synthetic-diamond maker in the U.S. The owner, Louis Pope, a successful business executive who worshipped Christ in his local church every Sunday for 60 years, felt he should give away much of his wealth to help those who suffer. Even as a young man, he always felt impressed by the words of Jesus to the rich young ruler. In Mark 10:17–22 we read: *"As Jesus started on his way, a man ran up to him and fell on his knees before him. 'Good teacher,' he asked, 'what must I do to inherit eternal life?' 'Why do you call me good?' Jesus answered. 'No one is good—except God alone. You know the commandments: "You shall not murder, you shall not commit adultery, you shall not steal, you shall not give false testimony, you shall not defraud, honor your father and mother."' 'Teacher,' he declared, 'all these I have kept since I was a boy.' Jesus looked at him and loved him. 'One thing you lack,' he said. 'Go, sell everything you have and give to the poor, and you will have treasure in heaven. Then come, follow me.' At this the man's face fell. He went away sad, because he had great wealth."*

In the case of my friend Louis Pope, he acted on a genuine commitment to do with his hard-earned wealth what the Savior admonished. That was, to give his money away. So, with funding from my associate, he, his family, and some of my friends and students began working with Kenyan villagers. Together, they helped establish a new social venture fund that invested financial and managerial support in social business start-ups in their area. Their mission was to combat poverty through enterprise. The core belief was that creating sustainable businesses that employ, serve, and empower Kenyans was the most effective tool in combating poverty. Among its projects are these:

a revolutionary, affordable housing project designed to make housing, clean water, and electricity accessible to rural Kenyans within a safe walking-community in villages outside Mombasa, thus filling a real need in a nation in which some 50 percent of families live in squalor because they try to survive below the national poverty line; serving some 26,000 rural Kenyan women entrepreneurs with capital to start and grow their microbusinesses through an NGO; Yehu Microfinance, which employed 65 workers and enjoyed a high 96 percent payback rate; bringing in U.S. engineers and students to create an organic-coconut oil mill designed to create employment both for farmers who harvest the coconuts and employees who process them and press the meat into edible oils for export (Coast Coconut Farms grew to employ 40 Kenyans and to provide livelihoods for some 200 farmers).

Through the years, Pope's Asante Foundation has continued to spin off additional, promising new ventures to organizations capable of growing and scaling businesses and also of incubating more innovative agricultural, housing, energy, and water businesses in Kenya. Among the latest are aquaponics sustainable fish farms to create better rural jobs and provide plentiful fish so that local folks have more protein in their daily diets. A central theme of this engineering effort? For this project, the old adage "Give a man a fish" was rephrased: "Teach a woman to fish, and she will sell the produce and have food for her children during a lifetime." Also, Asante has begun eucalyptus tree farms to assist hundreds of rural farmers who were living on empty lands with rich soil. After all, Africa has a multi-billion-dollar demand for wood products, along with an ever-dwindling supply and inefficient value-chains that have kept the industry in failure. But why eucalyptus? Because it's fast-growing, with straight trunks; it's also drought-resistant and pest-resistant; it gives high timber yields and is extremely profitable. Furthermore, eucalyptus stumps can regrow repeat harvests, providing decades of income. The economics of this venture so far have proven to be very strong. Thus, a new lumber mill has been built and is already a supplier of valuable lumber, produced with high-tech manufacturing equipment from China. As of 2021, not only was the lumber being shipped to other parts of Africa and Europe, but also the scrap from leftover pieces of wood is utilized for another business—that of producing briquettes for mass consumption in the regional villages where residents need them for clean cooking and heating.

Guatemalan Lorena Adobe Stove Projects: An instance of a hands-on intervention using simple, low-cost technology is that which emerged from a BYU Marriott School initiative called HELP International (HELP, 2019) that grew from my own microfinance course back in 1999 and that continues to expand today. It is an innovative example of utilizing engineering and social science student volunteers, local entrepreneurs, alumni, and faculty in mobilizing collective efforts to serve the poor in parts of Latin America. HELP began in response to the terrible destruction of 1998's Hurricane Mitch in Central America, and has led to more than 3,000 students from over 30 universities doing in-depth summer volunteer service to countries around the world.

This case began when several of my young women students took HELP's training before departing to spend a summer laboring in Guatemala. They especially wanted to empower Indigenous women in rural regions, so they were given extra training in how to build Lorena adobe stoves (which are called *estufas* in Spanish). The technology uses compacted earth or adobe rammed tightly together, then a simple chimney is made from soldered empty tin cans to channel the smoke from the residence. Once on the ground in Central America, one of the women students in particular became completely enthralled with this simple appropriate technology and so became the team's "stove queen" (*La Reina de las Estufas*), meaning the leader on the project in Guatemala, by first making and then teaching Mayan villagers how to construct their own low-tech adobe stoves. This was critical, because peasant mothers typically do the family cooking in an open pit in the middle of their simple shacks or shanties. The thatch roof might have a hole cut to supposedly allow some smoke from the fire to escape, but generally it is barely effective. Instead, the mothers and their family members are victims of thick smoke trapped in the enclosed space as well as in the outside air, thereby engulfing the community environment. The health results are tragic, as the smoke and tiny particles would get in family members' eyes, nostrils, and even clothes. From such conditions, some individuals grew blind at a young age, contracted lung or other cancers, and suffered appalling death rates. Globally, some three billion people suffer these problems, often leading to heart and lung disease. Smoke inhalation is a significant cause of death in children. Those kids who remain alive often spend hours each day scrounging for logs and other wood sources with which to heat homes or cook food, thereby missing educational experiences (*National Geographic*, 2017).

Inspired, and armed with simple engineering plans and medical knowledge to educate villagers, the HELP group began to change the culture with new insights for a better future. The "Queen" managed the team because of her leadership skills as well as her technical expertise. She managed the stove-building calendar of appointments, working closely with the local NGO leaders who arranged with the Indigenous communities to start building stoves. With a group of 6 to 20 of her colleagues, she would go to a village, working with its men and women, teaching them how to make low-cost adobe stoves by building one or more stoves with them. At the start, the volunteers built 14 stoves. Then the villagers went on to build more than 140 stoves that summer, benefiting some 500-plus people. Later, under her leadership, the volunteer teams moved on to another community, building about 45 more stoves. The villagers there then built over 400 additional stoves. As the summer wore on, stove-building requests increased and came from new sources as word of mouth spread about the benefits of stoves and the availability of training on how to build and use them.

Key elements of this NGO strategy included the following:

- Mastering the technical knowledge necessary to design and execute the project
- Partnering with NGO leaders and staff to create a series of small but complex projects
- Sustaining enthusiasm and commitment over a long period
- Building relationships with NGO leaders and staff, village leaders, mothers, and even children

- Doing ongoing, persistent, constructive coordination with NGO partners
- Exercising initiative, creativity, and project management
- Influencing without using authoritarian behaviors
- Using participation to build commitment and a sense of ownership
- Extending the project's scope
- Using temporary project teams with shifting membership and roles as HELP volunteers came and went
- Demonstrating openness to reflective thinking and feedback through the use of After Action Review, an action research and action learning technique
- Demonstrating innovation, flexibility, and adaptability

The result of this work was greatly improved health for many impoverished Mayan families, who came to understand the benefits of new, appropriate technology. On the part of the U.S. students, they felt an amazing sense of fulfillment in finding that hard work and simple solutions could actually improve the world. The good news is that various iterations of this stove technology are continuing into the 2020s.

Water Systems in Post-Earthquake Haiti: In 2010 a terrible earthquake destroyed much of the island nation of Haiti, resulting in some 20,000 dead, 20,000 missing, and a million homeless as the quake flattened or mostly destroyed nearly all buildings in the island nation. My microfinance class at Brigham Young University responded to my invitation for those willing to help, so we launched a small project that we called "Sustain Haiti." Throughout the semester, interest kept growing with students from across campus hearing about our plans and joining the cause in weekly meetings, even when not earning academic credit. The project took off in the spring of 2010 and is still functions today as an NGO. The dozens of students who volunteered in Haiti that first summer engaged in many activities, ranging from rebuilding orphanages and people's homes, to training Haitians in microenterprise creation, to offering microloans, to training folks in entrepreneurship, and much more.

One of the engineering projects we developed was helping design and install a simple water system for getting clean water through new pipes we bought, so that thousands of quake victims could have water to drink, cook with, bathe their children with, and so on. Not being water experts, the team of student volunteers considered several options for doing this:

- Go it alone.
- Partner with another NGO, such as Potters for Peace, which was operating in the neighboring country that shares the same island, the Dominican Republic.
- Design a new filter system for channeling pure water, beginning in the town of Leogane, which was the epicenter of the earthquake, while also building similar water systems for nearby towns like Jacmel.

Ultimately, it was decided to buy PVC and to engineer a new water system from area wells that would shoot clean water through makeshift pipes to the many tent camps where Haitian refugees were trying to survive. They were waiting in desperate conditions until major aid could arrive from the World Bank, USAID, the United Nations, and other organizations, as they worked to ramp up with big sums of money and as professional water engineers could design and build an entire new system.

The modest efforts of Sustain Haiti achieved yeoman results through the first two years of the island nation's recovery. Additional outcomes occurred both for factory workers and for the supply chain of materials needed to rebuild. Over that time period these student efforts were a boon to help thousands of families to have access to clean drinking water, along with less disease and death.

Brief Highlights of Additional Applied Tech Projects

In the following paragraphs I briefly summarize various other NGO interventions that used various approaches to technology, along with business acumen, to enhance the lives of people in developing countries around the globe.

Thailand Wave of Hope: In 2004, a massive 9.1 earthquake struck in the Indian Ocean, leading to a horrendous Asian tsunami. Together, these two disasters combined to lead to the deaths of some 230,000 victims, along with affecting millions more who survived but were injured physically, were made homeless from their destroyed towns, or suffered economically as businesses and entire communities were swept out to sea. Following the quake, 100-foot waves crashed onto the shorelines and swept inland for great distances in more than a dozen countries bordering the ocean. In my social enterprise course at BYU, which I started teaching in January 2005, some 90 students joined in my plea on Day One after the quake, to come together and mount a rescue effort by assisting to help any way we could. After our first few days of class, having all done a bit of research as to what and where needs were that we might offer to address, we determined to help rebuild villages in the coastal area of Khao Lak, in Thailand's Pang-Na province. Our efforts continued over a three-year period of recovery until major foreign aid and Thailand's own government was able to restore much of the physical infrastructure (roads, houses, fishing boats, and schools) that had been destroyed.

To help rebuild the country after the destructive waves that had wreaked havoc throughout the region my students and I decided to call our new NGO "Wave of Hope." It signified that it would strive for a more optimistic future for the people of Thailand. Volunteers gave thousands of hours of service to many different projects, and also worked with others from around the world. Many spent their days in the hot sun on house rebuilding efforts. They worked in the villages of Tap-Tawan and Lam Pom, preparing and pouring foundations, laying rebar, raising walls, building roofs, and applying plaster finishes. In all they helped in the construction of over 50 houses. The team also dug trenches and laid the pipes for a whole new water system to channel clean water into homes for the first time.

Our student Wave of Hope team also built a workshop, featuring new equipment for wood working, and more. It was named "Thaikea," combining the names of "Thailand," where the team was serving, along with the big Swedish company "Ikea." They helped build dozens of simple wooden homes to replace those destroyed by the tsunami. They taught local women how to design and make their own simple furniture, constructing and painting bookshelves, chairs, and play sets for schools and homes. Other volunteers helped by working on boats built for fishermen who had lost theirs in the tsunami. They applied waterproofing caulk and painted the boats, while also securing the necessary capital to purchase some 40 boat motors so that livelihoods could return to normal—could, in fact, be even better. Also, some volunteers taught English to schoolchildren, and even to adults who wanted to learn. An early analysis of the start-up of this project can be read at Woodworth (2008).

Equitech Cooperative: Within the BYU College of Engineering, a colleague and I mobilized business and technology students to design a worker-owned manufacturing cooperative, called the Equitech Co-op, to learn design, how to do graphic arts, how to make molds, and how to learn other skills by running our nonprofit firm to produce brass and other medallions and plaques for sale across many university departments, as well as in the neighboring community. This not only created new skill sets for our students, most of whom came from Peru, Brazil, Hong Kong, and Argentina, but also generated some employment for them as struggling, low-income international students. They learned technology skills, but also explored leadership, marketing, decision-making, accounting, and more.

Mali Rural Village Technologies: In the *arrondissement* of Ouelessebougou in West Africa, many of my colleagues and students have been committed for over 30 years to reduce poverty and empower struggling villagers in an area that is one of the three poorest nations on Earth. People have lived in mud huts with thatched roofs for hundreds of years, lacking even today such modern amenities as electricity, health care, schools, jobs, and many of the features of modern society. After decades of drought, lack of water and irrigation, and having been disconnected from the larger, but still impoverished, capital of Bamako, dozens of villages languish. So in the mid-1980s, a group of citizens in Salt Lake City formed an NGO to learn more of the plight of Malians, especially women and children, and the Ouelessebougou Alliance was born. Since then, hundreds of Utah college students, doctors, farmers, engineers, schoolteachers, entrepreneurs, Christian religious congregations, and Utah Muslim societies, along with other charities have mobilized their talents and financial resources to learn more about Mali and offer help.

Villagers in drought-ridden Mali planting women's cooperative vegetable gardens, which required digging wells for irrigation.

Since the Ouelessebougou Alliance began, having been structured as a partnership with Africa, many changes have borne fruit. Volunteer engineers, for instance, designed new reservoirs to capture precious water during the limited rainy season for storage through the year. They dug new village wells in some 40 communities, as well as drinking wells for the people and garden wells for agriculture. With simple designs, wells could be accomplished for $2,500 each, rather than the big, "gold-plated" traditional technology of wells proposed by huge organizations like Africare at a cost of $35,000 each. Other technicians used their simple yet appropriate technology to help plan and construct schools with 4 to 5 simple rooms each in every village so that children from age 6 up to 14 would have the chance at an education. Later, solar power technology was installed that would transform the dark and dreary classrooms, by accessing more light by day, but also village adults could attend literacy courses at night. Eventually, engineers and medical doctors from Utah built a rural pharmacy to dispense medicines, and two health care workers (a male and a female) in each village were taught to provide simple first aid, teach the need for handwashing, dispense mosquito netting for every household, and more. Today, statistics exist beyond the space of this chapter that document the improved levels of reading and writing capacities of most children, better nutrition for families, empowerment of women with their own cooperatives and microenterprises, and much more. People in Mali are now living longer, healthier lives.

Even during the current COVID-19 pandemic, the entire alliance continues to apply its tried-and-true methods for working with the global poor. We do so by designing appropriate technologies in collaboration with Indigenous women and men, so that they and their families can live more fulfilling lives. The actions we have taken, and will continue to take, from entry to the various steps below, include the following interventions:

- Develop Collaborative Partnerships with Local Women and Men Who Are Influencers
- Design Action Research Plans
- Carryout Steps Using Process Consultation
- Hold Strategic Direction and Governance Discussions
- Generate Capital Resources
- Manage Branding and Marketing Strategies
- Offer Individual Feedback and Coaching of In-Country Leaders
- Utilize Team-Building Techniques to Ensure Unity and Buy-In
- Continually Carry Out a Cultural Analysis
- Deal with Difficulties by Using Confrontation and Conflict-Resolution Techniques
- Employ Other Methodologies as Needed

Conclusion

As a professor teaching at international universities through four decades, I've saved anonymous feedback from students in most of my courses. I've never forgotten the words of one student who stood out in 2012. Here are the thoughts of a young engineering student who took my social entrepreneurship course, and then afterward spent three months as a volunteer working on the ground in Uganda. Said he:

> Ever since I was a little kid, I dreamed of living in Africa when I grew up. Now, I've spent the summer among villagers in Uganda, providing new, simple technology products for use in rudimentary schools (solar-powered energy, laptop computers, and Internet access). It's been so meaningful to install (these things), and also train the people so they might use them to improve their lives. I finally have a sense of how I can give ongoing services in my life and career to make humble families, especially mothers and kids, to enjoy more knowledge and security for their long-term futures.

As I conclude this chapter on appropriate technology, science, and engineering practices that can be used to improve the world, I'd like to reflect for a moment on the larger realities of God's majestic work. In John 1:3 we read: *"Through him all things were made; without him nothing was made that has been made."* And in Isaiah 42:5 we read: *"This is what God the Lord says—the Creator of the heavens, who stretches them out, who spreads out the earth with all that springs from it, who gives breath to its people, and life to those who walk on it."* I also admire the words of Psalm 104:24: *"How many are your works, Lord! In wisdom you made them all; the earth is full of your creatures."*

My colleagues, students, and collaborators in the various tech examples I describe in this chapter will surely agree that their work to design new instruments for social change was inspired by heaven. Whether developing solar panels for rural Africa, greenhouses for Peruvians high in the Andes, clean water in Indigenous India, or merry-go-rounds to generate electricity in Ghana, everything we have collectively done must acknowledge the inspiration of God. Of course, it took our own brains, education, physical labors, and money to do this work. But without Him, these humble projects and long-term programs would never have been possible.

Through all these innovations in appropriate technology that they have made over several decades, my university volunteers' lives have clearly been changed as they ventured out around the world and served thousands who could not help themselves. Likewise, the beneficiaries in hundreds of global villages were helped along in their own efforts to improve their quality of life, and were clearly blessed by the volunteers' efforts. Essentially, such efforts have been practical, "hands-on" collaborations of people of many nations, occupations, and professions—for the benefit of the entire world. All have surely been blessed by the God of Heaven and his son, Jesus Christ.

References

Brigham Young University. (2022). Accessed April 22. https://www.byu.edu/.

Empower Playgrounds. (2022). Accessed January 11. www.empowerplaygrounds.org.

Galatians 6:2.

Genesis 4:9.

H2O for Humanity. (2019). "Water purification social business in India." Accessed November 16. http://www.h2oforhumanity.com/.

HELP. (2019). HELP International, NGO. Accessed October 22. https://help-international.org/.

IDE. (2022). Accessed January 5. https://www.ideglobal.org/.

Illich, I. (1973). *Tools for Conviviality.* Through World Perspectives Publishing by Harper and Row.

Isaiah 42:5.

John 1:3.

Mark 10:17–22.

Marriott School of Business. (2022). Accessed March 9. https://marriottschool.byu.edu/.

National Geographic. (2017). "Three Billion People Cook Over Open Fires—With Deadly Consequences." August 14.

Polak, P. (2008). *Out of Poverty: What Works When Traditional Approaches Fail.* Berrett-Koehler.

Psalm 104:24.

Romans 12:10.

Schumacher, E. F. (1973). *Small Is Beautiful: Economics as if People Mattered.* Blond and Briggs.

SKDRDP. Shri Kshethra Dharmasthala Rural Development Project. (2019). Large Indian NGO with multiple development programs. Accessed December 22. https://`skdrdpindia.org/.

Smith, I., and Woodworth, W. (2012). "Developing Social Entrepreneurs and Social Innovators: A Social Identity and Self-Efficacy Approach." *Academy of Management Learning & Education,* vol. 11, no. 3, pp. 390–407.

Woodworth, W. (2008). "Youth-based Social Entrepreneurship: Post-Tsunami Crisis Interventions." *Social Science Research Network* (SSRN). Elsevier. March 8.

Yunus, M. (2010). *Building Social Business: The New Kind of Capitalism That Serves Humanity's Most Pressing Needs.* Public Affairs.

Microcredit Support Organizations (MSOs): Ways that American Christians Can Reduce U.S. Poverty

"If you spend yourselves in behalf of the hungry and satisfy the needs of the oppressed, then your light will rise in the darkness....The Lord will guide you always." —Isaiah 58:10–11

I now turn to the question of how we believers in Christ can do more than preach religion on Sunday. Are we relevant to the practical problems of society? Microcredit Support Organizations (MSOs) are an emerging innovation for Christians to accelerate the growth of microenterprise development in the United States. This chapter surveys the rise of this movement and its impacts, and analyzes the strengths and criticisms of these new social enterprises. I highlight three MSO cases with which I have been personally involved and have studied: one, with Grameen America (primarily aiding immigrant and minority women), a second among African Americans in Florida, and the third, an MSO serving Hispanic clients in the western U.S. I explore the relevance and significance of these nonprofits, propose implications for practitioners, and offer suggestions for further research.

Several questions arise from this chapter. For Christians, what is the relevance regarding microcredit and the MSO movement if we seek to adhere to Old Testament prophets such as Isaiah? What are some implications for aiding the poor as Jesus taught, being "our brother's keeper"? What are some current best-business practices we can employ to help the poor? Clearly, several important points need to be emphasized.

One point is that the findings discussed herein make the case for not simply reading the Bible or attending church services on Sunday. We need to do more to improve the world and reduce poverty. A relatively recent approach for doing this as individuals in today's world is using business tools to combat social ills and fight economic deprivation. Welfare and other traditional government programs have not, and evidently never will, solve the problems of society's have-nots. Simply giving away money, food, and grants tend to generate unintended results such as dependency. What is needed instead is investing in the poor—using grassroots capitalism to enable such individuals to lift themselves through entrepreneurial tools and methods. Thus, there needs to be a shift from dependency to dignity. Unfortunately, we could give away to people of the world all the financial resources the U.S. possesses, yet it would still be insufficient. Nor would its impacts last. Rather, the better practice is the facilitating of economic self-reliance within poor communities, so that they learn how to gain control of their own futures.

Another point is that Base-of-the-Pyramid (Prahalad, 2004) and similar MSO interventions are beginning to accelerate the growth of microentrepreneurial phenomena. For instance, huge firms like Deutsche Bank and MasterCard are channeling millions of dollars to empower the poor. Other firms ought to join in the cause. In recent years, I have consulted with many midsized firms that give microlending capital to MSOs in their local communities. Equally important, the firms' top executives donate some of their time and expertise to conduct group training sessions, or even to mentor a single microentrepreneur.

Christian executives who make these efforts report a real sense of religious and personal fulfillment. They demonstrate that a manager can make a personal and professional difference in someone else's life. They show that business leaders like themselves can enlarge their sphere of leadership and stewardship beyond their firms, with outside stakeholders, including the poorest individuals in society. By doing so, these socially responsible corporations are enjoying increased credibility, learning that they can not only do well financially but also just do good.

Introductory Story

Susana is a 43-year-old Hispanic immigrant who struggled for several years after arriving in the United States from Central America. As a practicing Christian, together with her husband and three children, they located in a small town in Utah hoping to find the American dream—secure careers, school for the children, a decent home, food security, and a better quality of life than before. But life was hard. Neither Susana nor her spouse was able to obtain a middle-class wage job. Poverty led to numerous stresses and strains. Eventually, the husband abandoned his family and moved on, leaving no forwarding address.

While the conflicts over money and other marriage issues declined, the terrors of a bleak future, unanswered questions, and practical matters like how to pay the rent all heightened Susana's worries. Unable to speak English, combined with having no income, led to her being forced to move to another dilapidated rental unit. This meant a loss of the children's few friends, as well as their having to begin anew in the middle of the academic year at a new school.

After further difficulties, Susana saw a flyer announcing the work of a local community nonprofit support organization, named Mentores para los Microempresarios (Mentors for Microentrepreneurs). That group was launching a program to train Spanish-speaking immigrants who sought to start income-generating projects. Beginning to feel she might not be successful in obtaining employment in the formal economy of Utah, she thought that becoming self-employed might be a viable alternative.

A year later, after small business training and a microloan of just $500, Susana was able to stand on her own two feet. She used the loan to purchase haircutting equipment: clippers, combs, electric hair-styling brushes, trimmers, a curling iron, razors, hair tonics, talc, gels, and a shoulder bag. She makes a living going door to door carrying the tools of her new trade. She solicits customers who would enjoy a low-cost, nicely done haircut within the comfort of their own homes.

While her family is not wealthy by any means, Susana was able to pay off her loan 100 percent, on time. She started out her microenterprise by bringing in around $300 the first month. With Mentors for Microentrepreneurs' ongoing consulting assistance, her business has grown so much that she now grosses as much as $1,500 per month. Her family has been able to remain in the same apartment so the children can continue to stay in the same school, keep their friends, and worship at the same church. All this gives the family both stability and a degree of security that they never had before.

Each month Susana saves a percentage of her income to maintain the business and prepare for a better future. Eventually, she hopes to go to beauty school and then open her own shop. She says she feels blessed by God, as well as by many good people on earth (Woodworth, 2019).

The case of Susana is real. It grew out of a project that several of my MBA (master of business administration) and MPA (master of public accountancy) students and I developed over recent years to address the challenges of family poverty in our own community. This chapter elucidates the growing phenomenon of U.S. microcredit support organizations (MSOs)—what they are, how they strengthen poor families, where they work, how they are structured, and the extent of their impacts.

Lifting the Poor through Microcredit Support

While many Americans experience the stress and strain of poverty, new solutions are being implemented to help overcome the debilitating effects of joblessness. One of the most innovative is microcredit support organizations (MSOs) to empower the poor and enable those who struggle to enjoy greater incomes, experience a sense of dignity, solidify family relationships, and improve their quality of life.

This approach differs from large-scale, expensive programs that broadly assert that their objective is to eliminate poverty, in general. Instead, it is a sort of boutique strategy that pursues narrower goals. It uses a business model, not charity, to lift the poor, and it accomplishes this, one family at a time. In doing so, the poor experience a better life, feel more dignity, and are not dependent on huge government programs. The phrase I often use in my consulting and working with microcredit support organizations is that they give the poor "a hand-up, not a handout."

To begin with, I will clarify several terms. First, microcredit is usually offered through *nongovernmental organizations (NGOs)*, an increasingly used term for what Americans typically have referred to as nonprofit foundations. The most commonly used word is *microcredit*, but in this chapter, when it is used, I mean "microlending" only—tiny amounts of capital loaned for income-generating projects. *Microentrepreneur* is the term for the recipient of microcredit, that is, an individual who seeks a small loan with which to start or expand one's business. *Microenterprise* is used to signify one's small business. Because of its minuscule size, it is usually operated by just one or two people, perhaps just a parent and her child. Such an entity is "micro" because it is much smaller than traditional definitions of U.S. small business (fewer than 50 to 100 employees and with annual revenues of under $1 million).

Microfinance is a more-encompassing word that may include microcredit for the microenterprise operated by the microentrepreneur. But microfinance may also provide additional economic services for the poor, such as a microentrepreneur's savings account. Other examples could include instruments like microloans for housing or education; microinsurance; small-scale agriculture loans for seed, tools, or animals; and so forth. NGOs that provide such credit or offer a broader array of financial services, I describe as *microcredit support organizations (MSOs)*. Basically, they are organizations offering a range of small-scale economic development programs to strengthen the informal economy and empower impoverished people. One may wonder where these new financial strategies came from, so next I offer some background.

Global Origins of Microfinance

Three financial experiments gave rise to this movement. One MSO that claims it was the first is *ACCIÓN* International, an NGO that was doing traditional development work in Latin America during the 1970s, focusing especially on Catholics, but also on the growing populations of evangelicals. It began to provide simple, tiny loans for start-up economic activity in 1972 in Recife, Brazil. Seeing that a small amount of credit could help a poor family improve, other people adopted the practice in their own program. In the early 1990s, *ACCIÓN* collaborated with a group of business leaders in La Paz, Bolivia, to establish the first for-profit, commercial bank dedicated to microfinance services for the poor, named Banco Sol. While *ACCIÓN*'s efforts were limited to Latin America until recently, it eventually began to expand—launching start-up offices in the U.S., Africa, and on to India and beyond.

Another pioneer was the Grameen Bank of Bangladesh, a huge Muslim nation; the bank is based in the capital city, Dhaka. It was the world's first microcredit organization to achieve major growth and substantial scale. It was founded in 1976 by Professor Muhammad Yunus, a decades-long partner of mine who is a U.S.-trained economist. He established the Grameen Bank by creating a peer-lending structure in which five to six women each received individual loans and jointly guaranteed all the loans in their group. Weekly payments were small and easy to understand, and all loans were for just one year. This group structure fostered self-esteem as well as and a culture of mutual accountability that supported high loan repayment rates, high savings rates, and low levels of business failure. Today it has more than 8 million clients, 97 percent of them women.

The third MSO, called FINCA International (Foundation for International Community Assistance), did not become a major organization in the emerging microcredit field until 1990. But the founder, my colleague Dr. John Hatch, was a key player in the efforts to generate interest and public attention for the MSO field, beginning in 1983. Indeed, without any knowledge of the Grameen Bank in far-off Bangladesh, or of the microcredit experiments by *ACCIÓN* in Latin America, Hatch invented a type of solidarity group that he called *Village Banking*. FINCA created a number of start-up programs over the next few years, giving workshops in which its Village Banking model and methodology were taught. The model was implemented in those early years in several Latin American locales, but more recently has expanded to Africa and the former USSR. Today it has some 600,000 clients collaborating in 24,000 village bank groups of mostly poor women living in 28 nations.

Microcredit has become perhaps the most innovative development tool to globally empower millions of poor families in recent years. It is impressive for several reasons. It defies the traditional assumptions that solutions are best invented in industrialized nations and that top-down development is required because national political leaders' support is essential for success. Instead, microentrepreneurship essentially turns traditional borrowing and finance for families upside down. Perhaps related are the words of Jesus when he declared that *"So the last will be first, and the first will be last"* (Matthew 20:16).

MSO Growth and Its Acceleration

From its humble, experimental beginnings, microcredit has grown into an innovative development strategy involving millions of poor women and a lesser number of men who are accessing the services of literally thousands of global microfinance institutions. These MSOs come in various forms. Most operate as microcredit practitioners, acquiring funds and providing microentrepreneurial support services. Some are commercial banks like Mibanco in Peru. These are specialized, for-profit banks set up to provide financial services to impoverished families. Many credit unions are also starting to participate in the movement as a different breed of MSOs.

As microentrepreneurship has been increasingly recognized for its contribution to poverty alleviation, many government and multilateral organizations (such as USAID, the World Bank, and the United Nations) have become involved. Likewise, a number of important microentrepreneurial industry research and policy organizations have begun helping to further the impacts. These MSOs include the Consultative Group to Help the Poorest (CGAP) and the Small Enterprise Education and Promotion Network (SEEP).

In 1997, microentrepreneurship began to accelerate through the establishment of an annual world Microcredit Summit that established the goal of extending microentrepreneurship to the planet's poorest families, hoping to impact a hundred million people. It has been reported that as many as 3,164 MFIs (microfinance institutions, another term for MSOs) had reached 92 million clients with microloans, benefiting more than 333 million individuals in poor families. The microcredit campaign has grown 776 percent since its inception in 1997, averaging a bit more than 36 percent annual growth. The world summit has continually expanded its outreach further over the years. In 2005, the UN even declared 2005 as the "International Year of Microcredit," and the movement has continued to grow.

U.S. Microcredit

MSO strategies emerged in America during the mid-1980s in response to the desires of low-income people—often women, minorities, and persons with disabilities—who wanted to achieve the American dream of self-employment. In a curious historical twist of the usual pattern in which U.S. aid organizations go abroad to advise countries in the developing world on how to improve their economies through "modern" innovations, in the case of microfinance, it was just the opposite. MSOs from poor nations came to North America to share their expertise on how the peer-lending approach to microentrepreneurship could be applied in the states, as well as in Canada (Nelson, 1994). Grameen and two other successful Bangladeshi MFIs led the discussions.

As the western organizations learned from Asian practitioners, innovations followed, in spite of the general opinion that so-called industrialized societies would never embrace group borrowing techniques. Over time, some applications of approaches in the developing world have succeeded in the U.S. Microentrepreneurship has helped people transform their family lives and also improved the economic well-being of their communities. The field has grown rapidly and now exceeds hundreds of programs operating in virtually all states and the District of Columbia.

Grameen America Case

One of the most significant U.S. examples of microcredit has been the establishing of Grameen America in 2008 to help increase women's financial mobility through its proven approach of engaging with and lending directly to women entrepreneurs. The Nobel Peace Prize Laureate Dr. Muhammad Yunus invited me to join his initial board of advisers in designing and rolling out its work. Since then, the organization has invested over $2.1 billion in more than 142,000 low-income women entrepreneurs and is positioned to reach more than half a million women by 2030. Grameen America uses its "social capital" model with 24 branches in 19 U.S. cities, including New York City where it started, as well as in Chicago, Los Angeles, Houston, and other cities. Its work is unmatched in terms of its national scale, financial sustainability, and mentoring relationships with its members (Grameen America, 2022).

Grameen America provides small loans to women living in poverty so they can invest in starting or expanding a small business. The program model is based on Yunus's theory that investment in a small enterprise enables women to generate income to pay back their microloan as well as to grow their business, and eventually to increase their income and improve the material well-being of their households. The model is based on the Grameen Bank program first launched in Bangladesh in the late 1970s with the aim of improving the lives of the rural poor. The original Grameen Bank model has since spread throughout the nonindustrialized world. When Grameen America was established in New York City, it hired Bangladeshi staff from its Asia operation and began rolling out the same lending model as the original program. Consistent with Grameen America's mission to empower women, the organization gives loans only to women entrepreneurs in the United States.

It uses a group lending model that requires potential borrowers to form a loan group of five women who live near and know each other before they are eligible to apply for loans. After forming such groups, women participate in five days of mandatory training. As can be imagined, many poor people in the U.S. don't well understand a lot about finances, banks, lending, interest or principal on loans, and more technical matters. So, the process of educating them to be successful occurs. It's called Continuous Group Training (CGT), during which they learn about the terms and conditions of the Grameen America loan, the rules of the program, and their responsibilities as borrowers. After the training is completed, the five-member loan groups are officially enrolled in the program. Each member of an approved group then receives her first loan, which is typically between $500 and $1,500, and with an interest rate of 15 to 18 percent. The average term of a Grameen America loan is some 6 months, or half a year. In recent years, because so many women have successfully started growing their microenterprises so well, the initial loan amount currently may start as high as $2,000, or quadruple the original $500 microloan.

Five or six loan groups come together to form loan centers, known as village banks in Bangladesh and most of the Third World. They usually consist of some 20 to 30 women, and the larger groups meet weekly,,often at the home or business of one of the borrowers, to make their loan payments. In other words, the loans are repaid gradually, in small amounts, that makes women borrowers' success greater than trying to pay the entire amount after a six-month period. Each woman in a loan group receives her own loan and is responsible for paying it back. Grameen America reports loan payments to several major U.S. credit reporting agencies to help borrowers establish credit histories. For a single woman to be able to receive a second, greater loan, all group members of her small group must be current on their payments. This process within each small group is called using "Social Collateral" as an effective way of encouraging the payback of one's borrowing. In this way, group vetting and group social pressure, as opposed to traditional loan underwriting, are used to ensure repayment. With time and growing business success, subsequent loans may become larger. Qualifying for a larger amount is designed to help members expand their businesses even further.

Grameen America continues to have strong impacts in blessing the lives of impoverished women in the United States. While it initially focused on single females, especially immigrants and refugees from around the globe, it has a new priority today. In 2021 it announced a significant new commitment to accelerate its goal of racial equity by raising and investing over $1.3 billion for microenterprise loans to more than 80,000 Black women throughout the next decade. It's a magnificent new initiative that will help reduce America's racial disparity (Philanthropy News Digest, 2021*).*

Microcredit Methodologies in the USA

In the process of such initiatives, U.S. microcredit has gained the attention of local, state, and even national legislators of both political parties. It has captured the interests of economic development, human services, and other professionals. The enactment of welfare reform laws in the U.S. in 1996, with their time limits and work requirements, has increased the urgency of creating new economic opportunities for low-income people.

Currently, a microenterprise in the American economy is usually defined as a business with five or fewer employees that is small enough to require initial capital of $35,000 or less. Most microenterprises are sole proprietorships, which create employment for the owner and, often, other family members as well. However, some microenterprises eventually grow into larger businesses that eventually employ more people.

There are several reasons why I and others view the rise of microentrepreneurship within the U.S. context as both viable and desirable:

- Self-employment allows people in low-wage regular jobs to supplement their income.
- Microcredit enables the entrepreneurial spirit to flourish among society's poorest families and thus promotes their development (Nelson, 1994).
- Structural unemployment, such as plant closings and corporate downsizing, has dislocated many workers, leading many to create their own jobs (Woodworth, 2021).
- Banks in the U.S. find it difficult to make profitable microenterprise loans under $35,000, most of which are not 100 percent collateralized. Reasons for this include the cost of conducting due diligence on loan applications, high transaction costs on loans, and compliance with "safety and soundness" issues of federal and state regulators.
- Women are only half as likely to receive a loan to launch their small business, compared to males, making their prospects more difficult (Hecht, 2021).
- For a low-income person, self-employment offers opportunities to use one's talents and find personal fulfillment. These opportunities may be difficult to find through low-wage employment (Nelson, 2000).
- Self-employment offers women the flexibility to balance work and family responsibilities through either part-time or home-based microenterprises, or sometimes both.
- Immigrants and refugees frequently lack the certifications, licenses, or English proficiency needed to obtain professional jobs for which they may actually qualify. Creating a

self-employment business related to professional training received in their native country is often preferable to taking a low-wage job in another field.

Thus, MSOs provide business development services to people who are currently operating a microenterprise or are interested in starting one. The programs are supported by a wide variety of nonprofit organizations. They range from those for whom microcredit work is their primary activity, to those whose programs include various other employment, economic development, and antipoverty strategies. Such organizations include community development corporations, loan funds, community action agencies, women's business centers, community development financial institutions, small business development centers, and many others. MSOs provide one or more of the following services:

Business Training and/or Technical Assistance: These programs help participants build the skills needed to plan, market, and manage their microbusinesses. The training and technical assistance usually results in the participants' developing their ideas into feasible enterprises through writing formal business plans. In addition to helping individuals learn to research the market, conduct financial analyses, and plan marketing strategies, the assistance addresses personal development issues such as family budgeting, control of personal finances, and appropriate managerial behavior.

Access to Credit: MSOs help participants obtain access to funding for their businesses. Many operate in-house lending programs. Others link participants with loans from collaborating banks, public loan funds, or other financing sources with which they have formal relationships. Most loans are made to individual business owners, while some programs use a peer-lending model. This assistance to accessing credit is crucial because federal and state banking regulations, along with underwriting criteria, often prevent commercial banks from making loans to poor families.

Ongoing Business Assistance: Many MSOs provide continuing consultations to microentrepreneurs after they start or expand their family firms. This assistance addresses issues that the businesses face as they move through each stage of development, as well as specific difficulties that they encounter.

Access to Markets: MSO assistance helps participants find markets that will increase sales and profitability. They often provide training in marketing and sales concepts. They may also encourage clients to participate in trade shows, develop catalogs of their products, and advertise their businesses on the Internet. Some programs have started incubators for certain types of firms, such as technology or food businesses. Incubators provide business owners with office space to operate their firms, as well as with support services, such as secretaries, telephones, computers, fax machines, and so on.

Asset Development/Economic Literacy: MSOs help clients increase their understanding of banking and savings principles. Some even offer participants the option to open Individual Development Accounts (IDAs)—savings accounts that low-income households can use for certain purposes, such as to purchase a home or start a business. These accounts are matched—usually $1 to $3 for every dollar saved—with funds from either private or government sources.

Microentrepreneurs may choose to form one of a wide range of businesses—usually ones that fit their interests and abilities. Common types of microenterprises are: repair services, cleaning services, specialty foods, jewelry, arts and crafts, gifts, clothing and textiles, computer technology, child care, and environmental products and services. While microentrepreneurship is expanding throughout the United States, it is not a simple process, nor is it easy to implement (Bhatt and Tang, 2001). Next, I will highlight some of the challenges and outcomes of several MSOs that support such small U.S. firms, by examining several cases of microentrepreneurship.

Micro-Business USA

Another American MSO that provides microcredit is based in the Miami area of south Florida. It was first established over a decade ago by my colleague Kathleen Gordon as a branch of an enterprise called Working Capital. Micro-Business USA (MB-USA, 2006) has grown gradually ever since and has come to serve multiple families in three languages: Creole, Spanish, and English. Its clients include low-income whites, African Americans, large populations especially from the Dominican Republic and Cuba, as well as Haitian and other Caribbean refugees.

From Gordon's presentations at my university, speeches to students in my courses, and personal conversations, the following picture about MB-USA emerges (Gordon, 2005). It provides microloans only to U.S. citizens or to permanent residents with low incomes. Most are self-employed, but a few also fill other jobs in the formal economy, so their microenterprise becomes a second income. The MSO's mission is to support financial self-sufficiency for low-income families. It is established as a not-for-profit corporation with the state of Florida, and is qualified as a 501(c)(3) tax-exempt firm with the I.R.S. This enables donors to claim a charitable tax deduction on their federal filings for moneys given to support microentrepreneurship in Florida.

MB-USA's headquarters is in Miami and it has additional offices in North Miami, Broward County, Fort Lauderdale, and St. Petersburg. It has provided training in peer-group-lending processes to some 6,000 individuals, given out more than 2,500 loans to microentrepreneurs, and achieved a rate of repayment in excess of 95 percent. Poor individuals begin the MB-USA program with 12 hours of training and a $500 microloan. Little by little, they build a credit history in the ensuing weeks and months as the loan is paid on time, until it is fully repaid. Clients also continue to participate in the MSO's microentrepreneurial training to learn marketing and sales, leadership, accounting, and other critical dimensions of entrepreneurship.

Many such firms are often part-time projects that generate income. Recipients develop their talents and skills, apply ideas, and enjoy the experience of nurturing their own microenterprises. They typically help overcome self-doubt and economic hardships, and begin to feel greater self-worth, according to Kathleen Gordon.

Microbusiness Mentors (Mentores para los Microempresarios)

One offshoot of Micro Business USA is that it has inspired other groups to design and implement community-based microentrepreneurship programs like the one my students and I established for poor families in our university town of Provo, Utah. With advice from Kathleen Gordon, who freely shared materials and her experience, in 2003 we began to design an MSO as a business school laboratory for service learning and outreach, as noted in this chapter's beginning, the vignette about Susana.

For my social entrepreneurship course, a team of my graduate students worked with others across campus to conduct a needs assessment of Provo's inner-city Latino community. What we found were a number of problems facing residents in that area, in contrast to other neighborhoods: median family annual incomes under $20,000, higher violent crime rates, lower high school grade-point averages, more public-assisted housing subsidies, official poverty rates of 52 to 84 percent in various sectors, family English mostly as a Second Language (ESOL) of 28 to 51 percent in that area's elementary schools, and student mobility that ranged between 50 and 64 percent (Dutton, 2002; Woodworth, 2002).

At the same time, we noted other challenges and opportunities. One key demographic revealed that the Hispanic influx to the region was huge: Immigrants had grown from approximately 8,000 in 1990 to over 26,000 a decade later. In our surveys of inner-city Latino families, we learned that 48 percent reported having zero savings and 71 percent had annual incomes of under $30,000. When we inquired about their potential interest in becoming self-employed, 81 percent answered in the affirmative. Likewise, 78 percent reported they would be interested in receiving business training. Yet surprisingly, only 55 percent expressed interest in obtaining a loan (Densley, 2003; Woodworth, 2003). Thus, we began to believe that the delivery of business skills might best be our first priority.

Out of all the above data, along with input from focus groups of Latinos and many interviews with city officials, social service agencies like Community Action, United Way, and others, we created MicroBusiness Mentors as an MSO. We initially designed a four-pillar system for operating its program:

- Training in entrepreneurial skills
- Group support as members help each other by sharing their efforts, difficulties, and best practices
- Mentoring as BYU student volunteers give of their time and business skills to help clients progress after getting their microloans
- The loans themselves, consisting of whatever amount of funding the NGO gave them to launch or grow tiny enterprises

Briefly put, from early surveys, training seemed to be of interest to 78 percent of Latino adults. So, we eventually designed eight modules, one to be taught each week for eight weeks. Interested parties would learn what microentrepreneurship is, how it works, what concepts such as principal and interest are, as well as covering other relevant topics: simple accounting and bookkeeping, sales and marketing, customer service, productivity, human resources, team-building, business English, and so forth. In addition, we decided that as learning grows and application occurs through the use of business cases, trainers would begin to help the participants design their own microenterprise business plan.

During these weeks, would-be microentrepreneurs learn about each other, work on training cases as a team, and share ideas and experiences. This system of mutual support builds solidarity and trust. If group members go on to complete the eight sessions of training and qualify for $500 loans, a graduation ceremony is held and certificates of completion are given, as well as the loans. Each member of the group signs a commitment to repay each other's loans, in addition to one's own, with the group thereby acting as social collateral. This technique is sometimes referred to as "peer-lending" or "solidarity group loans." Group commitment and peer pressure serve to minimize borrower default rates. Also, they teach responsibility and the importance of repayment on time and in full for the amount due.

MicroBusiness Mentors volunteers offering microcredit to the first clients
of our MPA class. Volunteers provided training and microloans to refugees
and immigrants in their Utah community. Each received $500 to establish
their own start-up for moving toward economic self-reliance.

After graduating and obtaining their first loans, our microentrepreneurs next turn to launching their tiny businesses, and each is assigned a volunteer mentor who agrees to coach them at least monthly throughout the next year. These mentors are older, experienced individuals who have enjoyed considerable business success, know how to operate within the realities of the U.S. business environment, and are fluent in Spanish language skills.

As of 2021, Mentors for Microentrepreneurs seems to still be succeeding with genuine impacts. Thousands of would-be microentrepreneurs have received orientation or training. Those who completed the training have received loans, started microenterprises, and, at least to date, a remarkable 98 percent of them have paid back their microcredit debts. Eventually, this MSO evolved beyond being a voluntary MPA class project to becoming a legally registered 501(c)(3) nonprofit so that it can expand its services and loan capital to greater numbers of poor families. We hope to eventually have the capability and resources to assist many more thousands of impoverished Hispanic families in our community so they can progress from the "underground" or "black market" economy to the point that they may qualify for larger-scale loans from regular banks in the formal U.S. economy.

But does this approach to alleviating poverty work beyond the cases cited above? I turn next to several more-systematic studies that suggest some answers.

Research on U.S. Microentrepreneurship

While numerous published articles have studied MSOs in the developing world (formerly, and patronizingly, called the "Third World"), U.S. research is limited. However, the following paragraphs synthesize nine major benefits and impacts from such efforts, revealing significant benefits for U.S. society. While it is often said that "Big is better" when it comes to business and life, I prefer the words of the British social innovator E. F. Schumacher (1973): *"Small is beautiful."*

1. Overall, the national numbers about microcredit and associated results are quite impressive. Small microbusinesses represent more than 92 percent of all U.S. enterprises. That includes some 28 million direct jobs, along with an additional 15 million indirect or induced jobs. These firms are defined as having five or fewer workers, including the owner, yet they make up 31 percent of the entire private sector, generating almost $5 trillion annually in economic impacts. At the same time, they collectively contribute some $135 billion to city, state, and federal budgets to keep America running (Association for Enterprise Opportunity, 2013).

2. Microentrepreneurship supplements family income. Research shows that clients of just one organization in the northeast, called Working Capital, a Massachusetts MSO, each enjoyed more than $5,000 in additional income annually—a considerable figure for many poor families (Ashe, 2000).

3. Microentrepreneurship increases family assets. An Aspen Institute study (Clark and Kays, 1999) found that average American household assets over five years grew by $13,623 among all study respondents. In contrast, a low-income subgroup of microentrepreneurs experienced a significantly higher increase in assets, averaging $15,909 during the same period.

4. Microentrepreneurial efforts pare down one's reliance on government welfare. Two studies, one by the Self-Employment Investment Demonstration (SEID) project (Raheim and Alter, 1995), and the other, the Aspen Institute (Clark and Kays, 1999), found that many welfare recipients who participated in microenterprise development programs left federal government Aid to Families with Dependent Children (AFDC), as well as left food stamps programs. In the Aspen Institute's study, 61 percent of the low-income group stopped receiving AFDC. In the SEID study, 43 percent were not receiving food stamps, and 52 percent of the study participants no longer received AFDC benefits.

5. Even in tough times such as the 2008–2009 Great Recession, or the disastrous economic impacts of COVID-19 in the U.S. in the early 2020s, microcredit services helped many families receive support for their microbusinesses in underserved communities (Brookings Institution, 2020).

6. Obtaining microcredit through group lending ensures greater entrepreneurial survival rates, including sales and profits, than in typical individual-based small businesses (Barsky, 2000).

7. MSO participants often serve as positive role models for their children as well as for the larger community. Many successful microentrepreneurs go on to become mentors and advisers to others who seek to become self-employed (Anthony, 1996).

8. Families and individuals in the MSO programs of *ACCIÓN* report more self-respect, dignity, and independence through group lending processes (Himes and Servon, 1998).

9. Explosive growth on MSO efforts has been reported across the U.S., including huge successes in Southern California (Microenterprise Collaborative, 2020), (Microenterprise Assistance Program of Nebraska, 2021), and so forth. The programs include city, county, and state programs; university efforts; federal government aid in agricultural regions (Rural Microentrepreneur Assistance Program, 2021); and many nonprofit programs from coast to coast, such as Maryland Capital Enterprises on the East Coast (2020).

MSOs as Tools for Bottom of-the-Pyramid Individuals

Over the past several decades, much to-do has been made in the press about providing business services and products to the poor, meaning those at the Bottom-of-the-Pyramid, also called Base-of-the-Pyramid (BOP). Stuart Hart, in 2005, and C. K. Prahalad, in 2004, have produced best-sellers about this phenomenon. The rise of American MSOs is a movement for addressing this new opportunity by focusing on underserved families who have had difficulty accessing business development services of credit through traditional institutions. The question is, can businesses serve the "unbankable?" The answer seems to be in the affirmative, as they channel their services toward a specific target population of the poor, such as women, members of minority communities, people with low incomes, immigrants, refugees, and welfare recipients.

A core assumption is that by supporting adult individuals in starting or expanding an income-generating enterprise, those examples may motivate their children later. MSOs can help them to increase their income, assets, and net worth. As a result, their reliance on welfare may be reduced, enabling them to move out of poverty. Self-employment activities can also result in individuals' increased self-esteem, improved quality of life, and greater involvement in their own communities. Such programs also benefit one's home town. They help to revitalize downtown areas, enhance regional economies in rural areas, and may lead to additional results for good.

A question often raised is how exactly are MSOs in the United States capitalized. Early in the movement, during the 1980s, funding for microentrepreneurship mostly came from foundations. Over time, however, existing agencies whose work focused on poverty alleviation, and who historically had relied on public funding, found that some of the public dollars available to them could support these efforts. By the early 1990s, microentrepreneurship was recognized as a distinct field, and supporting legislation and appropriations began to be passed by Congress. Today the federal government channels money through such avenues as the Small Business Administration (SBA) Microloan Fund, while other agencies such as the departments of Agriculture and of Housing and Urban Development also offer funding. In the latest fiscal year of federal funding for 2006, Congress authorized $12.7 million for SBA loans, along with $13 million in technical assistance for supporting microentrepreneurship. Also, corporations such as American Express and Levi Strauss provide philanthropic grants to MSOs, as do nonprofits such as the United Way. In addition, churches and individuals are becoming more motivated to help fund such efforts to empower families.

As to the scope of today's MSO programs, the size varies considerably, as do the types of agencies that host them, and also the extent to which they identify with the field. This makes hard data nearly impossible to ascertain. Various observers estimate there are between 500 and 700 formal MSO nonprofit programs sponsoring tiny businesses in America.

It is safe to conclude that microentrepreneurship is becoming institutionalized in America. It is increasingly supported by the business community. Members of both political parties have sponsored legislation and appropriations with the objective of strengthening the family through countering poverty.

Christian interfaith leaders have worked to combat poverty by addressing many problems across the United States. These include feeding poor children, offering affordable healthcare to families, and providing microcredit, among other strategies implemented by churches to help create more self-reliant families.

Interfaith leaders in Salt Lake City pressing their state government officials to develop additional initiatives that will fund new affordable housing programs.

Criticisms of Microentrepreneurship

While the growth of MSOs has been dramatic, some problems have also arisen. Several of the early organizational players have shut their doors. Symptoms of problems vary—leveling off of growth, board and staff infighting, inability to raise more grant money, and aggressive marketing by new MSOs entering the movement, among other factors. In certain instances, MSO managers belatedly realized that domestic applications of microentrepreneurship were more complex than global ones, necessitated greater sophistication, and so forth. For instance, FINCA spent three years and considerable money seeking to build a U.S. strategy, but finally abandoned the idea and refocused on its more successful global outreach. One notable case of MSO dissolution was the Coalition for Women's Economic Development (CWED) in Los Angeles, one of the seven core programs in the Self-Employment Learning Project (Huemann and Wiley, 1999). After some problematic years, CWED completely disintegrated.

Mainstream media sources also have doubts about microentrepreneurship. For instance, in 2001 the *Wall Street Journal* published one of the most widespread attacks on the movement. Its authors alleged that one specific MSO—Grameen Bank—suffered from loan repayment problems and lateness and/or nonpayment, and that its accounting processes hid financial irregularities (Pearl and Phillips, 2001). The world's largest MSO defended itself in the press by pointing out that it adheres 100 percent to Bangladesh's corporate accounting practices, and stressed out that the nation's Central Bank officials constantly audit its books, resulting in two decades without a single irregularity (Yunus, 2001). In fact, Grameen had continually published its financial information every month to anyone interested, making it one of the most transparent banks in the world.

With respect to late payments and nonpayment of some loans, Grameen reported that, indeed, it did suffer a onetime hit, but it was due to the devastating 1998 floods that inundated half of Bangladesh, killing thousands, destroying microenterprises, and leaving millions of homes under water for nearly three months. As a socially conscious MSO, Grameen then forgave thousands of microloans and wrote them off as an expense. Repayment rates had indeed dropped to approximately 90 percent, but rebounded within a year and were again operating at 99 percent (Yunus, 2001).

While the *Journal* debate has subsided, there are other skeptics and their criticisms. Two of the issues raised are the following oft-repeated assertions: tiny amounts of microcredit are too small to generate significant new jobs and lift the poor out of poverty; and there are many more youth and young adults unemployed globally; and microentrepreneurship is simply not sufficient to solve this crisis.

My frequent response to such critiques is the observation that microentrepreneurship is not a silver bullet with which to solve all problems. It is but one tool, albeit a radically different idea, for reducing poverty in many sectors of society. To complaints from critics who argue that small microentrepreneurship is insignificant in generating new jobs, I would agree to an extent, depending on what is meant by "insignificant." At one level, I argue that helping even just a few people is a good thing. Maybe empowering even only one individual is worth doing, to start to improve the world. But the impact problem of numbers is due to the lack of capital, not to the methodology. In the future, as formal financial markets further embrace this movement, I predict that we will see many more significant impacts on various national economies. For instance, in Bangladesh, where millions have received microloans, approximately a third of recipients have moved above the official poverty line (Yunus, 2000). I am told that similar impacts have occurred with Banco Sol clients in Bolivia and clients of Mibanco in Peru. As MSO access to larger amounts of capital becomes easier, more families will surely rise above poverty, including the U.S. poor.

With respect to the criticism that new employment creation is not keeping up with the demand, especially regarding worldwide youth, I concur. Yet the size of the problem is truly immense. So should we abandon traditional capitalist companies because they do not provide all the jobs that society needs? The International Labor Organization (ILO) estimates that there are some 200 million unemployed people globally, and nearly half are the ages of late teens and early adults. Even worse, the proportion has greatly accelerated in just the past decade, making the future even more bleak (ILO, 2004). So, I would suggest that MSOs are more needed now than ever. Microentrepreneurs, more so than huge multinational corporations, will help answer this challenge. Large companies have been downsizing for a decade in much of the world, and those jobs will not return. This is likely to become a growing crisis facing the U.S. economy, as well. One of the most viable solutions is clearly going to be microentrepreneurship. However, to meet the demand, MSOs must turn their attention to this growing new, younger target population—a group that typically has been overlooked. Doing this will require new strategies, youth-centered training programs, and other innovations in order to strengthen the next generation of microentrepreneurs.

So What?

Several questions arise from this chapter, including practical business and social policy questions, as well as religious issues. What is its relevance regarding the MSO movement? In practical terms, what are its implications for current best-business practices? From a Christian perspective, *what would Jesus do (WWJD)?* Clearly there are several important points to be emphasized.

From an economic perspective, one point is that these findings make the case for using business tools to combat social ills and economic deprivation. Welfare and other traditional government programs have not, and evidently never will, solve the problems of society's have-nots. Simply giving away money, food, and grants tends merely to generate unintended results, such as dependency. What is needed instead is *investing* in the poor, by using grassroots capitalism to enable such individuals to lift themselves through entrepreneurial tools and methods. Thus, there needs to be a shift from dependency to dignity. Unfortunately, we could give away all the financial resources the U.S. possesses, yet it would still be insufficient. Nor would its impacts last. Rather, the better practice is the facilitating of economic self-reliance within poor communities, so they learn how to gain control of their own futures.

Another point is that BOP and similar MSO interventions are beginning to accelerate the growth of microentrepreneurial phenomena. For instance, huge firms like Deutsche Bank and MasterCard are channeling millions of dollars to empower the poor. Other firms ought to join in the cause. In recent years, I have consulted with a number of midsized firms that are now giving microlending capital to MSOs in their local communities. Equally important, the firms' CEOs and other top executives are donating their time and expertise to conduct a group training session, for example, or to mentor a single microentrepreneur.

Executives who do this report a real sense of personal fulfillment. They demonstrate that a manager can make a personal and professional difference in someone's life. They show that business leaders can enlarge their sphere of leadership and stewardship beyond their firms, with outside stakeholders, including the poorest individuals in society. By doing so, these socially responsible corporations are enjoying increased credibility, learning that they can not only do well financially, but do good, also.

With respect to Christian values and what Jesus's perspective could be, I will briefly reference his life and teachings. We can first remember that in some ways, the Savior himself was a microentrepreneur. He worked as a humble carpenter in his earthly father's tiny microenterprise in Nazareth, a village in the Galilee. I'm pretty sure they never applied nor received a microloan to grow their modest enterprise, especially since that area was considered as a kind of bucolic backwater community where people eked out a hardscrabble existence. My guess is that the boy Jesus served as an apprentice, as was the case with most boys in his day who followed in a parent's footsteps or trade. There were no entrepreneurial training programs, no small-lending services, no other kinds of support. I'm sure there were challenges of hunger, disease, conflict, worries about weather conditions, access to drinking water for people and animals, and the problems of raising crops in such a hot, dusty region. Of course, the entire region known as Palestine suffered under the oppression of a foreign empire—Rome—that ruled with an iron fist.

Thus, I argue that today, in modern American society, we should reach out to our neighbors, as well as to strangers who may be jobless, lack incomes, and worry about their kids' lack of education and even of regular meals. Perhaps we all can practice our faith by reaching out to offer economic assistance. We should reach out even beyond our friends and family to help the stranger, the homeless, the once-incarcerated, and those sad figures trying to make a home on our community streets. Does our faith impel us to act?

Next Steps

Of course, there are numerous other issues regarding microentrepreneurship that I could address were it not for the constraints of space for this chapter. Among them are my personal concerns about MSO *mission drift*—that is, the tendency of U.S. microentrepreneurial services to flow to the upper-level segments of the poor rather than to those truly at the bottom. This phenomenon tends to occur because very poor individuals are perceived as higher risks, less educated, and therefore not really likely to be able to repay their loans on time and in full.

Still, I argue that considerable effort should be made to focus on members of America's most vulnerable population and that by designing effective strategies to help them they can, and will, be responsible clients. To what extent this is possible within the current U.S. economic context is clearly a matter of debate, owing at least, in part, to the cold reality that serving the poorest microentrepreneurs with tiny loans is not just risky, but also more expensive.

Future research, of course, needs to be done. But I think the data will bear out this assertion that the poor *can* become bankable. Better studies are badly needed on viable MSO tools for alleviating U.S. poverty. Which methods are indeed best? How may greater amounts of capital ramp up this movement within our own country? What works, and why? What succeeds the least, and which factors tend to correlate with difficulties? How might this be changed?

In addition, I would suggest that U.S. microentrepreneurship needs to move beyond government support and private donations. To build MSO strategies in the future will necessitate not only that they reach out to the poor, but that they become sustainable for the long run. Depending on government subsidies, fundraising campaigns and annual donor requests will not fully do the job. Market forces must come into play. Nor will simply reaching a break-even point be sufficient. Over time, MSOs in the U.S. may need to be transformed into institutions of the capital markets, in which they no longer operate as mere nonprofit foundations, but become morphed into for-profit companies working in parallel with the traditional banking sector.

Conclusion

All things considered, my sense is that microentrepreneurship has made genuine inroads for alleviating poverty in America. Whether the growing population of microentrepreneurs consists of either 10 or 50 million, it amounts to an economic self-reliance strategy that is here to stay. It is based on the premise of a business model, not an offering of welfare. If we envision economic development as a ladder, what we have had historically is rungs toward the top that served the upper-middle classes and elites—those who held decent jobs (or even great jobs), who had sufficient (or huge) wealth, or who worked for corporations, in government, or at the financial zenith of Wall Street. Such persons have enjoyed great access to banks and other upper-echelon financial services, reiterating the old adage that it takes money to borrow money.

In contrast, at the very bottom of the economic ladder are the poorest—the disabled, the unemployed, the immigrants. They have subsisted on the lower rungs through government antipoverty support tools such as job services, food stamps, AFDC, and other programs. Yet these tools have not been enough to help many of the poor climb up. Instead, many have stayed at the bottom—stagnant, dependent, unable to progress.

U.S. microentrepreneurship adds several new rungs to the ladder, above those of welfare, but still below the rungs of the upper and middle classes. It can be a facilitator for improving many people's quality of life. What is different, however, is that microentrepreneurship empowers the capital investment of poor people by generating microenterprise. As we have seen throughout this chapter, whether in Grameen America, south Florida, and the Hispanic West, microenterprise generates a sense of ownership and hope. Bit by bit, along with entrepreneurial training and consulting, in addition to a microloan, today's impoverished individual may rise beyond mere survival toward a sense of accountability tomorrow, and eventually may gain the capacity of controlling and improving one's own economic future. This is the promise of effective MSO sustainable services for poor American microentrepreneurs today.

References

Anthony, D. L. (1996). *Working: A Report on the Impact of the Working Capital Programs.* Mt. Auburn Associates, 1996.

Ashe, J. (2000). "Microfinance in the United States: The Working Capital Experience—Ten Years of Leading and Learning." *Journal of Microfinance,* vol. 2, no. 2, 2000, pp. 22–60.

Barsky, J. S. (2000). *Getting It Together: Working Capital's Group Model and Its Effects on Microentrepreneurs, Their Businesses, and Their Communities.* Working Capital, 2000.

Bhatt, N., and Shui-Yan Tang. (2001). "Making Microcredit Work in the United States: Social, Financial, and Administrative Dimensions," Economic Development Quarterly, vol. 15, no. 3, pp. 229–41.

Brookings Institution. Accessed October 11, 2021. https://www.brookings.edu/wp-content/uploads/2020/07/BrookingsMetro_RecoveryWatchEssays_Detroit-Small-Business_FINAL.pdf.

Clark, P., and A. Kays. (1999). *Microenterprise and the Poor.* Aspen Institute.

Densley, S. (2003). Provo/Orem [Utah] Chamber of Commerce data.

Dutton, M. (2002). Community Action Agency Statistical Report (unpublished). Provo, Utah.

Economist, The. (2006). "The Rich, The Poor, and the Growing Gap Between Them." Special Report: Inequality and the American Dream, June 17, pp. 28–30.

Edgecomb, E., and J. Klein. (2005). *Opening Opportunities, Building Ownership: Fulfilling the Promise of Microenterprise in the United States.* Aspen Institute.

Gordon, K. Presentations, speeches, and conversations with author W. Woodworth at the Marriott School of Business, Brigham Young University, Provo, Utah. Discussions between 1997 and 2005.

Grameen America. (2002). Accessed January 6, 2022. https://www.grameenamerica.org/.

Hart, S. L. (2005). *Capitalism at the Crossroads: The Unlimited Opportunities in Solving the World's Most Difficult Problems.* Wharton School Publishing.

Hecht, J. (2021). "State of Small Business Lending: Spotlight on Women Entrepreneurs." https://www.fundera.com/blog/the-state-of-online-small-business-lending-q2-2016, February 2.

Himes, C., and L. J. Servon. (1998). *Measuring Client Success: An Evaluation of ACCIÓN 's Impact on Microenterprises in the United States.* U.S. Issues Series, Document #2. ACCIÓN International.

Huemann, E., and J. Wiley. (1999). *The Challenge of Microenterprise: The CWED Story.* National Economic Development & Law Center.

ILO. (2004). *Global Unemployment Trends for Youth 2004.* International Labour Office. August 12.

Maryland Capital Enterprises. (2020). Accessed October 9, 2021. https://marylandcapital.org/services/business-loans/..

MB-USA. (2006). Micro-Business USA. Accessed May 28, 2006. www.microbusinessusa.org/programs.htm.

Microenterprise Assistance Program, State of Nebraska. (2021). Accessed November 11, 2021. https://opportunity.nebraska.gov/program/microenterprise-assistance-program/.

Microenterprise Collaborative. (2020). Report for 2020. Accessed October 12, 2021. https://microbizinsocal.org/wp-content/uploads/2021/03/2021-Microenterprise-Collaborative-Impact-Report-APPROVED.pdf.

Nelson, C. (1994). *Going Forward: The Peer Group Lending Exchange*. Calmeadow, November 2–4.

Nelson, C. (ed.). (2000). "Microenterprise Fact Sheet Series-Issue 1." Microenterprise Development in the United States: An Overview. Microenterprise Fund for Innovation, Effectiveness, Learning and Dissemination (FIELD) at The Aspen Institute, and the Association for Enterprise Opportunity (AEO).

PBS. (2000). "To Our Credit: Bootstrap Banking in America." Video documentary on U.S. cases of microcredit. Accessed April 26, 2014. www.pbs.org/tourcredit/stories_tmo.htm.

Pearl, D., and M. M. Phillips. (2001). "Grameen Bank, Which Pioneered Loans for the Poor, Has Hit a Repayment Snag." *Wall Street Journal,* November 27.

Philanthropy News Digest. (2021). "Grameen America Launches Black Women Entrepreneurs Initiative." https://philanthropynewsdigest.org/news/grameen-america-launches-black-women-entrepreneurs-initiative. May 14.

Prahalad, C. K. (2004). *The Fortune at the Bottom of the Pyramid: Eradicating Poverty through Profits*. Wharton School Publishing.

Raheim, S., and C. F. Alter. (1995). "Self-Employment Investment Demonstration Final Evaluation Report." University of Iowa, 1995.

Reed, L. (2015). *Mapping Pathways Out of Poverty: The State of the Microcredit Summit Campaign Report 2015*. Microcredit Summit Campaign.

Rural Microentrepreneur Assistance Program. (2021). Accessed December 9. 2020. https://www.rd.usda.gov/programs-services/business-programs/rural-microentrepreneur-assistance-program.

Schumacher, E. F. (1973). *Small Is Beautiful: Economics As If People Mattered*. Harper and Row.

Woodworth, W. (2003). "Latino Community Service Learning Data." Marriott Business School, Brigham Young University, Unpublished presentation to the Provo mayor and staff.

Woodworth, W. (2019). The Case of "Susana" from Central America. Unpublished paper.

Woodworth, W., et al. (2002). Provo Hispanic Inner City Report. College of Education, Brigham Young University (unpublished research), Provo, Utah.

Yunus, M. (2000). "The Grameen Bank Model for Lifting the Poor." In W. Woodworth and collaborators, *Small Really Is Beautiful: Micro Approaches to Third World Development—Microentrepreneurship, Microenterprise, and Microfinance.* Third World Thinktank, pp. 32–43.

Yunus, M. (2001). "The Grameen Bank, Micro-Credit, and the Wall Street Journal," *Wall Street Journal,* December 12.

CHAPTER 9

Salt and Pepper: Different Christian and Muslim Microfinance Strategies in East Africa (Yehu and Jami Bora)

> *"Is not this the kind of fasting I have chosen: to loose the chains of injustice and untie the cords of the yoke, to set the oppressed free and break every yoke? Is it not to share your food with the hungry and to provide the poor wanderer with shelter—when you see the naked, to clothe them, and not to turn away from your own flesh and blood? Then your light will break forth like the dawn, and your healing will quickly appear; then your righteousness will go before you, and the glory of the Lord will be your rear guard. Then you will call, and the Lord will answer; you will cry for help, and he will say: Here am I. If you do away with the yoke of oppression, with the pointing finger and malicious talk, and if you spend yourselves in behalf of the hungry and satisfy the needs of the oppressed, then your light will rise in the darkness, and your night will become like the noonday. The Lord will guide you always; he will satisfy your needs in a sun-scorched land and will strengthen your frame. You will be like a well-watered garden, like a spring whose waters never fail"* (Isaiah 58:6–11).

In this chapter I tell about two of my Christian friends who have given much of their lives to serving the suffering of gGod's children in Africa—Kenya in particular. For two decades, I've visited their projects, raised funding, and spoken on their behalf at multiple events to support their work. I describe several inspiring stories about their efforts through my field research into two nongovernmental organizations (NGOs).

One operates in Kenya's central mountainous region of urban Nairobi, where it has become the country's largest and fastest growing NGO. Most of its clients live in or near Kibera, Africa's largest slum, with estimates of a few hundred thousand to more than a million people. The other organization works in the southern rural area, along the Kenyan coast where members have enjoyed relative peace, but also endured extreme poverty. One-on-one client interviews have been conducted at the two research sites, along with observations of staff leaders, social services, village banking meetings, and so on. These materials became the sources of data gleaned during the study of both organizations. This study delineates similarities as well as differences among microfinance NGOs that provide economic and social development services to poor families in Africa, focusing on a variety of strategies, unique client services, and so forth. It shows how Christians of a variety of institutional faiths, though all are believers in the ways of Christ, can harness their faith and considerable skills to serve God—and others.

I conclude this chapter with an assessment of socioeconomic impacts, and I offer several suggestions for ways to reduce human suffering. The very act of integrating religious values, along with international development concepts and methodologies for reducing human suffering, can make a difference in the quality of people's lives.

Strategies such as social development and microlending have grown into a rapidly expanding global movement to reduce human suffering by providing education and social services, on the one hand, and small amounts of capital, known as microcredit, on the other. Microloans are given to impoverished individuals so that they may begin the process of lifting themselves out of poverty. The literature on this phenomenon that occurred during recent decades is expanding rapidly (Aghion and Morduch 2005; Counts 2008; Woodworth 2001; Yunus 2007).

Introduction to Kenya's Struggles

This chapter details highlights of my field research in two areas of Kenya, East Africa. I first offer a brief historical overview of the nation's history and its political and economic situations. I then outline a number of national development issues and social support systems, particularly that of microfinance. I go on to describe, analyze, and contrast the major differences between two nongovernmental organizations that seek to address African rural as well as urban hardships. The conclusion will suggest that while both organizations share similar objectives, still their areas of focus, the strategies used, and the outcomes are quite different. This supports my argument that there is no single "best" approach or "most universal" model by which microfinance may operate successfully in every part of the globe.

Kenya was a British colony for many decades, a place where Black labor was exploited and later a nation that provided immense natural resources to the British crown. Along with South Africa, it was one of the biggest success stories in Africa's history. The British had transferred elements of their education system and built a number of cities that were known for their cleanliness and order. They transported tens of thousands of laborers and technicians from India (another of Britain's colonies) to Kenya to build a railway system that would facilitate the transportation of goods. The nation continues to enjoy rich and fertile soils for its agricultural produce, and is known worldwide for the quality of its coffee and tea, among other products. It benefits from high mountainous regions in the north and the central part of the country, where the temperate climate is enjoyable because of the altitude. It also has a more tropical climate in the southern regions, and along the coastline.

In terms of Kenya's independence from the United Kingdom, this transition originated in the 1950s with the ferocious Mau Mau rebellion. When independence was declared in 1963, Britain sought to leave a portion of its systems intact so that Kenyans could benefit, as well as the British themselves.

African donations collected from churches and college students
who were members of the HELP Team.

The country has benefited from a relatively stable political system, with varying degrees of democracy and participation. It boasts a number of schools and universities, as well as a large cooperative sector of the economy. Nairobi, in particular, is home to various United Nations and other multilateral offices, which help to generate international awareness, as well as being a multicultural melting pot. Thus, Kenya has enjoyed considerable peace and plenty, especially in comparison with many other African nations.

While Kenya is still considered to be a developing country, its largest cities are somewhat modern, have functioning electrical grids, and boast a per capita yearly income of $1,600, roughly in the middle of its neighbors on the continent. Kenya's safari industry, owing to its extensive wildlife and national parks working to preserve its natural wealth, has been a huge boon to the country. A number of its unique cultures, such as the Maasai, have attracted scholars and tourists from around the globe seeking to study the many subcultures and languages of the country's wilder regions.

Although many features of Kenya are clearly positive, recent years have also brought troubling complications. For one, the nation suffers from hordes of refugees who have crossed some central African nations, where civil wars continue to rage, to the more-secure camps inside Kenya's borders. These masses have flooded to the cities looking for work, while also causing instability in smaller towns and rural areas along their path. Then there has been the complete collapse of Somalia's government to the east. Conditions along that border are much worse today, and much more violent. Along the entire coast of Kenya, in recent years there has also been the problem of pirate activity, including the hijacking of ships, as well as robberies and murders. Perhaps the most blatant illustration of public danger was a terrorist attack on the U.S. Embassy in 1998, which killed hundreds of people, injured thousands, and destroyed a section of downtown Nairobi. My visit there shortly afterward truly shocked me. Several Kenyan young people soon after applied to study business management at the school where I was a longtime professor, the Marriott School of Business at Brigham Young University, in Utah. Their stories of the dangers before and after the bombings were horrific, even to an experienced global traveler like myself.

Other tragic events during Kenya's modernization difficulties occurred at the end of 2007, when national elections were held. The regime in power, that of the president's Party for National Unity, suffered losses at the polls, but refused to step down. Chaos ensued and tensions between the opposition party and the president's grew into extensive hostilities. First came mass demonstrations by one side or the other, followed by shootings and roaming gangs of extremists, who invaded homes, wrecked businesses, and terrified the general population. Perhaps the most graphic and gruesome incidents were machete beheadings of individuals from the enormous Kibera slum, whose bodies were then laid in the middle of the road for everyone to see.

In spite of its problems, the population of Kenya has grown to approximately 55 million. Nearly half of the rural population and about a third of the nation's residents live below the country's poverty line, mostly as rural farmers. The unemployment rate ranges between 25 and 35 percent in different regions, and life expectancy is around 63 years.

In the mid-1990s, microfinance began to emerge as a promising strategy for helping to reduce Kenya's poverty. There are four commercial banks and a few other microfinance institutions providing most of the services for financing the poor.

The most prominent microfinance institutions (MFIs) are K-Rep Bank, WEDCO, Equity Bank, KADET Bank, and the Aga Kahn Foundation. Two others are Jamii Bora Trust and Yehu Microfinance, both of which provide not only microloans, but education and other tools as well. This chapter reports on my experiences and action research exploring these last two models of development by the respective NGOs.

Yehu Microfinance

> *"Give generously to [the poor] and do so without a grudging heart; then because of this the Lord your God will bless you in all your work and in everything you put your hand to. There will always be poor people in the land. Therefore I command you to be openhanded toward your fellow Israelites who are poor and needy in your land"* (Deuteronomy 15:10–11).

Yehu was launched from Utah in 2000 by a dear friend of mine, Louis Pope, the CEO of an industrial diamond producer, U.S. Synthetic. Together we had collaborated with other Christian business associates in launching an NGO called Unitus (for "Unite Us"), which became a microfinance accelerator in several countries, including India and Mexico. We worked to set up several worker-owned cooperative businesses in Nairobi, where my research revealed that among Christian congregations in the area of East Africa, some 82 percent of households had no viable employment, So the PRINCE Bakery—named for Christ, the Prince of Peace—was launched, as were other economic ventures for helping poor Christian families. These efforts drew on the Book of Acts in which we learn that *"All the believers were together and had everything in common. They sold property and possessions to give to anyone who had need. Every day they continued to meet together in the temple courts. They broke bread in their homes and ate together with glad and sincere hearts, praising God and enjoying the favor of all the people. And the Lord added to their number daily those who were being saved"* (Acts 2:44–47).

My friend Louis Pope had gradually learned about problems in the Third World (as it was haughtily called in those years) and had developed a desire to address them, especially the poverty of Africa. He joined the board of another NGO called CHOICE Humanitarian and became engaged in various projects in both Ethiopia and Bolivia. The more he learned about microcredit as a strategy for building the lives of rural families, he determined to launch his own project in Kenya. In particular, along with members of his family, he focused on the southeastern region of the country in the rural villages around Mombasa. After several years of small experiments using local consultants and Pope's financial resources, Yehu was transformed from simply a series of projects into a significant microfinance organization.

Yehu grew to eight microfinance branches, with some 60 employees, and had a client base of approximately 16,000 members. Thus far Yehu has given out over $8 million in microloans with a repayment rate of 88 percent. Loan sizes range between $71 and $2,000. The NGO has grown to have an outstanding portfolio of $375,000 (Woodworth 2007, Mombasa). Working with both Muslim and Christian women, Pope and his staff at Yehu Microfinance effectively managed the delicate balance between the two cultures.

The goal of Yehu is to help women and their families move toward self-sufficiency. Below is a summary of the typical Yehu client as of my last trip there:

- Years of schooling: 3.7
- Gender: 80 percent female
- Average age: 42
- Literacy rate: 54 percent
- Income under $2 per day: 97 percent
- Income under $1 per day: 83 percent
- Clean water access: 3.6 percent
- Pit latrines: 80 percent
- Electricity in home: 1.5 percent
- Children enrolled in elementary school: 95 percent
- Children enrolled in middle school: 25 percent
- Supporting more than six dependents on their income: 9 percent
- Supporting a terminally ill dependent: 11 percent
- Have had a recent death in the household: 21.5 percent

One of the ways Yehu has succeeded is that it has drawn on volunteer university interns, many of whom have been my MBA and undergraduate students who have studied microfinance in the courses I taught at BYU. Its Marriott School of Business has developed a number of initiatives to foster what we formerly called Third World development. Starting in 1990, the first NGO was created out of my courses, named Enterprise Mentors International, which operates in the Philippines and Latin America. Since then I have founded or cofounded some 40 other NGOs, either with friends or from the courses I taught. My classes typically functioned as a kind of NGO incubator, and led to practical programs like NGO creation and hundreds of field studies around the globe. These efforts have also given rise to numerous faculty/student publications, theses, and eventually the establishment of the Ballard Center for Economic Self-Reliance (recently renamed the Melvin J. Ballard Center for Social Impact).

Among other nongovernmental organizations designed and implemented with BYU involvement, a number of students have developed and implemented projects with Yehu Microfinance in Kenya. Yehu's internships, most of which feature volunteer labor and expertise funded by the students themselves, have helped to provide that NGO with considerable pro bono consulting services offered by students with a passion to change the world.

Another unique feature of Yehu Microfinance is that it inspired Louis Pope to establish his own Pope Family Foundation, which is now called the Asante Foundation. Five of his married children and their spouses have been involved with Yehu or Asante to various degrees. A son-in-law and one of Pope's daughters, for example, even moved to Mombasa and lived there in a tent for six months, where they helped design and implement the initial structures of Yehu as an organization. Another son, who earned an MBA from Cornell University, has been the ongoing manager of Yehu operations from his base in the US. All the Pope family members contribute of their personal funds, and most travel at least once a year to Kenya to volunteer with specific short-term projects for either the Asante or the Pope Family Foundation.

Additional admirable aspects of Pope's work are that he decided to establish for-profit business ventures in Mombasa that would create jobs and generate profits to further expand the microcredit NGO. One enterprise is known as Coast Coconut Farms, an economic development project launched in 2005. The company's mission is to provide sustainable employment, as well as management and ownership opportunities for rural Kenyans. This is done by giving the rural poor access to capital, equipment, and training, with the goal of refining organic coconut oil, which is harvested from wild coconuts growing along Kenya's coastline. The plan implemented was to use profits to help scale up Yehu's work, thus generating additional loan capital for further microfinancing. Coast Coconut Farms' vision is to create thousands of sustainable livelihoods for the rural poor using Fair Trade Principles (Woodworth 2006, Utah).

Essentially, Coast Coconut Farms functions as follows: Women and their children gather raw coconuts that have fallen to the ground in the bush. At their homes, they use the hard labor of their own hands to husk the coconuts, crack them open, and shred them. The shredded raw material is then taken to Pope's Coast Coconut factory in a nearby rural village. There it is pressed and processed to produce high-quality products. Some of it is sold as natural, organic oil for cooking and other consumption purposes in the United States as a healthy, natural food. The other platform is the product's transformation into natural oils and lotions for women's skin care that has no artificial ingredients, fragrance, or colors. In this form, it is bottled, labeled, and shipped to the United States, where it is sold as Basa Body Products, named after the women of Mombasa.

Kaye Woodworth in Africa, holding Fatimata, the new baby of the local NGO director, Djeneba.

Additional ventures have grown out of Pope's development portfolio, as well. In Utah, he purchased many acres for planting and growing sources to develop essential oils for a huge business, named doTerra, that has gained millions of clients globally. Pope also used several of my former students as interns to acquire land and construct fairly low-cost housing for Kenyan farmers that dramatically upgraded their comfort zones and lifestyles. Next, Pope acquired rural property outside of Mombasa, where he built a lumber company, purchased state-of-the-art sawmill equipment from China, and not only shipped it to the ports of Mombasa, but even flew Chinese engineers from Beijing to set the mill up and get it running smoothly. The business then began acquiring and shipping newly made lumber from regional eucalyptus plantations to saw and sell throughout East Africa. While difficulties frequently arise in such ventures as these, the indefatigable Louis Pope continues to move everything forward.

With the above background on Yehu Microfinance and related efforts as a case of East African rural development and microcredit, I now turn to another NGO model, one located primarily in an urban setting: Nairobi.

Jamii Bora Trust

In the Book of Proverbs, we read numerous admonitions for believers of the Bible to reach out and assist the downtrodden. Here are several citations to inspire and motivate us:

> *Do not withhold good from those to whom it is due, when it is in your power to act. Do not say to your neighbor, "Come back tomorrow and I'll give it to you"—when you already have it with you* (Proverbs 3:27–28).

> *Those who give to the poor will lack nothing, but those who close their eyes to them receive many curses* (Proverbs 28:27).

Apparently, the scriptures give us a heavenly mandate to do good. So another Kenyan example of helping those who suffer—meaning the world's have-nots—can be illustrated by a somewhat different NGO that operates, not out of Mombasa, but out of Nairobi, Kenya. The Jamii Bora Trust (JBT) was established in the latter city in 1999 by a Swedish Christian named Ingrid Munro. At the time, several individuals who had been beggars or slum dwellers approached her as the head of the African Housing Fund, and as a Scandinavian ex-pat, to help them improve their living conditions. After engaging them in a number of discussions, Munro became interested in the idea, and together these people launched a small savings program from which JBT has evolved into becoming the largest microfinance institution in the country. Having collaborated and also presented my research about her magnificent labors multiple times, (Woodworth 2006, Halifax),

I tell her story because it frames another case of people using their personal values to improve the world while serving God's children.

My friend Ingrid Munro was impressed by the pleas of the poor and agreed to help raise some initial funding to begin improving the housing and other features of her clientele. The primary targets of JBT are slum dwellers who live in Nairobi's largest shantytown, Kibera. Early clients were primarily alcoholics, street beggars, gang members, prostitutes, drug addicts, and others in similar situations. Many suffered from HIV-AIDS, and virtually none had jobs. Their wretched existence was somewhat typical of the "poorest of the poor" in large cities in the developing world.

In 1999–2000, when I started traveling to Kenya, I conducted considerable research on community poverty and family struggles in the greater Nairobi area (Woodworth 1999). The data suggested that in many neighborhoods de facto unemployment was 60 to 80 percent, far above the official government statistics. The poor lived in shanties overrun with two or three families crowded into a single unit built with scrap wood by their own hands. Many adults suffered from illiteracy, and their children lacked opportunities for formal schooling.

In 2003, I began interviewing JBT participants. I have held various meetings with members of its staff over the years since then, as well as discussed matters with Ingrid Munro herself not only in Africa, but also in New York, Spain, Canada, and Mexico. By 2004 Jamii Bora began to experience its first profits. These allowed the NGO not only to survive, but also to roll out additional programs and services. I spent several weeks in Kenya in 2007, and a part of that time was devoted to research and interviews at Jamii Bora's headquarters (Woodworth 2007, Nairobi). The main agenda of JBT was—and remains— to reduce human suffering in Kenya. Its holistic approach focuses on poverty alleviation, but in contrast to Yehu Microfinance, it initially served the urban population of one of Africa's biggest cities: Nairobi. Also, it has become quite large, in contrast to Yehu's smaller client base. By 2007, JBT had mushroomed to helping 167,000-plus individuals, while offering a variety of services and products.

With a range of social and economic programs gradually developed during the first several years, JBT has gained a national reputation for building positive changes in the lives of its members and clients. A number of the Jamii Bora staff with whom I have met to discuss its work are currently *ex*-addicts, *ex*-alcoholics, and *ex*-prostitutes who are successful managers and staff in the organizational structure of JBT. Another distinct feature of this organization is that, in contrast to most MFIs around the world, approximately a third of its clients are men. The very name, Jamii Bora, in Swahili means "good families."

One side of JBT's focus might best be described as providing services for achieving a social impact. It conducts rehabilitation programs such as orphan outreach, alcohol rehabilitation, street beggar transition, and family counseling. A large staff of what might be considered social workers provides JBT individual and marital counseling, literacy training, health care services, and multiple other support services. Whereas in industrialized nations, like the United States, federal and local governments provide these types of services, in much of the developing world they do not. Any and all such resources must therefore derive from the private sector. In this sense, JBT is a privatized social and health institution serving its growing clientele.

On the other hand, JBT has actually become Kenya's largest economic development institution, part of its overall microfinance sector. It offers microentrepreneurial training, business plan consulting, and microcredit loans. Its philosophy is to empower the poor by helping them become economically self-reliant. A client's initial loan may range between $80 and $800. After some success and growth of one's microenterprise, such individuals may later qualify for larger business loans ranging from $900 to $9,000.

While JBT was launched in the impoverished and violent slums of Kibera, with as many as one million people, it has gradually spread to dozens of other branches in virtually all large cities in Kenya. Two years ago, it established the JBT Business Academy to provide more-formal and sophisticated training for microentrepreneurs who are growing their businesses from tiny microenterprises into a category we may call "small businesses," where instead of one or two people work five to 10 may be employed.

Thus, larger amounts of capital are needed for financing and more-complex business skills are required.

By 2004, JBT's success had leveled off, with about 65,000 borrowers. It was unable to continue escalating its growth due to funding constraints. One of the MFIs I had cofounded, Unitus (which friends and I started in 2000), decided to help JBT expand more rapidly. Unitus operated a global strategy for accelerating microfinance, yet had no programs in Africa. After an in-depth assessment of JBT's operational systems and managerial abilities, we gave Munro's organization $1.4 million in new capital with the goal of speeding its growth, and ensuring that it could achieve greater scale and impacts. This joint venture became a major innovation in the microfinance movement. It assured Unitus that its model could achieve quick and significant outcomes, which, in turn, soon inspired it to create several other such partnerships. It also impressed other MFIs with large capital holdings to begin doing the same. In the four years since the Unitus-JBT partnership, the Kenyan organization was able to more than double its client base to over 180,000.

A recent JBT development on the social side is that of the *Tumaini* program. It focuses exclusively on providing social services to beggars on the street. One-on-one counseling, medications, and other products are provided to help those who otherwise are condemned to a degrading life of handouts. The ultimate goal of *Tumaini* is that of assisting beggars to enjoy a more acceptable quality of life by making better decisions and obtaining an education and employment.

Another innovation has been the development of *Kaputei*, a new housing community. The logic of this JBT strategy is that rather than bring people out of the slums, train them, help them start businesses, and then watch them go back to the conditions of the slum to live, the effort should be to give them a clean break. *Kaputei* is essentially the start of a fresh slate, a newly designed community started from scratch out in the rural, peaceful area away from the slums and the congestion and the chaos of metropolitan Nairobi. Thus, JBT raised significant funds and works with corporate partners in the design and implementation of this new community. The clients can buy fairly inexpensive, simple homes with their own sweat equity and a mortgage payment of some $20 to $35 USD per month. This is about the same amount as the monthly rental payments the poor already pay to live in the slums. Whether this new housing model will be able to grow to scale to serve tens of thousands of JBT clients is still uncertain. But the power of this idea—to establish a new start for JBT families who are on the road to a better future—is very impressive (Woodworth 2007, Nairobi).

Ingrid Munro once shared with me an example of truly Christian financing by relating what occurred after the Nairobi riots of 2009 during the presidential elections. Due to conflicts, crime, and crisis, over half of Jamii Bora borrowers lost everything in the violence that marred Kenya's post-election tragedies. However, the NGO itself was able to cover the lost costs of the destruction, and the institution itself miraculously became stronger. It wasn't the fact that JBT held significant reserves for such a crisis, but that the masses of clients, managers, and Munro herself all enjoyed the people's respect, even their hearts. Thus, a cell phone campaign for new funding was implemented to raise money that would help some 80,000 impoverished JBT members be reimbursed. None lost either their money or their credit rating. By contrast, other NGOs and even some banking firms went broke and had to shut down completely. However, as many people suggested, in that incident, Jamii Bora showed that it operated on empathy, not charity or sympathy.

Ultimately, reaching her retirement years, my friend Ingrid Munro moved back to her home country of Sweden. This occurred at the very time that JBT was weathering numerous challenges as Kenya—indeed, the entire world of banking—was in the throes of many difficulties. The global economic Great Recession of 2008–2009 had already made everything more stressful for financial services firms, especially those of developing nations. Eventually, Jamii Bora began the process of evolving into a more-established organization, not staying merely a humble Nairobi NGO. So in 2020 it began partnering with the large Co-operative Bank of Kenya, the fourth largest commercial bank in the country. Just what the future portends is not yet known, but because it is a cooperative organization dedicated to help its members, I hope its future will continue to be bright.

Conclusion

Both Yehu Microfinance and Jamii Bora Trust in Kenya have a number of similarities, as well as differences. Whether we study the larger, urban example of JBT or the smaller, rural case of Yehu Microfinance, they and the overall development industry throughout Kenya have experienced some successes along with surmounted many problems.

On a global scale, the microfinance movement has been greatly accelerated since my colleague and adviser to many of my NGO start-ups, Muhammad Yunus, who founded the Grameen Bank of Bangladesh, received the 2006 Nobel Peace Prize (Yunus 2008). Yet there are also many critics of microfinance, as evidenced by books such as *What's Wrong with Microfinance?* by Thomas Dichter and Malcolm Harper (2008);); David Roodman's *Due Diligence: An Impertinent Inquiry into Microfinance* (2011); Hugh Sinclair's *Confessions of a Microfinance Heretic: How Microlending Lost Its Way and Betrayed the Poor* (2012), as well as other works by scholars such as Becky Hsu (2017) and Lamia Karim (2011).

In the cases of Yehu and JBT, the interview and observational data I have collected all suggest a promising future. On the success dimension, both are operational and growing, and enjoying ever-increasing sources of funding and impacts. Kenya now has established a networking umbrella for these types of nongovernmental organizations, called the Association of Microfinance Institutions (AMFI). A draft microfinance bill to regulate the industry was finally passed by the country's Parliament and took effect in 2008. Countrywide awareness of microlending as a development strategy was greatly enhanced during the UN's International Year of Microcredit in 2005. Faulu, Kenya, became listed on the stock market as Equity Bank, a full-service microfinance organization.

In spite of such positive trends, development stresses and strains must be noted. Donor funds for Africa are still extremely limited, and all in all, there is little government support in most of the continent for the microfinance sector. Another challenge in Kenya in particular is the lack of technical skills of managers and staff for operating such NGOs.

Drawing on the examples of Yehu and Jamii Bora, I pose several suggestions for improving social and economic development in Kenya going forward. First, the national government should ease the process for establishing and registering microfinance institutions. The educational structure of Kenya, at the university level, needs to design courses and programs that will provide better training for a future generation of managers in operating NGOs in general, and MFIs in particular. Incentives such as certificates and diplomas ought to be established. Finally, both large Kenyan businesses and multinational firms operating in the country ought to develop partnerships that link their for-profit agendas with the goal of Corporate Social Responsibility in providing support and funding to lift impoverished communities in East Africa. If the government along with the educational and business sectors can collaborate more effectively, the result will be that not only will Yehu's and Jamii Bora's clients prosper, but also civil society as a whole will be strengthened, and the poorest of the poor will move in the direction of greater self-sufficiency.

In the meantime, let us reflect on the words of Jesus, who challenged us to serve the poor and needy. Said he: *"Give to the one who asks you, and do not turn away from the one who wants to borrow from you"* (Matthew 5:42).

References

Acts 2:44–47.

Aghion de, B. A., and J. Morduch. (2005). *The Economics of Microfinance.* MIT Press.

Counts, A. (2008). *Small Loans, Big Dreams.* John Wiley & Sons.

Deuteronomy 15:10–11.

Dichter, T., and M. Harper (eds.). (2008). *What's Wrong with Microfinance?* Practical Action Publishing.

Hsu, B. Y. (2017). *Borrowing Together: Microfinance and Cultivating Social Ties.* Cambridge University Press.

Isaiah 58:6–11.

Karim, L. (2011). *Microfinance and Its Discontents: Women in Debt in Bangladesh.* University of Minnesota Press.

Kattilakoski, H. (2020). *The Financial Sustainability of Micro-Finance Institutions in Sub-Saharan Africa.* Cologne Business School, Köln manuscript.

Matthew 5:42.

Proverbs 3:27–28; 28:27.

Roodman, D. (2011). *Due Diligence: An Impertinent Inquiry into Microfinance.* Center for Global Development.

Sinclair, H. (2012). *Confessions of a Microfinance Heretic: How Microlending Lost Its Way and Betrayed the Poor.* Berrett-Koehler.

Wangui, M. (2020). "Regulator Approves Co-op Bank's 90% Stake Acquisition in Jamii Bora." The Kenyan Wall Street. *Kenyan News.* Accessed August 12, 2021. https://kenyanwallstreet.com/co-op-bank-acquires-90-stake-in-jamii-bora/.

Woodworth, W. (1999 Nairobi). Community interviews and survey data, 1999–2002.

Woodworth, W. (2006 Halifax). Ingrid Munro interview about Jamii Bora Trust at the Global Microcredit Summit, Canada, November.

Woodworth, W. (2006 Utah). Louis Pope interview about Coast Coconut Farms, at BYU in Provo, April.

Woodworth, W. (2007 Mombasa). Interviews with Yehu Microfinance in villages outside Mombasa.

Woodworth, W. (2007 Nairobi). Jamii Bora Trust managers/staff interviews about structure and results, summer.

Woodworth, W. (2018 Mombasa). Yehu Microfinance interviews and site visits, Mombasa and surrounding rural villages, summer.

Yunus, M. (2007). *Banker to the Poor: Micro-Lending and the Battle Against World Poverty.* Public Affairs.

Yunus, M. (2008) *Creating a World Without Poverty: Social Business and the Future of Capitalism.* Public Affairs.

A Call to Action: Practicing Our Faith in Christ—Today

As I conclude this book's powerful stories of dedicated Christians improving the world and reducing human suffering, I want to explore several more passages of scripture that have motivated my life.

First, let's recall the amazing story in Acts 3:1–11 of the healing of a man born lame, a miracle that Peter and John performed at the gate of the big new temple built after the Babylonians destroyed the one built by King Solomon. It's a miraculous account of someone who suffered his entire life yet eventually being healed. I quote several verses (using their numbers, for clarity), summarize each one, and also inject my comments to explain.

1. Peter and John were making their way together up into the temple. It was the ninth hour of prayer. 2. At the entrance lay a man who had been born lame. From the day of his birth, his feet and lower legs were crippled and useless. Every day he was carried to the gate of the temple, the one named "Beautiful." As people would enter the house of God, he would beg for help meeting his needs. 3. One day, seeing Peter and John going in, he asked them for a gift. 4. Peter looked deeply into the man's eyes and said, *"Look at us!"* 5. The cripple gave them his attention, hoping to receive something (Acts 3:1–5). Clearly, he didn't expect a cure after eking out a miserable existence depending on the mercy of others who might give him a few tiny alms. He certainly never thought he would be fully healed after decades of struggling in squalor.

6. Yet Peter said to him, *"Silver or gold I do not have, but what I do have I give you. In the name of Jesus Christ of Nazareth, walk."* 7. Peter then took him by the right hand, and raised him to his feet. Immediately his feet and ankles were given strength. What a shock to that person's soul! Peter didn't toss him a measly penny or a half shekel. Instead, the poor soul received the power of God—the healing that comes from the Holy Spirit. 8. He leaped up, stood on his own two legs, and began to walk. He then went with Peter and John into the temple. He was walking, jumping, praising God (Acts 4:6–8). It was the first and perhaps the only time he had ever stood on his own two feet, after decades of lying forlornly in the dusty streets or perhaps on a bed of rags in someone's shanty.

9. When all the people saw him walking and praising God, they recognized him as the same man who used to sit begging at the temple gate called Beautiful, and they were filled with wonder

and amazement at what had happened to him. While the man held on to Peter and John, all the people were astonished and came running to them in the place called Solomon's Colonnade.... 10. They recognized him as the same man who used to sit begging at the temple gate called Beautiful, and they were filled with wonder and amazement at what had happened to him. 11. The lame man who was healed held on to Peter and John while all the people came running toward them into Solomon's porch. How greatly amazed they were (Acts 2:9–11). I can only imagine how surprised the crippled person was, as well as those in his community—even more so because he'd never learned to take a single step. Now he was striding, jumping, and shouting his thanks to God. Apparently, later, even Christ's enemies had to acknowledge the miracle, admitting *"we cannot deny it"* (Acts 4:16).

I've seen a few miracles of healing in my own life, including while preaching Christ in the *favelas* (slums) of Brazil, as well as when one of my daughters became terribly sick and our family prayers were immediately answered.

Equally important, I myself have many times been able to lift up the bodies and souls of impoverished people who were crippled physically, financially, or emotionally. Some seemed to be living in the same squalor of my efforts to serve others in Africa, Guatemala, Fiji, and so forth. But through microcredit, social entrepreneurship, and the building of schools, I witnessed lives being changed.

Several years ago, while working with a nongovernmental organization of Christians in India, I had the privilege to visit several leper colonies (see chapter 2) where three generations of people were struggling to survive despite being viewed as "undesirables." I found meeting with elderly people who had suffered over decades to be a heart-rending experience. Playing street soccer with young male teens was great fun, though, as I felt compassion because of their isolation from the outside world.

The most meaningful experience I had on that project was listening to the aged men in the dusty village square telling me about their long lives of trying to meet many challenges despite their affliction of leprosy. Ultimately, their nurses and caregivers asked if I could assist by donning latex gloves, washing their feet, and finally rubbing oil on their legs, backs, and feet to provide a bit of comfort. At that time, I became acutely aware of the great love and compassion Jesus had doing the same thing two thousand years ago in dusty Palestine. On that very day in the leper colony in India, my mind was flooded by the scriptures recorded in Luke 5:12–16. Readers will recall that was when Jesus descended after His marvelous Sermon on the Mount as large multitudes followed him. A man covered with leprosy approached, fell with his face to the ground, and begged him, *"Lord, if you are willing, you can make me clean."* The Savior reached out his hand and touched the man, saying, *"I am willing... Be clean!"* Instantly he was healed of his leprosy, and news of the miraculous blessing soon was spreading everywhere.

In my view, the efforts of our NGOs utilizing various social innovations, carried out by thousands of volunteers in recent decades, is a similar kind of Christian service. My volunteers and I have witnessed transformations occurring, women suddenly being able to stand and walk on their own two feet carrying heavy cans of water back to their tiny shanties. Children could drink clean water for perhaps the first time. Natural disasters were rebuffed, and villages were constructed anew. Such suffering will always be with us. Whether it's the Black Plagues of ancient Europe, or the Coronavirus pandemic of our own times, suffering abounds in many places around the world, and we who are able must act with charity and love. Whether it be the horrors of war in the Middle Ages or the ruthless carnage of Putin's hatred of Ukraine today, we can and must work for peace. Whether it be the current scourges of racism and resentment against minorities, women, and others, or today's pernicious politics of resentment and denial, we can and will reverse the suffering of millions.

In wrapping matters up, I want to suggest how our strategies for lifting those who suffer such as microfinance and social innovations are evolving and generating more and greater impacts. We will also report and respond to the negatives, the complaints by some that programs like microfinance don't attain their stated goals—in short, that the poor don't see improvements. Obviously, there are critics in all we do, and certainly weaknesses are evident whether we're discussing microenterprise or finance, social entrepreneurship or innovation, food for hungry stomachs, and the need to recover from floods and hurricanes or civil war. So below we discuss new trends, critical assessments, contrarian philosophies, academic debates, and more. At the end of this book, I seek your feedback. Please send your comments to me at www.https//warnerwoodworth.com.

Major Issues Relating to Social Entrepreneurs

In this final chapter, I will first discuss my own paradigm, developed over many years, which suggests enlisting a range of volunteers of various ages and conditions, and then going on to achieve developments beyond the scope of this book. The paradigm I would like to pass on to you includes several brief ideas for getting started in launching your own projects, as well as later gathering reports and responses to the various innovations analyzed in the book.

Let me first say that, obviously, none of my practices or proposals are perfect. I always apply humility when trying to make a difference in people's lives. Yet I hope and trust that all readers of this book, as well as those who may disagree with our work or success, will move matters forward to achieve deeper, long-term, sustainable impacts.

I will contrast those who do this work as one of two kinds of people: those who passively wait for natural social change to occur through churches, governments, and businesses, contrasted with those who courageously take action, not awaiting the Second Coming of Christ or a big solution instituted by billionaires like Bill Gates or Elon Musk. Instead of trying for huge solutions, the former pursue small-scale initiatives. The latter types merely hope, dream …or sometimes merely pray.

I have come up with a paradigm contrasting the two types of folks I've worked with over four-plus decades. You will notice the considerable contrast between somewhat traditional volunteers versus the more effective "movers and shakers" whom we call social entrepreneurs.

Table 10.1

Traditional Volunteers	Social Entrepreneurs
• Do what they're told	✓ Do what's needed
• Low energy/spend lots of time in the NGO offices	✓ High energy/work in the field
• "If it ain't broke, leave it as is"	✓ "If it ain't broke, break it"
• Focus on bureaucratic stuff: hours, pay, other benefits, and so on	✓ Focus on society's major challenges: poverty, illiteracy, poor nutrition, and so on
• Avoid the sweltering heat in developing nations by mostly working in air-conditioned offices	✓ Work in poor villages, coping with the sweat and dust while laboring in poor communities and seeing their hardships firsthand
• Fit in the system	✓ Alter the system
• Are assigned tasks by management	✓ Design new tasks with partners
• Endure lots of meetings and planning	✓ Enjoy laboring in the real world with peasants
• Run copy machines and computers	✓ Run people-centered projects
• Are cautious/Focus on lists in their Franklin-Covey planners	✓ Take risks/Focus on societal issues such as joblessness and hunger
• Are just hearers of God's word	✓ Are actual doers of the word
• If paid staff, the emphasis is on a salary and perhaps earning college credit	✓ Help by focusing on God's children, to transform human society
• Work in dull, boring assignments from 9:00 to 5:00, and then are done	✓ Engage in exciting, unpredictable work, often late into the night
• Shun responsibility	✓ Thrive on responsibility
• Conform to organizational demands	✓ Are free spirits who initiate new programs
• Operate despite having routine, traditional, conservative personalities	✓ Operate as wild radicals out to change or even overthrow the world

This typology is perhaps too stereotypical, but I'm hoping to suggest that attempts to change the world take high energy, gumption, and risks. In other words, passion is of the essence. This kind of work is a labor of love, and it can't be "trained into someone." As the much-admired Oprah Winfrey (2018) declared, "If you can find what is your passion, if you find what you love, you never get tired… and you would do it [what you love] for nothing." That's certainly been my experience as I've engaged with thousands of other folks in this work for over four decades.

To achieve the collaboration of others in our programs and outreach, I've sought to apply the concepts of self-efficacy in those who may be interested in helping to make a difference. It requires that I and other leaders try to instill in them a belief that they *can* help make the world a better place (Smith and Woodworth, 2011). This is a theoretical construct used in social science that I've found useful and applicable in mobilizing fellow Christians who may not initially see God's hand in our work. It helps them move forward with an open mind and open heart.

To illustrate, below are a handful of anonymous comments and feedback from friends, donors, Christian believers of several denominations, and college students whom I've recruited, trained, and mobilized to labor among the poorest people living on our planet. They suggest a mix of reflections as they sought to empower the poor, whether on the Navajo Nation's reservation in Arizona, in the flooded and wrecked villages of Mozambique in Africa, or in the leper colonies of India in Asia.

"This has been life-changing.… I am new in the social entrepreneurship world, although I feel that I was born for it."

"Having the opportunity to put my skills to practice by organizing our own projects will be perpetually beneficial. I will never forget the things I have learned."

"I've made way too much money and never knew what to do with it. Now I see it can be used to bless the lives of those who struggle."

"The [NGO design experience] helped me to look at the world differently—and look at myself differently!"

Social entrepreneurship "fulfills everything I have truly wanted to do with business and with my talents, and has helped me realize that I can do what I have always wanted to do."

"I'm looking for my life's mission and calling, and this [experience] really helped point the way there."

Volunteer social entrepreneurs, working as HOPE Humanitarian team members in Greece, provide food donations for Afghan and Syrian refugees.

Major Issues and Developments in Microfinance

In this final chapter I will highlight a number of updates, fresh insights, and trends in the giving of tiny loans to extremely poor people, especially to women in developing nations. As the number of projects extending loans to the global poor has increased in many parts of the globe, numerous innovations continue to occur that suggest the evolution of the process and promise ever-new changes. They include the following examples.

Types of Loan Products: Microcredit services are being offered above and beyond simply extending a loan to start a microenterprise. Some NGOs are giving innovative types of loans. For example, the Aga Khan Development Network, which operates in Egypt, Syria, and elsewhere, started providing health microinsurance for poor families at extremely low costs. Also, it now gives school loans so impoverished children can get an education. With support from the World Bank, the Aga Khan project grew from a fund of $35 million offering microcredit to small businesses of some 25,000 borrowers a year into a much larger MFI that now extends numerous types of financial loans to the poor. Other NGOs are offering housing loans to improve one's shelter, agriculture crop loans to insure peasant field work, and so forth.

New Banking Tools: Innovative tools for financial transactions are being provided through microcredit institutions in some countries. For example, in the Dominican Republic, ADOPEM—a partner of Women's World Banking—offers ATM services for its poor female clients. And in dozens of other countries, microentrepreneurs are able to obtain a Visa card or MasterCard to access needed capital for growing their enterprise, purchasing raw materials, and other activities.

New Institutions: Large new players are continuing to enter the field of microfinance. For one, the International Finance Corporation (IFC, 2022), which ignored microcredit during its early years, has now started funding up to 56 MFIs (microfinance institutions) in dozens of nations. In its early years it had a portfolio of more than $25 million and a client base of some 1.3 million households. IFC has continually expanded to amassing over $6.2 billion in loan capital for poor families through some 330 projects in 92 nations.

Measuring Microcredit: A dozen or more finance agencies have worked to create metrics and rate MFIs to determine their performance and assess their systems of effectiveness. They have learned to calculate risk and be able to predict future success. Such efforts play a major role in nations whose central banks are only beginning to implement microcredit programs. The Impact Assessment Center of the Microfinance Gateway and CGAPS's Poverty Assessment Tool both help to identify the poorest clients, provide loans, and then evaluate how much loans improve a family's quality of life. My home university, Brigham Young University, together with our colleagues at FINCA International, has been collaborating on field study impacts for years, to measure the results of microcredit. Opportunity International uses a performance and benchmarking system to compare its 40 partners around the world on such criteria as outreach, profitability, and sustainability.

Large-Scale Plans: In the early 2000s, major donor countries committed $34 billion to the International Development Association (IDA), which has been allocated over the last few years. The funds serve as low-interest loans as well as outright grants to a total of 81 of the world's poorest nations. The financing of small enterprise start-ups has become ever more significant, as have projects to aid a million extremely poor Africans (Trivedi, 2011).

Overseas Remittances: Immigrant workers in Europe, Japan, and the United States earn and send back more than $150 billion every year to their relatives spread throughout the developing world. Most of that money goes to very poor families struggling to survive. The capital from outside such nations greatly benefits some of those families, while in some cases the funds are squandered. Hence, Citigroup and other huge banks began attempting to capture some of the remittance total and channel it to MFIs, which then loan it to the poor, oversee its use, and ensure that the funds are used to climb out of poverty, not just to purchase consumer retail products. According to a study by the Inter-American Development Bank (IDB), the capital flowing from remittances like these is greater than the total amount of foreign aid given to certain Latin American countries. Tapping that source of money to fight poverty promises to generate further innovations in the future.

Government Initiatives: National governments have experimented with evolving approaches to microcredit. For instance, the government of Bangladesh has established the Palli Karma

Sahayak Foundation (PKSF), a national wholesale fund that, in turn, channels moneys to NGOs for microcredit purposes. So far it has extended well over $300 million to approximately hundreds of Bangladeshi NGOs, greatly expanding the availability of microcredit to the nation's poorest regions where, before PKSF, there were no such opportunities. As of 2020, it was assisting some 12 million households with various services, both financial and otherwise (PKSF, 2021). Because of this success, additional countries, such as Pakistan, Nepal, and the Philippines, have likewise created national wholesale finds, free of government influence, regulation, and corruption.

From NGOs to Banks: In a growing number of cases, what started as a nonprofit NGO providing humanitarian loans to the poor has evolved into a formal, for-profit bank. Depending on the legal environment and sociopolitical structures of a given national government, the trend for doing this has grown. The first example of this was ACCIÓN's project in Bolivia to transform itself, beginning in 1984. A partner NGO was organized, called PRODEM, and under the guidance of a native board of business experts and a skilled staff, training and loans began to be provided. Yet the demand for microcredit was so huge in a country so poor that PRODEM eventually determined it could simply not do the job as an NGO. A committee was formed to launch a new formal financial "institution," named Banco Solidário ("Banco Sol," meaning "Solidarity Bank"). It opened in the 1990s and quickly outgrew its need for donors and government support, which was often unpredictable. Instead, profits generated operating capital to fuel its growth. Today Banco Sol is the largest bank in Bolivia, providing a vast array of financial services to the country's poor, while enjoying a high rate of return on its loan portfolio. Banco Sol became the model for a similar formal microcredit bank in Peru, called MiBanco. Later came CARD (Center for Agricultural and Rural Development) in the Philippines and Nirdhan Utthan in Nepal, on similar lines. Pakistan followed by passing legislation to facilitate the country's so-called First Microfinance Bank. More such innovations continue to occur as MFIs and other NGOs work to establish formal financial markets around the globe.

Green Microcredit: In recent times, environmentalists began to partner with microcredit NGOs to provide financial services for the poor that are deemed ecologically appropriate and sustainable. Several of them teamed with Rotary International to send solar ovens to poor families victimized by the Asian Tsunami in Sri Lanka. Another three-way partnership is between FONKOZE, the major microcredit NGO in Haiti, a U.S. green NGO, and a solar energy vendor piloting equipment that generates electricity for Haitian microentrepreneurs. Numerous NGOs and universities are collaborating on research about pro-green policies for microcredit, as well as holding conferences and funding student internships in "green microcredit." HELP International, for example, trains its BYU student volunteers to implement square-foot-garden (SFG) methods, using compost, to double or even triple vegetable produce for poor families in several Central American countries. A number of other NGOs are giving loans to support environmentally sustainable projects like biogas systems, micro-drip irrigation, Lorena Stoves (to reduce in-house smoke particles), low-tech water pumps, and many more.

HELP International volunteers in Uganda, making mud adobe
to reinforce the huts of local microentrepreneurs.

Accelerating Microcredit: How to expand microcredit from its current important, though
limited, impacts into being an ever-growing and effective tool for empowering the poor has become
a matter of growing interest in many nations. So far, even though it provides loans to more than
100 million individuals, this figure represents a mere 16 percent of the projected global demand for
microcredit. Unitus has led the charge in showing that most microcredit NGOs serve an average
of only 2,500 poor clients. By contrast, a handful of major NGOs, such as FINCA, Grameen,
and ACCIÓN, now serve more than one million borrowers each. Thus, some 400 million poor
households can have access to capital. In 2000, Unitus launched an innovative acceleration model
to exponentially expand microcredit around the world. It evaluated high-potential NGOs that had
only few thousand clients and, upon deciding to partner with them, provided capital and consulting
services to enable them to dramatically expand. Unitus typically started investing $2 to $4 million
each for several new partners annually. Gradually, it fueled the growth of MFIs in Kenya, Mexico,
and India to a total of over 400,000 clients today. From there it mushroomed to securing MFI
capital of over $1.2 billion, thus helping to create jobs among the poorest of the poor, a number
that has risen to some 28 million people worldwide (Woodworth, 2021).

Hi-Tech Innovations: Providers of microcredit services are rapidly embracing the use of new technologies to expand their impact. These include computers and tablets, smart cards, personal digital assistants (PDAs), cell phones, and many other tools and apps. For instance, the Andhra Pradesh partner of Unitus, called Swayam Krishi Sangam (SKS), began using smart cards for each of its clients spread throughout the hard-to-travel rural areas of India. Before this, old pencil-on-paper manual ledgers were used. But SKS staff eventually began using PalmPilot-type handheld computers to record borrowers' efforts. The clients' loan and savings transactions were thus recorded automatically. Instead of paper passbooks and collection sheets, everything was computerized. This reduced meeting times, gave management up-to-date reports, cut errors, and so on. It also cut SKS's annual reporting costs and increased back-staff efficiencies so that personnel could visit more village banks each day.

In the early 2000s, PDAs were being used by numerous NGOs to manage MFI client data. While out in the field, staffers could review clients' readiness for upcoming loans, track all their financial transactions, use scoring techniques to predict customer behavior, identify borrowers whose repayments may be late, plan collection visits, and so forth. They could also fill out loan application forms. All this enabled the NGO to standardize credit practices and policies, improve data accuracy, and build loan officer efficiency as a benefit of improved management information systems (MIS). Then, as the cell phone technology took off, its technology made the need for earlier tools obsolete, both for MFIs and for rural villagers throughout the world.

For instance, in Uganda and Bangladesh, cell phones began to be used, not only to enhance client communication, but also as microenterprises that can sell "calling" minutes to the public. Such services became a hot commodity in rural villages that had no regular phone system. Some "phone ladies" in Uganda started garnering incomes of $1,000 per year, a sharp contrast to annual compensation of $300 when they were only raising goats. In Bangladesh, Grameen Phone was established in 1997 with a mere 28 village cell phones. Today it is the largest mobile service provider, not only in Bangladesh but in all of South Asia. There are hundreds of thousands of cell phones in Bangladesh villages, with over a million subscribers throughout the nation. In sum, smart cards, PDAs, cell phones, and other technologies are enabling microcredit practitioners to leapfrog from eighteenth century feudalism to twenty-first century hi-tech systems.

Coping with Disasters: What happens to NGOs when calamities strike the people of the world, like the December 2004 Asian tsunami, the 9/11 World Trade Center attacks in New York, or Hurricane Mitch in Central America? A number of NGOs have developed innovative policies and programs to better cope with such events. USAID, for instance, put together a five-phase series of interventions to help MFIs cope with overwhelming challenges. Katalysis, an NGO based in Stockton, California, prepared a manual titled "When Disaster Strikes," drawing on its experience after the 2001 earthquakes that hit El Salvador. It contained action plans for its U.S. headquarters, its regional field office, and local MFI partners. Similar recent strategies have been developed after Japan's 2011 magnitude-9 earthquake and tsunami caused the level-7 nuclear meltdown of the

Fukushima Nuclear Power Plant (Japanese National Police, 2019). Those disasters killed some 18,000, injured or made thousands more homeless, and became the costliest natural disaster in recorded world history, amounting to $235 billion, according to the World Bank.

Microloans for Street Beggars: In perhaps the most radical innovation of all, the Grameen Bank in Bangladesh responded to varying criticisms that microcredit doesn't actually target the "very poorest." Dr. Muhammad Yunus, who became my close friend over many years, launched its "Struggling Members" program in 2003, giving loans to street beggars. Frequent floods, a provider's or relative's death, or disability are often factors that may doom a Bangladeshi person to a fate of seeking charity from others. To buttress the claim that credit ought to be a "human right," as well as to serve those on the lowest rungs of poverty's ladder, Grameen started giving such people a small loan. Transcending the bank's rather rigorous rules for most borrowers, this innovation allows the beggar to not join a bank group, or even attend meetings if they don't want to or simply can't. The average loan is as low as $9.00 (U.S.), and no interest fees are charged. Repayment occurs when and as the borrower can make it. There is no rule, no pressure, and no collection agency. While most loan recipients continue to be on the street, now they have a product to sell, such as bread or candy, as well as earning a bit of extra capital. Grameen also provides blankets, mosquito nets, and other products to help street beggars be healthier and more comfortable. In the early years of this innovation, it loaned out approximately $500,000 (U.S.), of which nearly half was soon repaid. At the time, some 47,000 Bangladeshi "struggling members" received support, and many quit begging and were able to move up to operating their own microenterprise.

Additional Innovations: Finally, I must point out that the preceding innovations are only a *sampling* of the numerous creative solutions that MFIs are experimenting with around the world in 2022. Many of them are in the early stages of innovation that nevertheless holds the promise of future breakthroughs on a large scale. For example, a few years ago in Uganda, FINCA discovered that 80 percent of its 30,000 clients were raising at least one AIDS orphan, and that 75 percent of client incomes went to health care. So, it started offering health insurance to treat medical problems, as well as life insurance to mitigate the high burial costs for borrowers and their family members who may die. In Kenya, the Women Economic Empowerment Consortium (WEEC) chose not to give financial loans to its borrowers. Instead, it offered Maasai women, most of who were nomadic herders, their own cattle as the means for growing family income. WEEC bought many cattle at once to enjoy the advantages of bulk purchasing, and then the purchase price of the loaned cow was repaid from the individual's sale of milk. WEEC enjoyed a record of *zero* loan delinquency.

Even children have become microentrepreneurs. In Bangladesh, street children from 11 to 18 years of age go through training programs on health, AIDS, hygiene, and also financial well-being. When they graduate, the MFI called PMUK gives those who want to start a small microenterprise a tiny loan of $10 or so to shine shoes, sell flowers, or provide other services.

In the Philippines, Freedom from Hunger and the World Council of Credit Unions (WOCCU) began to partner with local credit unions in order to offer microloans to poor clients. WOCCU has seen its client base mushroom from 2,000 to hundreds of thousands of microentrepreneurs over the past several years.

In rural Slovakia, where people live widely spread out, making it difficult to set up an effective MFI operation in a central location, one NGO began taking its services to potential clients in the form of a "Traveling Road Show." The Integra Foundation (TIF) moved around the country, recruiting single mothers and abused women, providing training, accepting loan applications, and disbursing loans.

Having reported on and reviewed the range of microfinancing innovations, I next turn to some inevitable criticisms.

Microcredit Issues and Debates

While the microcredit idea of giving small loans to the poor has mushroomed into a large global movement, it is not without its critics. Like every good innovation, there are doubters and detractors, as well as ardent supporters. The paragraphs below highlight some of the main criticisms and points of debate. They are classified into three types of arguments: theoretical differences, practical disagreements over methods, and other basic questions about microcredit. I do not intend here to resolve the issues, but merely to raise them for the reader to consider.

Theoretical Debates: The conflicts over microcredit as a concept go back to its early years, when many bankers and economists rejected the very idea of giving loans to the poor. Such a proposition defied traditional assumptions that the poor were not worthy of loans, couldn't handle the responsibility, lacked collateral and education, and so on. But the U.S.-trained economist and eventual Nobel Prize winner Muhammad Yunus and others broke the mold of such theories when he realized his neoclassical economics education for a PhD degree did not adequately explain the complexity of impoverished communities in his native country of Bangladesh. He had been taught that the poor are simply lazy, and that poverty exists in developing countries "because people do not work." But he found that the realities of poverty clashed with the economic theory he had learned and was teaching his Bangladeshi students at Chittagong University, so he launched the Grameen Bank as a different model.

Most economists believe that self-interest drives all financial transactions. Microcredit argues a different paradigm—that altruism and helping others (that is, lifting the poor out of their suffering) can also explain economic behavior. The charitable motives of NGOs like ProMujer, Yehu Bank, Unitus, and others have always been explicit: *They sincerely want to reduce human suffering.* They are *not* using microcredit for self-interest purposes such as making money off the poor or gaining popularity in the media. They suggest an alternative to traditional economics that often leave the poor behind. And they show another economic model by which the impoverished are helped out of poverty.

Another conceptual debate is the question whether the best path to international development is large-scale, top-down funding of major projects, versus small-scale, bottom-up microloans issued to minor players. As a theoretical matter, this debate has raged for three decades, mainly between scholars and policymakers. For instance, as the most powerful player on the scene, the World Bank emerged after World War II to provide capital for reconstruction and development in the world economy, providing long-term credit to poor nations—mainly for building infrastructure like highways, bridges, dams, and other enormous projects to modernize such countries. The theory was that by investing in large-scale developments, a nation's ability to compete in the global market would increase and, as a follow-on result, the poor would gradually become better off. However, in many cases, such as Brazil, the theory simply did not work. Mainly, the rich in Brazil benefited, while the poor grew still poorer. Today Brazil is one of the most financially unequal countries on earth.

Many refugees flee their home countries for a better quality of life that microfinance offers to millions every year. Tamin's family walked hundreds of miles, seeking a new future, after crossing the Mediterranean Sea on a flimsy raft. Our volunteers hosted a dinner for them at a Syrian refugee camp in Greece. Later that night his family's tent burned to the ground.

Over the past decade or so, the theory supporting microfinance services to the poor at society's bottom has begun to be accepted by World Bank and scholars in other institutions. In recent years, these institutions have begun to focus more on poverty alleviation, emphasizing the issues of women, literacy, and microcredit. Thus, the World Bank has changed both conceptually and practically as the debate over microcredit has gone on. The World Bank's support for microcredit has changed, along with its theories: From a mere $2 million it furnished for microlending in the late 1980s, to $35 million in 1996, then to more than $100 million by 2000, its portfolio over recent years has climbed above $1 billion. By 2012, its portfolio reached a total of 24 million clients in micro, small, and medium enterprises (MSMEs). Today the bank has an active financial inclusion portfolio of over $3 billion, with lending and technical assistance projects in some 60 countries. It seems, then, that the debate is no longer whether or not microcredit is worthy of financial support. Instead, it's a question of *how much.*

Practical Debates: On the pragmatic question of microcredit, numerous differences arise in implementation and outcomes. The list of such matters is long, so I will highlight only a few here:

Gender: Male or Female? Should the loans go to only women, mostly women, or males and females equally? The trend over time has been toward giving loans primarily to female microentrepreneurs. The marginalization of women in the marketplace has been an age-old problem, based on the notion that women shouldn't have property rights, and so on. But the rise of democracy in nonindustrialized countries, as well as other forces, are gradually destroying such biases. It is now known that women compose a significant economic sector, especially in the informal economy, with huge potential impacts in helping a national economy to grow.

Hence, most NGOs, including Grameen and FINCA, that initially and primarily gave microloans to men, now almost exclusively channel their credit to women. They do this "because it is right," as some staffers say. They also do it because women tend to be better risks, they pay their microloans back at a higher rate, and they use their profits to grow the business or to help their children. Males often are not so responsible. However, some new NGOs, like BASIX in India, lend primarily to men. They argue that men can be responsible, too, and that loaning only to women upsets the traditional patriarchal structure in their culture, leading to unintended consequences, such as role loss, marital conflicts, and so forth.

Loans vs. Training? In scanning the horizon of microcredit, debate is ongoing about whether the NGO practitioner should only provide needed capital for microloans, or whether small business training ought to be included. Some MFIs, such as Grameen, simply provide microloans. They claim that the poor are in most cases trustworthy, capable, and merely need extra capital to start or grow their business ideas. Small organizations point out that training is costly and takes time, thereby reducing the growth in poor borrowers, many of whom can't afford the time or travel costs to attend seminars, even if such training events are free. Other NGOs argue the opposite, asking "What good is a loan if a person can't use it effectively?" They note the high rate of failure among new firm start-ups in most countries, and suggest that training lessens the likelihood that the microenterprise will fail. Visayas Enterprise Foundation illustrates this position. From its inception, its emphasis has been on training and management skills first, and credit later. Such NGOs admit training is costly, though the costs of microenterprise failure and resulting inability to pay back the loan are worse.

Organizational Model: Charity or Business? A major practical issue in the microcredit community is whether it ought to be a tool for social well-being on behalf of the poor, or be a new business model. Some scholars characterize the debate as the "institutionalists" (pro-business advocates) versus the "welfarists" (that is, humanitarians). Essentially, a typical charity-oriented MFI sees its mission as relieving human suffering, providing services, and donating goods to fill basic needs: food to relieve hunger, education to combat illiteracy, medicine to reduce disease. Thus, in their view, microcredit is simply an additional offering—credit to combat unemployment. Such organizations often depend on private donors or government subsidies. They reject calls to become financially sustainable and independent from foundations and other sources. Instead, they argue that the poor have a human right to credit. The role of NGOs and policymakers, then, is to reduce joblessness and poverty, and microcredit is seen as one more tool to give to the world's have-nots.

In contrast, the institutionalists argue that the welfare approach is far too small and too slow. They suggest, instead, that the need for financial services by the poor will grow to some *$100 billion by 2030.* Sheer charity from personal donations and foundations simply won't have the capacity to meet such a demand. Thus, microcredit efforts need to become part of the mainstream, operating as for-profit financial institutions that differ from traditional banks only in that they happen to target a poorer class of clients. While the welfarists dominated the movement for two decades, it seems that the institutionalists are now beginning to take the lead in the 2020s.

Credit or Other Services? This debate concerns whether a microcredit business loan ought to be the only offering to poor individuals, or whether additional services should be provided. Many NGOs claim that they should strictly focus on doing one thing—microcredit—and do it well. Their view is that organizations need to have a single, clear mission, but that many flounder by trying to offer multiple services, none of which is in fact extraordinary.

Conversely, other practitioners hold the opposite view. In their minds, microcredit is a necessary, but not sufficient, resource for the poor. They stress the need for additional programs for the poor that, if not provided, will likely cause them to slip back into their earlier suffering state. Perhaps the most well-known NGO advocating this view is Freedom from Hunger, a California-based nonprofit that pioneered the provision of various services (2010). Starting in 1946 with the enormous goal of "fighting hunger," in 1988 it shifted to integrate microcredit with nutrition or education. The result was its program "Credit with Education," which combines microloans with such things as HIV-AIDS awareness, polio vaccinations, family nutrition, women's health, literacy, and management skills. Eventually, in 2016 it merged with the Grameen Foundation in the United

States, to achieve greater synergies. At that time it had a $5 million annual budget and was serving many impoverished clients in some of the poorest nations of Latin America, the Caribbean, Asia, and Africa. While the integration of microcredit with other programs takes longer and is more costly, such advocates believe that the holistic approach greatly benefits the *whole woman,* not just her economic nature.

Other Practical Debates: Finally, it should be noted that there are numerous additional issues that differ between groups and experts doing microcredit. Lacking the space to explain them in full, I will simply list other issues below for readers to pursue according to their own interests:

- Does increasing microenterprise funding cannibalize other programs? Some worry that overemphasis on microcredit may be dangerous, because it could lead to cutbacks in other forms of poverty alleviation.

- How much time is required for one to rise from poverty? Critics feel concerned that microcredit takes too long to actually lift the poor from poverty. For example, one Grameen study reports that borrowers tend to receive loans for an average of period of *eight years* before they finally move out of poverty.

- Is microcredit exploiting women? Women bear the brunt of microcredit loans, thus becoming burdened with financial debt. Too often, the woman may not even control the use of such money, since the husband or other male family members may take her loan money for their own purposes.

- Are microenterprise products truly marketable? An ongoing debate concerns over whether products made by the poor are only sellable in weaker local markets, or whether they can be distributed beyond the village to international consumers?

- Work with savings or microcredit only? Some NGOs offer loans only, while others first require clients to start personal savings accounts as a way to learn money management and to build their own nest egg first. Then later, when loans are offered, the poor will understand some concerns like interest rates, principal, and other financial matters.

Additional Basic Criticisms: Finally, quite a number of researchers and policymakers argue strongly against what they call the "phenomenon" of microcredit. Their criticisms are summed up below:

- *Microcredit Hurts the Poor*—Some of them claim, quite forcefully, that microcredit exploits the poor by offering them loans to which they never had access to before, thereby "tempting" them with constant new offers and greater-and-greater debt. The adverse effects, they believe, may constrain those already suffering to a lifetime of deeper and deeper poverty.

- *Lack of Replicability*—Another critical argument is that microcredit only fits the informal economy of the developing world (formerly derogatorily called the "Third World"), not industrialized nations. Such claims have assumed that replicability is simply not possible in modern societies. While this was a major part of debate in the 1980s and 1990s, the evidence today is overwhelmingly to the contrary. Thousands of NGOs now operate in Europe, Canada, and the United States today, offering many successful models of microcredit.

Two Major Critiques of Microcredit

While I've long been an advocate and promoter of microcredit to the very poor, along with my longtime partner in such work, Professor Muhammad Yunus, the Nobel Peace Prize Laureate and founder of the Grameen Bank of Bangladesh, I'm well aware of some researchers' and government officials' concerns and complaints. So, I will use a few pages of this concluding chapter to balance the debates with several criticisms through the years.

Since the inception of the microcredit model in the 1980s, some "experts" have denied that a mere $60 microloan could do any good at all. Others claimed the process was a rip-off of the poor. Debates have raged now and then about the virtues of microfinance and other efforts to offer microloans, whether to use group-solidarity lending methods, whether an organization should become a for-profit or a nonprofit organization, and on and on into infinity. Two of the most recent hard-hitting attacks on microcredit are worth mentioning. One was featured on the front page of *The Wall Street Journal* two decades ago (Pearl and Phillips, 2001). Two reporters claimed that the MFI movement—and Grameen Bank in particular—did not play by traditional accounting rules and procedures that reputable financial institutions use. They charged that several other large-scale MFIs, as well as Grameen, really exist just to empower the poor, not make high profits as mainstream banks seek. But to those two reporters, apparently despite their having no training in pro-poor accounting systems of innovative microcredit programs, the system appeared cumbersome and ineffective.

In essence, though they called microcredit a "great idea," they went on to damn it with faint praise and then tried to dismantle it. But the *WSJ* staffers completely missed—or intentionally ignored?—the $3.2 billion by that time that impoverished rural Bangladeshi females had repaid to Grameen over the earlier two decades years. Instead, they emphasized the few millions of dollars in loans outstanding when they wrote their article. Part of the repayment problem their article complained about (but never confirmed) was due to the devastating Bangladesh floods that had engulfed half the country for more than two months. Some Grameen clients' businesses were destroyed, and millions of homes had water rising over their rooftops. So, Grameen responded with fresh loans to help victims dig out after the floodwaters receded and to get their microenterprises jump-started again.

In fact, since 2001, almost all that money has been repaid, and Grameen consistently has over *97 percent* of its more than 9.7 million borrowers paying their loans in full, on time, week after week, month after month, year after year. And that occurs among clients who are mostly illiterate, impoverished, and spread throughout distant rural areas lacking modern infrastructure, telephones, and even electricity. Many also suffer the ravages of natural disasters, mostly seasonal flooding, as well as civil strife and other instabilities—all factors quite different from the challenges faced by big U.S. banks. As of early 2022, Grameen Bank of Bangladesh had loaned out more than $35 billion to its country's poor. Thus, in fact, Grameen may enjoy a better record than Citibank or Bank of America, yet to outsiders seeking to diminish microcredit, no such comparisons were made in the *Wall Street Journal* article. Thus, the reporters set up a "straw man" of inefficiency and poor payment rates…and then knocked it down. Such criticisms against Grameen and other large MFIs may continue, though the resistance, along with countervailing data from the opposite side, ensure that microcredit is *not* about to collapse.

Most recently, another major American business journal, *Bloomberg Magazine*, has also tried to besmirch the microfinance movement (Finch, et al., 2022). The writers attempt to condemn MFIs in Cambodia and elsewhere, because there was corruption in some cases, as well as the struggles of peasant farmers in India and beyond who didn't pay back their microloans and ended up committing suicide. Those cases have been well documented and are certainly sad. But the reporters don't seem to realize that thousands of people commit suicide over debt from regular banks as well as well as "payday lenders." Experts are aware of the corruption that occurs now and then in major capitalist banks, which is likewise ugly and painful, whether we're talking about Wells Fargo or the big banks in Moscow. In fact, JPMorgan Chase, Deutsche Bank, HBSC, Standard Chartered, and Bank of New York Mellon were all accused of moving dirty money for over 20 years, despite evidence that they knew the funds were illicit. Will *Bloomberg Magazine* now move to close each of them and jail top executives? Of course not.

The fact is that Grameen and most microcredit institutions may enjoy a better record than Citibank or Bank of America. But to outsiders seeking to diminish microcredit, no such comparisons were made in either the *Bloomberg Magazine* or the *Wall Street Journal* article. Instead, the writers set up "straw men" of inefficiency, poor payment rates, borrower deaths, and government involvement in corrupt financial schemes, and then applied those bogus arguments to try to knock down the microfinance movement as a whole. The criticisms against Grameen and other large microfinance institutions may continue, yet the resistance, buttressed by countervailing data, ensure that microcredit is not about to die anytime soon.

While the criticisms, debates, and issues over microcredit rage, the behind-the-scenes reality is that the movement is in fact growing! Economists and other social scientists may fight over theories and concepts, but microenterprise development is increasingly being included in the curricula of numerous college courses on economics, as well as in research journals and the policies of large multilateral institutions like USAID, the World Bank, and the United Nations.

Differences in practical applications continue to grow as NGOs experiment, invent new models for offering help to people in need, and test the models and practices. While some see this as a weakness and wish there were one "grand system" that would work across cultures and diverse NGOs, others like myself feel delighted by the clashing controversies, because they yield new light and understanding, better methods, and future innovation. To such individuals, microcredit embodies the very essence of creating a new social invention. Like other technologies such as the telephone and computer, all the variations that will occur over the years to come mean promising options for microcredit practitioners, as well as sometimes-life-giving assistance for many thousands of consumers.

Finally, while the enemies of microfinance seek to halt, or at least slow, its course, their resistance will largely be irrelevant as the movement expands. Why? Because statistics from Action Against Hunger (2022), a report from the United Nations, suggest that currently some 811 million people globally live in "extreme" poverty, eking out an existence on less than $2.00 per person per day! Some 300 million-plus are children under age 18, and among them roughly 2 million die each year, most because of malnutrition. I can add other factors that make these data much worse, due to poverty and preventable diseases. In contrast, wealthy families across the world recently became richer than ever, and America itself has had a huge jump in those who were or now are billionaires.

To detractors who worry that microfinance burdens the poor with debt, so many more microentrepreneurs explicitly seek microloans *precisely so they can climb out of poverty*. To those who doubt microcredit's replicability and relevance in industrial nations, I suggest that virtually every modern country now has in place policies, funds, and practices for employing microfinance to mitigate its own economic problems. To hard-hitting critiques like those in *Bloomberg Magazine* or the *Wall Street Journal*, I offer the actual facts: Stories claiming that microfinance is "too good to be true," and that institutions like ACCIÓN and Grameen don't play by standardized U.S. rules, are contradicted by the fact that hundreds of new NGOs are springing up monthly around the globe. And they continue to outperform many traditional finance institutions!

Collectively, the growth of all these NGOs' has risen exponentially to more than 3,000 MFIs—which extend loans to *100 million of the world's poor*. Approximately 55 million are the very poorest people in their countries, while 82 percent are women. When the enormous impact of the microcredit movement is extended to include the average household family-size in the developing world, microcredit has now indirectly benefited some *400 million* men, women, and children.

Readers who wish to know about my lifetime of work among the poor around the globe may refer to my biographical details in *Appendix III*. It contains numerous links to sources of useful information on social entrepreneurship organizations that I have created or developed over my 48-year career.

Conclusion

As I reach the end of this humble little volume on how we all can work with God to help reduce poverty and allay suffering among the "poorest of the poor," I conclude with one last biblical verse—one that has given me impetus and courage in combating the ugly facts of people's always being hungry, suffering debilitating diseases, or trying to raise children in shantytown squalor in some far-off land. The courageous Apostle Paul declared, in II Timothy 1:7: *"For the Spirit God gave us does not make us timid, but gives us power, love and self-discipline."* We should never be afraid of changing the world. You and I—along with our families and friends, our neighbors and congregations—*can* draw on the powers of heaven to optimistically build a better world.

References

Action Against Hunger. (2022). "World Hunger Facts and Statistics" (from the UN's Hunger Report). https://www.actionagainsthunger.org/world-hunger-facts-statistics. May 12.

Acts 2:9–11; 3:1–11; 4:6–8; 4:16.

Finch, G., et al. (2022). "Big Money Backs Tiny Loans That Lead to Debt, Despair and Even Suicide." *Bloomberg Magazine,* https://www.bloomberg.com/graphics/2022-microfinance-banks-profit-off-developing-world/. May 3.

Freedom from Hunger. (2010). www.freedomfromhunger.org.

International Finance Corporation (IFC). (2022). https://www.ifc.org/wps/wcm/connect/industry_ext_content/ifc_external_corporate_site/financial+institutions/priorities/mesm/microfinance. April 14.

Japanese National Police Agency of Japan. (2019). "Police Countermeasures and Damage Situation associated with 2011 Tohoku district off the Pacific Ocean Earthquake." June 10.

Luke 5:12–16.

Pearl, D., and Phillips, M. M. (2001). "Grameen Bank, Which Pioneered Loans For the Poor, Has Hit a Repayment Snag." *Wall Street Journal,* November 27.

PKSF. (2021). Palli Karma Sahayak Foundation. "Citi Celebrates Successes of Small Businesses." *Daily Star,* April 16.

Smith, I. H., and Woodworth, W. P. (2011). "Developing Social Entrepreneurs and Social Innovators: A Social Identity and Self-Efficacy Approach." *Academy of Management Learning and Education,* vol. 11, no. 3, 390–407. http://dx.doi.org/10.5465/amle.2011.0016.

II Timothy 1:7.

Trivedi, R. (2011). The IDA to help a million Africans. http://www.microcapital.org/microcapital-brief.

Winfrey, O. (2018). "The signs you've found your passion in life." SuperSoul Sunday. YouTube video.

Woodworth, W. (2021). "Big, Bad, Audacious Unitus: Building a $1.2 Billion Social Business for Microcredit." *Noble International Journal of Social Sciences Research,* vol. 6, no. 4, pp. 48–55. https://napublisher.org/pdf-files/NIJSSR-6(4)-48-55.pdf. *gdSmart Content for Smart People* LA Progressive *A*

APPENDIX 1

TO LEARN MORE ABOUT MICROFINANCE AND HUMANITARIANISM

ACCIÓN International (www.accion.org)

ACDI/VOCA (www.acdivoca.org)

Adventist Development and Relief Agency/ADRA (https://adra.org)

American Indian Services (www.aisintl.org)

BRAC (www.brac.net)

BYU Center for Economic Self-Reliance (www.selfreliance.byu.edu)

CARE (www.care.org)

Care for Life (www.careforlife)

Catholic Relief Services (www.catholicrelief.org)

CGAP (The Consultative Group to Assist the Poor) (www.cgap.org)

Charity Anywhere Foundation (www.charityanywhere.org)

Chasqui Humanitarian (www.chasqui.org)

CHOICE (Center for Humanitarian Outreach and Intercultural Exchange) (www.choice.humanitarian.org)

Citigroup (www.citigroup.com)

Count Me In (www.count-me-in.org)

Financiera Compartamos (www.compartamos.com)

FINCA International (www.villagebanking.org)

Grameen America (https://www.grameenamerica.org)

Grameen Bank (www.grameen-info.org)

Grameen Foundation USA (www.gfusa.org)

HELP International (www.help-international.org)

Hope International (https://www.hopeinternational.org)

Intermediate Technology Development Group (www.itdg.org)

Jamii Bora (www.jamiibora.org)

Mentors International (www.enterprise-mentors.org)

MiBanco (www.mibanco.com.pe)

Microcredit Summit Campaign (www.microcreditsummit.org)

Microfinance Gateway (http://www.microfinancegateway.org)

MIX (Microfinance Information Exchange) (www.mixmarket.org)

Opportunity International/Women's Opportunity Fund (www.opportunity.org)
Ouelessebougou Alliance (www.sistercommunity.org)
ProMujer (www.promujer.org)
Reach the Children (www.reachthechildren.org)
Results International (www.microcreditsummit.org)
Samaritan's Purse (https://www.samaritanspurse.org)
Spandana (www.spandanaindia.com)
Swayam Krishi Sangam (www.sksindia.com)
Trickle-Up Program (www.trickleup.org)
United Nations (www.un.org; www.yearofmicrocredit.org)
Unitus (www.unitus.com)
World Relief (https://worldrelief.org)
World Vision (https://www.worldvision.org)
Yehu Bank (www.yehu.org)

Finding Other Microcredit Organizations

A single directory of all microcredit organizations worldwide does not exist. The following two organizations provide searches of their partner databases that can help locate microcredit organizations. Hence, these are *not* exhaustive directories:

> Association for Enterprise Opportunity (https://aeoworks.org/) primarily lists U.S. microcredit organizations.

> Microcredit Summit Campaign (https://results.org/mcs/ and https://www.devex.com/organizations/microcredit-summit-campaign-23552)

A directory of development organizations is also listed at www.devdir.org, with microcredit organizations marked with this symbol: **[M].**

Books and Articles on Microcredit

This list of books on microcredit contains some of the best introductory and more-advanced books on microcredit, written by or about people mentioned in the documentary named in the "Videos on Microcredit" section below. Other books on microcredit can be found at your local or online bookstore.

> *Banker to the Poor: Micro-Lending and the Battle Against World Poverty,* by Muhammad Yunus
> *Give Us Credit: How Muhammad Yunus' Microlending RevolutionIs Empowering Women from Bangladesh to Chicago,* by Alex Counts

Small Really Is Beautiful: Micro Approaches to Third World Development—Microentrepreneurship, Microenterprise, and Microfinance, by Warner Woodworth

The Miracles of Barefoot Capitalism: A Compelling Case for Microcredit, by Jim Klobuchar

Microfinance Distance Learning Course, by Heather Clark

Pathways Out of Poverty: Innovations in Microfinance for the Poorest Families, by Sam Daley-Harris (ed.)

The New World of Microenterprise Finance: Building Healthy Financial Institutions for the Poor, by Maria Otero, Elisabeth Rhyne (ed.)

The Price of a Dream: The Story of the Grameen Bank, by David Bornstein

Videos on Microcredit

Videos dealing with microcredit include the following, found at www.rooymedia.com/toourcredit/tapes.htm:

To Our Credit: Bootstrap Banking and the World (Part 1)
To Our Credit: Bootstrap Banking in America (Part 2)
Faces of Microcredit
In Their Words
Building Better Lives

Other online films or video programs include:

Good Works, Grameen and Microcredit— Muhammad Yunus: Banker to the Poor Interview. https://www.youtube.com/watch?v=krv385puXJU

To Catch a Dollar. One-hour documentary film. https://www.imdb.com/title/tt1541943/

Microfinance | BYU - Prof. Warner Woodworth. https://www.youtube.com/watch?v=APdODNs1rQw

The History of Microfinance. https://opportunity.org/learn/videos/muhammad-yunus-history-of-microfinance

With outside filmmakers, at BYU we made a one-hour PBS documentary, *Small Fortunes: Microcredit and the Future of Poverty,* which features some of our NGOs and partner MFIs around the world (Grameen, Acción, FINCA, and others). It also highlights concrete ways to establish action groups and fight poverty. See http://kbyutv.org/smallfortunes; or http://pbs.org/kbyu/smallfortunes; or www.selfreliance.byu.edu/store.cfm.

APPENDIX 2

SWOT ANALYSIS APPLIED TO ASSESSING AND/OR GROWING A NEW NGO

Below is a management consulting tool I have used to advise and assist a range of clients over the years, including corporate executives, labor leaders, public school administrators, state and city government officials, and religious leaders in improving their organizations. In a variety of cases, I have used these techniques with some of the nongovernmental organizations (NGOs) we have either launched or evaluated after years of social impacts. We have successfully applied these tools in Africa, Latin America, and Asia to discover new opportunities, as well as to manage and eliminate potential threats.

SWOT Analysis is a useful technique for understanding an NGO's **S**trengths and **W**eaknesses, and also to explore whatever **O**pportunities and **T**hreats it may face—hence, *SWOT*. Used in an organizational context, it may help to carve a sustainable niche in your social enterprise.

Social Business SWOT Analysis

What makes SWOT particularly powerful is that it can help uncover opportunities that your organization is well placed to develop. By understanding the weaknesses of your business, you can manage and eliminate threats that would otherwise catch you unawares.

More than this, by looking at your NGO using the SWOT framework, you can design a strategy that helps distinguish your nonprofit from others, especially when beginning a new project or program after, for example, Hurricane Maria's destruction in Honduras, or the civil conflicts in Mozambique, both of which catastrophes your new program could attempt to help.

To use this SWOT Analysis, answer the following questions:

Strengths:
- What advantages does your NGO have?
- What do you do better than anyone else?
- What unique resources do you have access to?
- What may others see in your efforts? Your strengths?

Consider these issues from an internal perspective, as well as from the point of view of outsiders, whether they be potential clients, village chiefs, donors, or even competitors. Be realistic: It's easy to fall prey to the "not invented here syndrome."

In looking at your strengths, think about them in relation to other successful groups such as volunteer skills, innovative services, and the like.

Weaknesses:
- What could you improve?
- What should you avoid?
- What are outsiders likely to see as weaknesses?

Do this from an internal *and* external basis: Do other people seem to perceive weaknesses that you do not see? Are other NGOs doing any better than you? It is advisable to be realistic *now,* and to face any unpleasant truths before things become more problematic.

Opportunities:
- Where are the good opportunities facing your NGO?
- What are the latest trends of which you are aware?
- How may you capture the positives?

Useful opportunities can come from such things as:

- Changes in government policy
- Changes in technology and markets
- Changes in social patterns, lifestyles, and population trends
- Local developments

The approach for looking at opportunities requires that you assess your NGO strengths honestly, and then ask whether they open up any opportunities. Alternatively, look at your weaknesses and consider whether new opportunities may emerge by eliminating problems.

Threats:
- What are the greatest obstacles your organization faces?
- What are other NGOs doing that you should be aware of?
- Are the requirements changing for successful humanitarian aid or microfinance?
- Is new technology challenging your work?
- Do you have financial problems?
- Could any of your weaknesses seriously threaten your nonprofit?

SWOT analysis can be illuminating by putting problems into perspective and then helping you determine what needs to be done to ensure future organizational success. **It should be emphasized that strengths** and **weaknesses** are often *internal* to your organization. By contrast, **opportunities** and **threats** often relate to *external* NGO factors.

A new NGO might draw up the following SWOT matrix:

Strengths:
- We can respond very quickly, since we have no red tape and no need for higher management approval.
- We can give really good customer care, perhaps because we have plenty of time to devote to that.
- The NGO leader on this project has gained strong skills from her or his academic education.
- We can quickly change directions if needed.

Weaknesses:
- Our new NGO is just starting up, so we may have little experience or reputation.
- Our small staff has only a shallow skill set.
- Because of a large disaster such as climate change, COVID-19, or other, our NGO is vulnerable to absenteeism, sick staffers, or frequent turnover.
- Our cash flow will be unreliable in the early stages.

Opportunities:
- The country's nonprofit sector is expanding and has new opportunities for impacts.
- The local council wants to encourage our kind of development work, because we provide good services
- Competing NGOs in the area may be slow to adopt new technologies, so we may get ahead of them.

Threats:
- Will rapid shifts in government policies affect our programs?
- How may new technologies change our plans beyond our ability to adapt?
- Might even small changes in political or other factors wipe out the actual impacts we achieve?

SUMMARY: **SWOT Analysis is a simple but powerful framework for analyzing an NGO's Strengths and Weaknesses, as well as the Opportunities and Threats needing to be faced. It is a useful tool that may assist your focus on organizational pluses and minuses while helping you take the greatest possible advantage of available opportunities.**

APPENDIX 3

Changing the World, One Person, One Family, One Community at a Time . . .

"Faith, Hope, and Charity"

"Never doubt that a small group of thoughtful, committed citizens can change the world. Indeed, it's the only thing that ever has." — Margaret Mead

Dr. Warner Woodworth, Global Social Entrepreneur (2022): My Social Innovation Work with the Poor Through Microcredit, Social Entrepreneurship, and Sustainability in Leading Global Change

Ever dreamed of changing the world? This appendix summarizes some of the microcredit work my associates and I have been doing over the past 40 years as change agents, entrepreneurs, professionals, college students, and friends to design courses, apply concepts, develop action models, and offer pro-bono consulting to fight poverty and address social problems. I hope they will suggest applications that more individuals like yourself may want to consider. These efforts grow out of the projects we have designed and implemented with our partners through the Marriott School of Business at BYU and other institutions I've worked with—teaching courses and offering mentoring and service-learning opportunities all while doing research and publication. Some of these social ventures have resulted in public recognition—including praise from President Bill Clinton's Global Initiative Award, Grameen Foundation's Practitioner Excellence Award, *Fast Company* magazine/Monitor Consulting Group's Social Capital Award, the Drucker Centennial Professorship at Claremont University, and the Faculty Pioneer Award for social impacts from the Aspen Institute in New York City. In some cases, we've had involvement of multiple partners—to help as project advisers, to provide service on various boards of directors of NGOs (nongovernmental organizations), and to donate their personal money as well as time.

The resources and links below show areas that may be of interest to you and your associates regarding our activities in Asia, Africa, and Latin America. They foster social entrepreneurship, scale up microcredit strategies, strengthen family well-being, build social capital, and generate Third World improvements. They show examples of how individuals, NGOs, and businesses may partner as resource systems for combating poverty, thus enabling networks, groups and organizations to become incubators in which to design, create, assess, and then spin-off social enterprises. We believe this will open a dialogue as to what others may accomplish as we collectively work to transform people's capacity for achieving economic self-reliance while helping to solve global problems.

Strategies: Social Entrepreneurship, Microcredit, Self-Reliance, Economic Development, Action Research and Learning, Cooperatives, Worker Ownership, Social Impacts, and NGOs

Where: Worldwide (1980s–2022)

Programs: Over nearly four decades, I have sought to recruit, train, and send over 3,400 university students out from universities such as Stanford, Virginia Tech, Utah, Portland State, Harvard, Brigham Young University, Yale, Colorado State, and many others, along with volunteers from Germany, the U.K., Brazil, Panama, Canada, and more, as global change agents—to partner with businesses, create new worker cooperatives and NGOs, work with existing social enterprises, and strive to foster sustainable strategies to empower the poor. Together, we have designed and implemented some 60 projects to build civil society and reduce poverty. As of now, 41 of them have become NGOs that operate in many countries. Others function today as social businesses that utilize leading-edge management tools *to serve the poor*, not to make a profit. In 2021 alone, through all these efforts, we collectively raised some *$29 million* in donations and investment capital, *trained over 264,000 poor women*, and grew their microentrepreneur base to *more than 8.2 million clients!* I'm a cofounder of Unitus, Mentors International, HELP International, and other NGOs. I invite you to also involve your friends and colleagues in these programs. In addition to providing new courses, training modules, student theses, and faculty mentoring, we have produced several tools for change. Much of this has occurred because of individuals' becoming committed to making a real difference in society.

What: Established a $3 million Center for Economic Self-Reliance (now the Ballard Center): http://marriottschool.byu.edu/selfreliance

- ❖ Held 12 years of annual conferences, bringing together top practitioners, donors, NGOs, students, and faculty: See http://marriottschool.byu.edu/selfreliance for more information.
- ❖ Published 12 books such as *Small Really Is Beautiful: Micro Approaches to Third World Development* (Third World Think Tank), Latter-day Saint volumes on using Christianity to improve the world—including books such as my new volume, *Radiant Mormonism* (2022); plus *Working Toward Zion* (Aspen Books–Modern United Order Practices); *United for Zion;* and others on management and social change such as *Industrial Democracy* (Sage); *Creating Labor-Management Partnerships* (Addison-Wesley); and more
- ❖ Founder of the *Journal of Microfinance:* http://marriottschool.byu.edu/microfinance
- ❖ Authored 300+ articles, and presented some 400 conference papers around the globe

Who: Dr. Warner Woodworth (Social Entrepreneur and Professor Emeritus)

Email: warnerwoodworth@gmail.com or warnersocialentrepreneur@hotmail.com
Website: http://warnerwoodworth.com
LinkedIn: https://www.linkedin.com/in/warner-woodworth-b775a4/
Facebook: https://www.facebook.com/warner.woodworth

"Earth provides enough to satisfy every Man's need, but not enough for every man's greed."
— Mahatma Gandhi

Social Enterprises and MFIs: Organizations we have started and/or been deeply involved with include:

- Sustain Haiti (Post Earthquake Haiti) http://www.sustain-haiti.org/
- Care for Life (Mozambique) http://careforlife.org
- Lifting Hands International (Collecting/shipping donations to the poor in Ukraine, Syria, Poland, and more) https://www.liftinghandsinternational.org/why-ship
- CHOICE Humanitarian (Nepal and 7 other countries) http://www.choicehumanitarian.org/
- Reach the Children (Tanzania and 8 other African nations) www.reachthechildren.org
- Hope Worldwide (Mobilizing volunteers to serve in refugee camps in Jordan, Greece, Bangladesh, and others) http://www.hopeworldwideutah.org
- Mothers Without Borders (Zambia) https://motherswithoutborders.org/
- H.E.L.P. International (Throughout Asia, Africa, Latin America, Belize, and others) http://help-international.org
- Ascend Alliance (Ethiopia, Bolivia, Perú, Ecuador) http://ascendalliance.org
- Cause For Hope (Honduras, Nicaragua) http://causeforhope.org
- Eagle Condor Humanitarian (Peru) http://eagle-condor.org
- Academy for Creating Enterprise (Philippines, Mexico, Ghana) http://creatingenterprise.com
- Charity Anywhere Foundation (Mexico) https://www.charityanywhere.org/
- Empowering Nations (Wave of Hope Thailand, Ghana, Panama) http://empoweringnations.org
- Serving Native Elders (Multiple tribes) https://www.anelder.org/
- PIN: Purpose Investor Network (Utah) http://pin-svp.org
- Mentores para la Microempresa (Utah Latino Community) http://microbusinessmentors.org
- Rising Star Outreach (Leprosy communities in India) http://risingstaroutreach.org
- DoTerra (Firm with social impacts) https://www.doterra.com/
- Mentors International (Central America, Africa, Philippines) http://mentorsinternational.org
- Ouelessebougou Alliance (Mali, West Africa) http://sistercommunity.org
- Globus Relief (Delivering healthcare worldwide) www.globusrelief.org/
- Yehu Microfinance (Kenya) http://yehu.org http://www.asante-foundation.org
- Grameen America (11 cities in U.S.) http://grameenamerica.com
- The Other Side Academy (TOSA) http://www.theothersideacademy.com
- Micro-Business USA (Florida immigrants) http://microbusinessusa.org
- Thrive Gulu (Uganda) https://thrivegulu.org/
- Mondragon (Basque country) www.mondragon-corporation.com/
- Microcredit Summit Campaign (Global) http://microcreditsummit.org
- Cotopaxi (Firm making outdoor gear for doing good) http://cotopaxi.org

- Rebuild for Peace (Jordan) www.rebuildforpeace.org/
- Ethikco (Musana Ugandan women's cooperatives) https://ethikco.com/
- Unitus (India, Mexico, Argentina, Indonesia, Philippines, Tanzania, Kenya) http://unitus.com
- First Hope (Orphanage in Nepal) www.firsthope
- Centre for Alternative Technology (CAT Appropriate Tech) https://cat.org.uk/
- Food for Everyone (Square Foot Gardening Methods) www.growfood.
- ProLiteracy (Global literacy NGO) https://www.proliteracy.org/
- WOW supports refugees) www.womenofworld.org/
- H20 for Humanity (Clean Water India) www.h2oforhumanity.com/
- American Indian Services (Native American Tribes) https://www.americanindianservices.org/

Other Smaller Projects/NGOs: SOAR (Sichuan, China), Acción Contra la Pobreza (Honduras), SOL (A sustainability NGO in rural Parana, Brazil), Liahona Economic Development Foundation (Lagos, Nigeria), Achatina Snail Farms (Rural Accra, Ghana), Nova Geração (Criciúma, Brazil), Paramita Group (Thailand and Asia), 100 Humanitarians (Kenya), and dozens more.

I have had the privilege of getting to know a number of associates from other collaborating NGOs and academic programs who, like me, are involved in research, funding, and promoting social entrepreneurship. I have advised or collaborated with some of them including the following:

- Aspen Institute (social innovation) http://aspeninstitute.org
- Program on Social Enterprise (Yale) http://mba.yale.edu
- Idealist Org http://idealist.org
- Harvard Initiative on Social Enterprise http://hbs.edu./socialenterprise
- Institute for Social Entrepreneurs http://socialent.org
- *Social Edge* (online magazine) http://socialedge.org
- Ashoka (Innovations for the Public) http://ashoka.org

- Wharton Business School, University of Pennsylvania https://socialimpact.wharton.upenn.edu
- Net Impact (MBAs doing good) http://netimpact.org

—◆—

Film: A one-hour PBS documentary we produced, *Small Fortunes,* is accessible on the web that features some of our NGOs and partner MFIs around the world. It also highlights concrete ways to establish action groups and fight poverty. See http://kbyutv.org/smallfortunes and/or http://pbs.org/kbyu/smallfortunes.

JOIN US IN BUILDING A MOVEMENT OF GLOBAL CHANGE AGENTS TO TRANSFORM THE WORLD!

"Each microloan is a voyage of self-discovery. All human beings have unlimited potential. These little monies give women an opportunity to discover their self-worth."
— Muhammad Yunus, Grameen Bank, 2006 Nobel Peace Prize Laureate

Having an awareness of how we are breathing and then maintaining relaxed, deep breaths brings forth the possibility of inner transformation.

When we consciously control our breathing, we can experience the reaction that occurs. As we breathe deep and slow, we create an inner calm and reconnect to the source of vitality *and* serenity.

The breath is also our connection to intelligent creativity. Breath and inspiration are breathed into us from the spirit, giving us divine guidance. Spirit inspires us to reach our full potential and find our purpose. This higher power is just the next breath away!

Meditation with Jesus teaches us to be aware of this life-enhancing source; it teaches us that God is with us in every moment and can literally breathe virtues, such as patience, into us. Try this: inhale as you silently spell *P-A-T-I-E-N-C-E* and then exhale. Repeat.

To illustrate the power and importance of the breath, many meditation practices or guided meditations begin with one of the following prompts:

Observe the breath.
Witness the breath.
Focus on the breath.
Follow the breath.
Concentrate on the breath.
Center on the breath.
Connect to the breath.
Take long, deep breaths.
Breathe in to a count of . . .
Breathe out for a count of . . .
Breathe fast.
Breathe slow.
Retain the breath.
Watch your breathing.

Breath is the sacred invisible power of God. It is meant to fuel the body, enliven the soul, and give us access to the spirit. "And the LORD God formed man of the dust of the ground, and breathed into his nostrils the breath of life; and man became a living soul" (Genesis 2:7 KJV).

INSPIRATION

Our breath is a gift. Breath is God's spirit and part of us in every cell we have. He's intimately within and around us, like the air we breathe. God used breath to make the first human. God uses breath to breathe new life into humanity. One day, we will surrender our breath to return to him. The breath of life is our link to our life source. With every breath we take, we are reminded that our lives exist because of a benevolent Creator. Consider that our breath, the air we breathe in and out of our bodies, is our direct connection to the spirit of God.

Remember, we are creating with every breath we take. Depending on how we breathe, we can create peace and harmony or we can create stress and anxiety in our bodies. We can use the breath to make our journey calm and peaceful or one filled with discord.

Our state of mind and how we breathe are inseparable. A calm and peaceful mind reflects calm and relaxed breathing. Long deep breaths feel like rest and safety, allowing us to access our thoughts consciously. This can give us more control over our thoughts. Taking short, shallow breaths or holding our breath can feel like fear and death, causing us to ruminate or make our thoughts scatter. Thoughts easily lead to emotions and then to actions. We can use our breaths to calm our souls and refocus ourselves on conscious, wise, deliberate actions.

I invite you to take time to experience the presence of God flowing in the breath as love. Breathe into your heart more love, and breathe out love for others and the world. Allow this loving spirit to fill you until you overflow with caring and compassion.

The breath of life is part of our identity and can help us to visualize that we are never alone. The breath feeds and nourishes us as it creates movement, pulsation, and vibration. It brings in vital nutrients and chemicals for our bodies to use. When we need more power, we can turn to the breath for a dose of spiritual power.

God's design is brilliant. We are given breath moment by moment to return our focus back to our hearts. As the breath goes deep, we contact the spirit of God, who dwells inside our bodies and souls. We have the privilege to have his spirit flowing in and out of us. This is the practice of receiving God, who gives us the self-control to pause before saying or doing something we might regret later. The ability to breathe deeply and relax is God's gift, enabling us to experience more peace, patience, and serenity. Through the breath of life, we can courageously face any obstacle with strength and wisdom, knowing that God is in each breath we take.

The goal is to stay consciously connected to the breath, the force of new life, God's spirit, and the higher power that he is. We stay calm and wise, letting the breath of life lead us into everything good. This can cultivate the virtue of goodness inside all of us.

INTEGRATE

Become aware of your breath, your connection to life. Take long, slow, deep breaths through your nose. Breathe deeply and rhythmically. Try the breath of peace. Inhale to a count of five (*P-E-A-C-E*) and exhale (*P-E-A-C-E*). Alternatively, attempt the breath of love. Breathe in *L-O-V-E*, hold in *L-O-V-E*, exhale *L-O-V-E*, hold out *L-O-V-E*, and repeat.

Imagine the breath as spirit, vitality, power, and inspiration. Imagine it purifying, calming, and healing as it creates feelings of safety, serenity, and a connection to your inner self. Inhale deeply and feel God enter. Exhale slowly and feel love exit.

Notice a feeling of calm and relaxation coming into the body. Breathe in and out of your heart. Allow the goodness of the breath to flow lovingly into your body, bringing you new life. Stay connected to the breath of life throughout the practice and into your day.

INQUIRY

1. Are you aware of how you breathe most of the time?

2. Is becoming aware of how you are breathing helping you? In what ways?

3. Do you move fast or slow? Talk fast or slow? Eat fast or slow? Breathe fast or slow?

4. Do you need to slow down, speed up, or find balance?

"To meditate with mindful breathing is to bring body and mind back to the present moment so that you do not miss your appointment with life."[13] (Thích Nhất Hạnh)

5. Do you normally breathe deep or shallow?

6. Can you commit to practicing a period of deep breathing every day for at least five minutes?

7. What is the most difficult thing about being conscious about breathing?

8. Do you believe that breath is the spirit of the Almighty? What is your experience?

"[A]ll things share the same breath—the beast, the tree, the man ... If all the beasts were gone, men would die from great loneliness of spirit, for whatever happens to the beasts also happens to man. All things are connected"[14] (Chief Seattle).

"[T]he air shares its spirit with all life it supports. It is the wind that gave our grandfather his first breath. It is the wind that receives his last sigh."[15] (Chief Seattle)

THE WORD—HARMONIZE

THE WORD

Joy

> For the word of God is living and active, and sharper than
> any two-edged sword, even penetrating as far as the division
> of soul and spirit, of both joints and marrow, and able to
> judge the thoughts and intentions of the heart.
> —Hebrews 4:12 NASB

As the breath gives us super inner powers, our words can give us inner *and* outer power. Our consciously projected words, fulfilled by actions, are another gift and higher power. Never underestimate the power of the Word and the power that words have in our lives!

Did you know Jesus is referred to as the Word of God? "In the beginning was the Word, and the Word was with God, and the Word was God" (John 1:1 WEB). The apostle John goes on to say, "So the Word became human and made his home among us. He was full of unfailing love and faithfulness. And we have seen his glory, the glory of the Father's one and only Son" (John 1:14 NLT).

Jesus called himself the Son of Man—a human representing all of humanity. He came to earth to elevate, lift, and bring love and peace to all human beings and to create a new generation with new ways of being human. He and his words are full of grace and truth.

Jesus teaches us how to find and be more like God and attain more power. One way we can do that is by using our words wisely.

Jesus spoke God's words. These highly energetic messages came from Jesus's heart and contained the keys to positive change. The messages were of peace, love, joy, unity, healing, mercy, justice, inclusivity, humility, and more. We can believe in Jesus and that he was sent by God to light our way, guiding us into truth and dying for us so that we could be set free.

We can meditate on his words until they renew and change the quality of our minds. These words can transform us by changing our mindsets, beliefs, and perceptions about ourselves and our lives. We can take these words in and let them flow out of us uniquely. By using these words, we begin to imitate Jesus in our actions, which can turn us into more powerful human beings. We find the words of Jesus in the Bible and the gospels of his disciples.

Even in modern times, the expression and experience of these words can lift and elevate our spirits and heal our souls. Heal humanity. When enough people on the earth transform their thinking, we can collaborate fully in serving one another. If we believe that God's words are true, we are open to receiving an advocate, a helper, who cooperates with us and works on our behalf.

Before Jesus died, he said to his followers, "And I will ask the Father, and He will give you another Advocate to be with you forever—the Spirit of truth" (John 14:16–17 BSB). Notice Jesus asked. That's because God doesn't force anything on anyone. We have "free" will, but if we believe in Jesus and ask for what we need, the spirit of truth can clarify God's words, guide our hearts, and bring us out of darkness into the light. Truth defeats and lifts darkness. In the presence of truth we become stronger. Jesus wants us to be enlightened, so he sends us an advocate who lights the path for us. He wants us to understand our identity. Truth is our identity. We have the power within, and truth can set us free.

When we meditate with Jesus, we start the day opening our hearts to receive and become grounded in God's unfailing love. We cleanse our hearts from the illusion that we are alone. We begin to surrender our words, which include our thoughts, fears, and limiting beliefs, to God's spirit of truth. We receive new possibilities and shifts in perspective that engage our souls' desire to thrive. New thoughts emerge, creating transformation within our minds. New thoughts bring new ways of feeling and being, causing shifts in how we act.

The gospel or teachings of Jesus are called the "gospel of the grace of God" (Acts 20:24 KJV). *Gospel* means "good news."[16] Jesus came to teach us how to acquire more grace, which is a sense of ease, flow, and blessings. Grace increases hope. When we have hope, we become inspired to follow a path further toward wisdom and dignity. His words teach us how to make our lives better, how to have internal harmony, and how to harmonize with others. His words eventually become our own.

Words have power and life because sound is vibration, frequency, and wavelength, which are movements of energy. Our words are an energetic and creative force. They have the power to create or disrupt. Imagine an opera singer with the power to shatter glass with her voice. Shattering is just one example of how sound can affect the physical material world, including our bodies.

Most religions agree that there is power in the word. Words can be used to create harmony. Unfortunately, words can also create disharmony. Therefore, we must be careful and responsible for what we say. Christ-centered meditation can help us observe our thoughts, giving us a quiet space to discern whether our thoughts should become words.

Science can prove that words are a powerfully creative force. Negative and demeaning words can cause a stress response in the body and disorganization and disharmony in our cells. Our words can hurt, or they can heal.[17] Science also shows us that our thoughts are creative. Thoughts are tiny packages of vibrational information that travel throughout our bodies[18] and can cause a physical reaction. Thoughts can create feelings, and feelings can create actions. Our actions can lead to either positive or negative consequences. As Dan Millman said, "Energy follows thought."[19]

INTROSPECTION

The sun was barely awake, and my candle and incense flickered and smoked in the dim light. I was sitting cross-legged on my cushion, eyes closed. It started as just another morning of singing songs to God until I heard a distinctly different voice from within. It called me to make my own devotional music using Bible concepts and scriptures. I heard this same subtle prodding for about half a year. I kept thinking, *Why do I keep hearing this message? How would I do this?* I wasn't a musician or a theologian. One day, I finally decided to stop resisting and rejecting this persistent yet gently encouraging voice.

I finally said yes to this "divine appointment" and began to follow the directions I heard. Once I did, songs poured out of me. I wrote them down during my meditation time or sometimes before getting out of bed. Early in the morning, new songs would sing to me. Shortly after, I met a musician who also wrote songs to God. Then a friend with a recording studio offered to help. And so it went.

God's grace flowed into my life because I answered his calling. And now I believe that's how it works. We hear the words and will of God, and if we say yes, he is there to help because it was all his idea. He wants it to be done; knows we can do it; and, therefore, gives us the power and grace to take his call to fruition.

God enabled me to create something I love, and now I help others too. People say my music gives them deep inner peace. Some say it keeps their family time in the car enjoyable, and others have said it helped them through a period of healing. It's all because I've learned to follow the voice and words of God. Often, God's will appears to be a daunting, almost-impossible task to tackle. However, accepting the challenge always makes us stronger and wiser and brings us more purpose in the end. You could say I'm devoted. But what does that mean exactly?

Devotion means a feeling of strong love.[20] When I start my day in devotion to God and bring my love to this time of meditation, I instantly feel love flowing in and around me. Before my mind has a chance to begin working on my to-do list, solving some of my problems, or planning the day ahead, I return to a dedicated space in my house where I can sit with God. In this space, I open my heart. I receive God's spirit of truth. I dwell in his love. The best part is that I never know what will be revealed that day. Unsurprisingly,

I hear God's voice the clearest during my time in the morning when I'm singing, chanting, meditating, listening, or reading God's Word.

As part of my morning routine, I take a quick shower, wrap myself in a robe, grab a cup of coffee or tea, and sit down to spend a little time with Jesus. It often feels like angels and saints are there with me too. It is a powerful way to start the day. I've been sitting with God first thing in the morning for many years now. This practice elevates my spirit and allows me to hear my soul and his voice in a clear, simple, and enjoyable way.

Singing and chanting harmonize and balance my body. It raises my vibration and prepares me for the inner work of meditation. After I sing, I can easily sit and explore the truth in my soul. I check in with my mind, emotions, and desires. I accept and allow who I am, my reality and my truth. Every day is different, and I never know what I will discover or uncover about myself. Sometimes I have to cry. Some days, I feel dark; on other days, I feel fine.

Regardless of how I feel, God always shows up with his love for me. When I connect to him first thing in the morning, my day always seems to be filled with grace, truth, and new possibilities. I can begin my day with a clear mind, allowing me to control my words. The days that I go without this morning practice are the days when I feel like I don't have as much grace or haven't refueled with God's light. Meditation is like a shower for my heart and soul. I start my day knowing who I am and who God is, and I always know he has my back. I stay connected. My only fear in life is that I will be cut off from his love and grace.

INSIGHT

If our words are powerful and creative, imagine the power in God's voice and words. God gives ordinary people assignments called divine appointments, and if we are listening and willing to follow them, magical things will happen. God's voice and words are alive and powerful. They can easily cut through the chatter, fears, and doubts in our minds. Resistance and an inability to move forward to a victorious life often come from a battle between our "free" will and God's will. Fortunately, we can learn to listen and find a deeper source of truth during meditation.

Christ-centered meditation helps us to slow down our thoughts, observe our thoughts, and choose our thoughts. This gives us the ability to have divine speech, enabling us to create more goodness in our lives and experience fewer negative consequences. If the mind believes something to be true, it can become true in our lives. Renewing the mind with new words and thoughts is, therefore, necessary. We can sing words of devotion from our hearts, meditate on the words and love of Christ, and receive help from the spirit of truth. By doing this, we transform the soul, raise our energy, and deepen our creativity. We begin to think and act more like Jesus from these spiritual practices.

Chanting, singing, speaking, reading, and praying can increase feelings of well-being.[21] Monks, nuns, saints, prophets, visionaries, doctors, and spiritual masters use words, music, and singing as tools for transformation. Science has shown that music and singing elevate thoughts and feelings to a higher vibration.[22] Positive words flowing through us in sincere devotion unite our bodies and souls through our hearts using the energy of love. Many cultures, religions, and meditation practices use the spoken word, chant, mantra, or singing to reach God.

Chanting, singing, worshipping, and praising have many physical, psychological, and spiritual benefits. The chant or song captures the mind, allowing the heart to open and express or release. These acts create a channel between the mind and the heart, opening communication and releasing endorphins, the body's happy chemicals. They, in turn, give us a feeling of connection and well-being. Internal harmony is created and new power is released every time the body, soul, and spirit unite.

INSPIRATION

The spirit of Christ lives in all of us. He wants our hearts to be his home—the place where he can move, live, speak, bring new life, and transform our bodies and souls. His light and words can raise our consciousness. And our energy! This can help us with the words we think and speak because his thoughts transform ours. His powerful words cleanse our minds of lower vibrational thoughts, such as fear and doubt, and elevate our thoughts into ones with higher vibrations, such as love and acceptance. Our word is one of our most powerful allies, yet it can also contribute to our destruction. Therefore, we must learn to use our words wisely. Jesus can teach us how.

Every morning, as we become still to meditate, chant, read, listen, or pray, we come home to our hearts. Meditating with Jesus allows us to see things in a different light and disrupt our old patterns of thought. Spiritual practices help us to slow down and observe our thoughts, emotions, and desires without having to act, thus helping us to gain more self-control. Most of us need to practice having self-control over our words. This begins with increasing our ability to witness our thoughts and remain in stillness and, if necessary, silence.

Thankfully, we can sit with God and seek his guidance. God loves to hear our voices, and prayer is using our thoughts or words to talk to God. God longs to be close to us. Talking and listening is a way to intimacy. The more we practice being honest with God, the more intimate and authentic we become. Also, the more blessings and grace we receive. We create our lives with the words and prayers we speak. We learn to watch, wait, and pray. We learn to pay attention. As we do, we have more discernment to make wise decisions. We listen to the whispers of God and wait patiently. This is mastery over self or self-control.

The highest vibration is that of God the Most High. He is above all and through all. Jesus, who is God's Word, was here on earth to serve humanity to elevate, lift, and bring glory—which is honor, prestige, and distinction—to human beings. Thoughts and words can be the mechanisms to change ourselves and inspire others. When we share our souls with God, when we talk or sing to him, he talks back to us and guides us. Through meditation and prayer, all of us can learn to walk confidently in the process of cocreating with God.

Jesus the Word gives us steps through his actions and *his words*, teaching us how to become better people. Hearing a divine appointment or God's voice is a blessing. It puts us on the pathway to becoming more spiritual, having a spiritual awakening, and knowing what to do today, right now, or at any moment. If you are reading this book, you are on the right path, so keep listening and following.

The goal is to use our voices and control our words in thinking and speaking. When we do, we use our words and God's words to cocreate. This can cultivate the virtue of joy inside all of us.

INTEGRATE

Select one of my YahLight devotional chants, or a worship song, hymn, or mantra that is repetitive, easy, and heart-centered. Once you start to sing, notice how sound creates vibration, movements of energy, balance, and harmony in your body. Listen to your unique voice. Witness your multidimensional nature singing, breathing, thinking, feeling, desiring, and listening all at once. Memorize the words to the song and close your eyes. Sing with joy and sincerity from your heart.

Imagine that God is listening and harmonizing with you. Sing at least one song for five minutes. Be willing to sit completely still and hold your body in a dignified position with your heart open. Resist the desire to move or stop singing. At the end of the song, take a deep breath in and hold it for as long as you can. Next, expand this breath into all areas of your body and release it slowly. While sitting, singing, and meditating, listen for the voice of God. Get to the point where you can sit and sing and meditate for longer periods.

Contemplate or memorize God's Word instead of or in addition to singing. Listen to a YahLight scriptural contemplation or select a Bible verse. Allow God's words to penetrate your heart and renew your mind with new thoughts.

EXPLORE STEP 4

Scan to get started with
YahLight *Devotional Chants*
and *Scriptural Contemplations*

scan me

INQUIRY

1. Did you realize words are powerful? How aware are you of your thoughts? The words you use?

2. Can you think of a thought that has created bad feelings for you? What words in the past made you cry?

3. Was there a person or people in your life who said negative, demeaning, or cruel things to you? What did they say? Do you say these thoughts to yourself? How does this make you feel?

4. What are the most critical things you think or say about yourself? Is it possible your thoughts or words are creating in your life? What thoughts can you begin to think that would create a better life for you?

"[Y]our ears will hear a voice behind you, saying, This is the way; walk in it." (Isaiah 30:21 NIV)

5. Before reading this book, did you know Jesus was called the Word of God? What does this mean to you? Would you like to, or have you, invited Jesus into your heart? What difference has this made in your life, or what do you think the changes would be?

6. Do you think in terms of good or bad? Can you change the words to *beneficial* or *not beneficial*? How would this change make a difference in your life?

7. Have you ever chanted? What are your beliefs about chanting? Are you willing to try?

8. What empowering words can you add to your life? For example, *I will, I won't,* or *I want.* Would these words help you? Hurt you? Do you have others you would consider using?

"When … the vibrational field of a particular human heart comes into spontaneous resonance with the divine heart itself, then finite and infinite become a single, continuous wavelength, and authentic communion becomes possible" [23] (Cynthia Bourgeault).

THE SPIRIT—CONNECT

THE SPIRIT

> But he that is joined unto the Lord is one spirit.
> —1 Corinthians 6:17 KJV

To go from powerless to powerful, it's critical to realize that we are born with a human spirit to connect to God, who is spirit. We can become joined as one spirit, enabling us to have a deep relationship with him. When we become conscious of how we are united with God's spirit, we can discover a place of deep inner stillness and stability that exists beneath and beyond our bodily sensations, thoughts, feelings, and desires.

This is where we find peace and power beyond understanding. It is incomprehensible by our limited mind and ego, yet it is real when we realize it in our hearts. When we find this place of peace and identify the instability of our souls, we can receive *and become* the fullness of all that Christ is: truth, peace, wisdom, power, kindness, goodness, joy, self-control, patience, faith, love, *and more.* The God of peace exercises his power to purify and cleanse our souls. Jesus Christ is the fullness of God.

God's goal is to transform us through the power of his spirit into becoming more like Jesus. God's spirit is holy, meaning divine. It is perfect. The work of God's Holy Spirit is to reveal to us the truth of our lives, the truth of Jesus, the truth of God, and more. It is the spirit that helps us to find our true identity and *spiritual* nature. Have you ever heard the phrase "mind, body, soul"? Thought leaders, yoga studios, and marketing companies fall short of defining our true identity when they leave out spirit.

In meditating with Jesus, we practice being *like* Jesus, a spirit consciously connected to the divine spirit. We sit in stillness and *practice* patience, self-control, love, kindness, faith, goodness, peace, wisdom, and truth. As we practice these virtues, we grow them inside our hearts. We all have godlike attributes and virtues inside of us that we can cultivate and grow. We are a spirit who desires to express our humanity and spirituality.

The moment we invite the spirit of Christ into our hearts, we transform into a new creation. This regeneration of the heart is the essence of the enlightenment I have been writing about, which is a state of unconditional love. The spirit of God, also known as the spirit of truth, dwells within our very core and has the power to bring us out of darkness and into the light.

We learn to bring God's light to areas inside our bodies that are hiding unresolved pain in delusion or darkness. Our human spirit can work with God's spirit to witness the brokenness that becomes stored in our hearts. While meditating, this wise spirit is our constant companion, comforting us and leading us away from suffering toward freedom. As Paul the Apostle wrote, "For the Lord is the Spirit, and wherever the Spirit of the Lord is, there is freedom" (2 Corinthians 3:17 NLT). Revealing the truth is the path to peace, and peace is what brings freedom.

Jesus was like us, human *and* divine. While on earth, he demonstrated a connectedness with a higher power, God's spirit, which let him shine his light on truth and live out his full potential as a spiritually evolved human being. He encouraged us to follow him into this infinite flow of divine light and grace.

Meditating with Jesus draws us inward to experience this union of love, which he never doubted, but we sometimes do. The invitation is inclusive of all so we may know and experience our true identity. We are made in the image of God, and since God is love, so are we. All of humanity is blessed to have God within. We are the human and the divine together, allowing us to remain in a position of giving love and receiving love.

God is somewhat undefinable because of our limited human capacities. Using the verb *to be* is how God referred to himself as he spoke to Moses: "I Am That I Am" (Exodus 3:14 KJV). He is more like a verb than a noun. A verb is an action, occurrence, or state of being, whereas a noun is an object. Contact with God creates movement. It affects our being.

We can all experience God. God is anchored to our souls. As we drift and doubt, he brings us stability, hope, faith, and truth. If we listen to who God says we are (versus the world or our own minds), we realize our *true* nature. In the Bible, God says we are loved, lovable, accepted, capable, and valuable and have infinite worth. He says we all have a purpose. God is an encourager who increases our inner strength. His anchor provides us the courage to face and overcome the inevitable storms of life.

In the Bible, God is described as spirit, love, light, and a consuming fire. His spirit is pure love, peace, patience, kindness, goodness, self-control, joy, truth, wisdom, strength, and faith. The use of *him* is ingrained in modern speech. But we could just as well use another form of the verb *I Am*. God's spirit is in *I, you, he, she, we,* and *they*. I'm not by any means saying you or he or she *is* God. To be a human being is who we are meant to be. We need only be ourselves, imperfect human beings experiencing being *joined* to God's perfect spirit.

We are co-heirs with Jesus, as sons and daughters, brothers and sisters, and children of the King, the alpha and omega. We are invited to accept our access pass to the kingdom of God. We are chosen to go backstage and hang with the band of angels and heavenly hosts. However, we must make the critical choice whether to join the group and be in God's family. With God, we can joyfully live in heaven; without him, we can struggle alone in a silent hell.

INTROSPECTION

About fifteen years ago, I discovered that I could connect to God more deeply through a daily practice of stillness, scripture, chanting, meditation, and prayer. When I turned within, the light of God in my heart *found* me. My soul became illuminated, and so did my ability to love. My life became established around consciously staying connected to the light of Christ. From this act of faithfulness, grace and creativity now flow to me, through me, and out into my life.

During my daily practice, I wake early to sing, talk, listen, read, and be guided by God. I now desire less and less of what the world offers and more of what God gives me: peace, stability, truth, guidance, and joy. I feel complete and satisfied. I experience Psalm 23:1 daily: "Yahweh is my shepherd: I shall lack nothing" (WEB). Life is an adventure of manifesting my dreams and overcoming my challenges. It is an enjoyable process as I seek God's guidance and help.

I've realized a certain hard-to-swallow truth: no one can do these things for me as God can. He knows all my secrets and embraces me. He sustains me with tenderness, mercy, and love. No human can replicate the depths of peace that I find with him. Buddhists say they find "refuge" in the Buddhist path, and I now understand this powerful word. With my God, I can rest in a sanctuary of serenity I never knew before and now cannot lose. I also realize no one can provide that place of safety for me—not a parent, a child, a beloved partner, a spouse, or a best friend. I am the queen, and he is my king. He is my beloved.

I experience his love, peace, and joy. I can also feel and hear when he wants me to change—when he's pushing me to transform my ways or follow the path he has laid out for me. Sometimes God gives me advice that goes against my will. I've noticed that before I comply with his counseling, a period of turning toward my resistance is inevitable. I listen to the objections from my will. I try to understand. However, I've also learned to trust his guidance; and after some debate in my soul, I surrender my resistance or rebellion. It always works out for my good.

I'm not afraid to be alone because I'm never alone. I don't have to care so much if people like me or don't because I know God loves and cares for me in all the right ways. Having a relationship with God has helped me to see what a good relationship feels like. Do I get lonely? Yes, sometimes I do. But I know how to quickly return to God. His spirit is inside of me. I only need to be still.

Tonyah Dee

INSIGHT

The Bible tells us that Jesus is the visible image of the invisible God (Colossians 1:15 NIV). He was with God at the beginning of creation. The Bible also tells us that God is good, holy, just, kind, loving, and faithful. He is spirit, love, light, life, and law. Jesus came to be the light for humanity. He came to reveal the truth of who God is—who we are, how to grow closer to God, where we can find him, how to see him, and how to know him.

God is the Creator, and whether we are conscious of it or not, our human soul and spirit long for an intimate relationship with the one who created us. At the center of our hearts, we also find God's Holy Spirit, the spirit of truth, which leads us into truth. Making this union conscious gives us a sense of completion and wholeness. God is inclusive. He is over all, through all, and in all. I find it interesting that AA defines the spirit as broad. It appears that God's spirit takes on many names and shapes. AA states, "To us, The Realm of Spirit is broad, roomy, all inclusive; never exclusive or forbidding to those who earnestly seek."[24]

How can we experience God? We must turn inward toward our hearts and ignite his light. However, we must also admit that we want to know him, that we need and want his help. We must invite his spirit to teach us to learn to be and love like Jesus.

Little by little, the spirit of truth helps us to transform and change our ways. He illuminates life in us, the light and the dark, helping us to see the truth. God wants the best for us and will help us if we trust him. God speaks to us in various ways; however, we must listen to it. His voice is a still small voice coming from inside of us. We hear it in our unique way and through scripture, music, people, nature, and contemplative practices.

But until we fully realize and manifest the power of our true identity, we may be lost in the darkness or have an identity crisis. Jesus and the spirit of God can lead us toward the best version of ourselves. We are guided toward the light to be enlightened by God's spirit and be set free. Our human spirit is the lamp of God; it shines on our inner parts and helps us to find places that need God's light and love. "The spirit of man is the lamp of the LORD, searching all his innermost parts" (Proverbs 20:27 ESV).

INSPIRATION

We take in the breath of life, and we consciously join with God's spirit in our hearts. We learn to remain stable, in a disposition of peace. We practice self-control, patience, and kindness as we get to know our personal truth. The spirit searches our inner parts, and God's spirit is a witness. In a place of stillness, we witness the soul, which is the mind (thoughts), emotions (feelings), and will (desires). We rise above the instability and unpredictable expressions of our souls and learn to see the beauty and sometimes bitter truth in all situations from God's perspective.

We learn to surrender and wait. We try to accept his guidance even though it might be challenging. We learn to faithfully return to a place every day where we can admit our struggles and then receive power, grace, and mercy. We learn to humbly accept his plan because it leads us toward our soul's purpose. We see our lives change; and we begin to have a new perspective—one that is broad, roomy, and good for all. Without being plugged into the power of God, we struggle to manifest these blessings.

Even in the dark places of our hearts or lives, we find the grace of God every time we trust him to help us. Grace is God's unmerited favor. We don't have to earn his love. Yet to be *so* loved even though we are *so* imperfect can be humbling and difficult to accept. Even so, God believes we are worthy of this type of love. We are his children, and he loves us unconditionally. Returning this loving attitude back toward him and others is our job.

Humility and acceptance are the attitudes to take. As AA states, "Nothing, absolutely nothing, happens in God's world by mistake."[25] Accepting things we don't want to accept challenges us to look for deeper meanings in our suffering or the suffering in the world. Acceptance is what helps to relieve our pain. Deep and sincere compassion unites us with others, given how we all suffer. With acceptance and humility comes the power to look within and change what we can in ourselves.

When we are vulnerable and can accept our circumstances—when we can admit the places where we are falling short, are being imperfect, are struggling, and are suffering—God gives us grace so we find peace, even in times of suffering. When we connect and communicate, he steps in and helps us. Our lives become easier, our pain is lessened, and we experience the providence and love of God.

Jesus demonstrated the ability to have acceptance, mercy, and compassion for himself and for others. He stayed in a state of power by accepting his situation, having faith, and humbling himself before God. This is what we all should strive for in our day-to-day lives.

The soul loves to test and experience life. We test and, at times, hide from the shame, guilt, or truth of what happened. But if we return to God, admit how the experience was, and speak the truth, we receive the compassion, mercy, and grace from God, which can restore our innocence. Our truth and his light, both powerful energetic forces, work together on our behalf as we both fall apart and trust in him to gather our shattered pieces to put us back together.

When we share our truth with God, we can find the path back to peace. This helps us to feel lighter. Peace becomes a barometer back to the serenity that only God can provide. And even during our challenges, we can become peacemakers, like Jesus.

The goal is to experience being spiritual—being human plus a spirit, with God's spirit filling us up to the point where we overflow. The ability to return to peace, stay connected, and continually listen to our helper, counselor, and guide builds more spirit and makes us more powerful, like Jesus. This can cultivate the virtue of peace inside all of us.

INTEGRATE

Take a deep breath in and hold it. Hold the spirit of God in and let him expand in your body. Relax with the breath held in. Exhale slowly. Relax deeply. Seek and find peace at the center of your being. Become aware of who you are on the deepest level, in the secret place of the Lord.

Find a place of peace and stillness that exists beneath and beyond your thoughts, feelings, and desires, a peace beyond understanding. Connect to God's Holy Spirit, who supports you, witnesses your soul, and illuminates new life in you. Imagine that God is with you and in you. Rest in his light and peace. Be still and know God.

Practice being patient, kind, gentle, and faithful; having self-control, thinking about good things; loving yourself; and loving God at the same time. Continue to inhale the breath of life (God's spirit), exhale, surrender yourself (your soul), and abide in his mighty presence.

INQUIRY

1. Do you believe that you are a spirit? Why? Is it intuition or intellect or both? What do you believe you are?

2. Have you ever heard that God is a spirit? What does the word *spirit* mean to you?

3. Is it hard to believe that we are given a spirit to connect to God, who is spirit?

4. What are your thoughts about Jesus Christ promising to send a spirit of truth to all who believe in his teachings? What does this mean to you? Can you receive this message? What resistance do you have, if any? Do you think you already have the spirit of truth in you?

"Those in whom the Spirit comes to live are God's new Temple. They are, individually and corporately, places where heaven and earth meet."[26] (N. T. Wright)

5. How hard is it for you to tell the truth to others? To yourself?

6. Are you confused about anything? Like what? Does admitting it make you feel better?

7. Is your past clear, or does it need some cleaning up? What can you release or let go of that is obviously draining your life force?

8. Do you believe in a force or source that knows all, sees all, and is in all? What do you call this? How have you experienced this in your life? What depletes or drains your life source?

"For God is Spirit, so those who worship him must worship in spirit and in truth." (John 4:24 NLT)

THE HEART—OPEN

THE HEART

Love, Kindness

Then Christ will make his home in your hearts as you trust in him.
Your roots will grow down into God's love and keep you strong.
—Ephesians 3:17 NLT

The heart is the power source of life. It is the spiritual center of the human. Everything flows in and out of the heart. What pours out and circulates in the heart is a field of electromagnetic energy that travels through the body, soul, and spirit and outward into the world. Sometimes this current gets blocked or disrupted as a result of certain life experiences, and we can lose our power.

When the light of Christ, which is pure love in our hearts, connects to the light and love of God, we have a powerful, benevolent field of energy that can help restore us and keep our hearts open so that love returns and remains flowing. Instead of living from a heart that opens and closes, we live with a heart that remains open in a graceful state of kindness, mercy, and compassion. Meditating with Jesus ignites and awakens the slumbering and dim spark of light that already exists in our hearts. This light becomes our foundation and source of spiritual illumination. We learn to return to this center to stay connected to God's love, keeping us strong.

The most important thing we can do, according to Jesus, is to learn to love. The spirit of Jesus Christ lives in our hearts, calling us to receive his love. When we answer the call, we find all that Christ is—a powerful, creative force and the embodiment of a higher power that can transform us. When we love God with all our hearts, love grows, and we can love ourselves and others.

Whenever we need more love, we can turn to God. As Jesus said, "Whoever does not love does not know God, because God is love" (1 John 4:8 BSB). During our time with God in meditation, we open our hearts and get to be born over and over in the womb of God's love. We are created to become our version of this love. It is our birthright and our journey, one of learning how to love. Jesus can show us the way.

The heart is meant to stay open and flowing, yet because life is so full of pain, our hearts can become hardened and cold. The good news is that God is at the center of our hearts and can transform our fear, pain, and darkness into faith, love, and light. When we meditate with Jesus, we merge our spirits with his healing spirit, healing our hearts while opening the door to love, peace, joy, and kindness. Inner evolution becomes an exciting journey.

Jesus is the true light. The Bible says about Jesus, "The true light that enlightens everyone was coming into the world" (John 1:9 WEB). He came into the world to show us how inner transformation happens in our hearts through his light. We become enlightened. We can go from being spiritually dead to spiritually illuminated.

Combined with the love of God, light is a molecule of high energetic force that can expose the darkness stored in our hearts, uncovering and revealing to us a powerful divine inner light that has always been inside us. This light energy gives us the power to heal and purify our hearts. As we turn to this light, it becomes easier to keep our hearts open and flowing. We also gain the power to overcome the temptations and distractions of the world that may lead us to a closed heart.

Jesus declared, "God is light, and in him is no darkness at all" (1 John 1:5 KJV). In meditation, we are allowing this light, the very essence of God, to see our hearts and souls. When we experience the release and letting go of the darkness, we undergo a metamorphosis, and increased awareness of our true selves.

When the light in our hearts shines brighter, we can see more clearly and have improved discernment. Jesus said, "Blessed are the pure in heart, for they will see God" (Matthew 5:5 NIV). Having a practice where we consistently purify our hearts will help us to see God everywhere and be happier.

In meditation, we learn to gently be in truth, however dark or painful. We can listen and recognize old thoughts and emotions that need to be brought to the light for inspection, validity, and healing. We embrace whatever we find, allow it to be, and let God's light work on it. We release judgment and let love into the darkness. Love and acceptance dissolve darkness. Allowing imperfection in ourselves helps us to see the whole human condition, the battle we all face with darkness and light. This helps us to understand how we all are struggling in some way, and the result is more compassion and kindness towards ourselves and others.

As discussed earlier, this process is often referred to in popular culture as doing the work. The work is always in our hearts. This work results in a pure and open heart. It heals and transforms the soul. It releases the old and unnecessary, making room for the new, energetic, sparkly, bubbly energy. This is the energy we need to reach our full potential. We learn that our hearts have limitless and vast amounts of love and compassion for ourselves and others. It becomes our source of authentic power, and this inner power is what helps us to live out our true destiny and purpose.

When we get off track, and our hearts become dark, broken, and cold, or we feel a lack of light, and our souls and spirits become weak, we can pray like the prophets in the Old Testament. King David prayed, "Create in me a clean heart, O God; and renew a right spirit within me" (Psalms 51:10 KJV). And Asaph declared, "My flesh and my heart fails, But God is the strength of my heart and my portion forever" (Psalms 73:26 WEB). When we meditate with the light of Christ in our hearts, we can be purified and restored by the divine essence of God.

INTROSPECTION

I have cried buckets of tears. Many times my heart has been broken, closed, and in pain. Meditating with Jesus has helped me develop new pathways in my heart and ignited a healing light of acceptance and unconditional love. I've learned to show myself compassion and kindness again and again. I understand the value of loving God with all my heart because love continues to grow inside me with every interaction. I've become less judgmental and more compassionate with myself and others.

Day in and day out, this attention to my heart has solidified a pathway that helps me to keep my heart open for longer periods. I allow any pain I'm holding in to pour out of me daily. I can sense when my heart is closing around a person or situation. The constriction feels bad. It indicates that I need to take action to return my heart to being open once again.

Often, I hear God give me the problem *and* the solution. His voice is at the center of my heart as conscience, wisdom, and counsel. I follow his directions, and sure enough, my heart opens back up. I feel better, lighter, and freer. And then I start the process over the next day. My life is easier now because I know I need more of God's spirit of truth whenever my heart begins to close.

As I learned to tune into and follow God's voice, I allowed myself to be led gracefully to my full potential and destiny. My inner life and outer life continues to change in positive ways. I experience more peace and joy every day. As I practice being with God, more and more of his virtues and characteristics grow inside of me. I've overcome so much already: anxiety, depression, eating disorders, substance use, codependency, an inability to express my truth, and feelings of unworthiness and isolation.

During my meditation and prayer practice, I attempt to be as real and honest as I can to live every day in reality. The reality is that my reality keeps getting better, so it's easier to be in it!

I spend time dwelling in the kingdom of heaven, renewing my mind about what is pure, right, and beautiful. It seems as if afterward, during my day, everything I need is brought to me. My heart is enlightened over and over. The light of Christ flows in and out naturally, and I can tell my light affects others as it lifts and elevates them too. Do I still cry? Yes, I do. Life is, at times, almost unbearably sad. But I'm lucky because I have someone with me who understands: Jesus.

INSIGHT

During meditation, we begin the process of total radical honesty and acceptance. Once we know how to connect to the consistent force of love in our hearts, whatever we find in our souls that we've been avoiding or judging can be transformed and released. The result is a consistent return to a lightness of being and inner strength to endure the rough times that inevitably come again. One of the ultimate goals of meditating with Jesus is to remain in the stability of God's unconditional love day after day until we become more like Jesus.

Christ-centered meditation is a purification process. We identify and admit our pain, weaknesses, and mistakes to God daily. Our hearts are released from the burden of keeping it all inside and hidden. Our flow of vulnerable truth keeps our hearts open. We learn how to accept our truth and practice being nonjudgmental.

In this position of humility and honesty, God is merciful and forgives us. We also learn to forgive ourselves over and over. This is one way we learn to love ourselves and our family, friends, neighbors, and enemies. We all fall short of who we want to be. But when we admit how imperfect we are and that we make mistakes, our spirits reopen, and we resume with open hearts. We can continue to love God and our neighbor only when we love, forgive, and fully accept ourselves.

We are all imperfect, all shaped by a past over which, at times, we had little control. We may still be acting from unconscious patterns of thoughts and behaviors. A Christ-centered meditation practice helps us to identify and be sensitive to disharmony in our minds and bodies. As we turn toward the powerful virtues of God within, we create new pathways to our hearts. These energies break through old repetitive patterns of information and false ways of thinking to create new ways of thinking, feeling, and behaving.

Meditation helps us turn inward to search for God in our hearts with all our hearts. Along the way, we may find blockages that keep us from the higher powers of Christ. But when we remain devoted to loving God, we learn self-love at the same time. The practice is learning to be still, observe, witness, listen, explore, submit, accept, and surrender all to a higher power. We learn to identify and then remove negativity from the soul, which purifies it, and makes room for more love, mercy, and compassion. As these qualities grow together, our hearts regenerate and are more easily able to stay open.

We can see God more clearly when we have open and pure hearts. We receive guidance and direction from within. When we choose to follow God's truth, it can lead our hearts back to peace. God always has a good purpose for us; he wants to restore us to sanity, serenity, and clarity. He does this by bringing his light, life, and love in and out of our hearts. This gives us clear eyes to see the beauty within and around us. A veil is lifted as we love God with all our hearts. "[A] veil lies on their heart. But whenever someone turns to the Lord, the veil is taken away" (2 Corinthians 3:15–16 WEB).

INSPIRATION

In meditating with Jesus, we spend time getting to know our hearts. This daily practice is about finding and living from an open heart. We return again and again to this divine center, which calls us back to receive unconditional love.

Imagine an image of Christ peacefully pointing to his heart. What he's doing is leading us home so that we can live in a place of love. This love energy cleanses our hearts. The outcome is a renewed sense of God's presence, where a dynamic shift in vitality occurs.

Jesus is the gate, the gatekeeper, and the door to the heart. He encourages us to have nonjudgment, mercy, forgiveness, compassion, and unconditional love to keep our hearts pure and to consistently see and hear God. He asks us to treat others as we want to be treated. These teachings initiate changes within us, bringing into our hearts more light, which is the light of life. Jesus says, "I am the light of the world. Anyone who follows me will never walk in darkness but will have the light of life" (John 8:12 CSB).

Having a reverent love for ourselves and Christ will make our hearts strong and open so that we pour out love to others and receive their love. The struggles we endure on the path to self-love and love for others unite us with all people. All humans desire to know this love and will struggle to have and keep it. It is why people often say love is a universal language. To speak it, every single one of us will have to first make the challenging yet rewarding journey to our hearts. Confidence comes when we can be out in the world, giving and receiving love and not hurting ourselves or others. That is what we accomplish when we learn to live and love like Jesus.

Our faith, belief, and practice can begin to change us, turning us into a new creation. We come to rely on God's truth instead of our thoughts. Our entire perception of life shifts, and we can perceive the changes that must occur, taking us from our old ways into newer and higher forms of being. The changes can be sudden or slow, but because we hear the truth in our hearts and decide to give our lives over to God and his love, we receive new life by way of insight, intuition, a new path, bold action, and a more positive outlook.

We're born again with a stronger, wiser new heart. This changes our nature to reflect the nature of God. And slowly, we become more like Jesus. We think and behave differently. We have a light that shines inward and outward from our hearts to ourselves and others, and it only continues to expand. This is the wonderful, sparkling, and eternal light of Christ. So let your unique light shine. Let there be light!

The goal is to make Christ in our hearts our safe place, our lifeline. Through Jesus, we learn to live from our hearts so that all our inner parts merge with love and light, flowing in an open and receptive way. Love binds all things together. We should, therefore, keep our hearts pure by seeing God in all things and situations. This can cultivate the virtues of love and kindness inside all of us.

INTEGRATE

Take a deep breath in and hold it. Let it fill your heart and then exhale slowly. Relax. Seek and find love in your heart. Remember something that gives you the feeling of love: a pet, a relationship, a hobby. Sit in this feeling of love.

God is love. Open and expand the healing light of Jesus coming from your heart, letting it flow through your body and soul. Allow unconditional love and light to search your inner parts. Bathe any pain with compassion and the breath of life. Notice anything constricted or heavy and bring your loving attention to it. Breathe in God's love to the hurt or dark places. Breathe out love. Accept your truth without judgment of good, bad, right, or wrong. Be cleansed by the love, kindness, and compassion flowing from your heart. Let go and let God in.

INQUIRY

1. What does being home with your heart feel like? Comfortable or uncomfortable? Do you have a practice to center yourself in your heart?

2. Has your heart been broken, or is your heart broken now? Why? When? How?

3. Are you aware of when your heart is open or closed? What are the different sensations?

4. Do you sometimes feel coldhearted? When? Around who or what? How does that feel?

"More valuable than treasures in a storehouse are the treasures of the body, and the treasures of the heart are the most valuable of all."[27] (Nichiren Daishonin)

Tonyah Dee

5. What do you think about Jesus as light, love, and life in your heart?

6. What do the words enlightened and empowered mean to you? Are these characteristics you have or would like to have? Why?

7. Do you have sufficient amounts of self-love? If not, what holds you back from loving yourself? Are you terrified or excited about love?

8. Do you judge yourself harshly? Have you forgiven yourself for being imperfect or unconscious and making mistakes?

"And so we know and rely on the love God has for us. God is love. Whoever lives in love lives in God, and God in them." (1 John 4:16 NIV)

THE SOUL—RENEW

THE SOUL

God, you are my God. I will earnestly seek you. My
soul thirsts for you. My flesh longs for you, in a dry
and weary land, where there is no water.

—Psalm 63:1–5 WEB

Being conscious of our unique souls is critical to being fully empowered. The unconscious, unknown soul is powerless to bring enlightenment or spiritual illumination but can alternatively be a powerful source of self-sabotage. The realization of self is, therefore, a higher power.

The human, according to the Bible, not only has a body but also has *inner* parts. Specifically, we have a body, soul, and spirit, and each part has an important role to play. As discussed earlier, the body is the temple of God's Holy Spirit. The soul is our unique self. It is our personality; and it includes these three powerful parts: the mind, emotions, and "free" will. The soul and the human spirit co-exist in the heart.

The human spirit, which connects to God's spirit, can light up and illuminate the heart, body, and soul so that areas of darkness within can be healed. During Christ-centered meditation, we allow God's love and light to flow through us to cleanse and purify us and, in turn, bring us new life. The powerful result is new ways of being, coming through an *inner* transformation in our hearts and souls.

In essence, God's spirit can bring our souls from darkness into light. Once the soul becomes illuminated and accustomed to being led by a higher power—one that is wiser, stronger, and more loving—it begins to yield and submit. It desires to be seen and in a good relationship with God's spirit. But it needs more power, which God's spirit can provide. Being led by God's spirit thus allows the soul to rest and relax. No longer feeling separate, the soul has a "helper" who is faithful, loving, accepting, and forgiving. This calms the soul. Like a child who is lost, needy, and seeking attention, the soul can be disoriented and disruptive without a divine parent.

To establish higher power living, we must surrender our souls to the higher consciousness and goodness of God's spirit. Unfortunately, this is easier said than done. The soul is powerful and may have become used to running the show. Therefore, if we want to improve our lives, the quickest and easiest way is to get to know the soul and make friends with it.

Exploring the soul in meditation is a daily journey of discovering, understanding, and embracing our authentic identity. The soul has been called many names. For me, it is the same as the ego, subconscious, and psyche. It is self-seeking, self-focused, and selfish. The soul is our self. It craves more power, and since God's spirit is the highest power, this can also be good.

The soul wants to do the right thing but is often incapable on its own. That's because the soul is unstable, weak, and always changing. It longs for stability, righteousness, and wisdom but can't always get there because of its innate nature. God's spirit can provide what the soul lacks as it remains the same, never changing, and ever-powerful. Meditating with Jesus can help us find that positive power.

Witness Lee writes that the Bible tells us the soul has three parts: the mind, emotions, and the will.[28] In daily meditation practice, we can experience this to be true, and it is of the utmost importance to understand. The soul is unpredictable and unstable because the mind (thoughts), emotions (feelings), and will (desires) are changing all the time.

The soul wants to experience life fully. If given the opportunity, it will seek new experiences and work hard to have more purpose and meaning. To that end, it stores information throughout our lives to help us on our respective journeys. One main job of the soul is to keep us alive and thriving. However, to survive, the soul also does what it can to avoid pain, including developing strong defenses and seeking pleasure. These defense mechanisms can inevitably thwart the soul's true intentions and purpose.

The soul is often like a child pursuing what will make it feel safe and happy. It may seek poor coping mechanisms to solve its problems in the short term. It has a mind of its own. The result is a sort of insanity, one that can make us feel cut off or separated from deeper aspects of the inner wisdom and truth in our hearts, the kind that can be provided by God's spirit, the divine parent to our souls.

The soul is also like a computer: it stores data, past experiences, defenses, memories, beliefs, thoughts, emotions, and desires. This data cycles through the soul, creating the same thoughts and feelings and causing the same actions and behaviors. Even when what used to work no longer works, the soul may default to using an old pathway first. This can cause the soul to get stuck in what I call the soul cycle.

The soul cycle works like this. Thoughts create emotions. Our will then makes choices, causing actions. Actions create feelings, and then come the thoughts. Next, thoughts lead to actions, which creates more thoughts and more actions. And around we go. We cycle through the same thoughts, feelings, and actions, unable to escape the soul cycle until we bring in a higher power to help us.

This might lead to overwhelming frustration and disappointment. As a consequence, we can reject or abandon our souls because we don't like our "selves." We don't like our thoughts, feelings, desires, or actions; and as a result, we try to deny, ignore, or repress parts of our souls instead of learning to have mercy, understanding, and self-compassion. However, learning to love our souls is possible because God's love already lives inside our hearts. By example and words, Jesus teaches us to be nonjudgmental, forgive, and continually return to God for guidance. This is love in action.

During meditation, as we find and accept abandoned, hidden parts of ourselves, we can become whole again. We develop integrity, and our inner parts start to work as they were designed to work: together, in unity. We can do as Jesus did and call on our Abba Father, a daddy to our souls. Being connected to the stability, wisdom, and power of God's spirit helps our souls to endure, thrive, and accept our imperfections as we learn from them and continue to move forward.

This is one way that Jesus saves us. This is what salvation means to me. We are saved from ourselves—the instability, feelings of separateness, the suffering of our souls—as we seek, find, and connect to the higher power in our hearts. Instead of being our own worst enemy, we learn to love the enemy inside. We begin to decrease the self-harm we inflict because we discover self-love instead. The enemy disappears as we accept all aspects of ourselves and learn to honor them. There are stories hidden in our souls that can help us to heal.

When we shine the light of Christ on our souls and seek more truth, we can gain insight into the past, present, and future and develop self-control. We learn to react less. We learn how to be still, witness, and become friends with our souls. This makes all the difference. We merge with the conscience and wisdom of Christ. We might be unaware of the satisfaction the soul gets from being led and loved by a wise friend with a higher power; but the soul learns to calm down, wait, and listen. We go from self-sabotage to ever-increasing amounts of self-love.

Our soul can become the part of us that works for us, not against us. We can learn to focus on taking the steps forward that are necessary to keep us on our unique and authentic paths. When the grace of God is cocreating and directing our souls, we experience an overall improvement in our well-being. This becomes fuel for staying connected to the source, which truly provides.

INTROSPECTION

Sixty miles from where I was raised, in a fetal position on the floor of my apartment, I lay exhausted in dry tears, hungover, and alone. I was a long way from home, the home in my heart. I had been a goal setter until then, going through the motions: set goals, achieve them, set new goals, achieve those. I kept on going without an end in sight. I achieved success in the goals I set, but they seemed to take me farther and farther in the wrong direction and away from peace. I was always on to the next goal, and the unrest I felt below the surface kept me from enjoying the present moment.

In my spare time, I passionately studied the art of survival: time management, stress management, nutrition, exercise, and lifestyle. I read most of the self-help books as they came out. I read my first self-help book at the age of seventeen. It was titled *Seeds of Greatness: 10 Best Kept Secrets of Total Success* by Denis Waitley. I was productive but not peaceful, and worse, I could be self-destructive. It was "self-help," all right, but the wrong kind, the kind that wasn't helping my soul.

That Saturday morning, alone in my apartment, I accepted Jesus into my heart. At twenty-four, at the prompting of a television evangelist, I got down on my hands and knees and cried out for help. I said yes to the man on the screen asking me if I wanted my life to change. Surprisingly, my life immediately (like the next day and the days after) changed for the better. The feeling of despair burned to ashes, and in its place, wonder and excitement took over. I jumped in with my intellect and learned all about Jesus. My mind became filled with new thoughts. These new thoughts led to new emotions of hope, peace, and power. This directed my will to create a new lifestyle and life.

For most of my life, I didn't know my soul, and it operated unconsciously because of that. When I surrendered my soul that morning to Christ, I connected to a higher power. My understanding of life changed as I began to understand God. My soul was made aware of higher ways of thinking and being. Christ led me into a new way of life, not a religion.

I transformed into a new person. I began to follow a pure lifestyle on a narrower path. Almost immediately, I had the power to let go of what was no longer beneficial to me. My faith grew, as did my blessings.

Years later, I learned to meditate with Jesus, which resulted in me befriending my true self, my unique soul. As a result, I found *more* of God. I began witnessing my soul—not believing every thought I had, accepting with love every feeling, and listening for wise guidance to direct my will. I was waiting on God *and then* taking action. I began to consistently listen from within. Eventually, I let go of emotional blockages and false thoughts. Good things continued to happen. My life became abundant, and I became more and more peaceful.

Once, I was busy planning. Now, I am resting more and trusting in God. I'm experiencing firsthand how God wants to preserve, deliver, and prosper me. He guided me into a life where I can experience my losses and victories, blessings and challenges, and do so while surrounded by love, acceptance, and forgiveness. My soul, under the control of God's spirit, is a soul at rest. In peace.

INSIGHT

The nature of the soul is always changing. The body is always changing as well. That's why we are encouraged to surrender our "flesh," the body and soul, to the spirit. In the Bible it is written: "The mind governed by the flesh is death, but the mind governed by the Spirit is life and peace" (Romans 8:6 NIV). Since thoughts create emotions, and emotions create actions, it's important to know the mind, emotions, and will, the three parts of the soul.

The mind is always working. So don't expect the mind to ever stop working, not even in meditation. It is the mind's job to think, analyze, judge, solve problems, discern, plan, learn, imagine, and store information. As we meditate, we can get to know our minds. Because the mind stores all information, true or false, what comes from our minds is not always true. Therefore, we need to constantly renew our minds with new thoughts and information and let go of false beliefs or thoughts that are not helping us. Fortunately, we can renew our minds with the thoughts and words of Jesus.

We learn to merge our minds with the mind of Christ. We learn to listen, observe, and discern our thoughts and not react to them. We learn to let false thoughts go and find the truth. With this ability to control our minds, we can express our words carefully using divine speech and create more goodness for ourselves and others.

We are emotional and sensitive beings, and because of this, our emotions can inform us of how we are experiencing life. Therefore, we need to listen to our emotions and not numb, escape, or distract ourselves from them. This part of the soul is trying to get our attention to share a truth. When we can accept and embrace and show unconditional love and compassion for our personal truth, we can release our emotions and become more compassionate and caring.

Every emotion has a distinct feel and often carries a deeper message specifically for us. If we learn to listen and value this part of the soul, we can experience life authentically. Our unique story unfolds. When we learn to share and express the truth of how we are feeling, it brings us closer to God and others. If we continue to struggle with loving ourselves and our feelings, we can always turn to God's unconditional love.

As we witness, allow, and express deep emotional pain, it is released. We then acquire new emotions that can elevate us: courage, trust, acceptance, love, forgiveness, and peace. Sometimes, however, emotion will come from a false thought and, therefore, cause false emotion. When we meditate with Jesus, he promises to take us from darkness to light by revealing the truth. In exchange, we must do our part: humble ourselves, admit our darkness and pain, ask God to help heal our emotions, listen for truth, and let the new emotions lead us to heal our hearts and return us to the light.

The will, our "free" will, is where we hunger, desire, and dream. It makes decisions and choices. Our will often sounds like I will, I won't, I want, I don't want, I wish, I don't wish. Often, we relentlessly and unconsciously become attracted to some things and repelled by others, which creates a sort of merry-go-round of seeking from the outside world what we want and pushing away what we don't.

As this occurs, the soul remains unsatisfied and goes on to the next thing that might fulfill the craving from deep within. We can spend our entire lives grasping for *things* to fill an inner hunger or void just to end up feeling unsatisfied. The Bible says our will hungers after and thirsts for God's spirit. Jesus makes his healing power clear: "But those who drink the water I give will never be thirsty again. It becomes a fresh, bubbling spring within them, giving them eternal life" (John 4:14 NLV). Jesus thus becomes our source of provision and satisfaction. When we thirst after God's spirit, we become satisfied in this relationship that gives what we truly need: inner peace, joy, and well-being.

We can learn to surrender our will to the will of God, which helps the soul. His will opens the door to power. The soul's desire is to express its unique design. God's will provides direction into what truly satisfies our souls and may amplify our souls' authentic calling. God's desire is to give us the desires of our hearts, and he can help us to manifest them. However, we must say, as Jesus did, *not my will* but "Thy will be done" (Matthew 6:10 KJV).

INSPIRATION

In meditation, we learn to be friends with our unique souls. If we surrender our bodies, minds, emotions, and wills, we can become open vessels and recipients of divine energy. We can be led into becoming a supernatural human being, who reflects the virtues and characteristics of Jesus. This is the concept of dying to ourselves to live a better life. We surrender the soul (ego) and become joined to God, who is spirit. We become more spiritual. We connect to a higher power to transform into better versions of ourselves to live our best lives and serve one another. All of humanity benefits.

There can only be a shallow understanding of ourselves without understanding how God works in us, how he created us, and what his plan is for us. Knowing our identity—the body, soul (mind, emotions, and will), and spirit—can take time, effort, and focus. But it is well worth it. When we realize we are united with God's spirit in our hearts, it equates to self-actualization, self-realization, an experience of the metaphysical and the realm of spirit.

We are all like Jesus, human and divine. It is, therefore, important to know all our *inner* parts. Meditation brings us home to our true selves and teaches us how to heal and transform our souls. It leads our hearts to freedom and liberation. God intends and promises to take us from our old selves to our new selves. God's plan is to bring us ever-increasing amounts of glory, which manifests itself as distinction, integrity, honor, and magnificence.

Jesus said, "[S]eek first the Kingdom of God and his righteousness, and all these things will be added to you" (Matthew 6:33 ESV). This kingdom is found within the heart. Peace, faith, love, joy, self-control, patience, goodness, joy, and kindness are only a few of the additions we can add to our lives. Attaining these inner virtues helps us to manifest our dreams with God's help and grace. We can learn to let go of old stories in our souls and become a vessel for serving God as he whispers to us our purpose and cocreates with us at a natural pace so we can move toward a life that is authentic and our own.

The goal is to realize that we live in a body, have a soul, and are a spirit and that we can awaken to being human and divine. We are supernatural and multidimensional. Being able to distinguish the voices in our bodies is power. There are two voices. We have a voice, which is the voice of our souls, and the voice of God's spirit. We can learn to recognize the different messages and befriend, not fear or reject, either.

Tonyah Dee

Some say the devil can speak through the soul. This theory is a prime example of how important it is to detect and identify the messages coming from our souls. When we do, it can result in an awakened understanding of who we are in the moment, who God is, and, most importantly, how to have authority over the messages coming from the soul. With awakened understanding, we can distinguish between the voices, giving us the wisdom to not act impulsively to all our thoughts, every feeling or emotion, or the desires that may be blindly driving us or seeking our attention.

Surrendering our souls to God's spirit can only bring us increased amounts of power. We begin to hear his voice more loudly and experience his wisdom. This can cultivate the virtue of self-control (soul control) inside all of us.

INTEGRATE

Take a deep breath in and hold it. Exhale slowly. Seek and find your mind. It is thinking, planning, analyzing, judging, and remembering. Notice how thoughts come and go. Thoughts can be random and not always true. The spirit of God gives you control over your mind. Surrender your mind to the thoughts of God. Silently recite a Bible verse or favorite positive affirmation.

Take another deep breath in and hold it. Exhale slowly. Seek and find your emotions. Pay attention to what your soul is feeling. Emotions seek light, love, and acceptance from your heart. Allow your truth. Use the breath to release dark or heavy emotions. The spirit of God understands you and brings you comfort. Surrender your emotions to the love of God.

Take a deep breath in and hold it. Exhale slowly. Now seek and find your will. It makes choices using the words *I, I will, I won't, I want, I don't want, and I wish*. Let the spirit of God hear the desires of your heart. Silently talk to God using those words. Then surrender your will to God's will. Say, "Father, Thy will be done."

Surrender your soul (your mind, emotions, and will) to the care of God's spirit. "But the fruit of the Spirit is love, joy, peace, patience, kindness, goodness, faithfulness, gentleness, self-control; against such things there is no law" (Galatians 5:22–23 ESV). Seek and find the truth.

INQUIRY

1. On a scale of one to ten, one being that you don't know anything about your soul self and ten being you know everything there is, what would you rate yourself?

2. Is it hard to be yourself? Make a list of what in your life is right for you and what makes you tired, keeps you down, or holds you back.

3. Do you abandon yourself for the expectations or desires of others? If yes, how does that make you feel?

4. What would you change about yourself?

"And what do you benefit if you gain the whole world but lose your own soul?" (Mark 8:36 NLT)

Tonyah Dee

5. What are the repetitive negative stories coming from your stored memories? Can you rewrite them in terms of what you have learned?

6. Are you anchored more in your mind, emotions, or desires? Which part of your soul is most active?

7. Can you anchor to something deeper, like the peace and stability of Christ in your heart? How?

8. Does it make sense that knowing your soul will help you to trust yourself? How?

"Those doing soul work, who want the searing truth more than solace or applause know each other right away"[29] (Rumi).

"Food for the body is not enough. There must be food for the soul."[30] (Dorothy Day)

PRAYER—BELIEVE

PRAYER

Patience

[W]hen you pray, enter into your inner room, and having
shut your door, pray to your Father who is in secret, and
your Father who sees in secret will reward you openly.
—John 6:6 WEB

Why do we have a daily spiritual practice of keeping our bodies still, consciously inhaling, and exhaling the breath, reciting God's Word, connecting to the spirit, opening our hearts, and surrendering our souls? It is so that we can pray. Prayer has the power to transform our lives. Prayer is the final destination of this eight-step practice.

Jesus had a pure heart. He could stay connected to God, communicating with him at all times. To communicate effectively, we must first become honest with ourselves so we can surrender to God in humility, vulnerability, and truth. God loves to hear from us.

Sometimes, the best prayer is a simple one, like "I need help!" But how can God help us if we aren't talking and listening to him?

As we meditate with Jesus, we learn to be *in* the spirit and pray *in* the spirit. In other words, we learn to be joined as one with God's spirit. We make room for this during meditation, cleansing our hearts so his spirit can come forward and be present with us. We let yesterday go and become present with him. Being present requires practice. Praying is that practice that helps us become better at being focused in the present moment and on our relationship with God.

It makes sense that prayer is a road to self-actualization since prayer is a journey we take inside, directly to the heart, where we are connected to God's life force. In this space, we fully understand our potential. This results in the possibility of actualizing our authentic souls and discovering our deepest dreams.

When we pray, we use our hearts and souls to commune and communicate with the Creator. Prayer is not meant to be a manifesting practice, but it turns out to be one anyway. When we are faithful and ask for what we need and then believe that God answers our prayers, we see the cocreating that takes place and the abundance that flows into our lives from it. God doesn't always give us what we ask for, but we might receive insight or a new perspective enabling us to answer our prayers. As promised, though, when we pray, we are rewarded.

When we have patience and unwavering faith to return to the unseen spiritual realm where we ask for and believe in a union with the great provider, Jesus Christ, we experience miracles, synchronizations, and supernatural coincidences. Even when we attempt to manifest goals or dreams using only our willpower through visualization, it requires a belief in the unseen. We project our visions and hopes, use words of affirmation, admit our truth, and then believe it's ours already.

We do the same in prayer. With God, we have an advocate, someone whose plan is to prosper us, not harm us. At first, prayer is something we do as a conscious and daily single act. Later, prayer becomes how we live our lives as we consciously walk in truth, praising, asking, believing, and trusting God every step of the way.

INTROSPECTION

All day, every day, a voice inside me says, "Praise God, hallelujah, and amen." For even the smallest blessings, I often respond silently with "Thank you, God." Because I now trust God, and my life is centered on faithfully praying to him, I have God's grace. He shows himself to me continually. God is good to me.

My life keeps getting better and better every day. So, I try to stay surrendered to his timing, guidance, and plan for me. The result is that blessings continue to flow into my life with ease. The challenges now are to maintain the endurance and strength I need to keep up with all the blessings, abundance, and opportunities coming my way and avoid the distractions that take me away from the flow of his grace.

I've experienced many of my prayers manifesting, always with God's perfect timing. Yet I know I can't control anything, even with prayer. God is in control. Always. It is merely my job to accept all my blessings and all my challenges and let go of trying to control the process or outcome. I give my requests to him and then wait. I wait because I believe that he might have a better plan than mine. Often, this is the case; and if I'm willing to wait, watch, and accept what comes my way, things seem to go in the right direction.

I start in the morning, and then it seems I'm praying all day long, even when I'm not praying per se. I pray in the sense that I'm always trying to listen, talk, and stay connected to God's spirit. This way of being sets a pace that is not hurried or stressed. The result is more and more synchronistic events. More "God winks." As Kathie Lee Gifford says, "[T]here is not a word in the Hebrew language for *coincidence*,"[31] the intimation being that there are no coincidences. Instead, everything happens according to God's plan. As a believer, I get to stand back to some degree and observe the miracle of God as he walks alongside me, though I still know God is in control.

I know this because prayer, worship, and praise to God are acts of noble surrender, where we are bowing to a higher power. It just feels right. It helps me feel that I'm a part of something large, worthy, and honorable. Prayer generates love and respect in my heart first thing every day. It takes over my body and soul. I abide, wait, and allow it. It is my addiction. It makes me want to praise and ask more. So, I do. I am gripped by this energy that is so much more powerful than myself.

Make no mistake, though: my life is hard. It's always changing. Like most people, my soul sometimes gets triggered, and I don't always react perfectly. Just like everyone else, I too have to face the consequences. Yet because of my relationship with God, I understand consequences are what I need to learn and grow into a better person. Learning to talk and listen to God has given my life a depth I didn't have when I was younger. I no longer have to tell everyone my issues or spend my time seeking the advice of others. I go right to God as my guide and counselor, and he answers me in some unexpected way that strangely makes sense, making the mystery of his omnipresence more intriguing.

Time and time again, change comes, doors open and close, yet I continually return to seek his stability and wisdom in prayer. Many philosophers and spiritual leaders have said that change is the only constant in life. Meditation and prayer practice can be the bridge we use to travel away from the old and into the new. Using stillness and patience, we cross over the turbulent waters of change with ease and grace toward a better future.

It is very much a faith and love fest. Love grows within as I learn to love daily and accept my reality. Love is activated. Love goes out. Love comes back. Everything passes through my heart, and I continue to change. For the better.

Since committing to my prayer practice, all my relationships mirror my intimate life with God. I express gratitude and am vulnerable to others. I can share my current pain and struggles. I express my needs and ask for what I want. I talk from my heart, not just my mind. I am patient and trusting. I listen, wait, and surrender control. I receive humbly and gracefully, and God rewards me with loving and caring relationships. What goes around does indeed come around. God is great.

INSIGHT

Jesus said, "Therefore I tell you, whatever you ask for in prayer, believe that you have received it, and it will be yours" (Mark 11:24 NIV). This Bible verse communicates that Jesus gives us the way to a more abundant life through faith and prayer. In other words, when we pray, we should consider our prayer already answered. We should feel what it would be like to have the thing or things we hope and ask for.

As Jesus did, after we pray, we can say, "Father, I thank You that You have heard Me" (John 11:41 BSB). By saying these words, we demonstrate how we have faith that our prayer has been heard and is now being answered even before we witness it. We show our trust that God is working on it and practice patience. With these words, we release any thoughts that what we prayed for is still an issue or a problem. We demonstrate our faith by moving on and doing what we can to improve our lives.

As in any good relationship, we talk *and* listen. The ability to communicate honestly cannot be underestimated. Prayer is as easy and possibly as difficult as talking to a good and close friend. In prayer, we choose to be vulnerable, honest, and real. This establishes a closer, friendlier relationship between God and us as it would with someone we trust. Granted, this seemingly simple act is far more difficult than it sounds.

The importance of being vulnerable is a relatively new concept in our society, and many of us have been programmed to do the opposite. Avoiding honesty, hiding our feelings, and not getting too close has been the message and the process. Many of us may need to deconstruct this false belief. Praying to God, as Jesus did, is a good way to learn a more honest way to communicate and get close to someone.

Every day, when we pray, we talk to the spirit of truth in our hearts. This keeps us in touch with reality, our humanity, and the bigger picture. At that moment of sharing the truth, we realize we have the ability and the power to overcome loneliness, embrace our inner reality, and admit our challenges and struggles. Without truth, we have no path to authenticity or a better reality. With truth, there's no need for judgment of good or bad. When we walk in truth, everything we do leads us into a deeper relationship with God and ourselves.

Truth ultimately brings us more power and authenticity. We can live and experience life without needing to withdraw or isolate ourselves. We can share our truth with others, and this brings us closer to each other.

We can build a practice of becoming vulnerable and honest by being thankful for our blessings as we, at the same time, admit and accept our struggles and challenges. This establishes neutrality in our hearts, which may equate to the peace of which Jesus spoke. He said, "Peace I leave with you. My peace I give to you; not as the world gives, I give to you. Don't let your heart be troubled, neither let it be fearful" (John 14:27 WEB).

Our hearts are cleansed when we release the truth. Fear turns into faith. Troubles become a natural part of life and are easier to bear because we don't hold them in as burdens. We receive the peace that comes from being true to ourselves. Living a lie destroys the soul as it slowly loses its ability to be who it is meant to be.

It is my experience that spiritual disciplines such as meditation, contemplation, singing, chanting, or praise can all be considered forms of prayer. So, too, can being in nature and simply being aware of God's creation. Whatever helps us feel the strong presence of God's spirit, where we feel like talking to God and hearing God's voice and wisdom, *is* worship and prayer.

INSPIRATION

Prayer is a matter of the heart. It feels great to be real with someone all the time. This is too much to ask from another person. However, God wants to hear what burdens us. Other people don't necessarily want to listen to the details of our daily trials because they have their own issues to work out. God's light carries our prayers and thoughts—those molecules of information from our hearts—throughout our bodies and out into the world. Since our words and thoughts are creative, manifestation in the physical world happens, but it is not always based on our timing or design.

The Bible encourages us to be thankful for our blessings and challenges, admit our mistakes and faults to ourselves and one another, and pray. Doing this keeps us healthy by cleansing and purifying our hearts. It is like a good shower for the soul. The heart becomes lighter when the soul is grateful and emptied of burdens such as guilt, shame, and anger. We can feel this lightness of being almost immediately.

The ability to confess our mistakes and admit our weaknesses is a powerful way to release the burdens caused by the shadows and heaviness of negative emotions. Shame and guilt can build up, creating darkness in our hearts. This may prevent us from experiencing higher, more elevated, and more peaceful feelings of love and acceptance.

Resistance to this process blocks our willingness to be real and thus experience the love that comes from intimacy. When we admit our struggles and mistakes, we become free to learn and be loved for our imperfections. With God, we are unconditionally loved. If we deny our mistakes and pretend we are perfect, we don't learn and lose out on the opportunity to receive forgiveness and grace. If we pretend for too long, we risk losing our authentic souls and becoming lost and alone.

In addition, acting perfect, self-righteous, or prideful can make others around us feel inferior. No human is perfect. No matter how many illusions a person may build around themselves to protect their ego from humiliation or shame, deep inside, we know how imperfect we are. To admit and confess makes us more relatable. God can then help us because he knows our stories and understands them.

When we turn to God and pour out our truth, we are rewarded with grace. Amazing! Jesus was well-liked because of his ability to be authentic and honest while showing grace and mercy to those struggling, imperfect, and nothing like him. I've found that giving people this kind of grace always circles back. People remember when you let go of judgment and remain in truth without condemning or rejecting them. Jesus was full of grace and truth. This combination heals the heart and soul. During our prayer time, we give our truth; and in return, we receive the fullness of Christ.

Without exposing the truth of our imperfect nature, we cannot receive the opportunity for growth and grace. We may create or remain in a false reality and thus darkness. We may continue to struggle with the same issues over and over, year after year. Our mental health may deteriorate.

Jesus wants the dark stuff to be revealed so that it can be healed. He wants us to go from darkness to light. He wants to transform and reward us with grace. Praying is giving and receiving. We give our truth, we receive grace, and our lives are blessed with his undeserved favor. Meditating with Jesus is not a practice we do once or twice a day; it is a way of living in the presence and awareness of God at all times. Prayer is an opportunity to connect to the current of faith and be delivered into the hands of grace. We can allow God to show us his goodness.

The goal is to have an intimate, honest, vulnerable, and authentic relationship with God. Our faith grows until we are sure we will overcome anything that keeps us from being filled with his spirit. We achieve constant cooperation with a higher power. We can listen for his guidance and learn to trust the still small voice and the whisper that is God's love. This can cultivate the virtue of patience inside all of us.

INTEGRATE

Bring your hands together before your heart in prayer, establishing unity within body, soul, and spirit. Pray out loud or silently. With gratitude, thank God for all he has done for you. Come to God with thanksgiving for all your blessings and your challenges. Thank him for what you do not have but want. Thank him for whatever bubbles up from your heart. Say out loud or silently, "Thank you, God, for your kingdom, power, and glory. Thank you for this day, this practice, and my body, soul, spirit, and heart."

Continue with "Thank you, Jesus, for your light, love, grace, and mercy" and "Thank you, Holy Spirit, for your guidance, help, wisdom, and truth." Thank God for whatever else you want to thank him for. Express your gratitude.

Confess and admit dark thoughts, struggles, mistakes, and behaviors. Ask for forgiveness. Forgive yourself. Feel forgiven.

Ask with hope for what you want and need. Pray for others in your life and in the world. Ask to be an open vessel for God's will to be done. Believe your prayer has been heard. Listen to your heart. Listen deeply for God's voice and guidance. Receive your authentic supernatural life. Receive hope and grace. Then, wait patiently. He is working for you, inside of you, through you, and around you.

Tonyah Dee

INQUIRY

1. Do you pray? Does prayer feel comfortable? What is comfortable or uncomfortable?

2. Can you first recall a time when you called out for God with your voice? Was it in celebration, praise, and love; or was it during a time of suffering?

3. Are you aware of a desire inside of you to share your truth with someone? How often do you push your truth deep into your heart and soul?

4. Did you have someone to talk to and someone who listened to you as a child? Do you believe that God longs to be close to you? Why or why not?

"The prayer does not change God, but it changes the one who offers it."[32] (Søren Kierkegaard)

5. Have you ever been in therapy? Can you see how praying could be considered divine therapy?

6. How difficult is it for you to be vulnerable and honest? To be intimate?

7. Do you believe God can hear your prayers?

8. What would keep you from daily prayer? How can you overcome this?

"Confess your offenses to one another, and pray for one another, that you may be healed. The insistent prayer of a righteous person is powerfully effective." (James 5:16 WEB)

CONCLUSION

The Light of Christ: The Highest Power

[T]he light itself is of importance to me, that it still shines upon me after
eighteen hundred years with undimmed brightness; but how to call it,
or of what it consists, or who gave it existence, is immaterial to me.[33]

—Leo Tolstoy

What does it mean to meditate with Jesus? It means manifesting with a higher power, hearing God's voice, finding our authentic souls, and praying in spirit and truth. Increasing conscious connection with the light of Christ restores a unified relationship with the body, soul, and spirit. This harmony and wholeness gives us that extra energy we need to pursue the dreams in our hearts. This practice cleanses and purifies our souls and can help us to resurrect a unique and authentic life as directed by the spirit of God, who wants us to use our unique gifts to serve others.

It is not a matter of trying to behave like Jesus or putting a lot of effort into changing our behavior, as in self-improvement, but allowing the spirit of Christ to live in and through us, giving us new life, new insights, perspectives, and creative paths. Perhaps we don't know God, Jesus Christ, or God's Holy Spirit. If our understanding is limited, we should know that God's ultimate goal is to transform us to live in perfect peace. We come to this higher power with whatever understanding we have currently, and he will help us gain the knowledge we need at a pace we can handle.

We can set our sights on the destiny of Jesus, not only on the journey of suffering but also on the miracle of resurrection. He suffered yet was resurrected to do great work in the world through believers who accepted his spirit into their hearts and followed his teachings. Jesus followed the will of God. It was a difficult and challenging journey, laden with physical and psychological pain; yet he was given a unique adventure and purpose, anointed to bring us the good news of God.

We, too, have our adventures. We can bear our cross, suffering, and pain to be miraculously renewed, transformed, and born again. We surrender our souls and begin to live by the spirit. We receive our anointing, empowering us to function supernaturally, making our journeys meaningful.

Meditating with Jesus means that we make the conscious choice to be guided toward our full potential as individual human beings. It is a decision to turn toward our inner truth and become honest and authentic. A daily practice of reconciling the relationship we have with God draws us closer to him and ourselves. This will perhaps shift our destination forever to where we can recover our authentic purpose and true nature.

We can renew our minds with the thoughts and words of God. Like Jesus, we can think or say over and over, "Thy will be done" (Matthew 6:10 KJV), "[D]o to others as you would have them do to you" (Matthew 7:12 BSB), "[F]orgive them; for they know not what they do" (Luke 23:34 KJV), "Peace be with you" (John 20:21 ESV), "[L]ove the Lord your God with all your heart" (Mark 12:30 ESV), "[L]et your light shine before others" (Matthew 5:16 NIV), and "[L]ove your enemies and pray for those who persecute you" (Matthew 5:44); "With man this is impossible, but with God all things are possible" (Matthew 19:26 ESV). We can learn many other verses to recite. These words become the way we function in the world.

As we change our thoughts, our words, emotions, and actions change too. We grow God's virtues inside of us, and we are better able to give and act from our hearts. In accepting the higher power of God, we find rest, balance, and ease, knowing we are *cocreating* our best lives. Life will never be perfect, but it is our own.

INTROSPECTION

I am not who I used to be. At times, it's disorienting. Going in new directions, letting people go, saying goodbye to aspects of my behavior that no longer work, allowing the past to be the past, releasing judgment, and walking courageously into open doors—none of it is easy.

That said, I've experienced a profound transformation in my life ever since I committed to meditating and praying with Jesus. No longer was I running, hiding, or numbing, Today, I'm inhabiting my body fully and always, allowing a slow and steady inner and outer transformation into all that is good and worthy. I am a spirit experiencing growth that began when I first allowed the power of the spirit of God to grow in union with my spirit.

After years of being led astray by who I am not—my false, sabotaging self—I've become willing to embrace God's spirit and my true self. I always try to listen for his voice and then try my best to follow the guidance I hear. I have to fight my resistance to this process. At times, I fail to listen and must forgive myself.

My perspective has changed such that I believe in the beauty of the unseen, which constantly pulls me into greater depths of faith and trust. This has made all the difference. I've stopped grasping, worrying, and judging. My anxiety has all but disappeared. I can rest. I'm creating and living, not just surviving. I'm cocreating, cohabitating, and codependent with a powerful force that has captured my heart.

When I tell people I used to have an anxiety disorder, they can hardly believe it. They say my energy is so calm and nice to be around, and it's hard to imagine me any other way.

In the book *Alice in Wonderland*, Alice discovers her true identity at the end of her extraordinary journey. She comes out from the rabbit hole, out from the darkness beneath the surface, and begins to immediately speak her truth. She goes on to pursue her dreams with the vitality and intensity of someone who has discovered a higher power.

Earlier in her adventure, Alice discovers lost parts of herself, and by befriending these parts, she is made whole. Our journey is like Alice's, and God is like the caterpillar, accepting us as we are but encouraging us to look deeper by asking, "Who are you?" However, God goes beyond the caterpillar, asking, "Who are you *really*? Who are you *now*? Who do you want to *become*?"

Recently, during a winter retreat in Costa Rica, I intentionally wrote down in my journal every time someone complimented me. This is what people told me: "Tonyah, you are brave, a bright energy, insightful, doing good things, my idol, on the path to bliss, gorgeous, a good listener, a soul sister, the most enlightened person I've met, finished seeking you have found, amazing, an apostle, fully balanced, have nothing missing, and are moving into maturity."

I claim that victory. I'm Tonyah, victorious in overcoming obstacles that get in the way of my union with God. I'm magnifying Christ more and more. Sure, I still face challenges, human suffering, and unrealized dreams, but I can be myself. I am that I am.

INSIGHT

God is light. "This is the message which we have heard from him [Jesus] and announce to you, that God is light, and in him is no darkness at all" (1 John 1:5 WEB). God's light is the unconditional love, presence, and blessing of God's Holy Spirit. It speaks to us from our hearts. It is a still small voice of wisdom and truth. Although unseen, it's the highest and purest form of energy. The more wisdom and truth we acquire, the lighter we become and the more we radiate light.

Scientifically, light is a type of energy known as electromagnetic radiation; it's an energy that travels in waves.[34] When light hits a surface, its energy can be absorbed, soaked up, and reflected; or it can be deflected, blocked, or changed in direction. The heart generates the same electromagnetic waves. When we merge our heart waves with the waves of God's light, we can absorb and soak up his light and reflect the light of Christ out to others and the world. It's no coincidence: God's plan is to restore the brokenness in the world through the hearts of those who reflect Jesus.

We are all born with a divine spark of light in our hearts. It is only a little spark. It is dim, but it is the light of Christ. Even though we are all born with this light, we can be spiritually dead. We may not have connected to God's spirit yet, which is light and life. We can still be living in darkness. We may have unintentionally or intentionally deflected, blocked, or caused God's light to change direction; and as a result, we are missing out on this energetic power that can transform our hearts. The goal is to connect our little lights and stay connected to God's light, his spirit, and then become spiritually alive, awake to our true nature and how we are meant to be.

We can find Christ—the light of life, the ultimate energy source—in our hearts. We can grow this light through daily spiritual practices like spending time in nature, being still, listening, contemplating, reading scripture, singing, fellowshipping with others, meditating, and praying. We can begin to live a life of belief, acceptance, courage, and laughter.

With the light and water of Christ, we can grow the fruits of God's spirit, which feed our bodies and souls peace, love, joy, goodness, kindness, self-control, patience, forgiveness, kindness, humility, and faith. Truth becomes our guide, and we learn to trust. Truth is not something to hide from but what releases more light into our lives. So much light that all the powerful words above can take on a life of their own inside of us.

We uncover, ignite, and empower the light by letting go of dark, repressed, denied, heavy, and false thoughts, emotions, and desires stored in our souls. As we let go and let God's light in, the dim spark of light begins to grow into the wonderful light of Christ, which shines brightly through our hearts. We can look into the faces of all people, of humanity, as we learn to look into the loving eyes of Jesus Christ.

Healing begins in having an honest face-to-face relationship. When we are with God's spirit, we no longer have to hide our shame or distress. He calls us to look to him in our time of weakness to find more strength; and because we are open to receiving, we receive more life.

When the spark of light inside of us becomes fully merged with God's light, and the Holy Spirit fully dwells in us, God's love grows in our hearts, transforming and giving us the ability to hear his voice and feel his presence. As dark or stressful times arise, we discover we have the tools to return to the light faster. We also know better how to protect ourselves from forces of evil or darkness. Because of that, we become attuned to what is good and brings light and what causes light to become dull or disappear altogether. We have the insight we need to empower self-control, the ability to resist, and the ability to welcome. This is self-mastery.

We are ultimately awakened, realizing we are human *and* divine. Upon awakening, we can witness sanctification and transformation. This keeps us in a state of hope and perseverance. As our inner attributes change, our outer world changes. We understand perfection is impossible, yet we are connected to perfection. Our suffering decreases as compassion and tolerance increase. Dreams come true and creativity flows as we continue to listen for God's voice. We find more meaning, purpose, and beauty. We become authentic and find our unique destiny. We are aware that God is good. God is great. And we thank him.

INSPIRATION

Don't worry if you haven't accepted God or Jesus into your life yet. You still can. You can seek God or find people you vibe with who seem to know God. You can get to know Jesus or be baptized. Search your heart. When you do, you will begin to hear inner guidance from God's spirit, the spirit of truth. You may even receive a vision of things to come. "However, when he, the Spirit of truth, has come, he will guide you into all truth, for he will not speak from himself; but whatever he hears, he will speak. He will declare to you things that are coming" (John 16:13 WEB).

Being still, meditating, and praying open our eyes to the truth. This is why it might be difficult in the beginning. The body and soul want to express, and we need to learn to listen and be available. Befriending the soul is possibly one of the most important things we can do for ourselves because it can result in self-love. Truth leads us to who we are. We change as God does his work of inner transformation, which sets us apart for special use or purpose. We are cleansed, unburdened, and then blessed. We remain conscientious about being honest. We can begin to live in reality and enjoy our truths—all of them—the suffering and the beauty.

In meditating with Jesus, we are invited to recognize, awaken to, and be aware of who we are as empowered and authentic human beings. The cost of not being authentic, of not being ourselves, can create dissonance, an inner death, and rob us of our life force. Instead, we can be enlightened and guided by the loving presence of Christ within us. With this help, we can stay true to ourselves and set into motion new patterns that create transformation, increasing our life force. An authentic life is the result.

Jesus points us directly to God's love. He points to God's heart in our hearts. When we believe and trust Jesus, we become heart to heart, spirit to spirit, with the liberating power of the Creator. God's voice speaks to everyone's personal situation. It is unique to each soul. It is faithful and available as a guide, helper, and counselor to each individual on earth.

We are called to become our version of what it means to be a spiritual person, a person filled with the spirit of God. The goal of Jesus is to take us out of the darkness that limits and anchors our hearts in the heaviness of pain, fear, and isolation and bring the power of light and love to open and create the flow of new life on the wings of compassion, forgiveness, acceptance, and faith.

In meditation, this is an experience, an encounter, in the present moment. A daily practice of being still to listen and observe our souls engage our spirits in the pursuit of truth. Energy pours forth; new abilities and ways of being excite our spirits, and our old lives fade away. We become spiritually empowered while dwelling in our human flesh. We become united as one with the highest power of all. Jesus the Christ is the spiritual director because of his intimacy and connection with God, his beloved Abba and our divine parent. He directs our paths and makes them straight when we follow his teachings.

I encourage you to try to listen to this higher power. Follow God by whatever name you use, but call on that name. Listen, and you might discover the great I Am is calling to you. Turn inside and surrender your soul. Raise your white flag and let God see you.

INTEGRATE

Practice meditating and praying with Jesus. Use the eight steps outlined in this book to keep your heart empowered. Enjoy the beauty and wonder of being a supernatural human being.

Be still in your body and consciously connect to the breath of life. Observe, witness, and understand the changing nature and messages coming from within. Resist relying on your soul's perceptions, opinions, thoughts, emotions, or desires; *they are of value* but not as valuable as God's. Choose your thoughts and words carefully. Put yourself humbly before the spirit of truth. Believe in and know the light, love, and life of Christ in your heart. Turn wholeheartedly inward toward your soul. Trust.

Remove the shadows and darkness blocking the flow of new life. Listen to a higher conscience, the voice of God deep within, and follow the guidance. Find truth. Surrender all to God's spirit. Give praise, admit, ask, believe, and receive. And then say amen.

Allow the light of God to heal you and shine through you. Live in the light. Grow, shine, illuminate. Become unique, transparent, and full of higher power. Know and express unconditional love. Ignite the true light within, and watch peace grow. Wait on YahLight, the light of the Lord. Spread your joy!

Tonyah Dee

INQUIRY

1. What will you change as a result of reading this book? Or what have you changed?

2. What was the most helpful chapter for you? Why? How?

3. What is the biggest insight for you? What is a mantra you can create for yourself?

4. How have meditation and prayer helped you?

"And you will know the truth, and the truth will set you free" (John 8:32 NLT).

Tonyah Dee

5. What was or is the most difficult part of meditating with Jesus?

6. Did you try chanting? What did you like? What was difficult?

7. Do you feel closer to Jesus? To God? To your soul? To your body?

8. Did you experience the peace, love, and light from God's spirit?

"[T]he journey into the light, which is synonymous with the true self ... is to make ourselves aware of the height, length, breadth, and depth of the love of Christ in taking on our human nature."[35]—Thomas Keating

PART TWO

MEDITATE WITH JESUS

8-STEP DAILY PRACTICE

As you now know, the first part of this book was all about using your mind and intellect to understand what makes *you* unique, powerful, and an integral part of humanity. Now that you have finished reading and have this knowledge at your disposal, the second part of this book will be devoted to integrating what you learned into an experience of the heart, which will lead to you use your knowledge to better your life and the world. Remember, meditating with Jesus is not about attaining perfection; it's about self-discovery, seeking the realms of God, and transforming into someone who can contribute to helping others.

Meditating with Jesus connects us to a higher power. It allows us to witness our souls, gain self-control, save ourselves from self-sabotage, and bring us to a place where we are empowered to light the way for others by positively influencing the world around us.

Practicing these eight steps, we can also discover authenticity, learn to surrender yet pursue our unique paths, and, little by little, contribute to Jesus's plan of learning to love and serve humanity.

To assist, I have included a cheat sheet, daily practice guide for the "8 Steps to Meditating with Jesus," and journal pages to chronicle forty days of your journey home to your heart. To support you in this highest of goals, I have provided daily prompts in your journal that you may or may not wish to answer. Record your experiences as you become still and go inward to be with your soul and a higher power. What truths do you uncover or recover? Are there moments when you notice your burgeoning relationship with the Creator of All bringing insight or making a difference in your day or life?

Are you ready for forty days of meditation and prayer? If you don't feel ready, don't worry. You may never feel that way. Just start where you are. Sometimes it takes a season to understand and embrace a change in lifestyle. It's also okay if you miss a day or days. I encourage you to return and complete forty days of practice, even if it's not continuous. Do the best you can and observe your reactions. Also, ask yourself: Are you loving and nonjudgmental or harsh and ready to give up because you didn't do it "right" or "perfectly" or as you intended to? This book teaches the skills you need to forgive yourself and keep on keeping on as you elevate your life.

Meditating with Jesus is not an impossibly big task. I give you steps to follow, as Jesus did. God wants to love us. But we need to turn to him and accept that love every day. I invite you to defeat any resistance to this process. With God's light, life, and love, you can be an overcomer and experience being victorious. You, too, can ignite, empower, and be the light!

Tonyah Dee

Cheat Sheet

DAILY PRACTICE

Step 1

restore

Faithfulness

THE BODY

Step 2

sanctuary

Gentleness

THE BREATH

Step 3

create

Goodness

THE WORD

Step 4

harmonize

Joy

THE SPIRIT

Step 5

connect

Peace

THE HEART

Step 6

open

Love, Kindness

THE SOUL

Step 7

renew

Self-Control

PRAYER

Step 8

believe

Patience

DOWNLOAD THE GUIDE

scan me

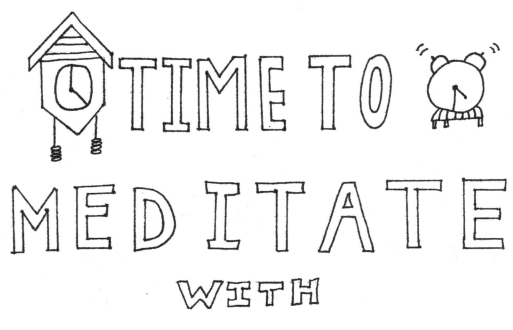

TIME TO MEDITATE WITH JESUS

CONNECT TO A HIGHER POWER
WITNESS BODY, SOUL, SPIRIT
PRAY, LISTEN, CO-CREATE

Daily Practice Guide

Step 1 — DAILY PRACTICE

Create a space, a "God spot," where you can be alone with God. Try establishing a morning routine. For example, set your alarm, shower, and then meditate. Decide in advance how you will sit. Will you use a chair, cushion, or couch? Have your favorite devotional chant, mantra, hymn, or instrumental music accessible. In addition, have a journal, a Bible or devotional, pencil, candle, and a place to set your morning beverage. Experiment with your best time to practice. Give early morning a chance, so that you can start your day being restored with faith and God's Grace. Resist the temptation to skip the practice. Instead, show up for yourself. There's no judgment. There's no right way or right amount of time. So, most of all, make the experience enjoyable.

restore

Step 2 — THE BODY

Create a sanctuary in your body. Gently become as still as possible in a seated position. Your spine is straight and your sitting bones stable. Your shoulders are back, heart open, and chin tucked in. The top of your head reaches upward, and your belly is soft. Now imagine a cross from Heaven to Earth and shoulder to shoulder running through your body. Next, find a position of dignity. Close your eyes so you can direct your attention to explore your inner world. Breathe slowly and deeply. Stay alert yet relaxed. Begin to experience your body as a temple of God's Spirit, where you can experience God's Presence and get to know your true nature. Resist the temptation to force anything. Be gentle with yourself. Breathing is slow, deep, and relaxed.

sanctuary

Step 3 — THE BREATH

Become aware of your breath, your connection to life. Take in long, slow, deep breaths through your nose. Breathe deeply and rhythmically. Try the breath of peace. Inhale to a count of five (P-E-A-C-E) and exhale (P-E-A-C-E). Imagine the breath as spirit, vitality, power, and inspiration. Imagine it purifying, calming, and healing as it creates feelings of safety, serenity, and a connection to your inner self. Inhale deeply and feel God enter. Exhale slowly, and feel love exit. Notice a feeling of calm and relaxation coming into the body. Breathe in and out of your heart. Allow the goodness of the breath to lovingly flow in and out of your body, bringing you new life. Stay connected to the Breath of Life throughout the practice.

create

Step 4   THE WORD

harmonize

Select a YahLight devotional chant, a worship song, a hymn, or a mantra that is repetitive, easy, and heart-centered. Once you start to sing, notice how sound creates vibration, movements of energy, balance, and harmony in your body. Listen to your unique voice. Witness your multidimensional nature, singing, breathing, thinking, feeling, desiring, and listening all at once. Memorize the words to the song and close your eyes. Sing with joy and sincerity from your heart. Imagine that God is listening and harmonizing with you. Contemplate or memorize God's Word instead of or in addition to singing. Listen to a Yahlight scriptural contemplation or select a Bible verse. Allow God's Word to renew your mind with new thoughts.

Step 5   THE SPIRIT

connect

Take a deep breath in and hold it. Hold the Spirit in and let it enliven your body. Relax with the breath held in. Exhale slowly. Relax deeply. Seek and find peace at the center of your being. Become aware of who you are on the deepest level, in the secret place of the Lord. Find a place of peace and stillness that exists beneath and beyond your thoughts, feelings, and desires, a peace beyond understanding. Connect to God's Holy Spirit who supports you, is a witness to your soul, and illuminates new life in you. Imagine that God is with you and in you. Rest in His Light and Peace. Practice being patient, kind, gentle, faithful, having self-control, thinking about good things, loving yourself, and loving God at the same time. Abide in His Mighty Presence.

Step 6   THE HEART

open

Take a deep breath in and hold it. Let it fill your heart, and then exhale slowly. Relax. Seek and find love in your heart. Remember something that gives you the feeling of love: a pet, a relationship, a hobby. Sit in this feeling of love. God is love. Open and expand the healing light of Jesus, letting it flow through your body and soul. Allow unconditional love and light to search your inner parts. Bathe any pain with compassion and the Breath of Life. Notice anything constricted or heavy, and bring your loving attention to it. Breathe in God's Love to the hurt or dark places. Breathe out love. Accept your truth with no judgment of good, bad, right, or wrong. Be cleansed by the love, kindness, and compassion flowing from your heart. Let it go, and let God in.

Step 7 THE SOUL

renew

Take a deep breath in and hold it. Exhale slowly. Seek and find your mind. It is thinking, planning, analyzing, judging, and remembering. Notice how thoughts come and go. Thoughts can be random and not always true. The Spirit of God gives you control over your mind. Surrender your mind to the thoughts of God. Silently recite a Bible verse or favorite positive affirmation. Take another deep breath in and hold it. Exhale slowly. Seek and find your emotions. Pay attention to what your soul is feeling. Emotions seek light, love, and acceptance from your heart. Allow your truth. Use the breath to release dark or heavy emotions. The Spirit of God understands you and brings you comfort. Surrender your emotions to the Love of God. Take a deep breath in and hold it. Exhale slowly. Now seek and find your will. It makes choices using the words I, I will, I won't, I want, I don't want, I wish. Let the Spirit of God hear the desires of your heart. Silently talk to God using those words. Then, surrender your will to God's Will. Say, "Father, Thy will be done." Surrender your soul, your mind, emotions and will, to the care and direction of God's Spirit, a Higher Power.

Step 8 PRAYER

believe

Bring your hands together in prayer. Pray out loud or silently. With gratitude, thank God for all He has done for you. Thank Him for what you do not have but hope for. Thank Him for whatever comes to your heart. Perhaps try: "Thank you God for your Kingdom, Power, and Glory. Thank you for this day, this practice, my body, soul, spirit, and heart. Thank you for my blessings and challenges." Continue with "Thank you Jesus for your light, love, grace and mercy" and "Thank you Holy Spirit for your Guidance, Help, Wisdom, and Truth." Confess and admit dark thoughts, struggles, mistakes, and behaviors. Ask for forgiveness. Forgive yourself. Feel forgiven. Ask for what you want and need. Pray for those in your life and in the world. Ask to be an open vessel for God's Will to be done in your life. Believe your prayer has been heard. Receive hope and grace. In your day, wait patiently and listen. God is working for you, inside of you, through you, and around you.

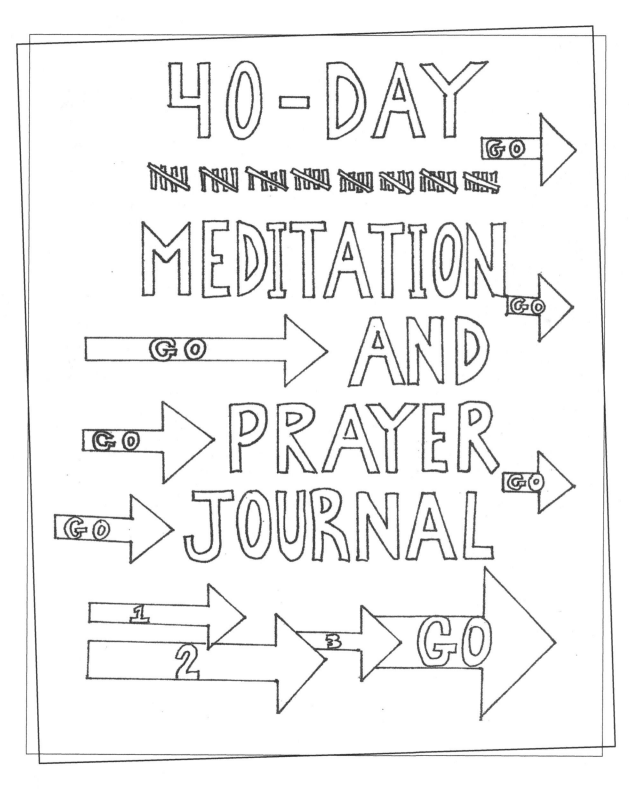

Meditation and Prayer

WHAT ARE YOU...

Resisting	Admitting	Avoiding	Needing
_____	_____	_____	_____
_____	_____	_____	_____

HOW IS YOUR...

Soul	Mind	Emotions	Will - desires
_____	_____	_____	_____
_____	_____	_____	_____

Body	Heart	Spirit + Still small voice
_____	_____	_____
_____	_____	_____

WHAT IS YOUR...

Truth/ God's Truth	What to surrender?	What are you praying for?
_____	_____	_____
_____	_____	_____

NOTES: _____
_____
_____
_____

DAILY

restore

Faithfulness

BODY

sanctuary

Gentleness

BREATH

create

Goodness

WORD

harmonize

Joy

SPIRIT

connect

Peace

HEART

open

Love

SOUL

believe

Self-Control

PRAYER

renew

Patience

Meditation and Prayer

DAY _____

WHAT ARE YOU...

Resisting	Admitting	Avoiding	Needing
_____	_____	_____	_____
_____	_____	_____	_____

HOW IS YOUR...

Soul	Mind	Emotions	Will - desires
_____	_____	_____	_____
_____	_____	_____	_____

Body	Heart	Spirit + Still small voice
_____	_____	_____

WHAT IS YOUR...

Truth/ God's Truth	What to surrender?	What are you praying for?
_____	_____	_____
_____	_____	_____

NOTES: _____

_____

_____

_____

DAILY	BODY	BREATH	WORD	SPIRIT	HEART	SOUL	PRAYER
restore	*sanctuary*	*create*	*harmonize*	*connect*	*open*	*believe*	*renew*

Faithfulness	Gentleness	Goodness	Joy	Peace	Love	Self-Control	Patience

Tonyah Dee

Meditation and Prayer

WHAT ARE YOU...

Resisting	Admitting	Avoiding	Needing
_____	_____	_____	_____
_____	_____	_____	_____

HOW IS YOUR...

Soul	Mind	Emotions	Will - desires
_____	_____	_____	_____
_____	_____	_____	_____

Body	Heart	Spirit + Still small voice
_____	_____	_____
_____	_____	_____

WHAT IS YOUR...

Truth/ God's Truth	What to surrender?	What are you praying for?
_____	_____	_____
_____	_____	_____

NOTES:

_____

_____

_____

_____

DAILY
restore

Faithfulness

BODY
sanctuary

Gentleness

BREATH
create

Goodness

WORD
harmonize

Joy

SPIRIT
connect

Peace

HEART
open

Love

SOUL
believe

Self-Control

PRAYER
renew

Patience

Meditation and Prayer

DAY _____

WHAT ARE YOU...

Resisting

_____

_____

Admitting

_____

_____

Avoiding

_____

_____

Needing

_____

_____

HOW IS YOUR...

Soul

_____

_____

Mind

_____

_____

Emotions

_____

_____

Will - desires

_____

_____

Body

_____

_____

Heart

_____

_____

Spirit + Still small voice

_____

_____

WHAT IS YOUR...

Truth/ God's Truth

_____

_____

What to surrender?

_____

_____

What are you praying for?

_____

_____

NOTES: _____

_____

_____

_____

DAILY

restore

Faithfulness

BODY

sanctuary

Gentleness

BREATH

create

Goodness

WORD

harmonize

Joy

SPIRIT

connect

Peace

HEART

open

Love

SOUL

believe

Self-Control

PRAYER

renew

Patience

Tonyah Dee

Meditation and Prayer

WHAT ARE YOU...

Resisting

_____

_____

Admitting

_____

_____

Avoiding

_____

_____

Needing

_____

_____

HOW IS YOUR...

Soul

_____

_____

Mind

_____

_____

Emotions

_____

_____

Will - desires

_____

_____

Body

_____

_____

Heart

_____

_____

Spirit + Still small voice

_____

_____

WHAT IS YOUR...

Truth/ God's Truth

_____

What to surrender?

_____

What are you praying for?

_____

NOTES: _____

_____

_____

_____

DAILY	BODY	BREATH	WORD	SPIRIT	HEART	SOUL	PRAYER
restore	sanctuary	create	harmonize	connect	open	believe	renew
Faithfulness	Gentleness	Goodness	Joy	Peace	Love	Self-Control	Patience

RETURNING

Definition: Come or go back, turn one's attention.[36]

"So as for you, return to your God, Observe kindness and justice,
And wait for your God continually" (Hosea 12:6 NASB).

Can you observe the kindness within yourself? Can you wait for your God?

Meditation and Prayer

WHAT ARE YOU...

Resisting	Admitting	Avoiding	Needing
_____	_____	_____	_____
_____	_____	_____	_____

HOW IS YOUR...

Soul	Mind	Emotions	Will - desires
_____	_____	_____	_____
_____	_____	_____	_____

Body	Heart	Spirit + Still small voice
_____	_____	_____
_____	_____	_____

WHAT IS YOUR...

Truth/ God's Truth	What to surrender?	What are you praying for?
_____	_____	_____
_____	_____	_____

NOTES: _____

_____

_____

_____

DAILY	BODY	BREATH	WORD	SPIRIT	HEART	SOUL	PRAYER
restore	sanctuary	create	harmonize	connect	open	believe	renew
					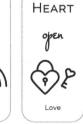		
Faithfulness	Gentleness	Goodness	Joy	Peace	Love	Self-Control	Patience

Meditation and Prayer

WHAT ARE YOU...

Resisting	Admitting	Avoiding	Needing
_____	_____	_____	_____
_____	_____	_____	_____

HOW IS YOUR...

Soul	Mind	Emotions	Will - desires
_____	_____	_____	_____
_____	_____	_____	_____

Body	Heart	Spirit + Still small voice
_____	_____	_____
_____	_____	_____

WHAT IS YOUR...

Truth/ God's Truth	What to surrender?	What are you praying for?
_____	_____	_____
_____	_____	_____

NOTES: _____

_____

_____

_____

DAILY
restore

Faithfulness

BODY
sanctuary

Gentleness

BREATH
create

Goodness

WORD
harmonize

Joy

SPIRIT
connect

Peace

HEART
open

Love

SOUL
believe

Self-Control

PRAYER
renew

Patience

Tonyah Dee

Meditation and Prayer

WHAT ARE YOU...

Resisting	Admitting	Avoiding	Needing
_____	_____	_____	_____
_____	_____	_____	_____

HOW IS YOUR...

Soul	Mind	Emotions	Will - desires
_____	_____	_____	_____
_____	_____	_____	_____

Body	Heart	Spirit + Still small voice
_____	_____	_____

WHAT IS YOUR...

Truth/ God's Truth	What to surrender?	What are you praying for?
_____	_____	_____
_____	_____	_____

NOTES: _____
_____
_____
_____

DAILY	BODY	BREATH	WORD	SPIRIT	HEART	SOUL	PRAYER
restore	*sanctuary*	*create*	*harmonize*	*connect*	*open*	*believe*	*renew*

Faithfulness	Gentleness	Goodness	Joy	Peace	Love	Self-Control	Patience

Meditation and Prayer

WHAT ARE YOU...

Resisting	Admitting	Avoiding	Needing
_____	_____	_____	_____
_____	_____	_____	_____

HOW IS YOUR...

Soul	Mind	Emotions	Will - desires
_____	_____	_____	_____
_____	_____	_____	_____

Body	Heart	Spirit + Still small voice
_____	_____	_____
_____	_____	_____

WHAT IS YOUR...

Truth/ God's Truth	What to surrender?	What are you praying for?
_____	_____	_____
_____	_____	_____

NOTES: _____
_____
_____
_____
_____

DAILY	BODY	BREATH	WORD	SPIRIT	HEART	SOUL	PRAYER
restore	*sanctuary*	*create*	*harmonize*	*connect*	*open*	*believe*	*renew*

Faithfulness	Gentleness	Goodness	Joy	Peace	Love	Self-Control	Patience

Tonyah Dee

Meditation and Prayer

WHAT ARE YOU...

Resisting	Admitting	Avoiding	Needing
_____	_____	_____	_____
_____	_____	_____	_____

HOW IS YOUR...

Soul	Mind	Emotions	Will - desires
_____	_____	_____	_____
_____	_____	_____	_____

Body	Heart	Spirit + Still small voice
_____	_____	_____
_____	_____	_____

WHAT IS YOUR...

Truth/ God's Truth	What to surrender?	What are you praying for?
_____	_____	_____
_____	_____	_____

NOTES: _____

_____

_____

_____

DAILY	BODY	BREATH	WORD	SPIRIT	HEART	SOUL	PRAYER
restore	*sanctuary*	*create*	*harmonize*	*connect*	*open*	*believe*	*renew*

Faithfulness	Gentleness	Goodness	Joy	Peace	Love	Self-Control	Patience

RECEPTIVE

Definition: Willing to consider or accept.[37]

"But examine everything carefully; hold fast to that which is good"
(1 Thessalonians 5:21 NASB1995).

What is it like for you to be receptive to your truth daily?

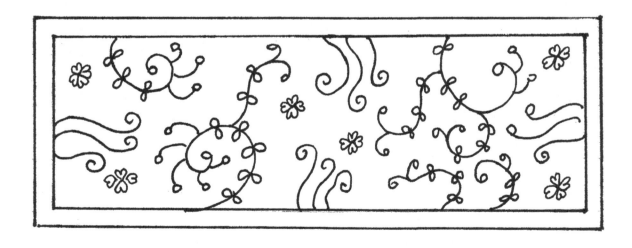

Meditation and Prayer

What are you...

Resisting	Admitting	Avoiding	Needing
_____	_____	_____	_____
_____	_____	_____	_____

How is your...

Soul	Mind	Emotions	Will - desires
_____	_____	_____	_____
_____	_____	_____	_____

Body	Heart	Spirit + Still small voice
_____	_____	_____
_____	_____	_____

What is your...

Truth/ God's Truth	What to surrender?	What are you praying for?
_____	_____	_____
_____	_____	_____

Notes: _____

_____

_____

_____

DAILY	BODY	BREATH	WORD	SPIRIT	HEART	SOUL	PRAYER
restore	*sanctuary*	*create*	*harmonize*	*connect*	*open*	*believe*	*renew*
Faithfulness	Gentleness	Goodness	Joy	Peace	Love	Self-Control	Patience

Meditation and Prayer

WHAT ARE YOU...

Resisting	Admitting	Avoiding	Needing
_____	_____	_____	_____
_____	_____	_____	_____

HOW IS YOUR...

Soul	Mind	Emotions	Will - desires
_____	_____	_____	_____
_____	_____	_____	_____

Body	Heart	Spirit + Still small voice
_____	_____	_____
_____	_____	_____

WHAT IS YOUR...

Truth/ God's Truth	What to surrender?	What are you praying for?
_____	_____	_____
_____	_____	_____

NOTES: _____

_____

_____

_____

DAILY	BODY	BREATH	WORD	SPIRIT	HEART	SOUL	PRAYER
restore	*sanctuary*	*create*	*harmonize*	*connect*	*open*	*believe*	*renew*
					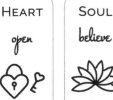		
Faithfulness	Gentleness	Goodness	Joy	Peace	Love	Self-Control	Patience

Tonyah Dee

Meditation and Prayer

WHAT ARE YOU...

Resisting	Admitting	Avoiding	Needing
_____	_____	_____	_____
_____	_____	_____	_____

HOW IS YOUR...

Soul	Mind	Emotions	Will - desires
_____	_____	_____	_____
_____	_____	_____	_____

Body	Heart	Spirit + Still small voice
_____	_____	_____
_____	_____	_____

WHAT IS YOUR...

Truth/ God's Truth	What to surrender?	What are you praying for?
_____	_____	_____
_____	_____	_____

NOTES: _____
_____
_____
_____

DAILY	BODY	BREATH	WORD	SPIRIT	HEART	SOUL	PRAYER
restore	sanctuary	create	harmonize	connect	open	believe	renew
Faithfulness	Gentleness	Goodness	Joy	Peace	Love	Self-Control	Patience

How to Meditate with Jesus

Meditation and Prayer

WHAT ARE YOU...

Resisting	Admitting	Avoiding	Needing
_____	_____	_____	_____
_____	_____	_____	_____

HOW IS YOUR...

Soul	Mind	Emotions	Will - desires
_____	_____	_____	_____
_____	_____	_____	_____

Body	Heart	Spirit + Still small voice
_____	_____	_____
_____	_____	_____

WHAT IS YOUR...

Truth/ God's Truth	What to surrender?	What are you praying for?
_____	_____	_____
_____	_____	_____

NOTES: _____

_____

_____

_____

_____

DAILY
restore

Faithfulness

BODY
sanctuary

Gentleness

BREATH
create

Goodness

WORD
harmonize

Joy

SPIRIT
connect

Peace

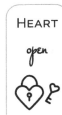

HEART
open

Love

SOUL
believe

Self-Control

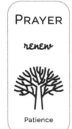

PRAYER
renew

Patience

Tonyah Dee

Meditation and Prayer

WHAT ARE YOU...

Resisting

_____

_____

Admitting

_____

_____

Avoiding

_____

_____

Needing

_____

_____

HOW IS YOUR...

Soul

_____

_____

Mind

_____

_____

Emotions

_____

_____

Will - desires

_____

_____

Body

_____

_____

Heart

_____

_____

Spirit + Still small voice

_____

_____

WHAT IS YOUR...

Truth/ God's Truth

_____

_____

What to surrender?

_____

_____

What are you praying for?

_____

_____

NOTES: _____

_____

_____

_____

_____

DAILY	BODY	BREATH	WORD	SPIRIT	HEART	SOUL	PRAYER
restore	*sanctuary*	*create*	*harmonize*	*connect*	*open*	*believe*	*renew*

Faithfulness	Gentleness	Goodness	Joy	Peace	Love	Self-Control	Patience

REUNION

Definition: Two or more people coming together again.[38]

"Therefore, we are ambassadors for Christ, as though God were making an appeal through us; we beg you on behalf of Christ, be reconciled to God" (2 Corinthians 5:20 NASB1995).

Do you have an increased sense of union and reconciliation with God and your body, soul, and spirit?

Tonyah Dee

Meditation and Prayer

WHAT ARE YOU...

Resisting

_____

_____

Admitting

_____

_____

Avoiding

_____

_____

Needing

_____

_____

HOW IS YOUR...

Soul

_____

Mind

_____

Emotions

_____

Will - desires

_____

Body

_____

Heart

_____

Spirit + Still small voice

_____

WHAT IS YOUR...

Truth/ God's Truth

_____

What to surrender?

_____

What are you praying for?

_____

NOTES: _____

_____

_____

_____

DAILY	BODY	BREATH	WORD	SPIRIT	HEART	SOUL	PRAYER
restore	sanctuary	create	harmonize	connect	open	believe	renew
Faithfulness	Gentleness	Goodness	Joy	Peace	Love	Self-Control	Patience

Meditation and Prayer

WHAT ARE YOU...

Resisting	Admitting	Avoiding	Needing
_____	_____	_____	_____
_____	_____	_____	_____

HOW IS YOUR...

Soul	Mind	Emotions	Will - desires
_____	_____	_____	_____
_____	_____	_____	_____

Body	Heart	Spirit + Still small voice
_____	_____	_____
_____	_____	_____

WHAT IS YOUR...

Truth/ God's Truth	What to surrender?	What are you praying for?
_____	_____	_____
_____	_____	_____

NOTES: _____

_____

_____

_____

DAILY	BODY	BREATH	WORD	SPIRIT	HEART	SOUL	PRAYER
restore	sanctuary	create	harmonize	connect	open	believe	renew
			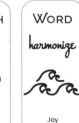		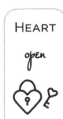		
Faithfulness	Gentleness	Goodness	Joy	Peace	Love	Self-Control	Patience

Tonyah Dee

Meditation and Prayer

WHAT ARE YOU...

Resisting	Admitting	Avoiding	Needing
_____	_____	_____	_____
_____	_____	_____	_____

HOW IS YOUR...

Soul	Mind	Emotions	Will - desires
_____	_____	_____	_____

Body	Heart	Spirit + Still small voice
_____	_____	_____

WHAT IS YOUR...

Truth/ God's Truth	What to surrender?	What are you praying for?
_____	_____	_____
_____		

NOTES: _____

_____

_____

_____

DAILY	BODY	BREATH	WORD	SPIRIT	HEART	SOUL	PRAYER
restore	*sanctuary*	*create*	*harmonize*	*connect*	*open*	*believe*	*renew*

Faithfulness	Gentleness	Goodness	Joy	Peace	Love	Self-Control	Patience

Meditation and Prayer

WHAT ARE YOU...

Resisting	Admitting	Avoiding	Needing
_____	_____	_____	_____
_____	_____	_____	_____

HOW IS YOUR...

Soul	Mind	Emotions	Will - desires
_____	_____	_____	_____
_____	_____	_____	_____

Body	Heart	Spirit + Still small voice
_____	_____	_____
_____	_____	_____

WHAT IS YOUR...

Truth/ God's Truth	What to surrender?	What are you praying for?
_____	_____	_____
_____	_____	_____

NOTES: _____
_____
_____
_____
_____

DAILY	BODY	BREATH	WORD	SPIRIT	HEART	SOUL	PRAYER
restore	sanctuary	create	harmonize	connect	open	believe	renew

Faithfulness	Gentleness	Goodness	Joy	Peace	Love	Self-Control	Patience

Meditation and Prayer

WHAT ARE YOU...

Resisting

_____
_____

Admitting

_____
_____

Avoiding

_____
_____

Needing

_____
_____

HOW IS YOUR...

Soul

_____
_____

Mind

_____
_____

Emotions

_____
_____

Will - desires

_____
_____

Body

_____
_____

Heart

_____
_____

Spirit + Still small voice

_____
_____

WHAT IS YOUR...

Truth/ God's Truth

_____
_____

What to surrender?

_____
_____

What are you praying for?

_____
_____

NOTES:

_____
_____
_____
_____

DAILY	BODY	BREATH	WORD	SPIRIT	HEART	SOUL	PRAYER
restore	sanctuary	create	harmonize	connect	open	believe	renew
Faithfulness	Gentleness	Goodness	Joy	Peace	Love	Self-Control	Patience

How to Meditate with Jesus

RESTORATION

Definition: Bringing back to a former position or condition.[39]

"And the God of all grace, who called you to his eternal glory in Christ, after you have suffered a little while, will himself restore you and make you strong, firm and steadfast" (1 Peter 5:10 NIV).

Do you sense God's spirit restoring you?

Tonyah Dee

Meditation and Prayer

WHAT ARE YOU...

Resisting

_____

_____

Admitting

_____

_____

Avoiding

_____

_____

Needing

_____

_____

HOW IS YOUR...

Soul

_____

_____

Mind

_____

_____

Emotions

_____

_____

Will - desires

_____

_____

Body

_____

_____

Heart

_____

_____

Spirit + Still small voice

_____

_____

WHAT IS YOUR...

Truth/ God's Truth

_____

_____

What to surrender?

_____

_____

What are you praying for?

_____

_____

NOTES: _____

_____

_____

_____

DAILY	BODY	BREATH	WORD	SPIRIT	HEART	SOUL	PRAYER
restore	*sanctuary*	*create*	*harmonize*	*connect*	*open*	*believe*	*renew*
Faithfulness	Gentleness	Goodness	Joy	Peace	Love	Self-Control	Patience

How to Meditate with Jesus

Meditation and Prayer

WHAT ARE YOU...

Resisting	Admitting	Avoiding	Needing
_____	_____	_____	_____
_____	_____	_____	_____

HOW IS YOUR...

Soul	Mind	Emotions	Will - desires
_____	_____	_____	_____
_____	_____	_____	_____

Body	Heart	Spirit + Still small voice
_____	_____	_____
_____	_____	_____

WHAT IS YOUR...

Truth/ God's Truth	What to surrender?	What are you praying for?
_____	_____	_____
_____	_____	_____

NOTES: _____
_____
_____
_____

DAILY
restore

Faithfulness

BODY
sanctuary

Gentleness

BREATH
create

Goodness

WORD
harmonize

Joy

SPIRIT
connect

Peace

HEART
open

Love

SOUL
believe

Self-Control

PRAYER
renew

Patience

Tonyah Dee

Meditation and Prayer

WHAT ARE YOU...

Resisting	Admitting	Avoiding	Needing
_____	_____	_____	_____
_____	_____	_____	_____

HOW IS YOUR...

Soul	Mind	Emotions	Will - desires
_____	_____	_____	_____
_____	_____	_____	_____

Body	Heart	Spirit + Still small voice
_____	_____	_____
_____	_____	_____

WHAT IS YOUR...

Truth/ God's Truth	What to surrender?	What are you praying for?
_____	_____	_____
_____	_____	_____

NOTES: _____
_____
_____
_____

DAILY	BODY	BREATH	WORD	SPIRIT	HEART	SOUL	PRAYER
restore	*sanctuary*	*create*	*harmonize*	*connect*	*open*	*believe*	*renew*
Faithfulness	Gentleness	Goodness	Joy	Peace	Love	Self-Control	Patience

Meditation and Prayer

WHAT ARE YOU...

Resisting
_____
_____

Admitting
_____
_____

Avoiding
_____
_____

Needing
_____
_____

HOW IS YOUR...

Soul
_____
_____

Mind
_____
_____

Emotions
_____
_____

Will - desires
_____
_____

Body
_____
_____

Heart
_____
_____

Spirit + Still small voice
_____
_____

WHAT IS YOUR...

Truth/ God's Truth
_____
_____

What to surrender?
_____
_____

What are you praying for?
_____
_____

NOTES: _____
_____
_____
_____
_____

DAILY

restore

Faithfulness

BODY

sanctuary

Gentleness

BREATH

create

Goodness

WORD

harmonize

Joy

SPIRIT

connect

Peace

HEART

open

Love

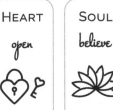

SOUL

believe

Self-Control

PRAYER

renew

Patience

Tonyah Dee

Meditation and Prayer

WHAT ARE YOU...

Resisting
_____
_____

Admitting
_____
_____

Avoiding
_____
_____

Needing
_____
_____

HOW IS YOUR...

Soul
_____
_____

Mind
_____
_____

Emotions
_____
_____

Will - desires
_____
_____

Body
_____
_____

Heart
_____
_____

Spirit + Still small voice
_____
_____

WHAT IS YOUR...

Truth/ God's Truth
_____
_____

What to surrender?
_____
_____

What are you praying for?
_____
_____

NOTES: _____
_____
_____
_____
_____

DAILY	BODY	BREATH	WORD	SPIRIT	HEART	SOUL	PRAYER
restore	sanctuary	create	harmonize	connect	open	believe	renew
Faithfulness	Gentleness	Goodness	Joy	Peace	Love	Self-Control	Patience

REMOVAL

Definition: Taking away or abolishing something unwanted.[40]

"For you were once darkness, but are now light in the Lord.
Walk as children of light" (Ephesians 5:8 WEB).

Can you identify and remove inner darkness, such as false or limited mindsets, buried or heavy emotions, and unbeneficial actions, which are affecting you or keeping you from an abundant life full of light?

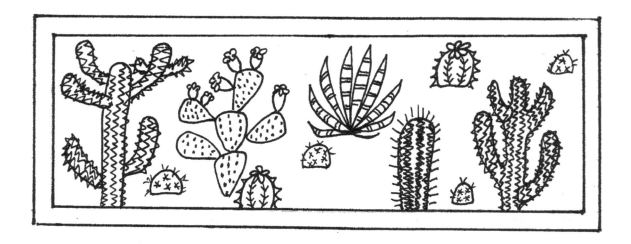

Meditation and Prayer

WHAT ARE YOU...

Resisting	Admitting	Avoiding	Needing
_____	_____	_____	_____
_____	_____	_____	_____

HOW IS YOUR...

Soul	Mind	Emotions	Will - desires
_____	_____	_____	_____

Body	Heart	Spirit + Still small voice
_____	_____	_____

WHAT IS YOUR...

Truth/ God's Truth	What to surrender?	What are you praying for?
_____	_____	_____
_____	_____	_____

NOTES: _____
_____
_____
_____

DAILY	BODY	BREATH	WORD	SPIRIT	HEART	SOUL	PRAYER
restore	*sanctuary*	*create*	*harmonize*	*connect*	*open*	*believe*	*renew*

Faithfulness	Gentleness	Goodness	Joy	Peace	Love	Self-Control	Patience

Meditation and Prayer

WHAT ARE YOU...

Resisting	Admitting	Avoiding	Needing
_____	_____	_____	_____
_____	_____	_____	_____

HOW IS YOUR...

Soul	Mind	Emotions	Will - desires
_____	_____	_____	_____
_____	_____	_____	_____

Body	Heart	Spirit + Still small voice
_____	_____	_____
_____	_____	_____

WHAT IS YOUR...

Truth/ God's Truth	What to surrender?	What are you praying for?
_____	_____	_____
_____	_____	_____

NOTES: _____
_____
_____
_____

DAILY	BODY	BREATH	WORD	SPIRIT	HEART	SOUL	PRAYER
restore	*sanctuary*	*create*	*harmonize*	*connect*	*open*	*believe*	*renew*

Faithfulness	Gentleness	Goodness	Joy	Peace	Love	Self-Control	Patience

Meditation and Prayer

WHAT ARE YOU...

Resisting

_____
_____

Admitting

_____
_____

Avoiding

_____
_____

Needing

_____
_____

HOW IS YOUR...

Soul

_____
_____

Mind

_____
_____

Emotions

_____
_____

Will - desires

_____
_____

Body

_____
_____

Heart

_____
_____

Spirit + Still small voice

_____
_____

WHAT IS YOUR...

Truth/ God's Truth

_____
_____

What to surrender?

_____
_____

What are you praying for?

_____
_____

NOTES: _____
_____
_____
_____
_____

DAILY	BODY	BREATH	WORD	SPIRIT	HEART	SOUL	PRAYER
restore	sanctuary	create	harmonize	connect	open	believe	renew
Faithfulness	Gentleness	Goodness	Joy	Peace	Love	Self-Control	Patience

Meditation and Prayer

WHAT ARE YOU...

Resisting

_____
_____

Admitting

_____
_____

Avoiding

_____
_____

Needing

_____
_____

HOW IS YOUR...

Soul

_____
_____

Mind

_____
_____

Emotions

_____
_____

Will - desires

_____
_____

Body

_____
_____

Heart

_____
_____

Spirit + Still small voice

_____
_____

WHAT IS YOUR...

Truth/ God's Truth

_____
_____

What to surrender?

_____
_____

What are you praying for?

_____
_____

NOTES: _____
_____
_____
_____
_____

DAILY

restore

Faithfulness

BODY

sanctuary

Gentleness

BREATH

create

Goodness

WORD

harmonize

Joy

SPIRIT

connect

Peace

HEART

open

Love

SOUL

believe

Self-Control

PRAYER

renew

Patience

Tonyah Dee

Meditation and Prayer

DAY _____

WHAT ARE YOU...

Resisting   Admitting   Avoiding   Needing

_____ _____ _____ _____

_____ _____ _____ _____

HOW IS YOUR...

Soul   Mind   Emotions   Will - desires

_____ _____ _____ _____

_____ _____ _____ _____

Body   Heart   Spirit + Still small voice

_____ _____ _____

_____ _____ _____

WHAT IS YOUR...

Truth/ God's Truth   What to surrender?   What are you praying for?

_____ _____ _____

_____ _____ _____

NOTES:

_____

_____

_____

_____

DAILY	BODY	BREATH	WORD	SPIRIT	HEART	SOUL	PRAYER
restore	*sanctuary*	*create*	*harmonize*	*connect*	*open*	*believe*	*renew*

Faithfulness	Gentleness	Goodness	Joy	Peace	Love	Self-Control	Patience

RECOVERY

Definition: Regaining possession or control of something stolen or lost.[41]

"I will restore your health, and I will heal your wounds,
declares the LORD" (Jeremiah 30:17 CEB).

Have you recovered lost parts of your soul or healed inner wounds?

Meditation and Prayer

WHAT ARE YOU...

Resisting

_____
_____

Admitting

_____
_____

Avoiding

_____
_____

Needing

_____
_____

HOW IS YOUR...

Soul

_____
_____

Mind

_____
_____

Emotions

_____
_____

Will - desires

_____
_____

Body

_____
_____

Heart

_____
_____

Spirit + Still small voice

_____
_____

WHAT IS YOUR...

Truth/ God's Truth

_____
_____

What to surrender?

_____
_____

What are you praying for?

_____
_____

NOTES: _____

_____
_____
_____

DAILY	BODY	BREATH	WORD	SPIRIT	HEART	SOUL	PRAYER
restore	sanctuary	create	harmonize	connect	open	believe	renew
Faithfulness	Gentleness	Goodness	Joy	Peace	Love	Self-Control	Patience

Meditation and Prayer

WHAT ARE YOU...

Resisting	Admitting	Avoiding	Needing
_____	_____	_____	_____
_____	_____	_____	_____

HOW IS YOUR...

Soul	Mind	Emotions	Will - desires
_____	_____	_____	_____
_____	_____	_____	_____

Body	Heart	Spirit + Still small voice
_____	_____	_____
_____	_____	_____

WHAT IS YOUR...

Truth/ God's Truth	What to surrender?	What are you praying for?
_____	_____	_____
_____	_____	_____

NOTES: _____

_____

_____

_____

_____

DAILY
restore

Faithfulness

BODY
sanctuary

Gentleness

BREATH
create

Goodness

WORD
harmonize

Joy

SPIRIT
connect

Peace

HEART
open

Love

SOUL
believe

Self-Control

PRAYER
renew

Patience

Tonyah Dee

Meditation and Prayer

WHAT ARE YOU...

Resisting

_____

_____

Admitting

_____

_____

Avoiding

_____

_____

Needing

_____

_____

HOW IS YOUR...

Soul

_____

Mind

_____

Emotions

_____

Will - desires

_____

Body

_____

Heart

_____

Spirit + Still small voice

_____

WHAT IS YOUR...

Truth/ God's Truth

_____

_____

What to surrender?

_____

_____

What are you praying for?

_____

_____

NOTES:

_____

_____

_____

_____

DAILY	BODY	BREATH	WORD	SPIRIT	HEART	SOUL	PRAYER
restore	sanctuary	create	harmonize	connect	open	believe	renew
Faithfulness	Gentleness	Goodness	Joy	Peace	Love	Self-Control	Patience

Meditation and Prayer

DAY _____

WHAT ARE YOU...

Resisting

_____

_____

Admitting

_____

_____

Avoiding

_____

_____

Needing

_____

_____

HOW IS YOUR...

Soul

_____

_____

Mind

_____

_____

Emotions

_____

_____

Will - desires

_____

_____

Body

_____

_____

Heart

_____

_____

Spirit + Still small voice

_____

_____

WHAT IS YOUR...

Truth/ God's Truth

_____

_____

What to surrender?

_____

_____

What are you praying for?

_____

_____

NOTES: _____

_____

_____

_____

DAILY

restore

Faithfulness

BODY

sanctuary

Gentleness

BREATH

create

Goodness

WORD

harmonize

Joy

SPIRIT

connect

Peace

HEART

open

Love

SOUL

believe

Self-Control

PRAYER

renew

Patience

Tonyah Dee

Meditation and Prayer

WHAT ARE YOU...

Resisting	Admitting	Avoiding	Needing
_____	_____	_____	_____
_____	_____	_____	_____

HOW IS YOUR...

Soul	Mind	Emotions	Will - desires
_____	_____	_____	_____
_____	_____	_____	_____

Body	Heart	Spirit + Still small voice
_____	_____	_____
_____	_____	_____

WHAT IS YOUR...

Truth/ God's Truth	What to surrender?	What are you praying for?
_____	_____	_____
_____	_____	_____

NOTES: _____
_____
_____
_____

DAILY	BODY	BREATH	WORD	SPIRIT	HEART	SOUL	PRAYER
restore	sanctuary	create	harmonize	connect	open	believe	renew
Faithfulness	Gentleness	Goodness	Joy	Peace	Love	Self-Control	Patience

REFULGENCE

Definition: A radiant or resplendent quality or state.[42]

"The Son is the radiance of God's glory and the exact representation of His nature, upholding all things by His powerful word" (Hebrews 1:3 BSB).

How is your practice helping you to become more like Jesus Christ?
Are you experiencing more light?

Meditation and Prayer

WHAT ARE YOU...

Resisting	Admitting	Avoiding	Needing
_____	_____	_____	_____
_____	_____	_____	_____

HOW IS YOUR...

Soul	Mind	Emotions	Will - desires
_____	_____	_____	_____
_____	_____	_____	_____

Body	Heart	Spirit + Still small voice
_____	_____	
_____	_____	

WHAT IS YOUR...

Truth/ God's Truth	What to surrender?	What are you praying for?
_____	_____	_____
_____	_____	_____

NOTES: _____

_____

_____

_____

DAILY	BODY	BREATH	WORD	SPIRIT	HEART	SOUL	PRAYER
restore	sanctuary	create	harmonize	connect	open	believe	renew
Faithfulness	Gentleness	Goodness	Joy	Peace	Love	Self-Control	Patience

Meditation and Prayer

WHAT ARE YOU...

Resisting	Admitting	Avoiding	Needing
_____	_____	_____	_____
_____	_____	_____	_____

HOW IS YOUR...

Soul	Mind	Emotions	Will - desires
_____	_____	_____	_____
_____	_____	_____	_____

Body	Heart	Spirit + Still small voice
_____	_____	_____
_____	_____	_____

WHAT IS YOUR...

Truth/ God's Truth	What to surrender?	What are you praying for?
_____	_____	_____
_____	_____	_____

NOTES:

_____

_____

_____

_____

DAILY	BODY	BREATH	WORD	SPIRIT	HEART	SOUL	PRAYER
restore	*sanctuary*	*create*	*harmonize*	*connect*	*open*	*believe*	*renew*

Faithfulness	Gentleness	Goodness	Joy	Peace	Love	Self-Control	Patience

Tonyah Dee

Meditation and Prayer

WHAT ARE YOU...

Resisting

_____
_____

Admitting

_____
_____

Avoiding

_____
_____

Needing

_____
_____

HOW IS YOUR...

Soul

_____
_____

Mind

_____
_____

Emotions

_____
_____

Will - desires

_____
_____

Body

_____
_____

Heart

_____
_____

Spirit + Still small voice

_____
_____

WHAT IS YOUR...

Truth/ God's Truth

_____
_____

What to surrender?

_____
_____

What are you praying for?

_____
_____

NOTES: _____
_____
_____
_____
_____

DAILY	BODY	BREATH	WORD	SPIRIT	HEART	SOUL	PRAYER
restore	sanctuary	create	harmonize	connect	open	believe	renew

Faithfulness	Gentleness	Goodness	Joy	Peace	Love	Self-Control	Patience

Meditation and Prayer

WHAT ARE YOU...

Resisting	Admitting	Avoiding	Needing
_____	_____	_____	_____
_____	_____	_____	_____

HOW IS YOUR...

Soul	Mind	Emotions	Will - desires
_____	_____	_____	_____
_____	_____	_____	_____

Body	Heart	Spirit + Still small voice
_____	_____	_____
_____	_____	_____

WHAT IS YOUR...

Truth/ God's Truth	What to surrender?	What are you praying for?
_____	_____	_____
_____	_____	_____

NOTES: _____

_____

_____

_____

DAILY	BODY	BREATH	WORD	SPIRIT	HEART	SOUL	PRAYER
restore	*sanctuary*	*create*	*harmonize*	*connect*	*open*	*believe*	*renew*

Faithfulness	Gentleness	Goodness	Joy	Peace	Love	Self-Control	Patience

Meditation and Prayer

WHAT ARE YOU...

Resisting	Admitting	Avoiding	Needing
_____	_____	_____	_____
_____	_____	_____	_____

HOW IS YOUR...

Soul	Mind	Emotions	Will - desires
_____	_____	_____	_____
_____	_____	_____	_____

Body	Heart	Spirit + Still small voice
_____	_____	_____
_____	_____	_____

WHAT IS YOUR...

Truth/ God's Truth	What to surrender?	What are you praying for?
_____	_____	_____
_____	_____	_____

NOTES: _____

_____

_____

_____

_____

DAILY	BODY	BREATH	WORD	SPIRIT	HEART	SOUL	PRAYER
restore	sanctuary	create	harmonize	connect	open	believe	renew
Faithfulness	Gentleness	Goodness	Joy	Peace	Love	Self-Control	Patience

REVELATION

Definition: Making known something previously unknown.[43]

"Blessed are the pure in heart: for they shall see God" (Matthew 5:8 KJV).

How are you seeing God?
How will you continue to know Jesus better?
How will you share the spirit with others?

Congratulations!

AFTERWORD

Many years ago, I began a meditation and prayer practice in the hope of eradicating my anxiety and the self-destructive behaviors that it triggered. Over time, almost without even realizing it, my anxiety disappeared, and I became a peaceful and joyful person. Most of the time, I forget about who I used to be.

The comment I receive the most is "You seem so at peace." Many add that I seem "happy and positive." I'm told I have good energy and am a bright light.

It's true. I have almost zero anxiety. Ever. No more. Gone. Even a slight backslide into self-destructiveness, self-sabotage, or fear is an immediate reminder to return to my spiritual practice.

In addition, I've been teaching my Christ-centered meditation and prayer practice to groups of women as a beta test before this workbook comes out. I've seen transformations happen and have been told by many women that the experience was a life-changing and positive one for them. Again, it's the comments that inspire me to continue doing what I'm doing:

> "Tonyah's practical, guided approach to meditation (listening to God) helped me more gently approach my morning time with my creator."—Donna Schuller

> "Through her teaching I learned how to quickly get into a more focused frame of mind and to discover how to hear God's prompting of his will for my life. I'm learning how to discern the difference between his will and my will with the practices she teaches."—Lisa Baker

> "My son died in 2020. Needless to say, I need to meditate, but in the past, it has been so hard to stay centered. The technique Tonyah teaches is gentle

and easy to achieve a meditative state of mind. I would recommend this Christ-centered meditation to everyone."—Mary Olds

They continue to ask me to teach my practice, and this is the confirmation that I'm on the right path to carry out God's will. It brings me joy to do God's work.

Some religious groups have called me New Age, and I've experienced marginalization. I now know what it feels like to be excluded and judged versus what I believe Jesus would want, and that is to be included and valued.

I was invited to teach at the largest Christian music festival in the United States for two years. The Wild Goose Festival is about supporting social justice, and because I took part, I learned what it means *for all people* to have a place to walk with and connect with God. I believe God wants me to understand the path to love and not just to understand religion. I'm sure the doors that continue to open for me is because I love like Jesus loved.

I'm still using the strategies outlined in this book because they continue to help me navigate through times of darkness and keep me elevated in the realms of peace, love, and joy. I continue to be led into greater amounts of abundance and freedom.

If we trust God or, as Jesus said, "don't let your heart be troubled. Believe in God. Believe also in me" (John 14:1WEB), we see, hear, and experience deeper realms of truth, which will set us free.

It's a lifestyle of higher-power living, which happens to be the name of the next book I am releasing. *Higher-Power Living* is a deep dive into spirituality, psychology, wellness, and the eight steps outlined in this workbook, which is *Higher-Power Living*'s precursor and companion.

I wrote the book in your hands so you can start immediately reaping the benefits of a daily Christ-centered meditation and prayer practice and begin living your life as God intended. If you would enjoy a deeper, more thorough dive into the Eight Steps, my next book, *Higher Power Living*, is coming soon.

May God bless you richly.

Much love,
Tonyah

APPENDIX

Resources for Your Daily Practice

YahLight Website

Tonyah Dee YouTube Channel

Tonyah Dee Website

Contemplations

Meditations

Music

NOTES

1   Debbie Gisonni, "Self-Awareness Increases With Meditation," *HuffPost*, August 29, 2013, https://www.huff- post.com/entry/meditation-tips_b_3830431.

2   *New World Encyclopedia*, s.v. "Abba," accessed May 18, 2022, https://www.newworldencyclopedia.org/entry/Abba.

3   David Wheeler-Reed, "What the early church thought about God's gender," *Conversation*, August 1, 2019, https://theconversation.com/what-the-early-church-thought-about-gods-gender-100077.

4   *Lexico*, s.v. "recovery," accessed May 19, 2022, https://www.lexico.com/en/definition/recovery.

5   William Griffith Wilson, *Twelve Steps and Twelve Traditions* (N.p.: Alcoholics Anonymous World Services, Inc., 1953), 96.

6   *Magnificent Obsession*, directed by Douglas Sirk (Los Angeles: Universal Pictures, 1954), https://www.criterion- channel.com/videos/magnificent-obsession-1.

7   Ralph Waldo Emerson, quoted in Susyn Reeve, *The Wholehearted Life: Big Changes and Greater Happiness Week by Week* (Berkeley: Viva Editions, 2014), chap. 18.

8   Carl Jung, trans., R.F.C. Hull, *The Archetypes and the Collective Unconscious* (Princeton: Princeton University Press, 1969), 335.

9   *New World Encyclopedia*, s.v. "Spirit," accessed March 1, 2022, https://www.newworldencyclopedia.org/entry/Spir- it#Etymology.

10 "Relaxation techniques: Breath control helps quell errant stress response," *Harvard Health Publishing*, July 6, 2020, https://www.health.harvard.edu/mind-and-mood/relaxation-techniques-breath-control-helps-quell-er- rant-stress-response.

11 James Nestor, *Breath: The New Science of a Lost Art* (New York: Riverhead Books, 2020), xix.

12 Ibid., 189-190.

13 Thích Nhất Hạnh, *Fear: Essential Wisdom for Getting Through the Storm* (New York: HarperCollins Publishers Inc., 2012), chap. 5.

14 Chief Seattle, "All Things Are Connected," in *Native American Testimony: An Anthology of Indian and White Relations: First Encounter to Dispossession*, ed. Peter Nabokov (New York: Thomas Y. Crowell, 1978), 108.

15 Chief Seattle, quoted in Rudolf Kaiser, "Chief Seattle's Speech(es): American Origins and European Recep-tion," in *Recovering the Word: Essays on Native American Literature*, ed. Brian Swan and Arnold Krupat (Berkeley: University of California Press, 1987), 531.

16 *Encyclopedia Britannica Online*, s.v. "Gospel," accessed March 21, 2022, https://www.britannica.com/topic/Gos-pel-New-Testament.

17 Masaru Emoto, *The Hidden Messages in Water* (New York: Atria Books, Hillsboro: Beyond Words Publishing, Inc., 2004), introduction.

18 Jane Fuller, "The Vibration Of Your Thoughts Create Your lives," *HuffPost*, January 12, 2016, https://www. huffingtonpost.co.uk/jane-fuller/your-thoughts-create-your_b_13318676.html.

19 Dan Millman, *No Ordinary Moments: A Peaceful Warrior's Guide to Daily Life* (Tiburon: H. J. Kramer, Nova-to: New World Library, 1992), 207.

20 *The Britannica Dictionary*, s.v., "Devotion," accessed March 28, 2022, https://www.britannica.com/dictionary/de-votion#:~:text=noun-,plural%20devotions,the%20quality%20of%20being%20devoted.

21 Paul Haider, "14 Proven Scientific Benefits of Chanting," *Sivana East*, n.d., https://blog.sivanaspirit.com/ sp-gn-scientific-benefits-chanting/.

22 Sarah Keating, "The world's most accessible stress reliever," *BBC*, May 18, 2020, https://www.bbc.com/future/ article/20200518-why-singing-can-make-you-feel-better-in-lockdown.

23 Cynthia Bourgeault, *The Meaning of Mary Magdalene: Discovering the Woman at the Heart of Christianity* (Bos-ton: Shambhala Publications, Inc., 2010), 61.

24 William Griffith Wilson, *Alcoholics Anonymous: The Story of How Many Thousands of Men and Women Have Recovered From Alcoholism* (N.p.: Alcoholics Anonymous World Services, Inc., 2001), 46.

25 Ibid., 417.

26 N.T. Wright, *Simply Christian: Why Christianity Makes Sense* (N.p.: HarperCollins Publishers, 2009), 129.

27 Nichiren Daishonin, *The Writings of Nichiren Daishonin, Volume 1* (N.p.: n.p., n.d.), 851, https://www.nichi-renlibrary.org/en/wnd-1/toc/.

28 Witness Lee, *Dealing with Our Inward Parts for the Growth in Life* (Anaheim: Living Stream Ministry, 2016), 28.

29 Rumi, quoted in Shaunna Menard, *Free to Heal: 9 Steps to a Successful, Soul-Satisfying Health Coaching Practice* (New York: Morgan James Publishing, 2020), Conclusion.

30 Dorothy Day, *Aims and Purposes*, February 1940, https://www.catholicworker.org/dorothyday/themes/ On%20Aims%20and%20Purposes%20(Dorothy%20Day).pdf.

31 Kathie Lee Gifford, *The Jesus I Know: Honest Conversations and Diverse Opinions About Who He Is* (Nashville: Thomas Nelson, 2021), 2.

32 Søren Kierkegaard, trans. Douglas V. Steere, *Purity of Heart is to Will One Thing: Spiritual Preparation for the Office of Confession* (New York: Harper & Row, Publishers, Inc., 1956), 51.

33 Leo Tolstoy, *My Confession and The Spirit of Christ's Teaching* (New York: Thomas Y. Crowell & Co., 1887), 152.

34 *Encyclopedia Britannica Online*, s.v. "light," accessed March 24, 2022, https://www.britannica.com/science/light.

35 Thomas Keating, *Consenting to God as God Is* (Brooklyn: Lantern Books, 2016), chap. 6.

36 *Lexico,* s.v. "return," accessed July 8, 2022, https://www.lexico.com/en/definition/return.

37 *Lexico,* s.v. "receptive," accessed July 7, 2022, https://www.lexico.com/en/definition/receptive.

38 *Lexico,* s.v. "reunion," accessed July 7, 2022, https://www.lexico.com/en/definition/reunion.

39 *Merriam-Webster Dictionary,* s.v. "restoration," accessed July 7, 2022, https://www.merriam-webster.com/dictio-nary/restoration.

40 *Lexico,* s.v. "removal," accessed July 7, 2022 https://www.lexico.com/en/definition/removal.

41 *Lexico,* s.v. "recovery," accessed May 19, 2022, https://www.lexico.com/en/definition/recovery.

42 *Merriam-Webster Dictionary*, s.v. "refulgence," accessed July 7, 2022, https://www.merriam-webster.com/dictio- nary/refulgence.

43 *Merriam-Webster Thesaurus*, s.v. "revelation," accessed July 7, 2022, https://www.merriam-webster.com/thesaurus/ revelation.

BIBLIOGRAPHY

Bourgeault, Cynthia. *The Meaning of Mary Magdalene: Discovering the Woman at the Heart of Christianity.*

Boston: Shambhala Publications, Inc., 2010.

Chief Seattle. "All Things Are Connected." In *Native American Testimony: An Anthology of Indian and White Relations: First Encounter to Dispossession,* edited by Peter Nabokov, 107-110. New York: Thomas Y. Crowell, 1978.

Chief Seattle. Quoted in Rudolf Kaiser. "Chief Seattle's Speech(es): American Origins and European Reception." In *Recovering the Word: Essays on Native American Literature,* edited by Brian Swan and Arnold Krupat, 530-532. Berkeley: University of California Press, 1987.

Daishonin, Nichiren. *The Writings of Nichiren Daishonin, Volume 1.* N.p.: n.p., n.d. https://www. nichirenlibrary.org/en/wnd-1/toc/.

Day, Dorothy. *Aims and Purposes.* February 1940. https://www.catholicworker.org/ dorothyday/themes/ On%20Aims%20and%20Purposes%20(Dorothy%20Day).pdf.

Emerson, Ralph Waldo. Quoted in Susyn Reeve. *The Wholehearted Life: Big Changes and Greater Happiness Week by Week.* Berkeley: Viva Editions, 2014.

Emoto, Masaru. *The Hidden Messages in Water.* New York: Atria Books, Hillsboro: Beyond Words Publishing, Inc., 2004.

Encyclopedia Britannica Online, s.v. "Gospel," accessed March 21, 2022, https://www. britannica.com/topic/ Gospel-New-Testament.

Encyclopedia Britannica Online, s.v. "light," accessed March 24, 2022, https://www. britannica.com/science/ light.

Fuller, Jane. "The Vibration Of Your Thoughts Create Your lives." *HuffPost*. January 12, 2016. https:// www.huffingtonpost.co.uk/jane-fuller/your-thoughts-create-your_b_13318676.html.

Gifford, Kathie Lee. *The Jesus I Know: Honest Conversations and Diverse Opinions About Who He Is.*

Nashville: Thomas Nelson, 2021.

Gisonni, Debbie. "Self-Awareness Increases With Meditation." *HuffPost*. August 29, 2013. https://www. huffpost.com/entry/meditation-tips_b_3830431.

Haider, Paul. "14 Proven Scientific Benefits of Chanting." *Sivana East*. N.d. https://blog. sivanaspirit. com/sp-gn-scientific-benefits-chanting/.

Hanh, Thich Nhat. *Fear: Essential Wisdom for Getting Through the Storm*. New York: HarperCollins Publishers Inc., 2012.

Jung, Carl. Translated by R.F.C. Hull. *The Archetypes and the Collective Unconscious.* Princeton: Princeton University Press, 1969.

Keating, Sarah. "The world's most accessible stress reliever." *BBC*. May 18, 2020. https://www. bbc.com/ future/article/20200518-why-singing-can-make-you-feel-better-in-lockdown.

Keating, Thomas. *Consenting to God as God Is*. Brooklyn: Lantern Books, 2016.

Kierkegaard, Søren. Translated by Douglas V. Steere. *Purity of Heart is to Will One Thing: Spiritual Preparation for the Office of Confession*. New York: Harper & Row, Publishers, Inc., 1956.

Lee, Witness. *Dealing with Our Inward Parts for the Growth in Life*. Anaheim: Living Stream Ministry, 2016.

Lexico, s.v. "receptive," accessed July 7, 2022, https://www.lexico.com/en/definition/receptive. *Lexico*, "recovery," accessed May 19, 2022, https://www.lexico.com/en/definition/recovery. *Lexico,* "removal," accessed July 7, 2022 https://www.lexico.com/en/definition/removal.

Lexico, s.v. "return," accessed July 8, 2022, https://www.lexico.com/en/definition/return.

Lexico, s.v. "reunion," accessed July 7, 2022, https://www.lexico.com/en/definition/reunion.

Merriam-Webster Dictionary, s.v. "refulgence," accessed July 7, 2022, https://www.merriam-webster.com/ dictionary/refulgence.

Merriam-Webster Dictionary, s.v. "restoration," accessed July 7, 2022, https://www.merriam-webster.com/ dictionary/restoration.

Merriam-Webster Thesaurus, s.v. "revelation," accessed July 7, 2022, https://www.merriam-webster.com/ thesaurus/revelation.

Millman, Dan. *No Ordinary Moments: A Peaceful Warrior's Guide to Daily Life.* Tiburon: H. J. Kramer, Novato: New World Library, 1992.

Nestor, James. *Breath: The New Science of a Lost Art.* New York: Riverhead Books, 2020.

New World Encyclopedia, s.v. "Abba," accessed May 18, 2022, https://www.newworld encyclopedia.org/ entry/Abba.

New World Encyclopedia, s.v. "Spirit," accessed March 1, 2022, https://www.newworld encyclopedia.org/ entry/Spirit#Etymology.

"Relaxation techniques: Breath control helps quell errant stress response." *Harvard Health Publishing.* July 6, 2020. https://www.health.harvard.edu/mind-and-mood/relaxation-techniques-breath- control-helps-quell-errant-stress-response.

Rumi. Quoted in Shaunna Menard. *Free to Heal: 9 Steps to a Successful, Soul-Satisfying Health Coaching Practice.* New York: Morgan James Publishing, 2020.

Sirk, Douglas, dir. *Magnificent Obsession.* Los Angeles: Universal Pictures, 1954. https:// www. criterionchannel.com/videos/magnificent-obsession-1.

The Britannica Dictionary, s.v. "Devotion," accessed March 28, 2022, https://www.britannica. com/ dictionary/devotion#:~:text=noun-,plural%20devotions,the%20quality%20of% 20being%20 devoted.

Tolstoy, Leo. *My Confession and The Spirit of Christ's Teaching.* New York: Thomas Y. Crowell & Co., 1887.

Wheeler-Reed, David. "What the early church thought about God's gender." *The Conversation.* August 1, 2019. https://theconversation.com/what-the-early-church-thought-about-gods-gender-100077.

Wilson, William Griffith. *Alcoholics Anonymous: The Story of How Many Thousands of Men and Women Have Recovered From Alcoholism*. N.p.: Alcoholics Anonymous World Services, Inc., 2001.

Wilson, William Griffith. *Twelve Steps and Twelve Traditions*. N.p.: Alcoholics Anonymous World Services, Inc., 1953.

Wright, N. T. *Simply Christian: Why Christianity Makes Sense*. N.p.: HarperCollins Publishers, 2009.

BIBLES

The Message: The Bible in Contemporary Language (MSG) New Life Version (NLV)

World English Bible (WEB) English Standard Version (ESV) New International Version (NIV)

New American Standard Bible (NASB)

New American Standard Bible 1995 (NASB1995) King James Version (KJV)

Berean Study Bible (BSB) New Living Translation (NLT)

Christian Standard Bible (CSB) Common English Bible (CEB)